PLACES MADE AFTER THEIR STORIES

Paul Carter is a highly acclaimed writer, public artist and interdisciplinary scholar. Among his best-known books are *The Road to Botany Bay* (1987), *Material Thinking* (2004) and *Meeting Place* (2013). His public artwork for Federation Square, Melbourne, *Nearamnew*, has attracted international attention. He is Creative Director of the Melbourne-based design studio, Material Thinking, and Professor of Design (Urbanism), School of Architecture and Design, RMIT University, Melbourne. With UWA Publishing he has previously published *Ground Truthing: Explorations in a Creative Region (*2010) and his first poetry collection, *Ecstacies and Elegies* (2013).

PLACES MADE AFTER THEIR STORIES

DESIGN AND THE ART OF CHOREOTOPOGRAPHY

PAUL CARTER

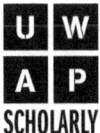

First published in 2015 by
UWA Publishing
Crawley, Western Australia 6009
www.uwap.uwa.edu.au

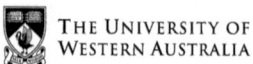
THE UNIVERSITY OF
WESTERN AUSTRALIA

This book is copyright. Apart from any fair dealing for the purpose of private study, research, criticism or review, as permitted under the *Copyright Act 1968*, no part may be reproduced by any process without written permission. Enquiries should be made to the publisher.

The moral right of the author has been asserted.

Copyright © Paul Carter 2015

National Library of Australia Cataloguing-in-Publication entry

Creator: Carter, Paul, 1951– author.

Title: Places made after their stories : design and the art of choreotopography / Paul Carter.

ISBN: 9781742587608 (paperback)

Subjects: Public spaces—Case studies.
  Public art spaces spaces—Case studies.
  City planning—Case studies.
  Urban landscape architecture—Case studies.
  Art—Appreciation.
  Art—Philosophy.

Dewey Number: 711.55

Typeset in Bembo by J&M Typesetting
Printed by Lightning Source

CONTENTS

List of Figures	vii
Acknowledgments	xi
A Word on the Name	xiii

Introduction

1	Material Thinking in the Meeting Place	3
2	Choreotopography's Prehistory	15
3	The Mythopoetic Catalyst	23
4	Planning, Poiesis, Pedagogy	30
5	Dramatic Society	35

Part 1

6	What Is Choreotopography?	43
7	The Designer as Dramaturg	55
8	The Measure of Encounter	68

Part 2

9	The Turbulence of Creation	89
10	The Dramaturgy of Encounter	101
11	Places Made After Their Stories	113
12	Listening to the Water Underground	128

Part 3

13	The Society of Trees	149
14	The Name of the Grove	164
15	Applying the Asterisk Principle	174
16	The Strategy of Ambience	188

Part 4

17	The Laws of Chance Meeting	213
18	Collective Attunements	222

19	Cosmetic Production	228
20	Fabricating Topographies	244
21	Fitting the Ground	256

Part 5

22	Improvising the Program	269
23	The Haunt of Ghosts	280
24	Exceptional Passages	295

Part 6

25	The Mission of Images	315
26	Options, Frameworks, Templates	327
27	Bicultural Senses of Place	341
28	Physical Gestures, Energy Patterns	356

Part 7

29	Pressure Cultures/Vacuum Cultures	367
30	Interweaving Bodies into Place	377
31	Learning Choreotopography	385
32	Patching Poetics into Politics	398
33	Feedback and the Movement Form	410
34	On the Importance of Personal Style	420

Bibliography	429
Index	450

LIST OF FIGURES

1 Material Thinking, 'Confluence of Goulburn and Broken Rivers', in 'River Connect, Reverse Brief', April 2008, pp. 1-12, p. 1. Photo: the author.

2 Leonardo da Vinci, 'An old man in profile to right, seated on a rocky ledge; water studies and a note, pen and ink', 154 x 216 mm, c.1513. *The Drawings and Miscellaneous Papers of Leonardo de Vinci ... at Windsor Castle*, ed. C. Pedretti, Harcourt Brace Jovanovich, London and New York, 1981, p. 48 r. Royal Collection Trust/© Her Majesty Queen Elizabeth II 2015.

3 Paul Carter, '*Nearamnew* Global Whorl: Wedge Interlock', pen and ink, 210 x 297 mm, June 2000. Copyright: the author.

4 Material Thinking, *Pearl*, 'Pearl, Masts, Shell: Preliminary Design Concept for Cultural Facility, Design Concept for Artwork, Landscape, Peninsula, Darwin Waterfront', digital render, November 2008, pp. 1-17, p. 10.

5 Deakin Motion Lab, Melbourne Ballet Company and Material Thinking, *Choreotopography*, Playhouse Theatre, Victorian Arts Centre, 3 December 2009. Reproduced by permission.

6 Dirk de Bruyn, *Opening*, video, Federation Square, Melbourne, 9 September 2011. An initiative of the Centre for Memory, Imagination and Invention, Deakin University. Reproduced by permission.

7 Soo Yeun You, '*Loops* improvisation', Federation Square, Melbourne, 17 July 2013. Photo: the author.

8 Dominic O'Brien/Fairfaxphotos, 'Federation Square', 2003. Reproduced by permission.

9 'Foamform 5', Kalimna Falls, Otways Ranges, 7 April 1999. Photo: the author.

10 René Descartes, 'Vortices', *Principia philosophiae*, Amsterdam, 1656, p. 129, New York Public Library, General Research Division. Reproduced by permission.

11 Material Thinking, 'Tree Drawings, Processes of Connection, Meander' in 'Red Ways: Alice Springs CBD Revitalisation, Design Options Framework', June 2008, pp. 1-70, p. 44, 46, 52

12 'The Lurianic Tree', adapted from Christopher Benton, 'Sefer Yetzirah, the Cube of Space, and the Emergence of the Tree of Life,' n.d., pp. 43-4. On line at http://www.maqom.com/journal/paper33.pdf. Viewed 26 February 2011. Drawing: Edmund Carter.

13 Material Thinking, 'Outline of University of Sydney Central (top) and Maze Green (circle) overlaid onto detail of Municipality of Darlington map (Sheet 28, 1884); Golden Grove Hotel cnr. Raglan and Alma Streets', 15 January 2006.

14 Material Thinking, '*Golden Grove* Template, University of Sydney, Darlington Campus historical map palimpsest with colour coded Pleiades overlay', 12 February 2006.

15 Taylor Cullity Lethlean, 'USYD Darlington masterplan, incorporating banded granite pavement', 31 March 2006. Reproduced by permission.

16 Taylor Cullity Lethlean/Material Thinking, 'Celeano, *Golden Grove* pavement spiral', detail. Photo: the author (18 July 2009).

17 Max Ernst, 'Printemps du ciel', 1963. Aquatint-etching in two colours, 230 x 167 mm. Copyright: ADAGP. Reproduced by permission.

18 Taylor Cullity Lethlean/Material Thinking, 'Electra, *Golden Grove* boardwalk illumination spiral'. Photo: the author (2 February 2009).

19 Taylor Cullity Lethlean/Material Thinking, 'Asterope, *Golden Grove*, proposed LED array', Student Services Building, University of Sydney, Darlington Campus. 21 February 2006.

20 Taylor Cullity Lethlean/Material Thinking, 'Atlas, *Golden Grove*, stele text', 2008. Photo: the author (2 February 2009).

21 Taylor Cullity Lethlean/Material Thinking, 'Alcyone, *Golden Grove*, ground spiral with text', 2008. Photo: the author (18 July 2009).

22 'Dandenong Municipal Building, Library and Civic Plaza', May 2014. Photo: Rush\Wright Associates. Reproduced by permission.

23 Material Thinking, '*Alterations 4*, programming Dandenong's new civic square', 4 March, 2013, 1-17, p. 2 (detail).

24 Material Thinking, '*Alterations 4*, programming Dandenong's new civic square', 4 March, 2013, 1-17, p. 3.

25 Material Thinking, '*Alterations 4*, programming Dandenong's new civic square', 4 March, 2013, 1-17, p. 4.

26 Material Thinking, '*Alterations 4*, programming Dandenong's new civic square', 4 March, 2013, 1-17, p. 5.

27 Material Thinking, '*Alterations 4*, programming Dandenong's new civic square', 4 March, 2013, 1-17, p. 6.

28 William Barak Wurundjeri, *Figures in Possum Skin Cloaks*, pencil, wash, charcoal solution, gouache and earth pigments on paper, 1280 x 820 mm, 1898, National Gallery of Victoria, accession number 1215A-5. Reproduced by permission.

29 'Dandenong Civic Centre and Square opening', 17 March 2014. Photo: Michael Wright. Reproduced by permission.

30 Material Thinking, '*Alterations 4*, programming Dandenong's new civic square', 4 March, 2013, 1-17, p. 8.

31 Material Thinking, '*Alterations 4*, programming Dandenong's new civic square', 4 March, 2013, 1-17, p. 9.

32 Material Thinking, '*Alterations* 4, programming Dandenong's new civic square', 4 March, 2013, 1-17, p. 7.

33 'Point Nepean Quarantine Station, looking north'. Photo: Deveraux-Gray Oral History Collection, provided by Point Nepean Community Trust. Reproduced by permission.

34 'Quarantine Station Point Nepean, New Disinfection Buildings', architect's drawing, c.1900, National Archives, B84_Folder 12.4. Provided by Point Nepean Community Trust. Reproduced by permission.

35 'Board Game', late nineteenth century, Point Nepean Quarantine Station Museum. Photo: the author (March 2008).

36 Material Thinking, '*Turning Point* concept sketch', overlay of Jean Houël, 'Plan de la Barrière de la Santé' (from *Voyage pittoresque des Îles de Sicile, de Malte et de Lipari*, Edizione per il Banco di Sicilia realizzata dalla 'Storia di Napoli et della Sicilia', Società Editrice, Palermo, 1977; orig. pub. Paris, 1782) on to Point Nepean Quarantine Station site plan, 28 January 2008.

37 Material Thinking, 'A New Body: Creative Template at Yagan Square', 7 November 2014, 1-11, p. 4.

38 Material Thinking, 'A New Body: Creative Template at Yagan Square', 7 November 2014, 1-11, front cover.

Material Thinking (established 2007) is a Melbourne-based design studio. Paul Carter is Creative Director. Edmund Carter is Senior Designer. The projects, designs and graphics featured in Figures 4, 16, 17, 18, 23, 24, 25, 26 are principally the work of Edmund Carter. The attribution of the remainder of the figures of Material Thinking works, graphics and design sketches is shared.

ACKNOWLEDGMENTS

The projects described in *Places Made After Their Stories* materialised through conversations with very many individuals. It would be better to think in terms of creative communities convening around temporarily shared regions of care. The many people who informed *Red Ways* are acknowledged in the Connecting Alice website. The Northern Territory Government no longer posts this document; it can be visited at www.materialthinking.com.au. In relation to the specific themes developed in *Places Made After Their Stories*, I owe a special debt of gratitude to Mike Gillam, Ken Hawkins (Northern Territory Government), Doris Kngwarraye Stuart and, above all, the Reverend Tracy Spencer.

Golden Grove was an integral part of *Fertile Ground*, the University of Sydney's Darlington Campus public domain design by landscape architects Taylor Cullity Lethlean. *Alterations* was a collaboration with landscape architects Rush\Wright Associates. The architecture office Lyons extended the invitation to be involved in the Dandenong Municipal Building and Civic Square development project in Melbourne. Lyons also led the successful bid to design Yagan Square in Perth. The guiding expertise of Scott Adams (Taylor Cullity Lethlean), Carey Lyon, Corbett Lyon and Neil Appleton (Lyons) is also gratefully acknowledged. For the opportunity to work on *River Connect* in Shepparton and at the Point Nepean Quarantine Station site I am indebted to Dr Lindy Joubert (University of Melbourne). From the same university, my colleagues Professor Ruth Fincher, Dr Paolo Tombesi and Dr Kate Shaw made 'Transnational and Temporary' happen. In 2013 the Institute of Interweaving Performance Cultures (Freie Universität, Berlin) offered me a twelve-month fellowship to work on my project 'The Dramaturgy of Turbulence'. Their generous support gave me invaluable writing time.

Dirk de Bruyn and Soo Yeun You improvised significant performances exploring choreotopographical motifs at Federation Square, Melbourne, and at the site now occupied by the new Dandenong Municipal Building and Civic Square. Soo Yeun You and Shaun McLeod collaborated on a number of indoor and outdoor movement improvisations, which Dirk de Bruyn recorded on film. Edmund Carter designed *Pearl*, besides playing a major role in the development of the designs for *Golden Grove*; he also contributed original concept sketches to *Red Ways* and *Turning Point*. Throughout, the dialogue between analogue and digital sensibilities has been the most important creative catalyst driving the work described here.

I am grateful to Jan Hendrik Brueggemeier (on behalf of the postgraduate student initiative 'Paper Tigers') for the invitation to run a masterclass at the Centre for Creative Arts, La Trobe University, Melbourne, in October 2012. Dr Richard Walley OAM made me welcome in opening discussions with the Nyoongar community through the Whadjuk Working Group in Perth. I am also grateful for the support of Mark Dorrian and Michael Tawa, whose invitations to lecture and whose own writings, design and pedagogical practices have provided continued critical support and creative inspiration.

Parts of Chapter 3 first appeared in 'Regional patterns: Narratives of "mere coincidence" and the production of sociability', in Robert Mason & Janet McDonald (eds), *Creative Communities: Regional Social Inclusion and the Arts*, Intellect Press, Bristol, 2015. Parts of Chapter 6 first appeared in 'Emargination: A pedagogy of the commons', in 'On the Margins', special issue, *Architectural Theory Review*, vol. 18, no. 2, 2013, pp. 150–63.

A WORD ON THE NAME

The title, *Places Made After Their Stories*, makes an obvious allusion to Geoffrey and James Bardon's 2004 publication, *Papunya, A Place Made After The Story*. In that book Geoffrey Bardon gives a first-hand account of the emergence of the Western Desert Painting Movement. Bardon had nothing but the deepest respect and admiration for the twenty five or so Pintupi, Anmatjira, Arrernte, Luritja and other artists whose work he documents in such careful detail; however, he was also conscious that the stories of place told through the painting designs were located inside another story. The great 'my Country' Dreamings, for example, were also records of country taken away: they had the poignancy of paintings done in exile. The abiding mythscape of central Australian Aboriginal cultures was located within the historical landscape of colonisation and its administrative legacy. This was not all. Within this doubled place of storytelling, a third irruption of the eternal into the temporal was occurring: this was the miraculous rebirth of creative expression itself. The artists who convened at Papunya, working with materials that Bardon provided to translate their knowledge of country into permanent patterns, were doing something new. Dreaming about the past, they were also inaugurating a different future. Doing this at that place and time, they were perhaps redeeming Papunya, hitherto a symbol of colonial dispossession and hopelessness. The revolution might be by night (invisible to the authorities) – 'Sometimes great dreams inhabit the place of their making in their attributes, appearances and forms'[1] – but it would signify the awakening of the continent as a whole to a new, hitherto neglected, future, one where places were at last made after their stories.

Places Made After Their Stories

*

Places Made After Their Stories borrows the idea of the threefold creation or re-creation involved in place-making and uses it in the constructive critique of master planning. Any place demarcated by government edict for redevelopment is a second place, a superficial territory carved out of a larger creative region. The creative region, where places are made after their stories, is like a human body, composed of sinews, nerves and skin. It accommodates the eternal movement forms of passage and return, arrival and departure: although mottled with historical events, it is also the matrix into whose surface these comings and goings are written. Enclosing and separating a patch of land, creating a territory within the flowpath of the creative region, master planning does not discover a place: it proposes to invent one. As a rule, the act of invention involves a prior act of disruption or destruction: the prior attachment to the larger country (the system of nerves and tendons that signify the living associations to the region that make any place an act of gathering) is cut; a blank canvas is substituted; and over this artificial blankness a new geometry of power is drawn. The suspension of this procedure involves reasserting the openness of the place to other places. It also entails recognising the present act of destruction involved in clearing the ground for redevelopment. Thirdly, it involves drawing the creative corollary; if master planning is found in a double destruction (of spiritual and physical place), then the act of re-creative placemaking must also be doubled. It will be an act of recollection (of the creative region) and an act of imagination, one that visualizes the old energies inhabiting new forms at that place. Out of this mythopoetic reworking of the received stories at that place can come licit inventions. These forms of place, comprising new physical arrangements, eidetic affordances and subtler catalysts for the continuing concomitant acts of transfiguration are inseparable from the collective creativity that brings them into being.

The collaborations described in *Places Made After Their Stories* are not intended as comparisons with the transformations of culture and design documented by Bardon. The comparison is structural, reflecting a recognition that the place-making technique described here also depends on a threefold historical judgement. Places are made after their stories in three ways: mythically and scientifically; historically and administratively; and creatively or mythopoetically. These three visions coexist, although this is rarely recognized or acknowledged. They constantly inform one another, bleeding like dream scenes across borders, where literal connotations regularly diffuse into widening analogical realms. But this tumult of images is resisted: the masters of instrumental reason fear to be mastered by their visions. Choreotopography, the art of design that emerges from the threefold flowering of places when their stories are mythopoetically rediscovered and transformed, therefore walks a perilous path. Reflecting on the legacy of Papunya, Bardon wrote, 'Sometimes nothing returns to the dreamer except the dream. Perhaps in spite of the nightmarish quality of our continent's recent history neither I nor any other can bring back a truth which does not wish to be known.'[2] There is no certainty that places made after their stories can survive. At the same time, as Bardon implies, what remains hidden is not necessarily lost. Indeed, in a time that identifies truth with exposure, when the authorities clear away every obstacle to progress, preferring to confront a desert rather than live with the swirl of weather, topographies and the intransigent reality of other bodies, it may be imperative to hide certain things away. An art of place making that secretes things in full view, that discloses rather than exposes what holds us together, may be vulnerable but inevitable.

Notes
1. Geoffrey Bardon and James Bardon, *Papunya, A Place Made After The Story*, Miegunyah Press, Melbourne, 2004, p. xxii.
2. Ibid., xxiii.

Introduction

1

MATERIAL THINKING IN THE MEETING PLACE

Places Made After Their Stories sits at the confluence of practical studies in material thinking and theoretical speculations about the constitution (and performance) of the contemporary meeting place. Reading an earlier book of mine, *Material Thinking: The Theory and Practice of Creative Research*, the United States–based design thinker Cameron Tonkinwise recognised that the collaborative art practices described therein yielded something useful to other practitioners and interested creative people, because they were all implicitly about place-making. The situated knowledge that artists discover through making a sculpture, a film, a painting or a dance has at its heart a dynamic process that can be communicated. The phenomenon of collaboration – between people, between artists and the non-human materials of their work – can create a microcosm of the transformational interaction that sociologists (and planners) associate with social innovation. However, Tonkinwise wonders what would happen if this special knowledge about place and placing were transposed from the studio to the street, from a domain where materials are malleable to one where they are collectively owned, disposed and renewed.[1] What is the value of material thinking in shaping, amending, retrieving, informing the places subject to political and economic determination?

Places Made After Their Stories is a critical and creative response to the discourse of master planning. It reports on landscape designs, civic space programs and urban revitalisation projects in which I have been engaged. In the tradition of *Material Thinking*, it derives insights about the nature of places and their production from the situation of their production, one that is generally under the jurisdiction of political agendas and circumscribed by functionalist criteria prescribed by government urban planning agencies. The political, and highly politicised, context of the studies published here creates a robust obstacle to speculative reflection. For example, a starting point of *Places Made After Their Stories* is that the term *place* is, as it circulates in planning literature, complicit in the devitalisation it seeks to redress. However, until our architecture and planning schools develop a philosophical and historical comprehension of what places can be, their graduates will continue to operate with wildly anachronistic and attenuated place lexicons. The point here, though, is that, in addition to meeting the challenge Tonkinwise extends – to find 'a poetics for this knowing-in-making-useful' – a designer has to navigate the rhetoric of what others consider useful. Where power resides with a professional clique that considers public space as a category of land that is blank for all practical purposes, the success of the project depends on being able to show planners that the ground they thought blank is, in fact, covered with inscriptions, a heritage, if you like, of future sketches. If present-day planners can be persuaded that the past already planned for the future, there is a better chance that what Tonkinwise calls 'affordances', the array of site characteristics that produce a *sense of place*, will survive the destruction normally associated with master-planned renewal.[2]

The proposition that past place-making practices were focused on the future development of the promoters, communities or other (self-)interest groups offers a useful criterion in engaging with inventories of material culture. For agencies investing in the development of the city, any evidence that the proposed site is not a blank sheet represents an obstacle to progress. Unless the buildings and artifacts the heritage historians and archaeologists find, identify and date can be contained and, ideally, used to brand the new development as a unique destination, they have no currency in the master-planned future place. However, it is different when the creative through line of certain past events is foregrounded; when patterns of passage, suggesting the rhythm of change or the turbulence of adaptation and growth, are made out, almost palimpsestically, in the physical and cultural topography of the location under consideration, it is easier to understand what has collected as the ballast of becoming at that place. An ethics of invention is inseparable from a care for this accumulated social labour; however, in the context of planning initiatives driven by an aversion to risk, evidence of earlier risk-taking that produced something durable is emotionally appealing. The powerful, in particular, like to feel that the past shared their interests. Public servants are flattered when their repetitious formulae somehow unearth an older creativity.

If the ambience of an environment or physical situation is to inform the design process, it needs to be materialised in the story of the place. It has to be verbalised through poetic concepts – multisensory affordances have to be translated into language. Even if the patchwork of story fragments that the rhapsodic artist-designer of *Places Made After Their Stories* assembles is representative of a multilayered local history, it cannot gain a place at the table of planning unless it can show its utility in visualising the future vitality of the place. This can lead to some paradoxical responses when master planners invite the rhapsode to turn the creative vision into a more refined planning document. However, the logical next step in bringing the heritage of regional or local affordances (physical, psychological and cultural) into the shaping of the future place design and program is not to leach it of its poetic style or generative function; it is to reverse the process of linguistic condensation by rewriting the storylines into the physical environment. This is possible because the critical through lines drawn out from the character of the place are movement forms or passages. As traces of passage, movement forms are like the wear friction produces. We learn that the Latin word *fricare* ('to rub off'), from which our word *friction* comes, 'turned into the Late Latin *frictiare*, meaning, 'walking and leaving footprints (just like animals do)'''. As the same source notes, 'Leaving tracks as you walk gave away who you are and where you're going, letting you be followed'. In an urban context it is interesting to discover that our word *traffic*, coming from a contraction of Latin *trans* + *fricare*, can be interpreted as 'friction across the road'.[3] The tracks left by traffic recall the enthusiasm of the Marxist philosopher Ernst Bloch for the tire patterns left on the as-yet unmetalled roads of Germany – 'Ice flowers here, Samarkands there – until both are washed away by the next rain'.[4] Graphically, movement forms exist somewhere between geography and choreography. It is this graphic return, or transformation into design, that enables a creatively interpreted cultural heritage to inform public planning. The site signature that emerges in this way is, true to its provenance, a hieroglyph, which maintains the possibility of future events taking place by veiling or keeping in reserve the full prophetic significance of what has been made.

There is, in my experience, a grave mismatch between the social and environmental philosophy implicit in a material thinking made useful (to repeat Tonkinwise) and the corresponding theory of planning. In practice, planners respond to the suggestion that creativity should be embedded in the design by treating it as an ideological attribute. The call to make place for things to happen is a summons to leave what is done unfinished, fuzzy round the edges, ambiguous and subject to growth and decay. Translated into the Benthamite mindset of most planning discourses, it becomes the public art brief or the basis of the community arts program. In these guises, creativity once again becomes epiphenomenal, an unpredictable occurrence whose manifestations are fully allowed for in the plan. In this unpropitious context, it is not surprising that our success in realising the proposals narrated in *Places Made After Their Stories* has been variable. I used to think that the derailing of public space design proposals that had successfully navigated the first two stages of persuasion (the rhapsodic and the graphic) reflected poorly on our project management skills. It took a while to grasp fully the cynical self-interest and associated short-term vision engendered by Australia's hectic electoral cycles.

The place-making collaborations discussed in *Places Made After Their Stories* are weak in the sense that they are vulnerable to misrepresentation or appropriation. But they have sometimes failed to fit the project delivery paradigm of master planning for another reason. They are creative collaborations that incorporate the collaborative process into the outcome; as a conversation may be broken off to begin again elsewhere, so with the projects of *Places Made After Their Stories*: they are passages within a larger creative trajectory. From the point of view of the rhapsode-maker, they are meeting places within a creative region. In *Material Thinking*, two kinds of collaboration are contrasted. In one, different specialisations converge on a common object: the result is an intensification of positive knowledge synthesised and applied. The recruitment of different professional subdisciplines to the task of delivering new infrastructure exemplifies this approach. It is planning's modus operandi, and the scope for collaboration is minimal. In contrast, with this weak form of collaboration, strong collaboration of the kind practised in material thinking 'places placing at the centre of the act of local invention. It defines place as the pattern emerging from the discursive crossweave of the collaboration'.[5] From this point of view, the weakness of the public place design collaborations discussed in this book is their strength: vulnerability to abandonment is a sign of commitment to 'the irreducible heterogeneity of cultural identity, the always unfinished process of making and remaking ourselves through our symbolic forms'.[6]

As this description suggests, material thinking implies reformed or creatively self-aware social arrangements. Taken out of the studio and onto the streets, it implies the governance of public space as well as its more narrowly defined administration and management according to rules established by our planning culture. It engages with the democratic project of self-becoming at that place. This, *Places Made After Their Stories* suggests, involves a form of turbulence that is, potentially at least, socially innovative: stirred up by public eros (and not simply individual rivalries and power struggles), society, or what Jean-Luc Nancy calls a 'multitude of singularities', and which organises itself choreographically, or at least with a clear intuition that our primary sociality depends on curating the space in-between.[7] Jean-Luc Nancy describes this mode of being with others in terms of 'exposures': or, as Marie-Eve Morin explains, 'The world is formed of limits or edges between singularities, of their articulations, of the play of their junctures "where different pieces touch each other without fusing together, where they slide, pivot, or tumble over one another, one at the limit of the other without the mutual play – which always remains, at the same time, a play between them – ever forming into the substance or the higher power of the Whole." The world is not the totalization of what is, an overarching horizon or a big container that would bring everything together. Yet, the world has a stance; it holds together the multiplicity of expositions between singularities, between worlds.'[8]

Here, an important insight from my earlier work *Meeting Place: The Human Encounter and the Challenge of Coexistence* intersects with the ambient design pursued in an applied material thinking. How is such a holding together achieved without reintroducing the coercive figure of the 'container'? It may be achieved when the meeting place is threaded with encounters. 'When it incubates encounter, it not only facilitates and multiplies opportunities of exchange but also sets the exchange rates. Both stable and unstable, it can be characterized as a reticulation of erotic zones.'[9] With its focus on the discursive construction of shared space – the way people talk, sing and dance places into being – *Places Made After Their Stories* is a theory and practice of sociability. Its object is to incubate opportunities for meeting. However, as *Meeting Place* discovers, meeting is not an unthinking transformation of individuals into crowds: the multiplication of encounters can and should foster a counter-formation, a widening galaxy of solitudes.[10]

Studies of historical accounts of formally staged meetings between Southern and Eastern Arrernte men outside Alice Springs in central Australia have shown that a primary function of these was to negotiate the conditions of living apart. This counterintuitive function of meeting – the maintenance of the conditions of non-meeting – was reaffirmed in discussions held in 2007 and 2008 with leading members of the Lhere Artepe Aboriginal Corporation. Asked whether they wanted a *meeting place*, they countered that they wanted a *talking place*; and one purpose of talking might, after all, be to veto well-meaning attempts to multiply opportunities for incompetent or unwelcome socialisation.[11] The spreading out into their own countries of visitors temporarily resident on Arrernte land that follows talking does not represent a traumatic truncation of social relations. The centrifugal return to other places, which balances the centripetal pull of the centre (the meeting place), breaks down the false opposition between the individual and the crowd. It makes possible what Elias Canetti calls a 'transformation': 'The human being must learn to be a plurality of beings, in a conscious fashion, and to hold them all together'. Canetti's 'vision of total and self-transcending opening to otherness' combined with a radical rejection of power – 'to become a city, a country, a continent, without conquering anything' – accurately evokes the social and political organisation of traditional societies in central Australia.[12] Because people are born together, they can separate without experiencing traumatic disfigurement. Because the intimacy they enjoy with their surroundings secures their command of the distance, giving them confidence to be apart, they can also meet again, for meeting might be an institution for the renewal of encounter, for *reinitiation* into the mysteries of the coexistence of the many, human and divine.

But, as *Meeting Place* observes, 'what Canetti welcomes as "the ability to transfigure the human condition into multiple worlds and the capacity to clear paths between them" is impossible without a release from the tyranny of spatial unification associated with modern cartography and the geometry of planning'.[13] The hybrid discourse of choreotopography seeks to address this deficiency. It reconceives material thinking as a kind of public space dramaturgy documented in the affordances that are the permanent traces of opening to the other. To insist that the place-making designs in *Places Made After Their Stories* constitute studies in the application of *material* thinking to real-world situations where new forms have to be *useful* may seem perverse. An early definition of *material thinking* is offered by Georg Wilhelm Friedrich Hegel in a historical context where '*das materielles Denken*' is a refusal to impose on what has happened any sense of pattern, direction or purpose.[14] Its narrative expression is a positivist chronology, a litany of facts supposed to speak for themselves. Transposed to the realm of place-making, the remote descendant of Hegel's materialist is the heritage historian whose detailed inventories of past material cultures suppose the relics of the past speak for themselves. The antithesis of this position is embodied in the planner's decision to sweep away every obstacle to progress. At the 'opposite extreme' from the '"contingent consciousness that is absorbed only in material stuff", a form of thought which is rooted in existing conditions and cannot see beyond them', the planner applies to the design of space 'the transcendental critical method of "argumentation" (*das Resonieren*), which involves "freedom from all content and a sense of vanity towards it"'.[15]

In this context, material thinking is, curiously, focused on the materialisation of the immaterial. Australian philosopher Michael Tawa takes this further, in the context of teaching architectural design recommending 'ana-materialistic thinking', the recovery from the materials of thinking certain immanent structures or tendencies towards higher levels of self-organisation. These 'assemblages' are simultaneously associations of ideas and the 'existential infrastructure for life'.[16] They are disposed to join together in new ways that are conducive to producing the conditions where life is lived twice, constructively and reconstructively, actively and reflectively. Ana-materialism can be characterised as a marriage of phenomenological principles of analysis to the inherent indeterminism of complex systems whose behaviour is, like the approach to design Tawa recommends, nonlinear – that is, both scripturally and ethically open, unfinished, receptive to innovation. Material thinking is in this formulation the study of *materialisation*, a mental as well as a physical phenomenon that is simultaneously an act of ideation and the discovery of pattern in matter. The discussion touched on here opens up a fascinating field for speculation: if the recommended approach to design is evolutionary, is its *bête noire*, master planning, applied creationism?

In *Material Thinking*, a materiality was advocated that borrowed inspiration from Georges Bataille's anti-metaphysicalist (and anti-materialist) notion of the *informe*.[17] Bringing this forward a couple of generations, one encounters Jean-François Lyotard's attempt to classify information as a form of the immaterial. The immateriality of information, accelerated in the last thirty years through the advent of digital systems of communication, refers to a phenomenon that is a variation on Marshall McLuhan's identification of message with medium. Immateriality is not the same as dematerialisation; it is what happens when attention is transferred from the transmitter–receiver model of communication (or cultural production and consumption) to the data flows themselves or the process of continuous informal production. To materialise the immateriality of information is to engage in a kind of choreography of information flows, to organise the technology of information display in ways that deform information or disclose its social construction. John Rajchman captures this logic when he suggests that Lyotard's 1985 Centre Georges Pompidou exhibition *Les Immatériaux* was 'conceived as a dramaturgy of information for the post-modern condition'.[18] An interface was designed between the physically imperceptible flow of digital information, the physical armatures that made it visible and the course of the spectator through this new phantasmagoric landscape. In this case, the impact of the exhibition, its residue of affect, was neither in the electromagnetic field nor in the material appliances used to translate its energy into perceptible signs, but somewhere in-between and around these ghostly–human interactions. Instead of being given signs showing the way, the public found themselves directed to be lost.[19] The troubling effect of this might best be described as the creation of *atmosphere*.

Notes

1 Cameron Tonkinwise, 'Knowing by being-there making: Explicating the tacit post-subject in use', *Studies in Material Thinking*, vol. 1, no. 2, 2008, viewed 3 June 2015, www.materialthinking.org/sites/default/files/papers/Cameron.pdf.
2 Ibid.
3 http://www.spanishetymology.com/disfrazar-and-friction-traffic/. Viewed 30 April 2015.
4 Ernst Bloch, *Literary Essays*, trans. A. Joron et al., Stanford University Press, Stanford, Calif., 1998, p. 356. For such marks as forms of 'dark writing' or ichnology, see Paul Carter, *Dark Writing: Geography, Performance, Design*, University of Hawai'i Press, Honolulu, 2008, pp.167–8.
5 Paul Carter, *Material Thinking: The Theory and Practice of Creative Research*, Melbourne University Publishing, Melbourne, 2004, p. 14.
6 Ibid., p. 13.
7 Paul Carter, *Meeting Place: The Human Encounter and the Challenge of Coexistence*, Minnesota University Press, Minneapolis, 2013, pp. 81–3.
8 Marie-Eve Morin, 'Nancy, Violence and the World, *Parrhesia*, Number 16, 2013, pp. 61–72, 63. The reference for the passage Morin quotes is: Jean-Luc Nancy, *The Inoperative Community*, trans. Peter Connor, University of Minnesota Press, Minneapolis, 1991, p. 76.
9 Carter, *Meeting Place*, p. 115.
10 Ibid., p. 103.
11 Ibid., pp. 104–7.
12 Ibid., p. 114, citing Jóhann P. Árnason and David Roberts, *Elias Canetti's Counter-image of Society: Crowds, Power, Transformation*, Camden House, Rochester, N.Y. 2004, pp.119–20.
13 Ibid., p. 114, citing Árnason and Roberts, p. 119.
14 Sean Sayers, *Dialectic and Social Criticism*, EServer, May 1992, viewed 3

June 2015, <http://govt.eserver.org/dialectic-and-social-crit.txt>, citing Georg Wilhelm Friedrich Hegel, *Phenomenology of Spirit*, trans. A.V. Miller, Clarendon, Oxford, 1977, pp. 35–6.
15 Ibid.
16 Paul Carter, 'Showing the Word', in Michael Tawa, *Theorising the Project: A Thematic Approach to Architectural Design*, Cambridge Scholars Publishing, Newcastle, UK: 2011, pp. vii-ix, vii.
17 Carter, *Material Thinking*, p. 185, citing Georges Bataille, 'Informe' in Documents, no.7, December 1929. Reproduced in Georges Bataille, *Visions of Excess: Selected Writings*, 1927–1939, University of Minnesota Press, Minneapolis: 1985.
18 John Rajchman, '*Les Immatériaux* or How to Construct the History of Exhibitions', *Tate Papers*, No. 12, October 2009, viewed 3 June 2015, <www.tate.org.uk/research/publications/tate-papers/les-immateriaux-or-how-construct-history-exhibitions.
19 'Rather than providing the viewers with a clear trajectory with a succession of visual artworks, they [the artworks of *Les Immatériaux*] staged "a labyrinth of questions that elicits a feeling of being lost and an incapacity to exhaust the possibilities for connections and meaning", where the viewers needed to rely in [*sic*] all of their senses' (Christina Grammatikopoulou, 'Shades of the Immaterial: Different Approaches to the "Non-object"', Interartive, n.d., viewed 3 June 2015, <http://interartive.org/2012/02/shades-of-the-immaterial/#_ftn10>, para. 13, citing Todd Jerome Satter, *The Black Box in the White Cube: Lyotard's Les Immatériaux as Machinic Theater*, 6 September 2011, viewed February 2012, web page no longer available.

2

CHOREOTOPOGRAPHY'S PREHISTORY

The first part of *Places Made After Their Stories* plunges us straight into the prehistory of the projects that form the book's case studies. A *process science* approach to urban design is proposed where people and place fuse into a common movement form. Contemporary descriptions of an expanded choreographic practice set the stage for this. They give back to the language of gestures a distinct social and ethical sense: abstract space retrieves its topological and affective senses with the result that predeterministic or utopian sociospatial schemata can be discarded. A description of public choreographies that recognise the social value of interweaving (and the nonlinear forms of interaction this involves) suggests a new role for urban designers. No longer designing a stage for prescribed social behaviours, they are dramaturgs instead, stirring pre-existing flows into more complex and turbulent conformations.

Places Made After Their Stories is a dialogue between recent and current developments in such fields as performance studies, social geography, post-linear design, public space governance and particular *forming situations*, place-making projects in which I have been creatively involved. The book proposes an intersection between the formal language of locomotion (choreography) and the physical characteristics of location (topography). A founding hypothesis of this is that situations are generative: local performances are not repetitions of what has happened elsewhere but can produce their own ground rules and distinctive social patternings. In this context, a case study (*River Connect*) is introduced to illustrate how a choreotopographical approach to place-making equips planners to think differently about their responsibilities: a *minor planning* sensibility would allow processes of complexification associated with the turbulence of human communication to shape public space.

River Connect introduces a theme that is also a thinking tool: water. The behaviour of flowing water, its aesthetic appeal and its human associations communicate the idea of thinking and acting fluidly, or going with the flow. In this book, the intelligence of water is recommended as a model of improved social awareness and interrelatedness. However, it is notable even in this project that water is considered in relation to trees: a branch dipped into the water recalls an image of turbulence; routes and roots are ancestrally as well as formally related. The corollary of minor planning would be a public art that fused figure and ground, and by withdrawing from view induced heightened (turbulent) flows. The global whorl pattern of the public artwork *Nearamnew* at Federation Square, Melbourne, was conceived in this spirit.[1] However, the object of *Places Made After Their Stories* is not to go over old ground; it is to narrate new developments which demonstrate the utility of this kind of concrete situated thinking in generating a richer urban design milieu.

The question with which Part 1 concludes is that of measure. How is the feedback between people and setting measured? A suite of choreotopographical experiments is described that tackles this issue. However, an observational technique suited to the study of behaviours that are intrinsically mimetic and interactive is challenging. A recent survey of the visitation rates to the twelve major institutions housed within Melbourne's art precinct revealed that over two-thirds of the total visits were concentrated in Federation Square.[2] This site represents only a small fraction of the arts infrastructure, and yet its distinctively porous spatial configuration, its openness to transient pedestrian flows and its adoption of a diverse cultural program have clearly attracted unprecedented levels of activity for an Australian public square. The popularity of Federation Square is symptomatic of the recent transformations in the relationship between public space and cultural activity.[3] But how is the success of such a place measured qualitatively?

Choreotopography takes its own etymology seriously: it *draws together* dance and place. The mechanism, the writing that translates between the *chorus*, or group of dancers, and the *topos*, or place, is storytelling. As the association of *chorus* with singing and *topos* with topic (or theme) suggests, storytelling means in this context the mythopoetic mechanisms societies use to understand themselves and the world they live in. If 'places are made after their stories' – to adapt the formulation of schoolteacher and artist Geoffrey Bardon for the way in which the Papunya Tula painting movement came into being – it is because the stories in question are poetic descriptions of place-making. Continuing the story of *Nearamnew*'s composition, Part 2 illustrates this point through reference to an Aboriginal Australian (Kulin nation) account of the formation of the land and water where Melbourne now stands. The tools Bunjil uses to carve the earth into its present form and to drive the people to their present places contrast strongly with the rule and measure of the colonial planner. The result is a non-programmatic opening up of space where coexistence may be negotiated. A feature of this mythopoetic narrative is the vortical constitution of the *chora*, with reference to the "city in motion", where the *chora* is perceived as a movement form, a feedback loop between movements or trajectories and the traces they leave, and therefore doubly constituted as a site of social attraction and repulsion.[4]

To say that places are discursive constructions is to give back to discourse its physical or choreotopographical sense as a rhythmically orchestrated to-and-fro between different positions. It is to define the character of the discourse as poetic, as the metaphorical mapping of relationships predicated on differences. Talking places emerge where the convening parties can find common symbolic (metaphoric) ground: symbols are inherently polysemous and lend themselves to further interpretation. They do not exhaust the potential of the in-between, and two people finding common ground can easily swivel to include new voices, views and interests. Engaging the imagination, symbolic narratives enable people to discover in their different founding stories convergent themes, images and interests. *Red Ways*, a four-year engagement with the Alice Springs community, is the main theme of the second part, and it serves to illustrate these points. It shows how in the project to build a meeting place symbolic identifications with trees were important. Trees in Alice Springs are not, though, symbolic in the sense of representing, say, a moral value; they are indexically tied to water. There is a direct, if hidden, relationship between their distribution and the key to the Centre's vitality, water, its characteristic periodicity, distribution and percolation. In a further turn of the mythopoetic enquiry, *Red Ways* was able to find common ground between the Arrernte notion of *utyerre*, or tie to country, and the concept of 'region' informing the observational science of Charles Todd, the Director of the Overland Telegraph project (1870–1872).

The role of the designer in this process of poetic reformulation recalls that of the classical rhapsode, cutting together different stories to produce a new emotional geography. But the symbolic capture is not simply poetic; it can produce a cartographic gesture or set of eidetic remappings and overlays that transcends the planner's talk of reconnection to produce instead, a subtler skein of ideas, complexified (folded together) images and tied-together creative regions that are related or gathered, rather than connected (because collected).

The discussion of *Red Ways* focuses on the mythopoetic dimensions of the engagement as these contributed most to the conceptualisation of Alice Springs as a storied network of living arrangements. However, the master lexicon of the period was certainly different. Not all projects are equal either in the extent of connections made or in their design. *Red Ways* began as an invitation from the Alice Springs Uniting Church to consider the redevelopment of Lot 74 on Todd Street Mall as a meeting place. Shortly after, this proposal got absorbed into the Northern Territory Government's *Moving Alice Ahead* strategy, part of which was the *Lifestyle* project (as I say, the lexicon had its own flavour), to 'develop strategies and infrastructure that make Alice Springs an even better place to live, work and invest'. A key component of the *Lifestyle* project was 'the redevelopment of the Mall and CBD [central business district] [to] revitalize the town centre'.[5] At the confluence of these events came my report *Care at a Distance*, with its observation that 'recent discussions about the redevelopment of the Alice Springs CBD have identified the need to underpin the physical design with a powerful metaphysical design, an overarching story that residents (Aboriginal and non-Aboriginal) and visitors (Australian and international) can recognize as uniquely distinguishing Alice Springs from other places and communities'.[6]

In retrospect, here at the outset was a tension between two discourses of place-making: one infrastructural, the other cultural.

If proof were needed that words matter, it was supplied by the Alice Springs Town Council, which objected to the title of the report on the grounds that it suggested the undue influence of Darwin on local decision-making.[7] Much of the original work for what became, in October 2008, *Red Ways: Alice Springs CBD Revitalisation, Design Options Framework* (by then our design studio, Material Thinking, responsible for delivering the project, had absorbed some of the planning speak which had come to dominate the conversation) took place in the context of developing a design concept for a visitors centre.[8] Although the proposal came to nothing, it was interesting for its fusing of infrastructure and program and for embedding both in the 'passage' between Todd Street Mall and the Todd River. The creation of a cellular event space connected by *axons*, or passages, mediated between Aboriginal Australian understandings of place as the embodiment of ancestral journeying and a broader community aspiration to 'reconnect' to the river. A direct relationship was proposed between choreography and topography, the two cleaving in the storying of the way itself. The proposed facility was not a 'centre' but a procession of minor meeting places strung along tracks that, in turn, spread in other directions to articulate a network of possible relationships. The design was dramaturgical rather than prescriptive. As the *Red Ways* report explained, 'One thing that distinguishes a Design Options Framework from a master plan is the attention it gives to non-material heritage. For example, the way different communities make places reflects the different ways they relate to one another; places reflect different systems of law, different ways of making decisions. To see this you have to watch, listen and wait. Sometimes the symbols used to depict places disguise these differences'.[9]

For the best part of two years, the mythopoetic underwriting of *Red Ways* kept up with the growing pressure to interpret *revitalisation* purely in terms of adjustments to the physical design of Todd Street and its environs. The advent of a new administration in 2009 changed that: without any investment in the previous government's goals, driven perhaps by a desire to differentiate their own initiatives, the new Northern Territory Government convened the Alice Springs Planning for the Future Forum, in March 2009. Out of this came two recommendations immediately relevant to *Red Ways*: a review of the development control clauses applicable to the CBD zone and the development of a framework plan for the revitalisation of Alice Springs' CBD. The 'framework' proposed here was very different from our design options framework. Reverting to the language of planning, it referred to the legal, administrative and environmental guidelines against which any revitalisation strategy should be measured. It was a framework for prioritising such competing needs as parking, pedestrian access, business opportunity and connectivity. Any notion of overarching storylines had gone. Any appreciation of the role design might play in drawing out and drawing together had disappeared. Finally, a greatly expanded revitalisation strategy, *Connecting Alice*, was delivered in early 2010. It was an odd document, awkwardly overlaying onto the local and regional governmental obsession with the 'upgrade' of Todd Street Mall the creative template of projects distributed across the centre of town, which together redefined the centre as a creative region, a string figure of meeting places and storied passages.

Notes
1 See Emily Potter's recent account, 'Postcolonial atmospheres: Recalling our shadow places', in Paul Ashton, Chris Gibson & Ross Gibson (eds),

By-roads and Hidden Treasures: Mapping Cultural Assets in Regional Australia, University of Western Australia Press, Perth, 2015, pp. 75–86.
2. Positive Solutions, 'Southbank Cultural Precinct Draft Audit', Melbourne, August 2012, p. 29.
3. See, for example, Nikos Papastergiadis, *Cosmopolitanism and Culture*, Polity, Cambridge, UK, 2012.
4. John Sallis, *Chorology: On Beginnings in Plato's Timaeus*, Indiana University Press, Bloomington, 1999, p. 127.
5. Northern Territory Government, *Moving Alice Ahead: Lifestyle*, brochure, Northern Territory Government, Darwin, 2007.
6. Material Thinking, *Care at a Distance*, March 2007. Available online at www.materialthinking.com.au.
7. Ken Hawkins, pers. comm.
8. Even this is only the barest summary. Between March 2007 and October 2008, for instance, the following important milestones were reached:
    - June 2007, Material Thinking, 'Care at a Distance, strategy for delivering the Moving Alice Ahead: Lifestyle, CBD Revitalisation'.
    - December 2007, Northern Territory Government adopts 'Care at a Distance strategy'.
    - January 2008, Material Thinking, 'Red Ways Visitors Centre Design Options Brief' and 'Adelaide House Museum, Draft Master Plan'.
    - March 2008, The Northern Territory Government Department of Planning and Infrastructure invites Material Thinking to develop the 'Red Ways' proposal.
    - July 2008, Material Thinking, 'Alice Springs CBD Revitalisation Progress Report'.
    - October 2008, Material Thinking, 'Red Ways: Alice Springs CBD Revitalisation, Design Options Framework'.
    - January 2009, Material Thinking, 'Flagging the Future: Red Ways: Alice Springs CBD Revitalisation, Design Options Framework Strategic Summary'.
9. Material Thinking, 'Flagging the Future: Red Ways: Alice Springs CBD Revitalisation, Design Options Framework Strategic Summary, January 2009', pp. 1–20, p. 16.

3

THE MYTHOPOETIC CATALYST

In contrast, the project outlined in Part 3, *Golden Grove*, had a conventional history. It, too, remains incomplete, but much of the original intention has survived the institutional amnesia inherent in the musical chairs of professional and political preferment. The choreotopographical impulses of *Red Ways* sprang from a number of place-making stories whose interpretation was informal and flexible. In a way, they sought to give back to development its older sense of unveiling: rather than erase older traces of passage, encasing the ground in a new pavement of concrete, we wanted to expose an everyday experience of passing, to suggest the energetic meeting places embedded in these ordinary traverses. The symbolic economy of *Golden Grove*, on the other hand, was remarkable for its frugality, as the entire scheme was generated from the poetic, cultural and historical associations of one root phrase, *golden grove*. Poetic research into the history of the Darlington campus of the University of Sydney had excavated a veritable Hill of Troy of overlapped strata of historical, cultural and environmental associations mediated through the name. The name thus suggested a creative algorithm, a generative place signature whose translation into a spatial template (through the astral golden grove of the Seven Sisters, or Pleiades) not only met functional expectations (the punctuation of passage, the illumination of the ways and eidetic re-enchantment or ambience) but translated these into a choreotopographically informed public artwork distributed throughout the landscape design, where its affordances (text, ground pattern and illumination) invited a performative interpretation.

Red Ways and *Golden Grove* were very different kinds of projects. However, when juxtaposed, they prove to have affinities we had not anticipated. The history of *Golden Grove* concludes with a discussion of the term *strategy*. An older non-militaristic sense of *spread* is foregrounded. The Alice Springs design options framework was strategic in this older sense, because it proposed a distribution of local projects, which, as they matured, spread out and joined up. A master plan that calls itself strategic misrepresents itself, as its object is to eliminate spread, to confine development to precisely defined operational rules and areas. Master plans usually fail because they do not indicate where to start. The point here is that the metaphorical foundations of the strategy found in *Red Ways* and *Golden Grove* are the same: both take their leads from the movement forms of the river and the tree. An intuitive identification is made between the anastomosing habits of central Australian hydrology and the typical profile of the eucalyptus. The physical resemblance between the bark pattern of the red river gum and the braided ochre and silver grey runnels of a desert creek after rain is obvious and well known. But under these external visual convergences, the poetic imagination perceives the rhythmic form of living time, creative nature. Roots and routes simply bunch time differently, their patternings representing different rates of spread. Whatever the pace, dissipation is not the waste of time but the multiplication of possible connections. The white tree against the red hill, the dendritic shadows in the sand: they are the traceries of passages that remain unfinished.

The Mythopoetic Catalyst

Places are made after their stories: material thinking enters the field of public space design discursively, through an original, mythopoetic interpretation of figures of speech. These may be names, metaphors, stories and the rhetorical gestures associated with them. Speech, like writing, has its flourishes: arabesques in the environment are the graphic residue of passage. Writing can be performative, denoting a habitual action at that place. Public signs can function in this way, as a choreography for strangers. When individual business names and shop window lists of services offered are mapped, they suggest the anonymous ebb and flow of capital, the endless materialisation of desire into economically mediated social relations. In *Golden Grove*, the mythopoetic catalyst was esoteric and obscure: the name had all but passed from local memory. In contrast, the figure of speech that generated *Alterations*, a public space design program and design developed for the new civic square in Dandenong, a south-east suburb of Melbourne, described in Part 4, might have been overlooked because it was so common: the 'alterations' service that many local businesses provided was unproblematically embedded in the everyday lexicon of exchange. However, on closer inspection, it proved to disguise a desire of transformation that comprehensively resisted the politics of multicultural self-identification.

Clothing alterations, like other forms of cosmetic disguisement and improvement, demonstrate the existence of a collective desire to fit in. They also, it turned out, disclose an awareness of what is fitting to the adornment of public space. Alteration was interpreted to mean the creation of a public domain where, in a local variation of Canetti's transformed community, people of different backgrounds could be public actors, commanding a plurality of beings, in a conscious fashion. The quality of public space that fitted such a community (that held it together) was described as 'ambience'. In maturing choreotopographical discourse *Alterations* was valuable because of the direct fashion in which it translated between choreography and topography: through the medium of the map qua cloth, it improvised a giant body; then, studying the disposition of the folds produced by this figure, and seeding this movement form with patches – eidetic affordances derived from the textiles on sale in Dandenong's fabric shops – it produced a ground pattern that could be imagined as the printout of the choreo- topo-graphical encounter.

As soon as the performative constitution of the meeting place is foregrounded, the question of what is materialised there arises. If the new public space design is not a set of objects, structures and functions, but something altogether more fluid – a set of shifting arrangements, interweaving paths and vortical moments of intensification – what patterning, Gestalt or other cultural imprint shapes the outcome or provides the rules of movement? What memories, histories and attitudes converge on them there? Although the new forms of behaviour that spin off from the collision of different bodies may be spontaneous, the forms themselves obviously retain the energy forms of what was brought into the situation. In fact, the new emphasis on the *placing* that occurs to produce places anchors the present firmly in a heritage of movement forms. Beside the present crowd, there is a shadowing crowd of preceding movement histories, defined by internalised habits of acceptable propinquity, space navigation and other spatio-temporal tactics associated with bumping into others, negotiating boundaries.

The ghost crowd that shadows the brightly lit, rationalised boulevards, interconnecting walkways and risk-free civic squares is architectural as well as anthropic. The materiality or gravity of new places partly resides in the sense they communicate of a former existence and of painful passage towards the present state of airbrushed functionalism. In Dandenong, interviews with local businesspeople anticipated the destruction of their premises. Our own performances danced around the edges of what in different circumstances would be termed a disaster. We factored in the ruin that is the prehistory of construction and proposed that the memory of passage be materialised in the public programming of the new civic square. Following this, in the two case studies in Part 5, located respectively in central Melbourne and at an isolated site on Port Phillip Bay, social fantasy and architectural functionality circle each other in a *folie à deux*.

'Transnational and Temporary: Placemaking, Students and Community in Central Melbourne' was a study carried out from 2006 to 2008 of overseas students' sense of place in their temporarily adopted country of educational residence. Led by colleagues at the University of Melbourne, supported through an Australian Research Council Linkage Grant and developed in association with the Melbourne City Council, the state Department for Victorian Communities and Department of Sustainability and Environment, it had a robustly positivistic stance and focus. Here, though, I record a negative choreotopography that eluded our methodological radar, a phantom community that students projected onto an abandoned site at the heart of the study area. In their state of postindustrial suspension, awaiting further destruction and redevelopment, the remains of the Carlton and United Brewery possessed an emotional magnetism quite missing from the anointed sites of gathering. The ghost community imagined there was considerably more lively than the one found in the commercial venues for socialising located in the busy central Melbourne shopping malls.

In ways not foreseen at the time, this insight informed our response to the second case study, which arose from an invitation to review the master plan prepared for the Point Nepean Quarantine Station in anticipation of the estate's transfer from federal to state ownership. However, the flavour of the connection is evident in the following passage from the reverse brief we presented to the Point Nepean Community Trust in January 2008:

> Our observation is that the genius loci of the Quarantine Station resides in the fact that it locates and institutionalises a unique kind of place. The function of the Quarantine Station was to stand in-between departure and arrival. It was a kind of non-place, interesting because it was commissioned by a society in order to secure their sense of place. The genius loci of the Quarantine Station is to possess a genius non loci. Its sense of place is bound up with the vision of another place, one whose interests it acts to secure. As an in-between or pre-place, the Quarantine Station exemplifies the idea of an 'imaginary construction'. In order to regulate arrival and control disease, the Station had to invent all manner of rituals. These played out the anxiety of the authorities, and those who wanted to gain entry had to be good actors in the social pageant. The Quarantine Station was associated with play. It was an intellectual as well as institutional front line – how do you visualize viruses? It was a place dedicated to education through the application of principles of social hygiene.[1]

Physically, the rationally arranged and carefully maintained quarantine buildings and the derelict site of the former Carlton and

United Brewery stood at opposite ends of the heritage spectrum, but culturally, they belonged to the same history of passage. In its *posthistoire* state, the brewery had become a no-man's-land where strangely invisible social hybrids passed through at night; however, in the full view of day, this had been the function of the quarantine station from the outset, whose barriers, checks and fumigation chamber staged the foundation of non-meeting at the heart of Western society's theory of planned sociability. 'This mechanization of movement was designed to create a place of meeting where no-one met. Goods passed over while miasmatic vapours were dissipated. In the clipped, rectilinear boustrophedon corridors of the barrier errancy was eliminated. Every step was taken to defer arrival, to keep the stranger walking backwards and forwards more or less on the spot. It is no accident that check-in counters of every kind use the same barrier system today. The object is the same: to transform the crowd into a linear queue, and to substitute for the protocols of meeting the discipline of waiting.'[2] Quarantine stations were primarily intended to inhibit the spread of plague, and as the methods they used to do so were ineffectual, they were often little more than turn-gates to the other world. Their linear descendant is the homeless man forced to march to the *ballet mécanique* of bureaucratic timekeeping.

Notes
1   Material Thinking, 'The Sense of Place @ the Point Nepean Quarantine Station, Reverse Brief to the Master Plan', 2008, p. 6. In the imaginary construction of the state, see Benedict Anderson, *Imagined Communities*, Verso, London, 1983.
2   Carter, *Dark Writing*, p. 67.

4

PLANNING, POIESIS, PEDAGOGY

If choreotopography has any consistency as an approach to place-making that fosters encounter, it should be reproducible. The final parts of *Places Made After Their Stories* explores this inference in two rather different environments: a major urban redevelopment project and a postgraduate seminar. The discursive construction of places, mediated through the designer as dramaturg, remobilises a symbolic economy. It involves a poetic sensibility alive to convergences of sense between different cultures and their sign systems. The advocate of places made after their stories enjoys a hybrid existence, part-anthropologist, part-artist. It is not immediately obvious that the choice of overarching metaphor made in *Red Ways* or *Golden Grove* could ever be arrived at inductively: at some point an affective leap is made, a connection that the designer finds significant (and can defend) but which without their intervention and advocacy would remain unrealised. The mythopoetic turn of mind that draws inspiration from the phrase *golden grove* or from resemblances between the concept of *utyerre*, or tie to country, and other forms of care at a distance displays a subjectivism that is too opportunistic to support a research program, say, let alone an approach to place-making that less-dramaturgically inclined architects, landscape designers and urban planners could adopt.

To counter this conclusion, *Places Made After Their Stories* describes various strategies for translating between planning and poiesis, between the instrumentalist rhetoric of the master plan and the creative community's vision of the place where it lives as a total work of art. *Red Ways* deployed a *design options framework*, while a *storyboard* was advocated as a way of organising the place-based knowledge invested in the Point Nepean Quarantine Station into a program that could generate the site's cultural redevelopment and associated economy. However, the formulation that has been most effective in creating a cross-disciplinary and cross-institutional meeting place has been the *creative template*. As we explained in introducing the concept to government and community stakeholders in the Yagan Square project in Perth,

> one object of the creative template is to broker common ground that allows creativity full rein. However, we ask readers to be patient with the language used in the creative template; it uses metaphors, patterns and other forms of resonance to build a sense of place. Some of us want narratives; others are suspicious of stories. The creative template identifies *increase sites* for the imagination: some will interpret these as branding opportunities, others as cultural stories – and others simply as artistic cues to investigate texture, form, arrangement and program.

As this statement implies, a primary function of the creative template was the stimulation of cross-cultural discussion about Yagan Square's symbolic meaning: what histories, stories, images and messages would it communicate? In this context, we explained,

> the creative template establishes a symbolic lexicon, a constellation of crosscultural convergences or likenesses. They are visual forms, physical gestures, narrative

structures, metaphoric associations and shared economic interests. The lexicon has a grammar in the sense that it articulates a particular myth of place. The myth is treated mythopoetically but at the heart of the discovery of convergent meanings is the resistance of the symbol to full translation of exposure. The mythopoetic site interpretation always shadows what can be seen. Mythic fictions have the advantage that they can simultaneously carry several different meanings. They also veil those meanings, which is an advantage since familiarity breeds contempt. Because the symbolic form is constitutionally polysemous, it allows a multiplicity of identifications. It is not exhausted by the proposed equivalences but can build new associations, significances and recognitions.[1]

The creative template is educative; it seeks to draw people out and in. When symbolic forms begin to coalesce into new topics, these can be compared to spaces that open up between *topoi*, or fixed places. These in-between spaces can also be elicited in the classroom. The last case study woven into the fabric of *Places Made After Their Stories* is an experiment in cross-disciplinary pedagogy undertaken at the Centre for Creative Arts at La Trobe University, Melbourne, in late 2012. Adapting Epicurus's hypothesis of *intermundia*, or spaces between worlds, participants in the masterclass were invited to explore convergences between their different interests. The convergences might be thematic, but they were more likely to be structural: the bias of the pedagogy was constructivist. I wanted to see how different materials and material logics could be combined. The definition of good combination would be *fit*, a sense of relational homology that would allow the newly improvised conceptual furniture of the *intermundium* to stand on its own feet. The playful ideational reduction proposed here was, in principle, repeatable: the objects coalescing in the different *intermundia* of the different groups could, in a second distillation or reduction, produce a further set of third-order objects. Although the success of the class must have depended greatly on the attitude and aptitude of the participants, we all had the definite impression that something repeatable had been achieved.

In the zigzag expository fashion used throughout *Places Made After Their Stories*, an intimate recollection of pedagogical play leads, finally, to a reflection on the broader political implications of a 'poetics for this knowing-in-making-useful'.[2] The discussion re-enters one of the earlier topical eddies: the association of choreotopography with the dramaturgy of change. With the polysemous potential of the clothing discourse from *Alterations* in mind, the notion of *crazy patching* is introduced: 'As one can build the crazy patchwork in any direction, the swarm of patches can be affected by an intervention at any number of places around the border; consequently the new order can group and reorganise itself in a number of different ways. There is not one master plan that piecing the pieces together discovers'. However, the last word of *Places Made After Their Stories* is that the insights of this discourse should not be professionalised beyond repair. Ideation – the process through which places of encounter may emerge – involves a feedback between the triad of memory, imagination and invention. While institutions commit themselves to cycles of collective memory loss, they are condemned to repeat themselves. This is the reason for master plans. But creative memory is *involuted*: it is remembering as imagining, and the trace of this combination is an arabesque, not a straight line. If a metaphor can be 'a kind of pirouette performed by an idea, enabling us to assemble its diverse names or images',[3] could not a symbolic discourse be a collectivity of such dance figures? A meeting place composed of these might resemble René Descartes's 'whirlpools or vortices of second element, rotating around their respective central stars to sweep along their planets like boats in a strong current'.[4]

Choreotopography is a place-making practice that demands of those who entertain its principles that they, too, remember, admit their histories, their shadows, their losses. Otherwise, there will be fluidity but no poise, routes but no roots.

Notes

1. Material Thinking, 'A New Body, Creative Template at Yagan Square', 2014, p. 2, citing Spike Bucklow, *The Alchemy of Paint: Art, Science and Secrets from the Middle Ages*, Marion Boyars, London, 2009, p. 168.
2. Cameron Tonkinwise, 'Knowing by being-there making: Explicating the tacit post-subject in use'.
3. Paul Valéry, 'Philosophy of the dance', trans. R. Manheim, in Roger Copeland & Marshall Cohen (eds), *What Is Dance? Readings in Theory and Criticism*, Oxford University Press, New York, 1983, p. 63.
4. John A. Schuster, '"Waterworld": Descartes' vortical celestial mechanics', in Peter R. Anstey & John A. Schuster (eds), *The Science of Nature in the Seventeenth Century: Patterns of Change in Early Modern Natural Philosophy*, Springer, Dordrecht, 2005, pp. 44–5.

5

DRAMATIC SOCIETY

I want to conclude this opening with a caveat, or perhaps an assertion of rights. The temptation, when taking material thinking into the meeting place, using it there to catalyse a dramaturgy of encounter, is to let it become professionalised. Finding 'a poetics for this knowing-in-making-useful', to return to Tonkinwise's expression,[1] easily becomes a question of looking for relevant cultural precedents or methodological analogues when, more properly, its origins are personal. In *Places Made After Their Stories*, useful parallels are drawn between the discursive production of places advocated in the book and the notion that places are made after their stories characteristically found in Aboriginal Australian cultures. The mythopoetic intertwining that can occur through the talking place of the creative template can discover genuinely shared cross-cultural common interests. It does not, though, provide a proper genealogy of the ideas. To speak personally, the intuition of the missed place-making potential of place-making stories and placenames goes back to the analysis of these in my earlier work *The Road to Botany Bay: An Essay in Spatial History*: placenames and their associations are compacted myths, the wish fulfilments of imperial fantasy, and establish colonisation as, from the outset, a mythopoetic campaign.[2] But behind this assertion is the personal experience of an English migrant reaching Australia in the 1980s, finding that the English language no longer served him.

In other words, the spatial history projected onto the Australian experience had one of its roots in a personal drama.

Such biographical vicissitudes may be legitimate baggage in an artist or writer, but they conventionally have no place in the professionalised practices of place-making. By the time that a poetic theory of a new society's coming into being at that place has been turned into a hybrid public art and public space design practice, it is expected to have achieved a certain level of scientific or at least operational objectivity. To meet this expectation, artists and designers have developed a sophisticated rhetoric, which represents the object, arrangement or program they have conceptualised *semiotically*. By a clever logical sleight of hand, the through line of the designer's interests (influences, aesthetic preferences, style) evaporates: the creative response is presented as simply another way of talking about what is already there. Any suggestion of innovation or individuality, any criticism that might attach to this, is neutralised by the claim that it responds directly to the functional brief. Colour palette, material choice and form, scale and arrangement can be rationalised (and rendered acceptable) when sourced from the immediate physical or cultural environment. Even flamboyant architects are careful to present their designs as representations of the client's intentions. Public artists (perhaps the most traditional material thinkers to work regularly in the public domain) present their work entirely in terms of one-to-one translations of stories into significant forms: their goal is as far as possible to contextualise the proposal so completely that the nervous politician can, if necessary, defend the work as invisible (making no difference at all).

There are some parts of the choreotopographical approach that can be preserved in generalisations or formalised as methods. The approach to creative community formation, or *weak collaboration*, the improvisation of graphic techniques for mediating between words and images, the reorientation towards the production of ambience through materialising the immaterial: these can certainly be taken over by the place-making professions and integrated into the design of place-making projects. There are other aspects, however, that remain contingent on the forming situation and whose emergence cannot be regulated. The role of the rhapsode, for example, presupposes a verbal dexterity and a rhetorical training that are rarely cultivated in the design professions. Even the development of dramaturgical skills will in all likelihood reflect the vicissitudes of upbringing and training. In this context of specialisation, where the feedback loop of personal reflection is discouraged, the professionalisation of choreotopographical insights, perspectives and techniques asks something of the profession itself. The translation of a spatial poetics into the language of administrative reason cannot all be one way. The users – those who will make material thinking useful – also have to learn something. They have to learn to know differently.

When I was growing up, in England, my father belonged to the local dramatic society. I never pondered the meaning of this name until I became myself an instrument in the production of a *dramatic* society. My father produced plays: the make-believe fascinated me, the coloured footlights, the stage props, the make-up, the costumes. But, more than the productions, I remember the after-parties, where, for the first time, I experienced ambience. Opening the door into a brightly lit and crowded room filled with noise, with laughter, with, as it appeared to me, alluring adults, I experienced ecstasy in the strict sense of being taken out of myself. At the same time, I compared these occasional rituals of conviviality with the social bleakness that generally pervaded the small town where I lived. The dramatic society had survived from a heroic period of postwar community revival. By the time I was growing up, most of the clubs, associations or activities established in that period had fallen into desuetude. Motor vehicles had taken over the formerly sociable streets. As in the old days when the victims of the Enclosure Acts were thrown to the edges of the roads,[3] we found ourselves avoiding the traffic, in our own marketplace thrown to the walls.

I felt the contrast between the animation of my father's stage productions and the *anomie* of local public life. I wondered how the drama of sociability had been pushed back from the streets into the theatre. As the theatre was a Nissen hut rented from the army, located obscurely on the outskirts of the town, the impression was reinforced that creative communities and the artificial production of sociability were marginal to everyday life. I glimpsed in the lit world behind the proscenium arch the truncated rituals of an older, richer society. In our town, the impact of the Enclosure Acts had fallen historically with the fullest weight; after the privatisation of the fields, public space had contracted to roads and pavements. Reflecting on the retreat of the theatre and the historical contraction of the commons, I reached the possibly spurious conclusion that they were connected. It followed, at least to me, that the theatre colluded in the land grab. By relocating the drama of society safely behind the footlights, it encouraged a kind of political quietism: the make-believe antics performed on the stage distracted from the everyday experience of being exiles in our own country.

This personal history illustrates the point that in becoming useful place-making knowledge choreotopography should not sacrifice the character of its origins and operations. The pressure to professionalise should not leach out expressive motivations. Its process is vortical and helical, a continuous resituating of old themes, an evolutionary overlaying of formerly separate motifs to produce new, more complex combinations. Choreotopography is the social art of spatial memory. Everyone who appreciates its value in the design of encounter enters its orbit through the activation of their own spatial histories. Its dramaturgy recasts the involute of a lifetime's body memories into the space of encounter. *My* choreotopography will always be motivated by a desire to repair the spatio-social schism observed a long time ago in southern England. It springs from the migrant experience in Australia. It is tutored by Aboriginal Australian theories and practices of place-making. Repeated exposures to the heat of sceptical planners temper it. However, it will always retain a personal signature, cryptically embedded in the script of the place. Historical enclosures (and corresponding exclusions) will always shadow its desire to disclose a richer social possibility.

Notes

1 Cameron Tonkinwise, 'Knowing by being-there making: Explicating the tacit post-subject in use'.
2 Paul Carter, *The Road to Botany Bay: An Essay in Spatial History*, Faber & Faber, London, 1987, chap. 3.
3 William Cobbett wrote of the situation near Faringdon, 'The labourers seem miserably poor... Their wretched hovels are stuck upon little bits of ground on the road side, where the space has been wider than the road demanded. In many places they have not two rods to a hovel. It seems as if they had been swept off the fields by a hurricane, and had dropped and found shelter under the banks on the roadside' (William Cobbett, *Rural Rides*, London, T. Nelson & Sons, 1923, p. 19.).

Part 1

6

WHAT IS CHOREOTOPOGRAPHY?

Choreotopography, a neologism intended to announce a new field of study, is defined as the phenomenon of feedback between sociability and setting. Evidence of sociability is the peaceful gathering and interflow of people in public space: the Italian *passeggiata*, a nightclub crowd dancing, the ordinary ebb and flow of people crisscrossing a nodal space in any urban landscape. The setting in this context is the form of the built space, together with the sensuous affordances it offers people to orient themselves and navigate it. The goal of choreotopography is to diffuse and possibly dissolve or transcend the figure-ground conception of behaviour in public spaces evident in this first definition: in choreotopography, a notion of self-organising flows or groupings is substituted for the theatrical representation of sociability as a phenomenon occurring on a pre-given stage. An ambiguity should be noted right at the beginning: in choreotopography, the 'multiplicity of singularities', as Jean-Luc Nancy defined the post-communitarian crowd, is self-organising, because it is open to influences from the setting or non-human environment.[1] In contrast, the theatrically imagined actors of sociological and group psychological theories are motivated entirely by drives – subjective apprehensions and interpersonal calculations – that are notionally independent of (closed off from) the surroundings. Sociability is, in this counter apprehension, the supplement of openness –

something like a willingness to *go with the flow* – which, it is proposed, certain milieux induce. Individuals and groups become self-organising when they exhibit a disposition to interact with their surroundings, an inclination to self-modification that is situational, improvisatory and creative.

David Hume attempted to introduce the experimental (or Newtonian) method of reasoning into moral subjects.[2] In a small way, choreotopography introduces process science into urban design. The 'fixed scientific cosmology' that Alfred North Whitehead attacked finds its counterpart in contemporary Western urban planning, which treats space as the passive container of objects that can be rearranged at will. Both presuppose 'the ultimate fact of an irreducible brute matter, or material, spread through space in a flux of configurations. In itself such a material is senseless, valueless, purposeless. It just does what it does do, following a fixed routine imposed by external relations which do not spring from the nature of its being'.[3] While scientific materialism was overthrown a century ago, what might be called *urban materialism*, manifest in the continuing authority granted to master planning, remains dominant in our training institutions and bureaucratic culture. In this recalcitrant context, the object of choreotopography is to materialise the immaterial, to assert the existence of a force that shapes the in-between into events, occasions (or encounters), and to argue that this force is nothing other than the interaction (or feedback) between conscious subjects and intervening surroundings. 'Mathematical physics presumes in the first place an electromagnetic field of activity pervading space and time. The laws which condition this field are nothing else than the conditions observed by the general activity of the flux of the world, as it individualises itself in the events.' The end result is that 'nature is a structure of evolving processes. The reality is the process'.[4] In its own way, choreotopography presumes a prior sociality,[5] studying the individualisation of its general activity in events. It supposes that the structure is not entirely internal to the subject, or entirely external: binding figure and flux is an erotic field of activity or movement form. A primary aim of choreotopography is to establish whether movement forms exist that express essential social configurations or patterns of mingling.

Various attempts have been made to elicit the character of the *movement form*, as the self-organising assemblage of people and place might be called. However, they tend to perpetuate the figure-ground binarism mentioned earlier. The effort to humanise space has led to attempts to define what is meant by such psychologically and emotionally charged terms as *home*, *belonging*, *identity* and *identification*. In the discourses of urban design and landscape design, some of the associations of these terms are evoked through the expression *sense of place*. However, as might be suggested by Michel Maffesoli's remark that a *sense* of place is given to places – buildings, streets, even vistas – 'by one of several imaginary constructions, whether tales or legends, written or oral memories, novelistic or poetic descriptions',[6] in these discourses, the objects composing the place remain inert. Definitions of *place* are endlessly changing: places morph into networks; networks interconnect real and virtual spaces. Even historically and culturally, places are always other places, imaginary doublings and performative redoublings of recollected ambiences or potential meetings. In my view, a more useful interpretation of *sense of place* occurs when *sense* is reconnected to the French word *sentier*, or footpath. Imagining a place as the accumulated trace of all the paths through it suggests that the flux can be patterned: a network of occasions, a reticulated event space is imaginable. The writing or notation of this situated sociability would correspond to a new kind of indexical choreography. However, even this trace of interaction remains after the event and does not influence the evolution of the processes.

Similarly, attempts to adapt choreographic understandings of human movement to the public domain tend to take the ground for granted. In place-based knowledge discourses, the relationship between peoples and places is said to be ecological, in the classical sense of referring to 'the whole science of the relations of the organisms to the environment including, in the broad sense, all the "conditions of existence"'.[7] However, the translation of this into a practice of particular situations or occasions remains undeveloped. The Finnish choreographer Riikka Theresa Innanen describes dance as an 'ecology of creativity, constituted by the body-mind in motion, interacting with the world through a visceral, aesthetic and kinesthetic interface'. She looks to create an expanded choreography that can interact with the wider 'dance' of the world, including perhaps 'the traffic infrastructure in [a] city, personal relations in a family or swarms of people moving through space'.[8] Her expanded definition of dance as a kinaesthetic art form certainly allows for a creative interaction with the 'odd', the other and the unexpected. Yet it remains tied to an assumption that the containing environment of the new social processing is passive.

A link is proposed between the individual skills of the dancer and certain *embedded structures* – which I take to be something like movement forms – which can be compared to the algorithms that drive the emergence of new, more complex forms in intelligent systems. Applying 'strategies from [Gregory Bateson's] Double Loop learning', Innanen describes a 'negative choreography' of movements that dissolves the performer–audience distinction and suggests a kind of 'Social Choreography' or dramaturgy.[9] The mechanism of this induced sociability or social self-organisation is mimicry. In a way, the feedback loops performed by the dancers produce comparable sites of self-transformation that take those in the vicinity out of themselves. However, while these investigations describe an expanded, ecological approach to the dance, they are predicated on a contracted sense of place. The fit of parts – the sense that the different elements can form patterns of increasing 'intelligence' and complexity – is internal to the system. However, as Constantinos Doxiadis points out, ekistics, a form of ecological thinking applied to the human setting, finds that the fit is also external: 'To serve Man best, Shells and Networks must follow the forces of external structure, which require that physical units of the same order, which are parts of any structure, should fit together in the best possible way'.[10]

Perhaps what is needed is a revived 'rhythm analysis', to use Henri Lefebvre's term, a new poetics grounded in 'spatial practices that challenge the "nature" of capitalist space, a practice that rejects the separation of our *bodies* from the *spaces we inhabit*'.[11] Laura Elrick finds neurological support for this possibility in the hypothesis of mirror neurons. If watching someone else perform an action activates the same sensorimotor areas of the brain activated when one performs the action oneself, then *'each of us might actually embody the acts of others'*. But, again, it remains unclear how such a 'reappropriation of the body',[12] while (theoretically) reappropriating capitalist space for the joyous labour of sociability, informs our interactions with the non-human environment. What is needed is another hypothesis that argues for a primary relationship between ourselves and our environment, one that integrates a multisensory wayfinding apparatus with an intuitive grasp of the physical relationship between objects and self: the 'eido-kinetic intuition', as I have called it, meets this need.[13] Ball players illustrate this faculty when they accurately project a missile into an opening; athletes who leverage their performance off equipment and even the everyday walker who successfully avoids bumping into another: all demonstrate the fact that navigation of the world involves a kind of echo location, an incessant calculation of distances, trajectories and landing places, but for which orientation and the successful fit of individual bodies to form a larger, self-organising movement form would be inconceivable.

What is the advantage of bringing the choreotopographic dimension of sociability into play? If a direct relationship between group behaviour and the design of the environment could be established, it would not necessarily promote the adventure of encounter. Instead, it might advance the cause of functionalism, providing a further encouragement to think of design in starkly reductionist behaviourist terms. Treating groups as susceptible to stimuli, it would simply add to the equipment of public control and containment. Alternatively, the discovery that the identity of the crowd and the sense of place were one and the same might merely recapitulate the apprehension of fourth-century-BC Athenians, whose term *agora* referred to both the place of assembly and the people who assembled there. The commonsense experience is that a simple stimulus–response model is not applicable to the way individuals, groups and masses move, mingle, amass and disperse. Social, cultural and political factors outweigh the subliminal impact that streets, squares and other sites of association have on social behaviour; at the same time, it is also observable that convivial arrangements of space are recognised and readily occupied. The background affect of such places can be called their *ambience*, a term that can be reinterpreted as the *steady state* of a people–place assemblage that has high choreotopographic potential.[14]

It seems clear from this reflection that a non-functionalist model of reciprocity between the social and its setting will have difference inscribed into its midst. The *inter esse*, or in-between, will not only have an operational value but as the precondition of flux will be essential to the existence of the process of sociability. Difference, which Emmanuel Levinas controversially describes in terms of the difference between the sexes, is not simply a logical or semiotic necessity; in the discourse of public space, it endows moving bodies with volume and faces. Participation in social production is not a reconciliation of differences (fed by the adventure of difference); it 'conditions the very possibility of reality as multiple'.[15] While the identification of this mystery with the feminine may be sexist, the deeper truth remains: that the 'mode of being' described here is 'modest' and embodies 'hiding [as] the way of existing'.[16] This idea can be developed later in the context of describing the materiality of *turning away*, which Levinas evokes in his distinction between touch and the caress.[17]

A better understanding of the value of measure, of the rhythmic adjustments that inform the gathering and dispersing of people, and of the relationship of these informal figures to the lie of the land or urban setting, might have an ethical dimension. The injunction to turn the other cheek alters its meaning, coming to refer instead to the flexibility moving people show in relation to one another and to the arrangement of objects throughout the ground shared in common. The same disposition to turn aside, so often interpreted as a sign of moral vacillation or weakness of will, also changes its meaning, becoming instead the essential inflection of sociability. In it strongest form, to turn one's back on someone is not necessarily to dishonour them. Instead, it may be an act of modesty or discretion, as when Aboriginal people refuse to return the whitefella's gaze or when Moslem women refuse the proffered handshake.

Turning away, or breaking off conversation preserves the distance at the heart of meeting. It negates Sigmund Freud's vision of an 'ultimate unity',[18] defining the crowd instead as a 'multiplicity of singularities', which coexists but is very rarely together.[19] Tergiversation is not an antisocial act but the social arabesque within the Brownian motion of the meeting place, the algorithm of separation, that ensures that bumping into people (socially), we do not bump into them (physically). Even together, people need to keep their distance. Separation coexists with coming together. It is the principle that differentiates a multitude of singularities from the historical crowd of Gustav Le Bon and Elias Canetti.[20] Singularities are individuals considered in the context of meeting, subjectivities as they appear to another. Together with a desire of association there goes, like a double, a desire to transcend the limits imposed by any historical meeting place. To traverse the erotic zone of all possible meetings is to be like Tadeusz Kantor's actor: all doors.[21]

With the house-carrying snail in mind, Arakawa and Madeline Gins talk of the 'organism-person-environment', the subject who literally knows where they are by carrying themselves over from one place to another – these 'places' being 'landing places' where perception and cognition coincide. They refer to this process as 'metaphorical mapping', and its respect for the trails we leave behind and the shadows we cast ahead sharply contrasts with the remorseless pressure to face each other characteristic of holistic social planning.[22] Such attempts to dissolve the figure–ground opposition and to conceptualise movement form inscribe distance into nearness, turning away into turning towards. Such formulations have an ethical dimension – tergiversation insists on the value of the veil – not from a misguided multiculturalism but because the realm of the hidden shadowing what faces us discloses in the field of visual perception a rondure: the volume of the world but for which there would be no drama of disappearance. This 'pre-visual apprehension' of the curvilinear ways inscribed into the 'gulf' between us explains the haunting power of Alberto Giacometti's groups.[23] They discern there a kind of erotic chiasmus, a vanishing point where Being and Becoming, Love and Death, meet.[24] And these implications are also political: at the heart of the agora assemblage (the fused mass of political agents and the place of their amassing) is a counter-impulse to resist amalgamation and unification.

The act of turning away is, in another guise, the apostrophe within the movement of the poetic dance, a moment of poised arrest, a node in the network of movement forms. But the apostrophe is also the name of speech addressed to one who is not there or who remains invisible. It acknowledges the ever-present possibility of death's irruption. It is the turning place where the limits of human power over change are made manifest. And such deviations are not simply part of choreography's symbolism; in another form, they embody a political philosophy, one of direct relevance to the question of public planning and its totalitarian tendencies. Commenting on the liberalism of Karl Popper, John Gray writes, 'A holistic approach to the methods of the social sciences further suggests the necessity of a *holistic* or *Utopian* approach to social engineering…which "aims at remodeling the 'whole of society' in accordance with a definite plan or blueprint"'.[25] The terms in which Popper rejects the design of society apply equally to the design of public space: the pretensions of the master plan 'to make predictions about the social and political development of man'[26] should be rejected.

In this sense, it is when choreography and topography fuse to create an interference pattern that dance can fulfil Susan Leigh Foster's ambition that it should 'gesture towards other fields of meaning'. According to Foster and the co-editors of *Corporealities*, in its original designation, discourse derives from the experience of dance itself. 'Bodies do not only pass meaning along…[but] develop choreographies of signs through which they discourse: they run (or lurch, or bound, or feint, or meander…) from premise to conclusion; they turn (or pivot, or twist…) through the process of reasoning; they confer with (or rub up against, or bump into…) one another in narrating their own physical fate.' The compilers suggest the discourse of dance can make up for 'that broader interest in the body that still awaits development in language'.[27] But also, choreotopographers would say, development in place for, at the very least, what bodies talk about is an expression of where they find themselves.

Notes

1. On Jean-Luc Nancy's theory of community, see Ignass Devisch, *Jean-Luc Nancy and the Question of Community*, Bloomsbury, London, 2013, p. 113.
2. John P. Wright, *The Sceptical Realism of David Hume*, Manchester University Press, Manchester, 1983, pp. 197–202 for discussion of this claim.
3. Alfred North Whitehead, *Science and the Modern World*, Cambridge University Press, Cambridge, UK, 1926, p. 22.
4. Whitehead, *Science and the Modern World*, pp. 90, 190.
5. Ben Malbon draws attention to the way Michel Maffesoli contrasts sociality with sociability, describing 'the fabric of tactile or proximate forms of communality [in contrast with] the strong "contractual" forms of community that characterise "the social"' (*Clubbing: Dancing, Ecstasy and Vitality*, Routledge, London, 1999, p. 26). Sociality has various definitions according to the ideal society of the writer. Maffesoli, for instance, derives it from a Dionysian theory of orgiastic unification: 'The orgiastic metaphor is the expression of this poetic rhythm which above all good and evil intends to unite, to fuse the elements of a heterogeneous totality' (*The Shadow of Dionysus: A Contribution to the Sociology of the Orgy*, trans. Cindy

Linse & Mary Kristina Palmquist, State University of New York Press, Albany, 1993, p. 72). Emmanuel Levinas, instead, speaks of 'all the surplus or all the goodness of a lost sociality' (*Ethics and Infinity: Conversations with Philippe Nemo*, trans. Richard A. Cohen, Duquesne University Press, Pittsburgh, 1985, p. 11).

6   Michel Maffesoli, *The Contemplation of the World: Figures of Community Style*, trans. S. Emmanuel, University of Minnesota Press, Minneapolis, 1996, p. 98.
7   Gregory J. Cooper, *The Science of the Struggle for Existence: On the Foundations of Ecology*, Cambridge University Press, Cambridge, UK, 2003, p. 5.
8   Riikka Theresa Innanen, *The Ecology of Creativity and Evolution of Choreographic Strategies*, Helsinki Meeting Point, 2011, viewed 3 June 2015, <www.helsinkimeetingpoint.com/riikka/paper2.pdf>, paras 1, 5.
9   Ibid., paras 14–16.
10 Constantinos A. Doxiadis, 'The Ekistic Elements and the Goals of Ekistics', 1964, reprinted in *Ekistics*, vol. 33, no. 197, April 1972, p. 242.
11 Laura Elrick, '*Poetry, Ecology, and the Reappropriation of Lived Space*', The Brooklyn Rail, 12 June 2006, viewed 4 June 2015, <www.brooklynrail.org/2006/06/poetry/poetry-ecology-and-the-reappropriation-of-lived-space>, para 11 (original emphasis).
12 Ibid., paras 15 (original emphasis), 18 (citing Henri Lefebvre, *The Production of Space*, Blackwell, Oxford, 1991, p. 167 and also with reference to Michael Steinberg, *The Fiction of a Thinkable World: Body, Meaning, and the Culture of Capitalism*, Monthly Review Press, New York, 2005, pp. 70–5).
13 Carter, *Dark Writing*, pp. 268–71 where these affective qualities of public space are attributed to an 'eido-kinetic intuition'.
14 The thermodynamic allusion is deliberate: public space management has traditionally been seen as a technique for minimising any ambient variation that might cause the crowd to heat up and agitate.
15 Emmanuel Levinas, *The Levinas Reader*, ed. Sean Hand, Blackwell, Oxford, 1992, p. 48.
16 Ibid.
17 Emmanuel Levinas, *Totality and Infinity: An Essay on Exteriority*, trans. Alphonso Lingis, Martinus Nijhoff Publishers, The Hague, 1978, section 4, p. 89.
18 'Civilization is a process in the service of Eros, whose purpose is to combine single human individuals, and after that families, then races, peoples and nations, into one great unity, the unity of mankind. Why

this has to happen, we do not know; the work of Eros is precisely this' (Sigmund Freud, *Civilization and Its Discontents*, trans. James Strachey, W. W. Norton & Company, New York, 1930, p. 69).

19 See Wilhelm S. Wurzer, 'Nancy and the political Imaginary after Nature', in *On Jean-Luc Nancy: The Sense of Philosophy*, eds. D. Shephard, S. Sparks, and C. Thomas, Routledge, London, 1997, pp. 91–102. For application of Jean-Luc Nancy's thesis to a choreotopographical work, see Paul Carter, *Mythform: The Making of Nearamnew at Federation Square*, Miegunyah Press, Melbourne, 2005, pp. 5–6.

20 See Paul Carter, *Meeting Place*, pp. 108–14.

21 Tadeusz Kantor, *A Journey through Other Spaces: Essays and Manifestos, 1944–1990*, trans. Michael Kobialka, University of California Press, Berkeley, 1993, p. 101.

22 Christina Makris, *The Mapping of Meaning in Madeline Gins' and Arakawa's Architectural Body*, Arizona State University, 2005, viewed 4 June 2015, <www.asu.edu/pipercwcenter/how2journal/archive/online_archive/v2_3_2005/current/in_conference/makris.htm>.

23 For discussion of Giacometti's sculptural groups and their implications for public space design, see Carter, *Meeting Place*, pp. 196–206. The allusion here is to D. H. Lawrence's meditation on the gaze exchanged between Mother and Child in Italian religious painting: 'It is a gaze by no means of innocence, but of profound pre-visual discerning. So plainly is the child looking across the gulf and fixing the gulf by very intentness of pre-visual apprehension, that instinctively the ordinary northerner finds him antipathetic' (*Psychoanalysis and the Unconscious*, W. H. Heinemann, London, 1923, pp. 100–1).

24 For a discussion of the Giacometti installation in the Fondation Maeght, Saint-Paul de Vence, see Carter, *Meeting Place*, pp. 196–206.

25 John Gray, 'The Liberalism of Karl Popper', 1976, reprinted in *Philosophical Notes* No. 9, Libertarian Alliance, 1988, viewed 14 February 2008, <www.libertarian.co.uk/lapubs/philn/philn009.pdf>, p. 2 (original emphasis), with reference to Popper's critique of the historicist doctrine of the social sciences. (See Karl Popper, *Stanford Encyclopedia of Philosophy*, Section 6, para 2. http://facstaff.uww.edu/mohanp/popper.html. Accessed 12 December 2008.

26 Ibid., p. 3.

27 Susan Leigh Foster (ed.), *Corporealities: Dancing Knowledge, Culture and Power*, Routledge, London, 1996, p. xi.

7

THE DESIGNER AS DRAMATURG

Places Made After Their Stories aims to give complexity a good name. Complexity as an expression of nonlinear movement patterns is associated with turbulence. In this context of induced but unpredictable sociability, the public space designer is 'the dramaturg of turbulence, someone who steers the performative techniques associated with particular times and places out into the broader public domain, enacting what Nigel Thrift characterizes as a "processual sensualism" throughout the subtle induction of new movement forms and arrangements in the comings and goings of the public'.[1] Choreotopography takes this theoretical position out into the marketplace of urban design and tests its practicability. It explores the nexus between discourse and design where the discourse is consciously poetic. Usually the discourse of design is stripped of poetic or mythopoetic content. It does not pay attention to the performative dimension of everyday speech: the rote consultation that is a feature of government-sponsored place-making projects discounts the creative and performative aspects of speaking. As places are, at least from an emotional, political and spiritual point of view, made after their stories, this disregard for the information about places embedded in symbolic narrative is disastrous. Eliminated are the great images, the symbolic equipment for linking parts together and discovering shared personal and collective coordinates.

Places Made After Their Stories is not a casebook of success stories. It is a record of steering through difficult institutional, administrative and ideological territory. Describing the different fortunes of projects that aimed to build mythopoetic place-making principles and practices into the fabric and program of urban space, it records relative failures and relative successes. *Red Ways*, in Alice Springs, is the result of an invitation to help shape a new bicultural meeting place. *Golden Grove* is a mythopoetically informed public artwork at the University of Sydney embedded in a landscape design where it functions as a lighting strategy. *Alterations*, in Dandenong, Melbourne, also integrated into a landscape design, is conceived as an eido-kinetic affordance, a ground pattern that communicates a sense of ambience. *Passenger*, at Yagan Square, Perth, a public artwork offspring of the creative template, is an emblem of choreotopographical sensibility. It responds to a creative template that, in turn, illustrates certain principles of minor planning. 'Nothing but the main form of a work will resist the vicissitudes and calamities of presentation', Ezra Pound remarks,[2] and what is true of a theatre production applies within even greater force in the domain of urban design. In compensation, the twists and turns produced by competing interests, understandings and powers can, if incorporated into the design, produce an analogue of processual complexity even when the object of those with authority is to eliminate turbulence.

Failures to agree can be valuable. At least they provoke a determination to clarify the issue at stake, not by an intensification of fixed, conflicting positions but through the recuperation of terms that have different valencies. The status of turbulence is a case in point. Turbulence is symptomatic of a world where reason's capacity to control the forces it has unleashed are repeatedly tested. Ever greater technological predictability produces correspondingly greater realms of murderous, as well as ecstatic, desire. Or, to put it another way, turbulence is inherent in information flows, for the design of public space extends to the virtual domain of the World Wide Web. The discourse of physical spaces, always vortical, interstitially vulnerable and ambiguous, has its counterpart in the viral unpredictability of the social media; and the feedback between virtual and physical worlds, recently foregrounded at Tahrir Square, Cairo, means that the new dramaturgy of public space also stirs up disorder. Authorities seek to curb and control turbulence; the artists, the revolutionaries and the dispossessed see its potential differently. If the uprising of the oppressed is not to lead to a new, neocolonialist authoritarianism, it must command a new language as well as program. The new discourse will rehabilitate the poetic; otherwise, it perpetuates the same logic of dissociation already evident in planning logic.

Agencies of reduction mistrust communities of elaboration. These correspond respectively to *vacuum* cultures and *pressure* cultures. Characterising master planning culture as a vacuum culture, one that sucks turbulence out of the urban atmosphere – thereby creating regions of imbalance that are ultimately unstable – I suggest that the value of repressurising our vacuum culture is not that it licenses a new eroticism indifferent to the larger suffering of the excluded: it is to activate the common air as a tool of social communication, to appreciate it as a universal gesture (and not simply a medium). A dramaturgy of public spaces that released this productive turbulence would pioneer new (or very old) forms of non-verbal communication; it would cultivate a civility of glances, approaches and mutuality. Mingling impression and expression, it would in principle redemocratise public space; climates of opinion, currently determined by powerful interests, would be instantiated in public performances. Such demonstrations of self-organising sociability resist the evacuation of public space characteristic of a vacuum culture: they enact the conviction that the public space precedes the public; like the breath of the gods, it permits their self-becoming.[3] If Rosalind Deutsche is right, and public space is where 'meaning continually appears and continuously fades',[4] then such informally directed 'dances' would (far better than architecture) make a lasting impression on the urban fabric.

Breakdowns in communication can be professionally grim; but they are, as I indicated, intellectually stimulating. They highlight the need to redefine contested terms and to mint concepts adequate to the social innovation intended. The invention of the expression *minor planning* illustrates this. It arose from a mismatch I witnessed in north-eastern Victoria between Aboriginal and non-Aboriginal understandings of place and, consequently, of place management. Ironically, the confusion arose because of the good intention to develop a master plan for the design, management and interpretation of the Goulburn and Broken rivers in the vicinity of the town of Shepparton. A key document in advancing reconciliation between the Aboriginal (largely Yorta Yorta) community and its non-Aboriginal neighbours was an Aboriginal oral history project. Incorporated into the master plan, the oral histories would, it was hoped, translate into 'an iconic program of regeneration of the Goulburn River frontage and local catchment to be undertaken by the Indigenous community in partnership with local Indigenous bodies and non-Indigenous groups and Authorities'.[5] In reality, incorporation proved difficult, because the design value of the place-making stories told through the oral history project was not realised. Instead of being understood as templates for human action, they were interpreted as items of cultural heritage to be represented by other means. A narrative of intermingling flows and catchments applicable to the past

The Designer as Dramaturg

and present formation of the water landscape came into collision with a 'dry' planning and management practice that divided the environment into different closed objects defined by property boundaries and economic function (see Figure 1).

Figure 1 Material Thinking, 'Confluence of Goulburn and Broken Rivers', in 'River Connect, Reverse Brief', April 2008, pp. 1–12, p. 1. Photo: the author.

To mediate between these differences implied a double translation. On the one hand, the regional principles underlying local place-making stories had to be articulated. On the other hand, the dry classification of the environment into discrete themes, operations and timeframes had to be dissolved. I suggested a middle ground in which planning yielded to design and design rediscovered its discursive roots in the act of drawing out (as in telling a story). There emerged from this mediation an image of the region as a system of fluid relations whose meaning was embedded in the way these were narrated, performed and maintained. Instead of a new master plan, I recommended developing a design options framework, a network model of functions and tasks in which the craft of land and water care was inseparable from concomitant tasks of education, recreation and art. The regeneration program was inseparable from participation in the communication of values. Design was strategic in the old sense of strategy, spreading outwards as water does periodically across a flood plain. Planning renounced its anxiety to fix things in place and eliminate unpredictable change.

Unfortunately, the proposal was not adopted. This led me to ponder an alternative planning framework that would make the comprehension of process possible and the delegation of agency over the management of becoming (all unpredictable phenomena associated with the seasonal variability of water flow and distribution) acceptable and even desirable. In an interesting article called 'Whither science? A science without origins: Nomad, minor science and the scientific method', Paulo and Alexandra Correa discuss Gilles Deleuze and Félix Guattari's distinction 'between Royal Science and "a kind of science, or treatment of science, that seems very difficult to classify"', which they call 'minor science'.[6] One part of their discussion seems particularly relevant. The minor science of flow, passage, network and even feedback –

the debt of Deleuze and Guattari to A.N. Whitehead is well known, and this article therefore led back to foundational questions for choreotopography – is able, the authors say, to explain its own explanations. Instead of calling on general principles, it derives sense from the operations themselves. From an ethical point of view, they write, what matters is not the motion–non-motion antithesis but the 'which motion?': 'Striated motion along straight lines, light rays or rehabilitated geodesics, motion that counts Space in order to occupy it – or vortical motion, wave motion, motion with intrinsic measures, that occupies Space as it generates it, in the strictest of senses'.[7]

Their argument is ethical but also aesthetic: promoting a science that reintegrates sensation and sense, they see a parallel between minor science and an equally innovative 'minor art'. 'The real challenge of science is its minor becoming, but in the precise sense of a search for the functions, the energy functions, which create the thing or the event – which creates the "thing-event" *and* the immanent "sense-event" of thing or an event'. This goal corresponds to the production of an artwork when it 'provides the intrinsic logic of the composition of that artwork – a logic which is not separable from the knowledge of the logic of sensation… and which can only be conveyed by the knowledge and mastery of media, materials and the elements of composition'.[8] But this goal might also correspond to a form of planning that puts design first, for design by its very nature always follows one line rather than another. Design answers the question 'which motion?' with a stroke that has longitudinal flexibility and duration, a line that, like the arabesque, can incorporate turbulence into the fabric of what is and what will appear.

A design-led minor planning is not simply master planning with gaps; it demarcates a different, choreotopographically formed environment. In this, the designer does not enclose and divide but instead follows the line of growth. Following the analogy between Deleuze and Guattari's minor science with its focus on 'the constant transformation or alteration of beings, their becomings, transitions and heterogeneities, the dynamics of processes'[9] and the nature of a place, it scores turbulence, graphically notating or outlining the phenomenon of continuously evolving, self-dividing and reforming growth lines that collectively constitute the vitality of a place. Thought of as meetings of heterogeneous elements – how else can places differentiate themselves from their surroundings? – places are always curvilinear deviations from the straight. In this spirit, Correa and Correa suggest Deleuze and Guattari's minor or 'eccentric science' can 'be defined by the proposition "from *turba* to *turbo*" – from the bands or packets of atoms or inert matter, to the vortices they populate while being ordered into jets'. The crowd in this model is not an aggregation of particles forming a solid region; it is imagined after the physics of flux found in the pre-Socratic philosophers – in, for example, Anaxagoras of Clazomena's 'theory of chaos and ordered turbulence, or *nous*'.[10] A dynamic region of this kind is not contained; it generates its own volume.

Transposed into the realm of public space design, Correa and Correa's 'minor science of becoming' dissolves the figure–ground distinction, which, in planning discourse, defines (or confines) the real-world application of design. Instead of measuring space, quantifying and fixing intervals, proportions and relations, a turbulent practice produces its own space, one that, while remaining topologically consistent, is elastic, variable and alterable. The design is wherever the designer and their forming situation are; and everyone, or at least the 'public', is involved in its vortical infolding and unfolding. The public space designer of this type can be compared to the new breed of dramaturg who, in certain kinds of post-theatral performances, replaces the traditional director. In his influential paper 'The Deep Order Called Turbulence: The Three Faces of Dramaturgy', Eugenio Barba describes a 'dramaturgy of changing states' charged with anxiety and ambivalence, as inherently ambiguous and instinctual physical movement wrestles with the conventionally delimiting constraints of symbolic language, generating what he effectively calls 'turbulence'. Unpredictability is written into the new script, but what emerges makes a new kind of sense, for turbulence is vortical: 'It engenders vortexes that upset the current of narrative action. In the absence of these vortexes the continuity, rhythm, and narrative risk lapsing into the obvious, into mere illustration'.[11]

Contributors to 'On Turbulence', a recent issue of *Performance Research*, amplify and apply these remarks in a wide range of different contexts and practices.[12] Most of the turbulent situations they evoke could, however, be performances of design process. In its essence, the line that departs from itself, that curves under pressure from an outside influence in the manner of Lucretius's unpredictable swerve, or *clinamen*, is the script of such performances. As the 'falling' atom is deflected, so it deflects.[13] The sum of all such swerves constitutes what is called *Brownian motion*, which, as D'Arcy Wentworth Thompson observes, can be scaled up to describe the behaviour of the human crowd.[14] The tracks formed in this way are feedback loops. They do not loop back to the site of original collision or bifurcation; they carry forward this impressed energy into every other reaction. The history of such events is Moivrean, rather than Humean: 'A Moivrean event is a set of complete paths through the tree, while a Humean event is a more localised collection of individual steps or chains of steps…A Humean event is most local when it consists of a single step, and then the alternatives are other steps from the same starting point. The alternatives to a Moivrean event include all other paths through the tree, and these may spread out in space and time'.[15] Thomas De Quincey gives this turbulent motion a proto-dramaturgical character when he reflects, 'Every intricate and untried path in life, where it was from the first a matter of arbitrary choice to enter upon it or avoid it, is effectually a path through a vast Hercynian forest, unexplored and unmapped, where each several turn in your advance leaves you open to new anticipations of what is next to be expected, and consequently open to altered valuations of all that has already been traversed'.[16]

The new 'Hercynian forest' is the internet and the interactive app that enable individual navigators to modify their paths in response to information about other paths. Such a capacity becomes turbulent when the other paths respond to the modified path, producing a kind of maelstrom of mutually altering and converging paths. In performance, a turbulent state obtains when the phenomenon of mutual modification becomes the basis of the work. A place-based app can show many people where they are in the city in relation to various phenomena; accordingly, it influences their navigation of the city.[17] However, it becomes a turbulent event only when the individuals using the service start to modify their behaviour in relation to one another, whereupon a collectivity begins to emerge, self-organising and unpredictable. The iSkyTV project of the Institute for Infinitely Small Things seems to work across these levels of self-awareness and self-organisation.[18] Comparable self-aware feedback loops occur in the transitional zone between ritual and historical re-enactment – and between both these layers of twice-remembered behaviour and the situation where the participants are collectively responsible for devising the new work. This observation applies to certain kinds of performances,[19] but also to the dynamics of cross-cultural encounter. In such cases of mimetic self-modification, a potential exists to improvise new rules of sociability.[20]

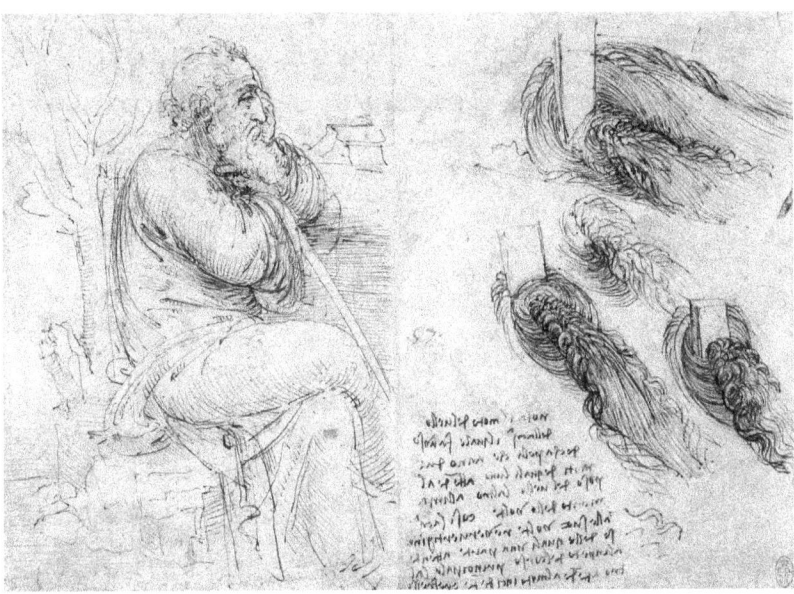

Figure 2 Leonardo da Vinci, 'An old man in profile to right, seated on a rocky ledge; water studies and a note, pen and ink', 154 x 216 mm, c.1513. *The Drawings and Miscellaneous Papers of Leonardo de Vinci ... at Windsor Castle*, ed. C. Pedretti, Harcourt Brace Jovanovich, London and New York, 1981, p. 48 r. Royal Collection Trust/©Her Majesty Queen Elizabeth II 2015.

Such interactions are obviously creative, but their power to invent new rules of coexistence adequate to the complexity of the situation depends on the willingness of the participants to reflect on their habitual behaviour. In pedagogy, this self-reflexive and self-organising potential corresponds to Gregory Bateson's already mentioned idea of learning about learning, or deutero-learning.[21] Chris Argyris discusses 'double-loop learning',[22] and, in another spatio-choreographic metaphor, the psychologist Kurt Lewin speaks about a theory and practice of social action involving a 'spiral of steps'.[23] When feedback leading to turbulence, or complex cascades of events that cannot be prescribed occur, the 'director' yields to the 'dramaturg': instead of actors passively following directions, the new organiser is like Leonardo da Vinci's old man pondering the whirlpool, experimentally lowering a staff into its chaos to observe the effect (see Figure 2). The feedback loops produced through this intervention are not foreign to nature. All the dramaturg has done is expose the turbulent potential of the medium and its capacity to self-organise at a higher level of complexity.

Notes

1. Carter, *Meeting Place*, p. 192, citing Nigel Thrift, 'Movement-space: the Changing Domain of Thinking Resulting from the Development of New Kinds of Spatial Awareness', *Economy and Society* 33: 4 (November 2004).
2. Ezra Pound, *Antheil and the Treatise on Harmony*, P. Covici, Inc., Chicago, 1927, p. 129.
3. See Paul Carter, 'Pressure: the political economy of air,' *Journal of Architecture*, vol.19, no.2, 2014, pp.168–86.
4. Rosalind Deutsche, *Evictions: Art and Spatial Politics*, MIT Press, Cambridge, MA, 1996, pp. 324–5. See also Carter, *Meeting Place*, pp. 144–6.
5. *Greater Shepparton – Community Action Plan, Proposal to Department of Victorian Communities*, Greater Shepparton City Council, Shepparton, Vic., July 2006.
6. Paulo N. Correa & Alexandra N. Correa, 'Whither science? A science without origins: Nomad, minor science and the scientific method', *Journal of Science & the Politics of Thought*, vol. 1, no. 2, 2009, p. 2, citing Gilles Deleuze & Félix Guattari, *A Thousand Plateaus*, University of Minnesota Press, Minneapolis, 1987, p. 361.
7. Correa & Correa, 'Whither Science?', p. 37.
8. Ibid., p. 40 (original emphasis).
9. Ibid., p. 2.
10. Ibid., p. 3.
11. Eugenio Barba, 'The deep order called turbulence: The three faces of dramaturgy', trans. Judy Barba, *The Drama Review*, vol. 44, no. 4, 2000, p. 61.

12 'On Turbulence', special issue, *Performance Research*, ed. Paul Carter, vol. 19, no. 5, 2014.
13 W.H.D. Rouse, 'Introduction', Lucretius, *De Rerum Natura*, trans. W.H.D. Rouse, London: Heinemann, 1966, vii-xxi, ix. See also main text Book II, lines 216–237.
14 D'Arcy Wentworth Thompson, *On Growth and Form*, vol. 1, Cambridge University Press, Cambridge, UK, 1942, p. 76. For a discussion of its application to human behaviour, see Carter, *Dark Writing*, pp. 178–9.
15 Glenn Shafer, *The Art of Causal Conjecture*, MIT Press, Cambridge, MA, 1996, p. 24.
16 Thomas De Quincey, *The Collected Writings of Thomas De Quincey*, ed. David Masson, vol. 3, A. & C. Black, London, 1896, pp. 314–15.
17 See, for example, Esmeralda Kosmatopoulos's *Mark-It* project: *The Project*, Turbulence, n.d., viewed 4 June 2015, <http://archive.turbulence.org/Works/MARK_IT/project.html>.
18 See Institute for Infinitely Small Things, 'The analysis of infinitely small things research report', *Performance Research*, vol. 11, no. 1, 2006, pp. 76–81.
19 The Aboriginal Australian music theatre work *Trepang* is a good case in point. See Peta Stephenson, *The Outsiders Within: Telling Australia's Indigenous-Asian Story*, University of New South Wales Press, Sydney, 2007, pp. 51–7.
20 This is explored in Carter, *Meeting Place*, esp. pp. 103–7.
21 See Max Wisser, 'Gregory Bateson on deutero-learning and double bind: A brief conceptual history', *Journal of the History of the Behavioral Sciences*, vol. 39, no. 3, 2003, pp. 269–78.
22 Chris Argyris, 'Double-loop learning, teaching and research', *Academy of Management Learning & Education*, vol. 1, no. 2, 2002, pp. 206–19.
23 Kurt Lewin, *Resolving Social Conflicts: Selected Papers on Group Dynamics*, Harper & Row, New York, 1947, p. 206.

8

THE MEASURE OF ENCOUNTER

Through a constellation of interrelated activities, a group with which I am involved has been exploring ways to turn choreotopography into a heuristic device. The idea in its simplest sense has been to devise tools able to detect the interplay between human movement in a public space and the character of the public space. This ambition was inspired by observations made over a period of years at Federation Square, Melbourne. Highly popular with the public, Federation Square is unusual among comparable gathering places in the Western world because it has *inscribed into its surface* a pattern suggestive of sociability (see Figure 3). As the designer of the global whorl pattern, I speculate that it

> worked as a catalyst of sociability if it helped engineer a new kind of meeting place. But the character of the meetings occurring there was up to the future: the movement traces scored and mosaiced into the surface of the plaza provided the initial conditions of a different political space. They prescribed a space of becoming without saying what would happen there. More positively, the tradition of *peripateia* that wandering the site might induce could perhaps incubate new ways of thinking about democracy; for the vitality of public space is an index of the political health of a community.

The interlocked but heterogeneous elements of the plaza might model a democracy which, instead of seeking to concentrate power centrally, committed itself to the distribution of agency and, through this, the recognition of 'extra-parliamentary' talk about placemaking and the formation of collective identity.[1]

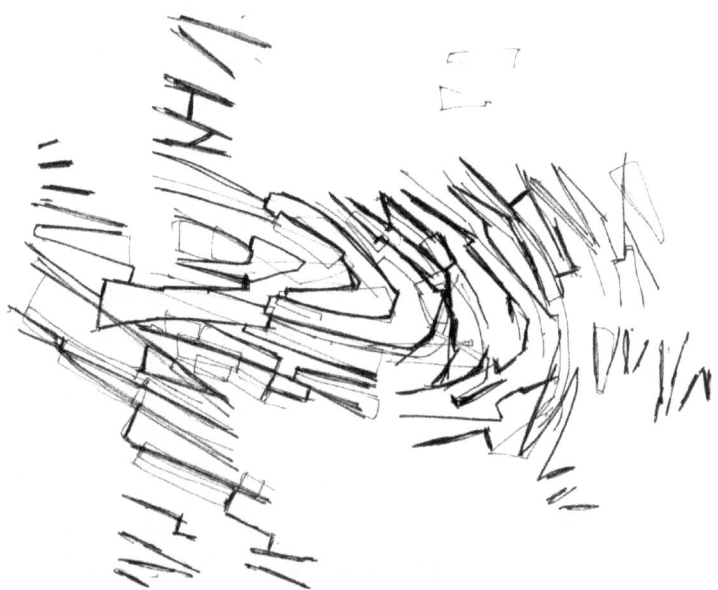

Figure 3 Paul Carter, '*Nearamnew* Global Whorl: Wedge Interlock', pen and ink, 210 x 297 mm, June 2000. Copyright: the author.

The object of the inscriptions that ride in the whorl pattern like rafts of letters was to dissolve the figure–ground distinction in public space design. 'To read the history secreted there is to perform a movement, perhaps to retrace the eddies and footprints of ancient traces: to read this place successfully, it is necessary to participate in its present meaning – not to interpret but to copy…It is to emerge from the monumental tomb of signification into the common place of poses, of marked coming and going.'[2] In short, the aim was to induce sociability, not prescribe it, to underwrite it, not program it. But the questions are: Does this ambition – to create a mimetic feedback between *eidos*, or the easily recognised pattern in the ground, and *kinesis*, or the movement of people – work in practice? And, if it does, how might such induced flows of sociability be detected? The object of *Nearamnew* was to avoid a 'holistic approach', to veil its instructions, to elide with the landscape so that its patterns should be barely more discernible than eddies in water or evolutions in cloud. In addition, the ground pattern and associated typographical knots encourage a reflective relationship between self and space: in contrast with the vibrant, positive connection Susan Leigh Foster and others want to establish between discourse and dance, *Nearamnew* explores a far subtler feedback loop, between reading and treading. Instead of promoting a robust social choreography of animated exchange, it invites a communion likely to produce a meditative eddying aside from the main throng. Finally, the square possesses a multitude of alternative affordances, destinations and attractions, any and all of which might affect the spacing and timing of human passage.

Although Laura Elrick's call for 'a practice that rejects the separation of our bodies from the spaces we inhabit' raises the question of the place-making practice that must go with it, it does at least endorse a testable hypothesis, from Henri Lefebvre, that 'the whole of (social) space proceeds from the body'.[3] If this statement is true, it ought to be possible to transpose the motions of bodies to the design of architecture. One could guess, in the other direction, that the 'new' architecture would be the amplification of gestures derived from essential through lines of figures in motion. Such formulations are extremely rough: they leave unresolved the relationship between the totality of the body in motion and the repertoire of gestures that provide the discourse of sociability. Equally, the number of lines that can be drawn out of the moving body is infinite, and none of them necessarily enjoys a superior expressive value. However, there was enough of a hint in these speculations to justify a first pass at materialising the choreotopographical principle, in the form of a collaboration between Deakin University's Motion Lab, my design studio Material Thinking and the Melbourne Ballet Company, in 2010.

The proposition of this collaboration was that the generation of 3D stereo-projection images from the live motion capture of performers' movements offers a virtual bridgehead from the dancers' pathways, actions and movement inflections to the volumes, passages and walls of an architectural milieu. The architectural milieu selected in this case was *Pearl*, a design proposal for a major new cultural facility in Darwin, whose nearly concentric rings and periodic distortions of these created a sense of turbulent through and cross flow, consistent with the trope that the building occupies a tidal zone and seeks to 'filter' the public through a maze of spaces (see Figure 4). *Pearl* came more than halfway aesthetically – that is, to the kinds of patterns one might expect the extrapolation of dancers' movements to produce. For this reason, it was plausible to speculate that the visualisation of the extrapolated dancers' movements would, when projected onto the animations of the architectural shell and its passages, produce enough of a fit or convergence of curvatures to stimulate the dancers to modify their movements until these created the illusion of threading the architectural spaces. The outcome of this feedback would be the generation of new movement forms that would meet Lefebvre's condition, for when, once again, the z axis, or movement towards and away from the observer, was activated, the dancers would appear to visualise in virtual space a building – that is, *Pearl*.[4]

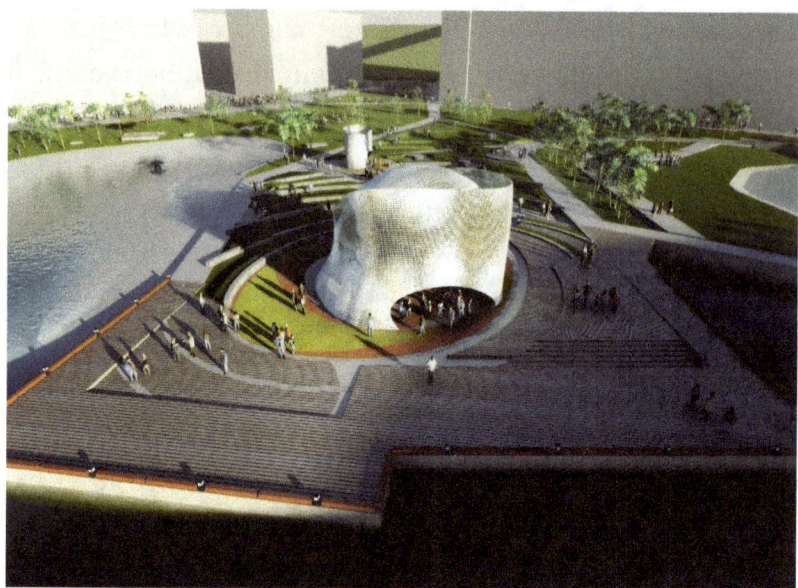

Figure 4 Material Thinking, *Pearl*, 'Pearl, Masts, Shell: Preliminary Design Concept for Cultural Facility, Design Concept for Artwork, Landscape, Peninsula, Darwin Waterfront', digital render, November 2008, pp. 1–17, p. 10.

The attempt to extrude architectural forms from the pathways of dancers proved elusive. The decision to choreograph the movements, or at least to envelop them within a composed soundscape, limited the capacity of the dancers to find their way: it reinstated the conventional subordination found in most theatre of scenography to action. On the other hand, the time lapse arabesques of light created by tracking the movements of sensors attached to the dancers' bodies vividly suggested the production of virtual bodies, ghost gyrations and eddies, and provided a kind of enveloping movement form that progressively shaped, contained and directed the pathways adopted (see Figure 5). It became possible to envisage a relationship between bodies and spaces defined in terms of a dialogue between actualised movements and remembered movements, rather than in terms of corporeal reactions to architectural programs. Ghosts were produced or negative choreographies defined by a pattern of recent departures or imminent convergences. Of course, choreography uses mimetic desire, the tendency to mirror the other, as a dramatic device; however, in this case, a third person seemed to be present. The accumulation of the light paths suggested a dramaturgy of space detached from any psychological narrative unfolding between the dancers, enjoying a kind of intermediate existence between the ephemeral evolutions of bodies and the volumes suggested by architecture when these are actualised in movement. Disembodied but embodied, it indicated the intelligence of the in-between, a certain propensity of the environment to think in geometrical patterns.

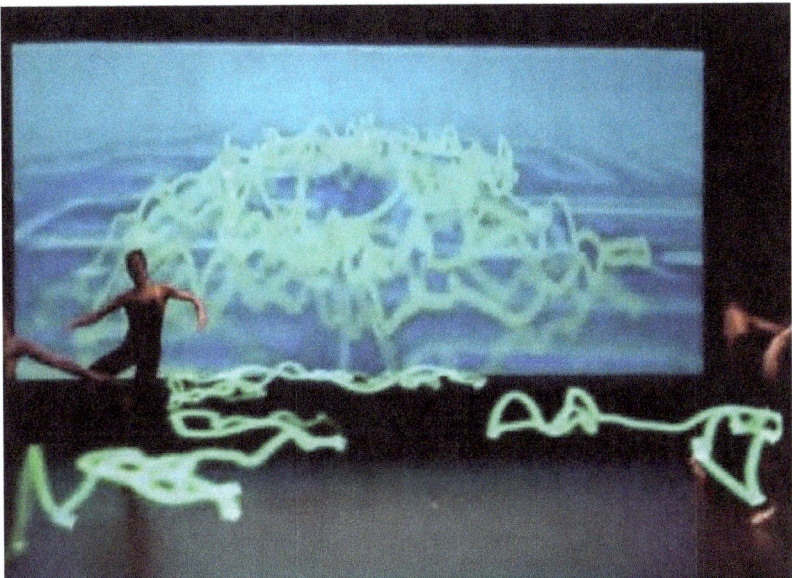

Figure 5 Deakin Motion Lab, Melbourne Ballet Company and Material Thinking, *Choreotopography*, Playhouse Theatre, Victorian Arts Centre, 3 December 2009. Reproduced by permission.

A limitation of the motion capture lab apparatus is that it cannot easily be adapted to the unconscious choreography of groups in public space. First, there is the practical (and psychological) constraint of attaching photosensitive devices to the body and installing external sensors to register the presence of these devices. Second, there is the fact, mentioned before, that, even if (theoretically) these constraints could be overcome, motion capture technology is not designed to capture the choreography of the group: its primary function is to notate the gestural language of trained dancers responding (usually) to a choreographer. In public space, however, it is not the individual (or even the ensemble) style that is of interest but the essential through lines of interweaving bodies. As these evolve mimetically, through an endless and kinetically-speaking proprioceptive feedback process, it is doubtful whether an array of fixed sensors can provide critical information. It would seem that the best way to notate these swirlings, interfoldings and passages is through participation; rather than stand outside the scene, the witness to these choreotopographical variations is more logically a participant in them. They may even be an agent of them, a provocateur. The proposition here is that the *inter esse* has a body or movement form and that an alignment with the evolutions of this is essential if the reason (the discourse) of bodies in relation to one another is to be discerned.

There was a further consideration. To describe dance as *discursive* is to imply a kind of subject matter suitable to its medium of presentation – one that arbitrarily-introduced music can only obscure. The discourse of bodies is not like that of speech. Perhaps it should be compared with the language of the Deaf community, Sign Language, which, Oliver Sacks speculates, 'has a different origin from speech, since it arises from gesture, spontaneous emotional-motor representation'. While 'the formal properties, the deep structure, of Sign allow the most abstract concepts and propositions to be expressed, its iconic or mimetic aspect allows it to be extraordinarily concrete and evocative in a way, perhaps, which no speech can be'.[5] In this case, dance is rendered mute when it is set to music. On the other hand, it might grow more articulate when performed over a ground already sensitive to its formal properties or deep structure. Such a ground would itself need to have a mimetic aspect – to be, for example, imitative of a movement form. However – and this is a key point – the expectation is *not* that the dancers or strolling members of the public 'perform' this pattern, physically following its chromatic grooves: the ground pattern is not a score to be slavishly followed. Rather, the spatial gesture or flourish performed expresses an 'abstract concept'. Such a concept cannot be static, a fixed and isolated position: in the nature of a movement language, it must be an idea of movement or process. It will be the outline of an action, the embodiment of a forming situation.

At Federation Square, I made the bold assumption that stories could be told or at least communicated kinaesthetically through the graphic design of the ground pattern. The global whorl pattern, which the polychromatic bands of cobbles bring out, is informed by an Aboriginal Australian drawing from northern Victoria, a bark etching, collected near Lake Tyrrell in the late 1860s and 'said to represent the eddying, whirling flow of water as it flooded Lake Tyrrell and overflowed its bounds'.[6] However, it transpired that the pattern had a larger, cosmic significance:

> There is circumstantial evidence to suggest that the artist's design may allude to the sky as well as the earth, that it not only images the whirling, infolding eddies of water in flood but the nebulous zone of the Magellanic Clouds. All of these facts suggested a work made in circumstances convergent with the historical and

environmental legacy we wished to celebrate. Its duplication of lines, some merging into others, others folding under, and yet others excessively drawn out, produced a graphic form that, while suggestive of place-making, rendered a process rather than an outcome. It was the integrity of the graphic trace that *Nearamnew* sought to carry over. Preserving its irregular and asymmetrical character was a way of avoiding inventions of our own or imposing upon it a symbolic rationalisation.[7]

A pattern of this kind might be the landscape design equivalent of an abstract concept in Sign Language, an idea of sky–earth reciprocity which, because of 'its iconic or mimetic aspect', is able to be 'extraordinarily concrete and evocative'. In this case, the story being told is that of place-making; the making of a gathering, sheltering or meeting zone is an appropriate story for this graphic discourse, because its articulation involves an essential movement form: the irregular and always turbulent vortex integral to the dynamics of association.

As a branch of material thinking, mythopoetic research is always tied to concrete situations.[8] The elucidation of the way people renovate and revise inherited patterns of behaviour and explanation starts from an instance of this in action. When I discussed with filmmaker Dirk de Bruyn how patterns of sociability at Federation Square might be documented, it quickly became obvious that our own identification with the situation of the design was integral to the way we observed and interpreted what was happening. For example, the overarching perspective within which place-making at Federation Square is conceived is a *migrant* one. The ground pattern may represent a doubling of sky and earth characteristic of Aboriginal Australian notations of place, but more obviously its gathering swirl implies that the people gathering there come from somewhere else. Many of the inscriptions engraved into the surface of the plaza allude to this reality: it is suggested that the social performances at Federation Square are primary negotiations of sociability because the ground they occupy is unceded (unsettled). They represent unfinished business in the positive sense of recognising that the future remains open, its community still evolving. Threading the opening to one another that the future represents will depend on how we conduct the dance of the present. The choreography of the future will involve a creative reinterpretation of inherited topography.

De Bruyn suggested that a mythopoetic rendering of sociability at Federation Square might begin with an interleaving of archival imagery derived from the evolution of the design for the ground pattern and footage shot on site. The global whorl pattern evolved over two or three years, and hundreds of drawings exist of its progressive iterations. Instead of treating the drawings as stills in a kind of flicker book presentation, Dirk suggested I perform their evolution through a simple improvisation where I reconstructed the whole pattern using the individual pages of the drawings. In the animation, the hand of the author, together with details of feet and shadow, are integral parts of the reconstruction (see Figure 6). The physician is always enjoined to 'heal thyself'. In a way, we were transposing this advice to the choreotopography project. Before attempting to understand the language of public sociability, we saw what kinds of movements the design would produce in the designer. It was a playful interlude but one that underlined the importance of embodiment in any methodology aimed at finding through lines or movement forms. Because of this, we began to reconsider which footage from Federation Square would represent a counterpoint *in the same symbolic register*.

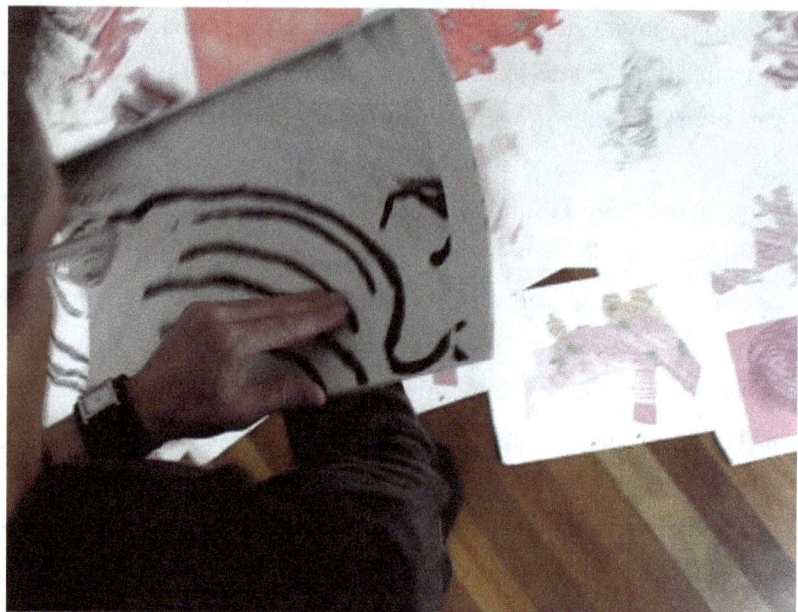

Figure 6 Dirk de Bruyn, *Opening,* video, Federation Square, Melbourne, 9 September 2011. An initiative of the Centre for Memory, Imagination and Invention, Deakin University. Reproduced by permission.

The short answer to this is that a comparable phenomenon at Federation Square would be one whose movement forms were the expression of mimetic desire. Just as my improvisation with the graphic archive was *homeopathic* in a way, the movement that the pattern desired to induce being *internalised* in my own spiralling path, so, it might be imagined, a migrant scenario might find in those travelling lines and swirling vortices the expression of an archetypal story. It was in this context that two apparently unrelated circumstances seemed to have a metaphoric identity and offer a poetic mechanism for inducing mimetic self-awareness in the Federation Square public. One of these was the opening of a dialogue with South Korean–Australian dancer and choreographer Soo Yeun You. The other was a parallel investigation I was undertaking of the association with Lake Tyrrell of the white Australian poet John Shaw Neilson. In an abstract but 'extraordinarily concrete' way, both dancer and poet embodied in their practice *footage*, the self-conscious actualisation of one foot placed in front of the other. You's traditional training emphasised the gravity that can characterise the act of making contact with the ground: her ground is neither given nor planar but appears to rise to meet her and to possess a resistant pressure that transfers upwards throughout the legs, trunk and arms (see Figure 7). Neilson had, as I show in *Ground Truthing*, *planted* his feet in the very remarkable sense of reforesting the Victorian landscape with 'trees' – poems that channelled the whisperings of nature: 'Neilson wrote a metrical history of the Mallee; by night he replanted the Mallee…In relation to the natural footfall of the traveller, trees are the ictus, the pre-inscription of the beat that indicates its direction and placing'.[9]

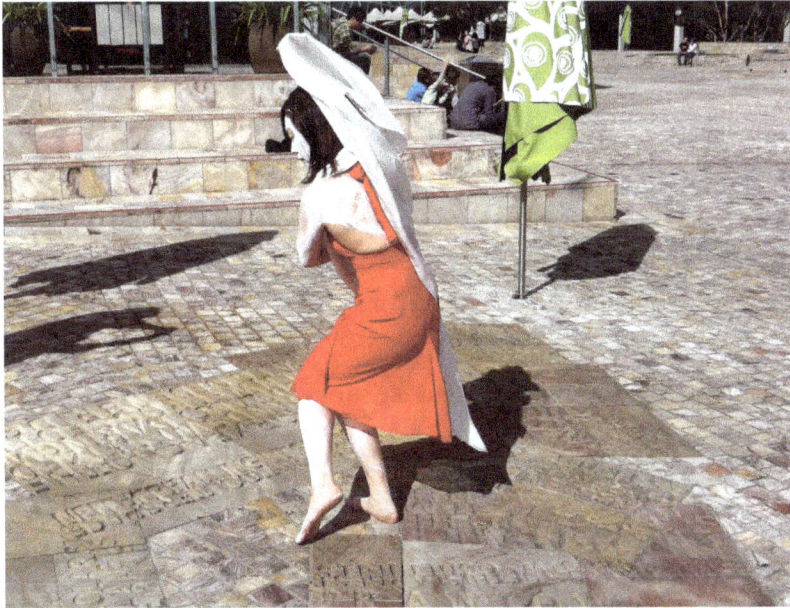

Figure 7 Soo Yeun You, '*Loops* improvisation', Federation Square, Melbourne, 17 July 2013. Photo: the author.

Here, another ingredient must be mentioned: the animation technique that de Bruyn used to shoot the global whorl graphic archive improvisation. The stutter effect, reminiscent of the jerky motion of early silent films, curiously mimicked the subject matter being recorded. The smooth progression from early, primitive sketches to later, more detailed, articulated and definitive drawings was brought into question. The tremor of the digitised cuts through what I was doing acted as a kind of temporal archaeology, excavating the origins of the creative narrative, conveying the contingency of one choice over another. In notes made shortly after the improvisation, I wrote:

> The stutter of the stills revisits a technological feature of the early silent movies and their digital imitation produces an expressive effect. It is as if the images are constitutionally in suspense, only contingently related one to the next. The question of temporal succession is posed and dramatised as the evidence of a creative process that is by its nature ever unfinished, inclined towards a destination or narrative cohesion that continually eludes it. The deferral of meeting is repeatedly announced; the meeting place represented is in a state of becoming that never resolves into a definite image or figure of sociability. The entire series teeters between an autistic withdrawal and a drunken veering towards.[10]

This observation suggested that an apt name for the second iteration of the choreotopography project would be *Opening*.[11] The object of *Nearamnew*, the public space design of which the global whorl pattern is a part, was to make concrete the principles of the *chora* (whose Aboriginal Australian counterpart is the concept of *tirille*, from which the name *Tyrrell* comes) – that is, to instantiate the principle that space is not a passive container of *topoi*, or functionally defined activities, but a creative process of placing, a strange attractor precipitating an endless opening to the other, a multiplying culture of sociability.

So we called the film animation *Opening*, referring to its ambition to stage the creative environment of storytelling, the precondition of individual narratives (and journeys) forming at that place. The story that we told would not be one of many but a kind of invitation to identification. Its abstractness, conveyed paradoxically through the 'extraordinarily concrete' character of the actions we performed, would provide a pattern or symbolic scenario that allowed identification or entrainment such that familiarity with the scenes depicted would be unnecessary to the emotional power of what they communicated. There followed a number of expeditions to Lake Tyrrell and the adjacent town of Sea Lake, as well as visits to Federation Square (whose trees, incidentally, consist of Mallee species). We visited sites associated with Neilson; in particular, we focused on the 'Red Sadie' poems, an enigmatic sequence associated with the poet's time in Sea Lake that obliquely notates a period of intense erotic suffering. I sourced a red dress at a weekend market and yards of fabric; we used flickering lights and nocturnal bush settings on the edge of Lake Tyrrell and were blessed with an uninterrupted night-time streetscape in Sea Lake that recalled a Russell Drysdale painting where You glided between street lights with a crimson parasol and de Bruyn circled her like an awkward beast animating her gestures with the counter-choreography of the hand-held camera.

The digital animation techniques de Bruyn used to film You's and my improvisations draw attention to the construction of the narrative illusion. Instead of animating what is inert, the acceleration of sequences of stills (captured with different time lapse settings) suggests that the actors are puppets, agitated into motion by stimuli from outside the frame. It is a frequent criticism of digital animation techniques (and of the digital manipulation of imagery more generally) that they reinforce a dissociation between imaginal consumerism and eidetic memory: an enlarged capacity to create plausibly lifelike computer animations creates a phantasmagoric accompaniment to everyday life that undermines our investment in the affective qualities of public space. In this context, de Bruyn used digital animation techniques to make palpable the artificiality of the new visual order. He used digital stop frame techniques to create flickering effects analogous to those that were integral to the technology of the silent film. The Viennese novelist Robert Musil's adolescent persona Törless likens a sense of 'restlessness and uneasiness' he feels to 'watching cinematographic pictures, when, for all the illusion the whole thing creates, one is…unable to shake off the vague sensation that behind the image one perceives there are hundreds of other images flashing past, and each of them utterly different from the picture as a whole'. And Musil adds that this is a state of mind 'that nobody forgets, when there is a failure of that power of association which generally causes our life to be faultlessly reflected in our understanding, as though life and understanding ran parallel to each other and at equal speed'.[12] It was exactly this sense of dissociation that de Bruyn learnedly recovered using digital techniques.

Dissociation, in Musil's analogy, offers access to an imaginal unconscious, to a world of other streams of imagining, interleaved with the narrative stream of which we are mainly conscious. This sensation can be transposed to public space where an interruption to one's thoughtless progress produces a sudden and disconcerting awareness of an *environmental unconscious* composed of all the other pathways that, in the interests of faultlessly integrating life and understanding, is normally repressed. In *Repressed Spaces*, I suggest that the design of public space could also induce a 'movement inhibition'.[13] Törless's sense of uneasiness was not confined to the early cinema: it was experienced in public spaces designed by modernist urban planners, in which the attempt to create utterly smooth and functional expanses had the paradoxical effect of petrifying the walker. In this account, the condition of agoraphobia, or space fear, was a reasonable response to an alienation experienced as a loss of agency over the choreography of everyday life. People who feel themselves to be manipulated by powers beyond their control become restless puppets, their perfect motion (which is also a kind of perfect immobility, like running on the spot) expressing a Kleistian detachment from external contingency.

In the context of our work, de Bruyn used a technique for creating the illusion of continuous movement *against itself*, reintroducing the flicker as a dramatic, psychologically significant device. The interest of this device as a technique for understanding how figures construct the footage of their surroundings, self-consciously enacting a gestural choreography within a field of others, other positions and possible trajectories arose from the fact that de Bruyn allied it to his own performative interaction with the performers (in this case me and the dancer Soo Yeun You). When he engaged in a kind of pas de deux with our movements and used the camera gesturally, mimicking gestures or constructing a negative choreography of counter-arabesques, the distinction between actor and observer was obviously dissolved. Although this manipulation of the camera clearly recalls Dziga Vertov's idea of the *kino-eye*, it would be perhaps more accurate to describe the result as a *kinaesthetic film*, as the motion of the camera was indexically related to the muscle sense of the cinematographer –

whose movements were, in turn, *mimetically* stimulated. The vertiginous circling of the subject performed by the camera or its rapid alterations of angle, where close-up alternates with framing landscape (the transitions being sutured rhythmically rather than through any intuitive continuity of subject) suggest the hand in matter rather than the eye. The sequences record what the conductor's hand would see if a lens were embedded in its palm. The larger organisation of matter visualises the human movement form as it makes its way through the world.

Another way to put this is to say that the cinematographer acted like a dramaturg, translating between the performance and the world beyond it. In the mimetically-induced dramaturgy of turbulence was materialised an elemental choreotopographical relation. It seemed to us that this insight made sense of the logic of dissociation that characterises the cutting together of the different sequences. The name of the work, *Opening*, discovers its relevance in this context, which is to articulate the intervals in perception when the connection of elements remains in suspense. We perceived an analogy between this problematisation of the montage technique and the enigma of sociability. At the heart of the project of meeting there is the possibility of not meeting. Meeting and the functionally designed meeting place presume an unproblematic sociability, but there exists prior to this and surrounding it the distance from which people come towards one another and whose culmination is exemplified in the encounter that occurs between two perfect strangers. Such an encounter, as is argued in my subsequent book, *Meeting Place*, derives its rules from the mimetic improvisations peculiar to the situation itself.[14] In these gestures, the opening to the other is materialised as a social praxis of making room. In this sense, not by any theatrical narrative but through a concomitant mode of production, *Opening* documents a distinctively choreotopographical phenomenon: the restless desire of encounter that always exceeds what can be represented.

Notes

1. Carter, *Mythform,* 2005, p. 21. The reference is to statements by the architects of Federation Square (Peter Davidson and Donald Bates) about the situation of architecture and the promotion of civility 'after democracy' (p. 6).
2. Paul Carter, 'Inscriptions as Initial Conditions: Federation Square (Melbourne, Australia) and the Silencing of the Mark,' in B. David & M. Wilson (eds), *Inscribed Landscapes: Marking and Making Place*, University of Hawai'i Press, Honolulu, 2002, pp. 230–9, 238.
3. Laura Elrick, 'Poetry, Ecology, and the Reappropriation of Lived Space', citing Henri Lefebvre, *The Production of Space*, trans. Donald Nicholson-Smith, Blackwell, Oxford, 1991, pp. 213–18.
4. This 'ground-breaking collaboration between Deakin University, the Melbourne Ballet Company and leading 3D design company Autodesk' is described in Deakin Research Communications, *Choreotopography!*, Deakin University, 6 December 2010, viewed 4 June 2015, <www.deakin.edu.au/research/stories/2010/12/06/choreotopography>.
5. Oliver Sacks, *Seeing Voices*, Harper Perennial, New York, 1990, pp. 122, 123.
6. Carter, *Mythform*, p. 13.
7. Ibid., p. 20. See also the discussion in Paul Carter, *Ground Truthing: Explorations in a Creative Region*, University of Western Australia Publishing, Perth, 2010, pp. 210–17.
8. *Mythopoetic* is used here in the critical sense described by Harry Slochower of a demythologisation of inherited thought patterns and behaviours that uses poetic techniques to produce better stories (*Mythopoesis: Mythic Patterns in the Literary Classics*, Wayne University Press, Detroit, 1970, p. 15).
9. See Carter, *Ground Truthing*, pp. 230–1, where it is explained that John Shaw Neilson worked as a labourer by day, clearing trees, and composed his poems of symbolic reafforestation at night.
10. Paul Carter, 'Choreotopography: algorithms of sociability', unpublished project notebook, 2011, pp. 1–3, p. 13.
11. Dirk de Bruyn (camera and film direction), Paul Carter (concept and dramaturgy) & Soo Yeun You (dance and choreography), *Opening*, film animation, 38 mins. The premiere, at Federation Square, Melbourne, on 10 September 2011, was followed by a one-month season in Federation Square Atrium and on Federation Square's Big Screen.

12 Robert Musil, *Young Törless*, trans. Eithne Wilkins & Ernst Kaiser, Pan Books, London, 1987, p. 135.
13 Paul Carter, *Repressed Spaces: The Poetics of Agoraphobia*, Reaktion Books, London, 2002, p. 16.
14 Carter, *Meeting Place*, pp. 129–132.

Part 2

9

THE TURBULENCE OF CREATION

In the Introduction, I described a suite of creative research inspired by the global whorl pattern at Federation Square, Melbourne (see Figure 8). The swirling Magellanic Cloud of coloured cobbles was designed to induce a comparable movement in the human crowd. Occupying a sloping, subtly undulating terrain, dissolving sharp divisions and colour coding, as it were, variable degrees of warmth (from the palest cream to the deepest flame-coloured ochre), the whorl pattern is a drawing of sociability. It describes an imaginary gathering, the accumulated passage of many feet drawn to its magnetic field by a mimetic desire to fall in with the tracks made by other passers-by. The basis of the pattern is an analogy with water. I studied the way foam gathers at the foot of waterfalls, the chains of bubbles revolving along the edges of the current and the strings of foam forming meandering patterns as they flow downstream. Sometimes, the conglomerate of these tiny frogspawn-like rafts is a slowly turning nebula of foam stretching across the entire face of the lake, inevitably flinging out arms of white dust to the point of disappearance back into the dark surface. Involution is twinned with evolution, infolding with unfolding (see Figure 9). These observations suggested the behaviour of crowds, and the ground pattern at Federation Square is in this sense an algorithm of sociability, a fundamental formula describing the twinned conditions of meeting.

Places Made After Their Stories

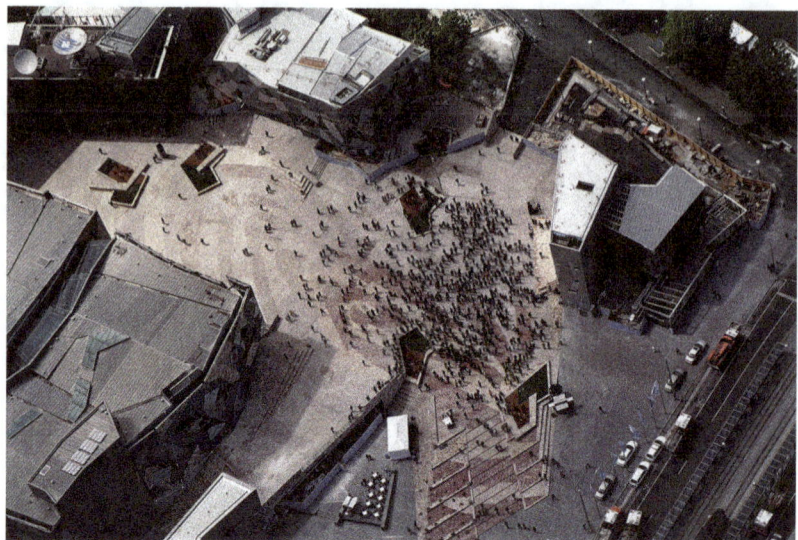

Figure 8 Dominic O'Brien/Fairfaxphotos, 'Federation Square', 2003. Reproduced by permission.

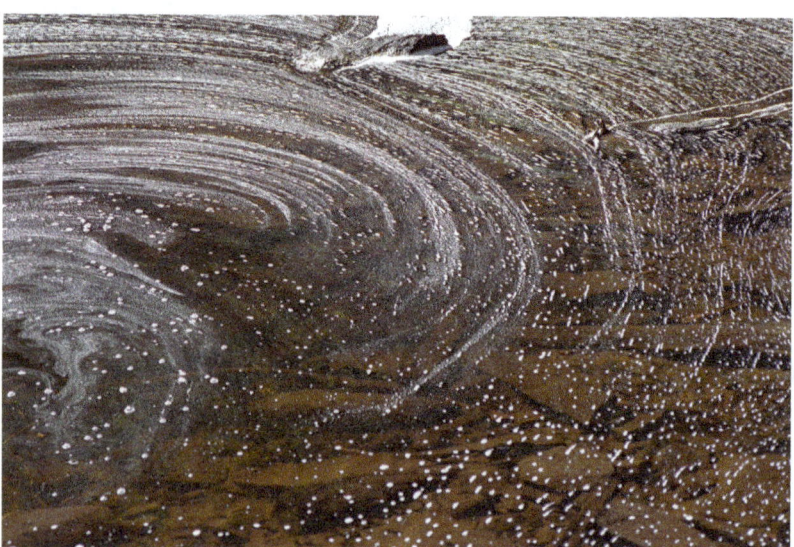

Figure 9 'Foamform 5', Kalimna Falls, Otways Ranges, 7 April 1999. Photo: the author.

The figure of drawing out and drawing in was not, though, solely based on a possibly fanciful analogy between turbulence in water and the eros informing sociability. It had a discursive dimension. Stories can come in many forms: the wordless performances that Soo Yeun You and Dirk de Bruyn carried out at Federation Square were miniature spatial histories; they were readings of the ground plane, where reading and treading elided. Such performances materialise the potential for encounter and can in principle become part of the future tradition of the place. However, in the case of the Federation Square site, adjacent to the Yarra River, we have other indications that vortical energy forms are traditional there. One of these is a creation story, an Aboriginal Australian (Kulin nation) account of the formation of the land and water where Melbourne is now situated and of the origins of the people who came to occupy it. It is, in fact, a second creation story, the description of the introduction of a new order on the basis of the destruction of the old one – and it takes the form of a whirlwind. According to the story the creator-figure Bunjil, or 'Pund-jel', 'became very sulky, when he saw that men and women were many and very bad. He caused storms to arise, and fierce winds to blow often. In the flat lands there arose suddenly whirlwinds of great force'. At the same time, with his knife, Pund-jel

> cut this way and that way; and men, women, and children he cut into very small pieces. But the pieces into which he had cut the men, women and children did not die. Each piece moved as the worm (*Tur-ror*) moves. *Bullito, bullito, koor-reen, pit-ker-reen* (great, great storms and whirlwinds) came and carried away the pieces that moved like worms, and the pieces became flakes of snow. They were carried into the clouds. The clouds carried the pieces hither and thither over all the earth; and Pund-jel caused the pieces to drop in such places as

he pleased. Thus were men and women scattered over the earth. Of the good men and good women Pund-jel made stars.[1]

This is a choreotopographical myth. It makes an equation between the lie of the land and the distribution of people. The mechanism of this social dramaturgy is the whirlwind. The identification of good men and women with stars suggests that social harmony can be likened to the geometry of constellations, clear in their stellar illuminations but characterised by dark intervals where subtler dust clouds of light may be made out.[2] Some have discerned in the story's punishment motif a Christian influence. This may be correct, or it may be an interpretation placed on the story by the colonisers when they tried to make sense of it in their own terms. However, more intriguing from a choreotopographical perspective is the fact that Bunjil possessed two complementary creation tools, neither of them exactly like the tools of the colonial planner. There was a cosmic knife; in his 1876 compilation of information obtained from colonists about Victorian Aboriginal peoples, from which the story is quoted, Robert Brough Smyth gives the Woiworong word for Bunjil's knife as '*bullito kul-pen-kul-pen gye-up*', where *bullito* means, among other things, 'total, universal, all, vast, very great, exceeding, satiate, full',[3] connotations that identify unity with a state of saturation. But there was also 'an instrument named *Ber-rang*, with which he could open any place or any thing, and in such a way as to make it impossible for any one to know how or whether or not it had been opened. No one could see the opening he made'.[4] These tools suggested to me a theory and practice of place-making very different from the enclosure acts performed by the colonial and contemporary planners. Instead of flattening space, and rendering it into finite units to be controlled, manipulated or alienated at will, Bunjil operates at the heart of the storm and in the midst of a topography that consists of openings.

The polemical importance of this alternative place-making tradition emerged in early 2001 at a moment in the construction of Federation Square when a newly elected government seemed intent on sabotaging the architects' vision. Driven by a negative desire to wreck an initiative of the previous government, the incoming Bracks ministry confronted the challenge of replacing a critical element of the scheme with an alternative object. If the Shard, an angular building that was to be one of the federation of buildings forming the square's constellation, was to be removed, something else must be put in its place. The alternative proposal could have been predicted: in the absence of an animation stemming from the growth forms embedded in the urban topography, a fountain is always the fallback position. Pumped-up water gives a superficial impression of life; but, cut off from living sources, it soon comes to signify another failure of connection. In the end, an attenuated version of the Shard was preserved and the symbolic water flow of *Nearamnew* allowed to proceed,[5] but the episode dramatically illustrated the reckless abstraction of the master planning sensibility. In contrast with Bunjil's wand-like knife, stirring up a multiplicity of living forms, the planner's ruler assumes a blank page onto which a pattern of inert lines forming right angles is drawn. In contrast with the *ber-rang*, translating the lie of the land into a human choreography, the colonial plan is a prescription for acts of levelling, draining, blasting and bridging. At that time, I wrote,

> The forces that have worked destructively to preserve a precinct of monuments picturesquely framed in nostalgia's past could have learned from Bunjil, the

place-maker, whose *Ber-rang* is, I speculate, and in the absence of contemporary testimony to the contrary, connected with the Woiworong word *Brrering*, a name applied to the Yarra valley and the water flowing in it, and meaning *mist*, and which in another mutation furnishes *Prahran*, the present name of a Melbourne suburb. To think of a place coming into being incrementally, its parts woven together like the hair of water, here eddying, there turbulent, now shallow now deep, and to observe the tidemarks briefly ringing the ground during its period of retreat – this is to observe the initial conditions of a process in which making and marking are contemporaneous; where, as nothing has been destroyed, nothing has to be monumentally restored.[6]

In contrast with the blank canvas theory of clearing, Bunjil uses his knife creatively, to carve the earth. Cutting into the land's living flesh, he creates scar tissue. Initiating it by this means into the realm of becoming, his *ber-rang* produces the hills, valleys and creek lines, the spread, the fold and the convergence – in short, the lie of the land. But Bunjil not only carves; he moulds. Whether or not Bunjil uses the *ber-rang* to stir up storms, he clearly possesses the power to shape the air and command the weather. He conjures up whirlwinds of great force. Again, though, the impulse is creative: to produce a revolution. Together, the carving and moulding techniques mobilise the stuff of the world, *extracting* from it different elements that are whirled about until a physical world is created that is coherent and all of a piece.

One myth tends to recall another as fundamental human gestures are in play. The way in which a commons comes into being (mythopoetically foreshadowed in Bunjil's foundational acts of place-making and community formation) strikingly recalls the cosmogony of the fifth-century-BC Ionian philosopher Anaxagoras, where the vortical figure is foundational. The process by which the parts of the universe came into being did not, according to Anaxagoras, consist of a 'separating off, in the crude and simple sense of cutting or chopping off of parts of the Urstoff' or original constitution of the world when 'everything was in everything'; it more resembled a process of chemical extraction such as can be observed when milk is transformed by churning into butter. In other words, 'We do not generate a new stuff, but only bring into perceptible form some portion of a pre-existent stuff'. Whether or not this explanation is scientifically adequate, it is psychologically plausible in the context of creating places where people can both spread out and meet: if new public spaces can be brought into being, their design will *extract* what was there before, rather than discard it. The movement that causes extraction to occur is rotatory: 'Cosmogony begins when the *Ur-mass* is "moved"...its characteristic form of locomotion is "revolution"... and as a result of the revolution or vortex certain stuffs "come together"'.[7]

Transposed to the place-making process, this theory of formation suggests an interesting modification of the Platonic account of space's coming into being. It also has a dramatic impact on the way we imagine social innovation, the emergence of a sociability that is more than the sum of its parts. The word *chora* is associated with a verb that has the active sense of *making room for*. But how does this happen? Robert G. Turnbull suggests that the *chora* makes room 'for the numbers or, equivalently, the geometric solids...When the Receiver is somehow mixed with the intelligible numbers (or shapes), the product is a spatial array of figures'.[8] Julia Kristeva likewise understands it as a place-making process, analogous to the emergence of the subject in writing. The subject in process, she says, 'experiments with or practices the objective process by submerging in it and emerging from it through the drives. This subject of expenditure is not a fixed point – a "subject of enunciation" – but instead acts *through* the text's organisation (structure and completion) where the *chora* of the process is represented'.[9] In these definitions, the *chora* is produced by cleavage (Turnbull's splitting open to make room) or by expression (Kristeva's emergence, which is analogous to Anaxagoras's extraction). The physical theory of separation corresponds to Bunjil's activity with his knife; the chemical model of purification corresponds to what Bunjil can do with his stirrer, the *ber-rang*.

Common to both modes of place-making is the recognition that places are atmospheres. They come into being when they acquire the property of drawing things together. The means of this is a psychophysical organisation of energy that at once individualises and unifies, holds together and holds apart, scatters and constellates. The celestial counterpart of this dynamic theory of mutual attraction and repulsion would be René Descartes's vortical mechanics. 'Descartes imagined whirlpools or vortices of second element, rotating around their respective central stars to sweep along the planets like boats in a strong current.' In this theory, 'local vortices form around the planets orbiting stars',[10] which stabilise the planets' centrifugal impulse so that they neither shoot further outwards (where in any case their motion will be impeded by entering another vortex field) nor fall towards the surface of the stars. The figures in Descartes's *Le Monde* and *Principia philosophiae* designed to communicate these ideas may illustrate a mistaken physical theory, but they remain intriguing materialisations of social fields of attraction and repulsion (see

Figure 10). They anticipate, for example, in a quite remarkable way, Kurt Lewin's regional theory of human behaviour, where the life world is composed of *'regions* with boundaries between them, some regions being "neighboring" to each other (*i.e.,* having common boundaries) some not'.[11] There is, in particular, a striking conceptual resemblance between Descartes's notion of a 'surface envelope'[12] and Lewin's theory of a 'boundary force' acting on a person coming from region A 'in order to prevent the person entering region B when he is in the "boundary region"'.[13]

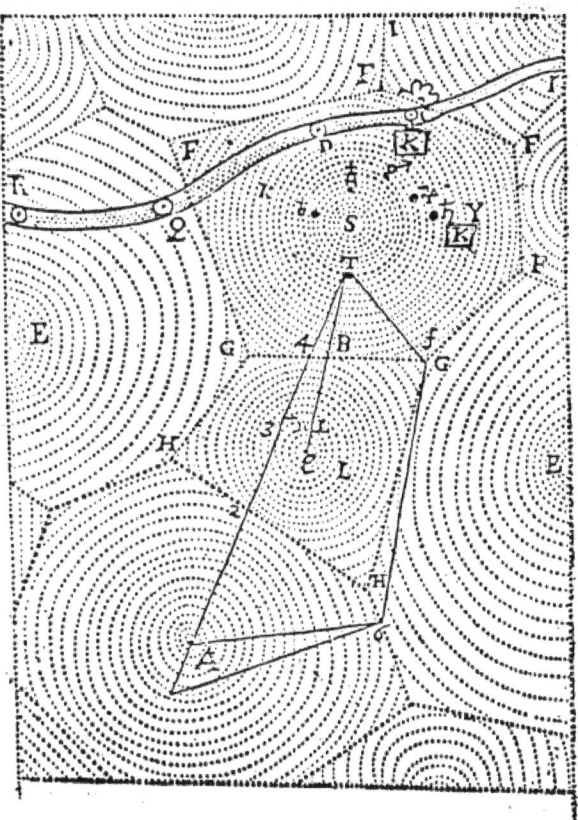

Figure 10 René Descartes, 'Vortices', *Principia philosophiae*, Amsterdam, 1656, p. 129, New York Public Library, General Research Division. Reproduced by permission.

Leaving aside these technical resemblances between celestial and psychological mechanics, when Descartes's diagrams are transposed to the dance floor, this celestial choreography suggests a room filled with whirling waltzers. When we learn that 'comets are objects extruded from vortex to vortex, first "falling" into a vortex and being extruded out',[14] it is any kind of traditional round, chain or ribbon dance where dancers weave in and out, exchanging one arm for another, that comes to mind. In such formations, the boundaries, although invisible, mark serpentine zones of dynamic stability where centrifugal and centripetal tendencies are reconciled or continuously sculpted into place by passing bodies. Edgar Wind refers to these as '"hedges" or *umbraculae*, belong[ing] to an intermediate state, which invites further "complication" above, and further "explication" below'.[15] These are not simply discursive figures – emerging, for example, from a *chora* imagined like Kristeva's 'space' with 'no thesis and no position', possessing only a 'kinetic rhythm';[16] they can be choreographed. However, the choreography will not (to continue Kristeva's analogy) impose a 'symbolic order' on the 'semiotic *chora*'. It will not, for example, attempt to say what the *chora*, or public space, is.[17]

In Ben Jonson's masque *Pleasure Reconciled to Virtue* of 1618, 'when "complication" reaches its height, and the opposites become indistinguishable, all multiplicity vanishes in the One beyond being – the absolutely familiar, for which there is no fitting image or name'.[18] This could be an illustration of Anaxagoras's theory of cosmogony. But the emergence of meaningful relationships with others and objects in the *chora* depends on a self-splitting that is continuous, a cleaving in the double sense it has in Bunjil's practice, which at once separates and binds.[19] The personality of such a place might be chiasmatic. Discussing one of the earliest forms of thought, the *chiasm*, Rodolphe Gasché explains, 'It allows the drawing apart and bringing together of opposite functions or terms and entwines them within an identity of movements'. When Emmanuel Levinas speaks of 'a pleasure of contact at the heart of the chiasm', it is clear that a form of physical as well as mental movement is understood. And in this form, the movement is timed as well as spaced, corresponding to a relational and differential space of the in-between, which in terms of what happens is *'always already* and always not yet'. Andrzej Warminski contends that such chiasmatic environments are not blandly or neutrally ambiguous but are sites of 'radically undecidable difference', a distinction that also illuminates the enigma of meeting.[20]

Notes

1. Robert Brough Smyth, *The Aborigines of Victoria*, vol. 1, Government Printer, Melbourne, 1876, p. 428.
2. On the importance of the dark sky, see Carter, *Ground Truthing*, pp. 69–84.
3. Smyth, *Aborigines of Victoria*, vol. 2, p. 135.
4. Smyth, *Aborigines of Victoria*, vol. 1, p. 423.
5. For a discussion of this controversy, see Carter, *Mythform*, p. 17.
6. Paul Carter, 'Participating forms: The place of myth in urban design', unpublished paper, 2001, citing Smyth, *Aborigines of Victoria*, vol. 2, p. 188; Paul Carter, *Living in a New Country*, Faber & Faber, London, 1992, p. 205 n. 7. See also the alternative spelling *Boorrang* (fog, mist) in Smyth, *Aborigines of Victoria*, vol. 2, p. 101. Evidently, this is the same word as *boorong* (see Carter, *Ground Truthing*, index entries *Boorong* and *boorong*, p. 327).
7. Jonathan Barnes, *The Presocratic Philosophers*, Routledge, London, 1982, pp. 339–40. Ur-stoff is defined as 'an undifferentiated mixture of stuffs, wearing the external appearance of "air" and aether".'
8. Robert G. Turnbull, *The Parmenides and Plato's Late Philosophy*, University of Toronto Press, Toronto, 1998, p. 149.
9. Julia Kristeva, *Revolution in Poetic Language*, Columbia University Press, New York, 1984, p. 126. Emphasis in original.
10. John A. Schuster, '"Waterworld": Descartes' vortical celestial mechanics', pp. 44–5.

11 Kullervo Rainio, *Kurt Lewin's Dynamical Psychology Revisited and Revised*, Goertzel.org, 2009, viewed 4 June 2015, <http://goertzel.org/dynapsyc/Rainio-Lewin's-psych-pdf-6–8-09.pdf>, p. 4.
12 Or, strictly, John A. Schuster's notion of 'a term of hermeneutical art', which he introduces to explain why similarly sized planets may circle their star at different distances. The size of the surface envelope will determine the resistance of the planet to its own centrifugal tendency ('Waterworld', p. 54). Similarly, Kullervo Rainio interprets Kurt Lewin's 'boundary' as referring to the phenomenon of 'the resistance to psychic locomotion' (*Kurt Lewin's Dynamical Psychology Revisited and Revised*, p. 6).
13 Rainio, *Kurt Lewin's Dynamical Psychology Revisited and Revised*, p. 5.
14 Schuster, 'Waterworld': Descartes' vortical celestial mechanics', p. 54.
15 Edgar Wind, *Pagan Mysteries of the Renaissance*, Penguin, Harmondsworth, 1967, p. 206.
16 See S. K. Keltner, *Kristeva: Thresholds*, Polity, Cambridge, UK, 2011, p. 30.
17 Julia Kristeva, *Revolution in Poetic Language*, Columbia University Press, New York, 1984, pp.25–6.
18 Wind, *Pagan Mysteries*, p. 206.
19 See Carter, *Meeting Place*, p. 100.
20 See Rodolphe Gasché, *Of Minimal Things: Studies in the Notion of Relation*, Stanford University Press, Stanford, Calif., 1999, pp. 271–3 (citing Emmanuel Levinas, p. 271), (citing Andrzej Warminski, p. 273).

10

THE DRAMATURGY OF ENCOUNTER

Places are discursive constructions. They enact narratives of place-making. Discourse in this context retains its physical sense of a running hither and thither. A place emerges when the crisscrossing paths made by discourse as it circulates begin to assume a stable form. These paths open up a space; then they begin to weave a string figure or constellation of different positions that make sense in relation to one another. Such places are not places in the planner's sense of definable enclosures; they are creative regions, which can be scaled up or scaled down to discover further creative chains of connection and dispersion. They are discursive but also recursive, growing and self-transforming in the telling. Hence, stories or myths of a society's coming into being are not simply fables; they present in a concrete fashion philosophical insights into the conundrum of being and being together. In particular, the parabolic character of stories means that they always lie alongside another reality. Storytelling is at once an act of memory and invention, constitutionally double. It is Janus-faced, looking back as it goes forward. Unlike the language of instrumental reason, whose denotative function is singular and authoritative, intended to eliminate ambiguity, the language of story is open to many interpretations. The meaning of a story lies in-between the figures (metaphors, symbols) and episodes from which it is composed. Symbolic forms are designed for sharing, interpretation and improvement. They encourage identifications, generate new insights and invite further interpretation. Places made after their stories are in this sense without bound or finish. They can be compared to the contract between actor and audience, where the sense is in the performance.

It is in this context that my four-year engagement with communities in Alice Springs, in central Australia, should be understood. Early in 2007, I received an email asking if I was interested in creating a 'Federation Square in Alice'. As my role in the Melbourne project, led by Lab Architecture Studio and landscape architects Karres en Brands, had been extremely modest, I sought clarification. The Uniting Church in Alice Springs was, it turned out, keen to create a meeting place in the centre of town. The story-based design of *Nearamnew* might offer, it was suggested, a culturally appropriate approach to the making of a physical space where Aboriginal and non-Aboriginal people, outsiders and insiders, could meet on more friendly terms. The early comment of Arrernte people I met through their representative body, Lhere Artepe Aboriginal Corporation – that the proposed place should be a talking place, not a meeting place – indicated that this commitment to establishing the initial conditions of meeting was, indeed, on the right track. From a choreotopographical point of view, a place where people meet is an analogue of the discourse bringing it into being. It is a re-enchantment of symbolic attachments, which ideally are shared across different communities, cultures and traditions. Poetic identifications of this kind do not replace, or obscure, historical traumas that may remain to be addressed, but they suggest therapeutic alternatives to, for example, the onerous and usually dispiriting prosecution of land claims through the federal courts. At a neighbourhood scale, they can offer practical reconciliation mediated through symbolic forms.

An example of the challenge this approach represented emerged early in the discussion about protocol. As *Meeting Place*, a book whose central theme is richly informed by the Alice Springs experience, indicates, meeting cannot be taken for granted. It cannot be assumed that people want to meet – or that meeting signifies the same thing across different cultures. Non-Aboriginal peoples may take a different view: both for cultural and historical reasons – colonisation has hardly led to the development of shared understandings of place – they may regard the function of meetings as the determination of the protocols of non-meeting. They will certainly not regard the ground as given or ceded; and where the land has been violently taken, the first conversation will be likely to turn on this fact. Such differences of cultural expectation, whether political, historical or legal, are not to be disregarded. Nor are they to be turned into proof of cultural and historical determinisms beyond reconciliation. On the contrary, as is argued in *Meeting Place*, a concept of meeting as talking place has the potential to develop a symbolic vocabulary based on shared interests. Such meetings are based on a necessity to resolve differences, to find common ground. One of their chief functions might be to secure a coexistence that does not depend on a centralised authority but which flourishes best through a distributive and more egalitarian sense of local government. Meeting understood in this dynamic and performative way might be able to enact a relationship to country that balances centripetal and centrifugal tendencies. Interestingly, this understanding of place as the product of discourse or storytelling, and therefore as a fusion of poetic and political interests, *did* offer a justification for the otherwise rather pretentious 'Federation Square' reference, as the federal model of good governance celebrated in *Nearamnew* had obvious parallels with the way in which Arrernte residents of Alice Springs understood the value of meeting.[1]

The practical challenge of fostering a place of meeting, then, was a poetic one. An early illustration of this was the view expressed by people of all backgrounds at an early community consultation. Whatever else the meeting place did, they said, its primary function should be to reconnect the centre of the town to the Todd River: the inward-looking cast of the central town's grid plan and the associated defences against the river's occasional flooding had not only severed an important environmental tendon, it had stopped an important memory laneway. Participants in the initial conversations remembered playing as children in the dry Todd River bed. Non-Aboriginal and Aboriginal children had played together, and the experience of unforced sociability contrasted poignantly with what had happened when 'shades of the prison house',[2] or differential secondary education, had erected increasingly impenetrable social and cultural barriers. When the same participants expressed the view that the most important step in revitalising the town was reconnection of the central north–south spine of Todd Street Mall to the river, it was immediately clear they were referring to the restoration of old shared story places as well as improved sightlines.

The significance of this call to restore a lost psychological and emotional landscape resided, though, in the fact that it was symbolically mediated. To express their sense of attachment, both to a place and to one another, Aboriginal and non-Aboriginal representatives alike spoke of the importance of the red river gums that grew along the river – as play places, as shelters, as the homes of birds and insects, as emblems of steadfastness in the flood. These were trees and groups of trees essentially identified with human arrangements; perhaps in those childhood games they provided the laws of certain social relationships, standing for boundaries, destinations, prospect sites and refuges. In any case, there is nothing strange about this identification: it is presumably common to all cultures. But here, of course, a fateful bifurcation occurs. While the sacred landscape of Aboriginal centralians remains (really or potentially) in full operation all around them, in non-Aboriginal Australian cultures it has been contracted to the golden age of childhood, where it sits under the baleful glare of Enlightenment reason as a pitiful remnant of those 'fables, myths, legends, fit only for women and children'.[3] Commenting on the generally hostile attitude of the Alice Springs Town Council towards Aboriginal Australian tree attachments, Alice Springs resident, photographer and environmentalist Mike Gillam observes that what he characterises as a long-term and concerted council-led attack on sacred sites has deep roots in foreign soil; it is driven not by reasons of economy, aesthetics or convenience but by a profound xenophobia: 'I've come to realise that denigrating or damaging sacred sites or the heritage of another is part of the ongoing culture war being waged in this country'.[4]

Talking about the meanings of the red river gums, and finding shared emotional ground, was therapeutic. It demonstrated that stories are active producers of meanings, not simply received symbolic narratives defined anthropologically or culturally. Focused on identifications rather than on impermeably, defensively wrought boundaries, all parties found themselves once again in a state of wonder or anticipation; an active recollection was occurring that materialised meeting as a quality of openness to the other, as a state of conditional receptiveness. Viewed from the distance of adulthood, the human encounter played out in the riverbed was framed in the perspective of loss. This was important. It allowed the meeting place to accommodate trauma; it let ghosts and the living cohabit. As the community psychologist Craig San Roque puts it, 'Between the *Tjukurrpa* [the knowledge of country embedded in creation stories] and the European dream', there is 'a region of psychic pain' – which, informally, we were also touching.[5] Our first community discussions represented a momentary achievement in collective ideation that reminded me of Jacques Rancière's notion of the 'emancipated spectator', where 'the theatrical privilege of living presence' is questioned and all are brought back 'to a level of equality with the telling of a story'. It promises 'the institution of a new stage of equality, where the different kinds of performances would be translated into one another'. For, in all such performances, 'it is a matter of linking what one knows with what one does not know, of being at the same time performers who display their competences and visitors or spectators who are looking for what those competences may produce in a new context, among unknown people'.[6]

But what applies to the symbol also applies to the symbolic narrative in which it is placed. The red river gum is not a signifier of sociability, for wherever there is one tree there is another; and wherever straggling rows or lines of gums are found in the Todd River bed or elsewhere through the centre of Alice Springs, they follow the traditional paths down which water flows after rain. The red river gums form chains, groups, patterning the landscape with memories of water behaviour stretching back half a millennium. In Western planning language, the object of good place-making is always reconnection: places that have been disconnected (like Todd Street in Alice Springs and the Todd River) are connected again, usually by breaking through the barriers that have grown up and creating a new connector (road or path). In this idea of place-making, a particularly prominent or venerable tree can easily serve as the terminus of the connection. The other terminus may be a crossroads in the town. But the function of the tree in this role is purely to signify connection. No symbolic value attaches to it – or, to put it another way, the tree allowed to contribute to the planner's scheme is not related in any way to its surroundings. There is no chance, for example, that the subordination of trees to planning convenience might be reversed and the direction of future development follow the orientations and indications of the tree lines and groups. This would be to cede control to the environment and, as Gillam points out in the already cited article – since the order of the environment is the foundation of Aboriginal Australian cultural identity – to acknowledge another authority.

In this sense, the red river gum is not a signifier of connection; it is a symbol within a symbolic narrative. It does not stand for something unlike itself (the idea of connection, for example); it relates things of its own kind (other relations). While the sign can be replaced, the symbol's value resides in the transaction it permits with what lies about it. The point was made very simply by Mbantua elder Doris Kngwarraye Stuart. Referring to a time when red river gums were distributed more closely down the Todd, she said, 'You can trace your stories from the trees, but now there are only isolated pockets'. According to Stuart, red river gums are related to her wellbeing in two ways: they embody the spirit of people who have passed away, and they also represent family histories. Human beings are related to trees because of the relations trees have among themselves. To remove trees from where they belong, to cut down groves of them or otherwise destroy their arrangement, is equivalent to an act of historical destruction. Such story-bearing trees presumably possess the same kind of spirit as other sacred sites. Reflecting on the fact that she had been chosen by her family to be its conscience, its historian, the one who had primary responsibility for protecting sacred sites, Stuart explained the psychic burden under which she laboured. 'For every damage', she said, 'we have to lose a life', and 'after damage my ancestors come to me'. They come in troubling dreams, but they also gather around the damaged site and regard her. This is the context in which she remarked, 'Why re-create when we already had the thing?' This is also to say, you cannot bring back the dead.[7]

Arrernte elder and teacher Margaret Kemarre Turner has made extensive observations about the double existence of trees: 'Might be the Ancestors came through from other countries and stopped here on their journey. And they became another tree here, left part of his – what do you call it? – *image* there. A plant or tree became them as they walked past and became who they are. And then they changed into another one. They might have dropped seeds there and other trees came out of those Ancestors before they travelled on'.[8] In contrast with the anthropologist T. G. H. Strehlow's statement about the absolute identification of totemic ancestor with the totem,[9] Turner seems to suggest that either of two transformations determined the identification: the Ancestor could come to a place, stop and become a tree; alternatively, because of a tree where they stopped, the tree might become them and be them as they travelled on. Identifying with a tree in this way, the Ancestor could leave his image behind as a tree wherever he stopped. It is this double aspect of becoming a tree that Wardaman (Kimberley) elder Bill Yidumduma Harney invokes when, with the remark 'Many trees move around during the night',[10] he conjures up a ghost community that is mobile, doubly human, integrating the physical and the metaphysical.

At issue in this mismatch of cultural attitudes is not necessarily a racialised dispute about the importance of trees but a more profound question of symbolisation. Non-Aboriginal residents were thus perfectly well able to sympathise with Stuart's position. Graham Piper said to the Reverend Tracy Spencer, who collected much of the information on which this chapter is based, 'What's the point of me telling you where everything used to be, or even what people would like to see. If we don't have the stories, then we'll only have the can'ts and buts'.[11] Here, Piper makes a clear connection between the loss of stories and the culture of planning: when the human region formed of intersecting stories and human and non-human associations is destroyed, a new theory of region, characterised by regulation, prohibition and separation, intervenes. Another contributor to our research, Bruce Deans, put this in a historical perspective, reflecting how, 'in the 1980s, this small population was over commercialised, raped and pillaged…it lost its heart and soul'.[12] A symbol in this context is not simply a more sophisticated or complex sign. It bears an indexical relationship to the thing it represents. Hence, the historian of classical myth Carl Kerényi questions whether the stylised meander patterns found on Greek vases are 'symbolic' representations of the labyrinth: 'Symbols demand an interpretation, whereas…the meander is itself an explanatory sign that was immediately understood'.[13]

In some way, trees are indexical traces of what has happened. They are forms of mimetic writing; as animations of the spiritual landscape, they are essential expressions of its choreotopography. Their symbolic potency stems from the fact that they are properly placed and related. It is this distinction that explains why the bland assumption of planners and landscape architects, that new picturesque plantings will create a sense of place, is not justified. The conventional approach to the design of a new meeting place involves a pleasing arrangement of shade trees, the provision of a water feature, perhaps, even a public art commission symbolising the goal of social inclusiveness. However, a landscape design of this kind, while convenient aesthetically, overlays a pre-existing place with the representation of a place. If, as is the case in Aboriginal Australian painting and story, the region is composed of a network of sitting-down places and travelling lines, a picturesquely constructed garden or landscape erases a prior society of spaces: although it appears to re-create the conditions of sociability, it perpetuates the colonial mindset that the land is vacant and may be freely cultivated. In the interests of tying people together, it overlays existing networks or, more brutally, cuts through their tethers. Even if the new meeting place involves planting new trees, its instrumentalist approach to place design is quite consistent with the removal of trees elsewhere. In contrast, from an Aboriginal Australian point of view, the location of a tree is at least as significant as its human function: where trees, groups of trees or other green upstanding flora occupy a place in a song line or ancestral Dreaming story, their removal creates a gap in the narrative. The replacement of trees deemed to be a public danger with others planted elsewhere may maintain the number of trees in a given area, but poetically it produces confusion, noise and chaos.[14]

Notes

1 For further discussion of Arrernte protocols of meeting and their global implications for the renegotiation of the terms of coexistence, see Carter, *Meeting Place*, pp. 103–14. For the relevant *Nearamnew* inscriptions and their interpretations, see Carter, *Mythform*, pp. 72–7.
2 William Wordsworth, 'Intimations of Immortality from Recollections of Early Childhood,' *Poetical Works*, ed. T. Hutchinson: Oxford University Press, Oxford, 1969, p. 460. The poem also contains the following apposite lines: '-But there's a Tree, of many, one,/ A single Field which I have looked upon,/ Both of them speak of something that is gone…'

3   Jean-François Lyotard, *The Postmodern Condition: A Report on Knowledge*, trans. Geoff Bennington & Brian Massumi, Manchester University Press, Manchester, 1984, p. 27.
4   Mike Gillam, '500 year old red gums are being lost through neglect – but the trees can't speak', *Alice Springs News Online*, 19 January 2012, viewed 4 June 2015, <www.alicespringsnews.com.au/2012/01/19/500-year-old-red-gums-are-being-lost-through-neglect-and-the-trees-cant-speak>.
5   Craig San Roque, 'Coming to terms with the country: Some incidents on first meeting Aboriginal locations and Aboriginal thoughts', in Maria Teresa Savio Hooke & Salman Akhtar (eds), *The Geography of Meanings: Psychoanalytic Perspectives on Place, Space, Land, and Dislocation*, International Psychoanalytical Association, London, 2007, pp 1–31.
6   Jacques Rancière, 'The emancipated spectator', paper presented at the Fifth International Summer Academy of Arts, Frankfurt, 20 August 2004, transcript at Maryland Institute College of Art, n.d., viewed 4 June 2015, <http://digital.mica.edu/departmental/gradphoto/public/Upload/200811/Ranciere%20%20spectator.pdf>, [p. 11].
7   Doris Stuart, pers.comm, Alice Springs, 1 September 2008. See also, Material Thinking, 'Notes towards "The Society of Trees", a meeting place in Alice, 1 September 2008'.
8   Margaret Kemarre Turner, *Iwenhe Tyerrtye: What It Means to Be an Aboriginal Person*, IAD Press, Alice Springs, 2010, p. 154.
9   T. G. H. Strehlow, *Songs of Central Australia*, Angus & Robertson, Sydney, 1970, pp. 180–4.
10 Hugh Cairns & Bill Yidumduma Harney, *Dark Sparklers*, H. C. Cairns, Merimbula, 2004, p. 65.
11 Tracy Spencer, 'Stories from the Street: Todd Mall/Todd Street, At the heart of Alice, July 2008', p. 1–17. Paper prepared for Material Thinking. Available from author. Piper quotation: p.8. Deans quotation: p.11.
12 Ibid.
13 Carl Kerényi, *Dionysos: Archetypal Image of Indestructible Life*, trans. Ralph Manheim, Princeton University Press, Princeton NJ., 1976, p. 91.
14 Note that this is not to suggest a lack of cultural pragmatism or the absence of creative mechanisms for incorporating the new. Dick Kimber argues that the older indigenous landscape changed radically in the nineteenth century (Dick Kimber, 'Placenames of central Australia: European records and recent experience,' in *Aboriginal Placenames: Naming and Re-Naming the Australian Landscape*, eds. H. Koch and L. Hercus, Canberra: Australian National University epress, 2009, pp. 287–322,

311), while T. G. H. Strehlow tackles head on the question of what happens when sacred trees die (T.G.H. Strehlow, *Songs of Central Australia*, pp. 574–6).

11

PLACES MADE AFTER THEIR STORIES

The design of a meeting place that fulfilled this program of reconciliation marked the beginnings of what became the *Red Ways: Alice Springs CBD Revitalisation* project.[1] As this name indicates, the Uniting Church's desire to make land it owned on Todd Street Mall available for a new meeting place was taken up by the Northern Territory Government and the Alice Springs Town Council. Absorbed into the *Moving Alice Ahead – Lifestyle, CBD Revitalisation* initiative, announced by the Northern Territory Government in 2007, it soon became decisively associated with physical modifications to the spatial syntax of the centre of town. In the conventional manner of planned urban interventions, *revitalisation* was, in the hands of the planners, engineers, councillors and media, construed purely in terms of improved connectivity, embodied in revised streetscapes and in the provision of public art offering a symbolic overlay or interpretation of the town's heritage. It can be said that the entire struggle of the ensuing four years stemmed from Material Thinking's resistance to this pre-emptive identification of improved opportunities for sociability with the redesign of urban hardware: our object throughout was to demonstrate how places are made after their stories, and meeting places occur where stories meet, find common ground, are exchanged and modify one another.

Given this evolution, should we have been surprised that relating soon lost out to connecting? There is always a temptation to personalise these conflicts, especially where power appears to be wielded in the face of reason and compassion. Yet, in a way, the destructive consequences of bringing the places made after their (water) stories into the arena of planning were systemic rather than due to the influence of particular personalities. They reflected a collision of sacred geometries. For, just as tree-clearing is coeval with colonisation, so is planning. Colonisation without the grid and the Euclidean temper that lays out, divides and conquers is unimaginable. Craig San Roque explains the impact of this mindset: with white settlement, 'the needs of traveling Aboriginal families, native animals and their sources of food, were simply passed over. The incisive movement of trucks, trains and road graders across the Ancestral dreaming tracks or "songlines" ruptured the cosmological order and lives of the resilient secluded desert people, exposing them to new stories, lives and forms of death'.[2] The present grid of north–south, east–west streets forming the CBD of Alice Springs is the legacy of this pre-planned, prescribed 'incisive movement'. Politically, San Roque notes, the present situation is much as it was in 1979, when the anthropologist W. E. H. Stanner wrote, 'Aborigines are administered, controlled and educated by people who know almost nothing about them'.[3] It continues. The same mentality that planned the non-human urban grid continues to grid plan – segment, disconnect and disparage – human life. Picking up the pieces – usually through the medium of further strategic plans – becomes bureaucracy's self-perpetuating raison d'être. The tragic waste, spatial, social and spiritual, deepens, and the experts with their executive summaries explaining how in five easy steps dignity and pride of place can be achieved are baffled to understand why the little children continue to 'inhabit an environment which appears to be the rag and bone shop of the heart'.[4]

Our project was neither hopeful about further top-down government intervention to ameliorate present social distress nor designed to promote its purposes. Here, then, the political implication of our poetic approach became at last quite plain. Unless it reinvested the language of the talking place with a symbolic dimension, discussion about the location, shape and program of a new venue to effect bicultural understanding and reconciliation was doomed to fail. The different symbolic investments in the red river gums illustrated the point that a meeting place consists of non-human associations as well as human ones. The setting of improved sociability contributes to the 'business' of the meeting place; after all, one obvious topic of the Alice Springs talking place might be agreed protocols for looking after the trees. In contrast with the planner's meeting place, a site denuded of prior associations and therefore in need of a new social script, the new meeting place that attracted identifications from across the different communities would need to be choreotopographical in nature, based on the recognition of a relationship between the emerging character of the new place and the existing network of associations resident in the setting. The feedback loop between storytelling and the emergence of a design where shared symbolic understandings of place might be fostered would not be an imitation of Aboriginal Australian creation stories; it would be founded in the demonstration of fundamental spatio-temporal orientations and environmental dependencies inscribed into place-making stories. The outcome of eliciting these convergent patterns of social organisation would be the materialisation of a third place, a choreotopographically conceived score, ground pattern or performance.

Often, what is under your nose is hardest to see. The most obvious thing about Alice Springs is its name. It is not on the face of it propitious or poetic. It is one of an overlay of place names (Todd Street, Todd River, Charles River, Emily Gap, Heavitree Gap) that obsessively and onerously commemorate Charles Todd, an immigrant engineer and director of the Overland Telegraph project (completed in 1872), who never visited the settlement largely named for him, his relatives and his home country. This is not propitious for a bicultural dialogue, for reasons the anthropologist and linguist T. G. H. Strehlow explains in a short appreciation of the nineteenth-century explorer John McDouall Stuart. Strehlow greatly admired Stuart (whose route the Overland Telegraph largely follows), because of his endurance in crisscrossing the so-called red centre a number of times, but he had one major reservation: Stuart failed to understand the fact that the land was occupied and governed by the strictest visiting protocols. 'The family groups of which each local group was made up kept in touch with each other by sending up smoke signals whenever their wanderings took them away from the main camps. Any visitors coming in from outside groups had the duty to announce their approach in the same way.' As soon as the camp came in sight, 'the visitors would sit down, place their weapons with their backs turned towards the camp of their hosts, waiting for some of the local men to come forward and welcome them as visitors'. Strehlow explains, 'Though this aboriginal visiting etiquette may appear strange to us at first, its purpose was exactly the same as our own: we too insist that visitors must not sneak up on us, but must announce their presence by knocking on the front door...Nothing would offend us more than if our visitors would rudely burst in upon the privacy of our homes uninvited'.[5] Just so: and in the wake of Stuart's lack of good manners, the telegraph similarly ploughed through the human ties that regionalised the country and made it an archipelago of dwelling places. Instead of proceeding hand over hand, carefully following protocol, the new line cut the old ties apart. Inaugurating communication at a distance, it seemed to sacrifice the possibility of communion in the present.

And yet, propitious or not, the name Alice Springs identifies the fundamental shaping feature of the central Australian landscape and its people: water, its appearance, distribution and periodicity. After all, what our community respondents were articulating when they asked for reconnection to the Todd River was not simply a new memory lane to the red river gums of childhood; it was a new opening to the source of life. While the gums might represent people, they also tracked the flow paths water followed after rain. Behind the memory of people was a deeper spatio-temporal orientation to the behaviour of water. The federal distribution of Aboriginal Australian clans across the region, each with responsibility for a different 'estate', maps directly the distribution of water. In each 'estate', Dick Kimber writes, citing Strehlow, 'there is always a key totemic site, called *pmara kutata*, perceived as "an everlasting home" with the life forces of the totemic ancestors eternally present. It is normally a very distinctive feature (not necessarily large), often with a reliable water-source… Alice Springs Waterhole, Emily Gap and Simpson's Gap are some of the best-known of such sites'.[6]

The distribution of water not only determined the spatial organisation of central Australian societies; its changefulness over time influenced where people resided, why they travelled and when they met. In contrast with the European conception of water as a resource, Aboriginal Australians identify with the snake-like energy of water's self-manifesting. 'In Central Australia the summer rains mean life', Strehlow writes. But, as his description of rain coming at Jay Creek in January 1937 shows, rainfall is neither planned nor manageable: 'Its fury burst upon us: rain, water, rivulets, torrents, foam, the tempestuous rush of flood waters... Suddenly a deafening roar could be heard approaching from the north, as though a tornado had suddenly leapt into life. We rushed outside into the streaming rain. The Jay was rising suddenly...The thunder of the flood made attempts at conversation almost futile. All we could do was to watch in silence the roaring, turbulent water of the re-awakened Jay – waters that were foaming, curling, breaking, tossing, leaping, and tearing with the eyeless fury of a primeval giant'.[7] Such turbulence is not only an impressive natural phenomenon; it has an emotional impact on those who witness it. There is a sense of being carried away, drawn back into a larger body – in short, a sense of reconnection. It is a sensation all may share: 'The highlight was always when the river flowed; rain in the hills behind St Philips sent water down the Todd, and in each backyard in Todd Street was the strange seeping sound of water moving through the earth'.[8] And this non–Aboriginal Australian memory not only refers to a temporary environmental transformation; it describes the fantasy of reconnection, when the 'backyards', no longer separated and self-enclosed, are reopened and rejoined through the caterpillar seepage of water to the larger body of the country. Water spreading in this way is an image of eros. Its turbulence is like the mixture of anticipation and panic associated with plunging into the unknown of new social relations, as when strangers approach unexpectedly. Water bursting its banks, making all the country one, is a natural dramaturg: relating human choreography and natural topography, it is a choreotopographical agent of change.

In his excellent survey 'Cultural Values Associated with Alice Springs Water', Dick Kimber writes about Wenten Rubuntja, one of the 'old custodians' that he came to know in the 1970s: 'I recall that, referring to the Aboriginal and "white" populations of Alice Springs, he once said to me, "We must work together, my good boy. We got to be like the two train-lines. That train, he cannot run on just one line"'.[9] In *Red Ways*, we interpreted the simile by investigating two seemingly dissimilar phenomena: the Overland Telegraph and the Aboriginal Australian concept of *utyerre*, or tie to country. It turned out that these two ways of storying country, these two storylines, exhibited parallels. Both could be shown to be predicated on the idea of water-based creative regions. Just as the course of the Overland Telegraph line was determined by the location of soaks, springs or waterholes, so the spreading principle of *utyerre*, joining one 'estate' or neighbourhood of local responsibility to another, leads from one source of water to another. The value of juxtaposing these parallel story tracks emerged when a reinterpretation of the Todd legacy disclosed hitherto unnoticed aspects of his work and inspiration. Through a mythopoetic investigation of Todd's interests and motivations, we were able to discover a regional sensibility that made possible a third place, an in-between space of cross-culturally shared interests.

Todd, it appears, considered the new technology of the telegraph as an instrument of *regional development*. At its maximum reach, the telegraph connected the edges of the continent, and these to London. Prior to this, though, Todd understood the potential of the telegraph regionally, establishing a network of telegraph or repeater stations in South Australia with the explicit purpose of collating meteorological data received almost instantaneously from these to build up weather maps.[10] In other words, the distance inscribed into the telegraph could take the form of a front, a pressure differential or even a region of these, sampling and bringing into regional correspondence local atmospheric differences. The object of this regional system of remote weather stations was not in the first place to link one point on the globe to another in a linear fashion; it was to create an internal network whose region was defined differentially, for, if the weather across the region were selfsame, its sampling at different sites would be unnecessary. The object was to measure rates of flow and, by comparing and collating these, to build up a picture of regional turbulence. Todd was doing with the telegraph what Charles Mountford observed in 1940 at Aparina, in the Musgrave Ranges of northern South Australia, in Pitjantjatjara country: the choreographing of a rain-making ceremony. 'Our rain-maker estimated that rain would fall in three days, but if the rain was further away than estimated, or if not enough time had been spent on the ceremony, then it would be necessary for the rituals to be repeated.' The skies were clear when the ceremony began; five days later, 'heavy wind and thunderstorms swept up the gorge'. There was, Mountford thought, no 'logical explanation for the success of this ceremony'.[11]

Todd was interested in passage, in rates of change, and wanted to plot them in order to make their effects more predictable. In this task, the region did not precede its mapping; on the contrary, the region (a climatically predictable zone) came into being experimentally as a function of the emergence of certain meteorologically regular patterns. Livingston argues that the development of the intercolonial telegraph system was critical in determining the later decision of the colonies to federate.[12] In turn, the federalising of telecommunications was critical in ensuring that postal, telegraphic and telephonic systems were not privatised but remained publicly owned. In other words, inside the story of linear conquest over space, there is another story of relating, one in which relative positions and local differences matter.

Beside being an expert in telegraphy, Todd was an astronomer. Beside orbiting the globe with telegraph lines, he was interested in the orbit of the Sun's planets. To study the satellites of the Sun, Todd had to take advantage of the tiny moment in time when, occasionally, a planet crosses the Sun's face. These transits let the astronomer make calculations about the planet's orbit. Extrapolating from the moving silhouette of the planet crossing in front of the Sun, the astronomer can work out the physics of the Solar System.[13] A tiny visible transit holds the key to the organisation of a vast invisible region. These studies also had practical value. James Cook's studies of the transit of Venus, in 1769 were intended to help fix the position of lines of longitude and thus improve the reliability of colonial survey. Todd studied the transit of Venus as well as the transit of Mercury. The measurements he made were useful in fixing precisely the position of the Victoria – South Australia border. Todd also studied the transit of Jupiter's satellites across the face of Jupiter. Of one series of measurements, he wrote, 'I was much impressed on some nights with the sudden and extensive changes in the cloud belts, as though some tremendous storm was in progress on the planet's surface, changing the form and dimensions of the cloud belts in an hour or two, or even less'.[14]

Here is a sensibility somewhat removed from the conventional picture of Todd as a typical imperialist, a servant of empire intent on gridding the planet on behalf of Britain's commercial and territorial interests. And it also suggests a surprising parallel with the theory of the creative region embodied in the Aboriginal Australian concept of *utyerre* mentioned earlier. While this term expresses a distinctively Aboriginal Australian understanding of region and relationality, it appears able to comprehend non-Aboriginal Australian systems of communicating and relating. Eastern Arrernte elder and artist Margaret Kemarre Turner likens her tie to the land to 'a big twirl of string that holds us there with our families'.[15] The tie or string is called *utyerre*, and its seed connotation appears to be that of tying. This connotation allows Turner to incorporate the telegraph (now in the form of the telephone) into an Arrernte ontology: 'That *utyerre* means a telephone. And when he's hearing on the telephone, that person can see – in his mind he knows it – what that line runs, they can see it, where the message's coming from, like a string'.[16] Seizing on an extensive convergence of function, Turner finds a place for electrically mediated communication. Her brilliant analogy has, though, the effect of regionalising the telephone. *Utyerre* is the concept of connecting, but '*utyerre* also is like a vein, a vein in yourself, and in your country', and it is the root of the yam that leads you to the root of another yam. In the same analogy, *utyerre* is the root that joins two adjoining homelands: 'The spirit of each country goes deep into the ground and joins up with the spirits of all those other countries in *apmereyanhe* to make one big root down there'. To be related to someone else might be expressed as having a 'bloodstream or bloodline' inside you – '*Utyerre* contains something running through it' – it is both the vessel and the flow path. The *utyerre* connects you to country historically as well as spatially: 'You gotta follow your straight line, where your string is, where your bloodline lays in the country. Like what country you're really tied to. What is really your connection. What line, what stream runs in from you to there'.[17]

What would regionalisation of the Overland Telegraph mean? In the first instance, it would renarrate it as a host of possible meeting places; and, second, it would narrate these as passages or talking places. The marking of passage and its potential to create meeting places would not lead to representations of precious associations but enact them in the choreotopography of these periodic flows and catchments. The turbulent overflowing of boundaries expanded the territory available for meeting. Different totemic creatures presided over the creation of different landscape features. 'The crucial element, though, remained the fact that the trails followed lines of waters, so that after heavy rains people could spread widely out over their homelands, return to the longer-lasting waters as the hot weather set in, and had retreat lines to the rare permanent waters in time of drought.'[18]

Anthropologist Barbara Glowczewski brings out the choreotopographical significance of this: in Warlpiri experience to the north of Alice Springs, 'geographical elements can shift: sand dunes travel with the wind, creeks can change their flow during floods, water which comes up when digging can disappear when soaks are dry'. The Warlpiri 'perception of desert space is that it is always moving, breathing they would say'. This mobility, the breathing capacity to go in and out, to expand and contract, extends to the whole of what some would characterise as a distinctive desert knowledge: 'The number of trails between two places is infinite; there are as many itineraries as there are ways to travel, track game or collect food. Metric distance is not necessarily meaningful in the desert; people measure space in time rather than kilometres'. Depending on the weather, the number of people travelling and the availability of resources, 'the perception of the desert expands and contracts accordingly'.[19]

Glowczewski makes a further point: Warlpiri people consider that Tjukurrpa trails 'are not just intertwined over a flat space – that is, the surface of the land – some go underground (those of small marsupials, reptiles or roots), others travel in the sky (like birds and rain). In this three dimensional web there are a lot of common places which have two or more trails – two or more totemic species and their custodians'. And this fact of interconnectivity itself implies that knotting and spread go together generatively and regeneratively. Thus, 'If the Rain Dreaming is the responsibility of one group, rainmaking benefits everybody'.[20] In this philosophy of place, water is multimodal; it may manifest itself in the sky, underground and at the surface. Understood dynamically and transformatively, it is a metaphor of sociability, the environmental phenomenon that makes a strategic conception of social existence possible. Roger Benjamin writes, 'The Water (Ngapa) Dreaming is one of the great Dreamings of central Australia. One of its "songlines" runs from Adelaide on the Southern Ocean thousands of kilometres to Darwin in the tropical north; another moves from the west to the east, a great storm front passing through Kalipinya. On these songlines great events occurred at different sites with the Dreaming crossing many different Aboriginal nations; it has interconnections with Rainbow, Hail, Wind and other Dreamings. The Water Dreaming is a generative principle crucial to the life cycle of the desert country'.[21] More specifically, Fred Myers notes, in the work of many artists of the Papunya Tula movement, 'there is an emphasis on watercourses or water channels, and these are seen as the paths of Ancestral snakes, a common mythological identification of sinuous channels as the "tracks" of Dreaming snakes'.[22]

But dependence on the manifestations of water has not only shaped central Australian Aboriginal cultures; it has profoundly informed their historical experience. Strehlow's expeditions in 1931–32 to locate Aboriginal people who remained outside the Hermannsburg mission or the cattle station economy occurred in the midst of a seven-year drought – the same drought that inspired Pastor Friedrich Wilhelm Albrecht to build a water pipe from Kaporilja Spring to the mission.[23] One reason why those whom Strehlow interviewed were willing to hand over sacred *tjurungas*, or ritual objects, was that their precious waterholes were occupied and sullied by cattle, and they could see no prospect of remaining in their homelands or maintaining their ceremonial lives.[24] Strehlow's elegiac writing about this period may read as an account of epochal and irrevocable change. From another perspective, however, his narrative is really a spatial history of drought. In another season, when water ran everywhere, an entirely different journey would have been undertaken. Different places, different people and different songs would have been encountered.

Similarly, Geoffrey Bardon may have regarded the flowering of art at Papunya in 1971–72 as a unique cultural reaction to an onerous colonial regime, but, from another point of view, it was the outcome of meteorological providence. The eighteen months that the white teacher spent at the government settlement northwest of Alice Springs were among the wettest on record. Bardon attributed the extraordinary sequence of Water Dreamings that Johnny Warrangkula Tjupurrula painted in October to November 1971 to the pleasure the artist felt in seeing the rain come. Rain dissolved separations and drew everywhere together: 'After rain seagulls and egrets could come with the Indian Ocean storms and Johnny Warrangkula Tjupurrula would paint Water Paintings of this phenomenon'. Such paintings were not representations of visible objects but symbolic actings out of revitalising events. Bardon notes that Warrangkula's 'dotting or stippling technique' was taken up by many artists, creating a performative language for human reconciliation: 'The iconography of the earth upon which we all stood was a literal meeting and reconciliation place of different tribal groups'.²⁵ In any case, the place made after this story was a score or script: it assumed a mimetic commitment and competence, a willingness to copy a gesture and relate it to another.

Notes

1. It is interesting to reflect on the origins of the revitalisation metaphor. In the context of anthropomorphic readings of place, it can be traced back to efforts to modify human biology. The Steinach Operation, for example, much touted in the 1920s, 'was essentially a vasectomy, but promised physical and mental rejuvenation' (Chandak Sengoopta, '"Dr Steinach coming to make old young!" Sex glands, vasectomy and the quest for rejuvenation in the roaring twenties', *Endeavour*, vol. 27, no. 3, 2003, pp.122–6). Sengoopta comments, 'The revitalization of individuals was not merely a medical task but the key to reviving a tired civilization and redeeming humanity, especially after World War I, which had robbed Central Europe of a large part of its young male population' (p. 126). Parallels with the devastation currently experienced in the Alice Springs community due to the incarceration of young Aboriginal males are uncomfortably close.
2. Craig San Roque, 'The yard', in Ute Eickelcamp (ed.), *Growing Up in Central Australia: New Anthropological Studies of Aboriginal Childhood and Adolescence*, Berghahn Books, Oxford, 2013, pp. 156–179, p. 158.
3. Ibid., p. 159, citing W. E. H. Stanner, *White Man Got No Dreaming: Essays 1938–1973*, Australian National University Press, Canberra 1979, p. 341.
4. San Roque, 'The yard', p.159.
5. T. G. H. Strehlow, *Comments on the Journals of John McDouall Stuart*, Libraries Board of South Australia, Adelaide, 1967, p. 7, 8, 9
6. Dick Kimber, *Cultural Values Associated with Alice Springs Water*, Department of Land Resource Management, Northern Territory Government, 2011, viewed 4 June 2015, <http://lrm.nt.gov.au/__data/assets/pdf_file/0020/118181/Cultural-Values-of-Alice-Water-Kimber-2011.pdf>, p. 34, citing T. G. H. Strehlow, *Aranda Traditions*, Melbourne University Press, Melbourne, 1947, pp. 143–4.
7. T. G. H. Strehlow, *Songs of Central Australia*, Angus & Robertson, Sydney, 1970, pp. 445–6.
8. Tracy Spencer, *Stories from the Street*, July 2008, p. 8.
9. Kimber, *Cultural Values Associated with Alice Springs Water*, p. 1, citing Wenten Rubuntja.
10. Charles Todd's first responsibilities were focused on building a new

'intercolonial connection', establishing telegraph lines between Adelaide and Melbourne (see K. T. Livingston, *The Wired Nation: The Communication Revolution and Federating Australia*, Oxford University Press, Melbourne, 1996, p. 46).

11 Charles Mountford, *Nomads of the Australian Desert*, Rigby, Adelaide, 1976, pp. 277–8.

12 Livingston, *The Wired Nation,* chapter 6.

13 P. G. Edwards, 'Charles Todd and the Adelaide Observatory', *Proceedings of the Astronomical Society of Australia*, vol. 10, no. 4, 1993, p. 351.

14 Charles Todd, 'Observations of the phenomena of Jupiter's satellites at the observatory, Adelaide, and notes on the physical appearance of the planet', *Monthly Notices of the Royal Astronomical Society*, vol. 37, 10 November 1876, p. 285.

15 Turner, *Iwenhe Tyerrtye: What It Means to Be an Aboriginal Person*, p. 15.

16 Ibid, p. 16.

17 Ibid, pp. 16–19.

18 Dick Kimber, 'Tjukurrpa trails, A cultural topography of the Western Desert', in Hetti Perkins & Hannah Fink (eds), *Papunya Tula: Genesis and Genius*, Art Gallery of New South Wales, Sydney, 2004, p. 273.

19 Barbara Glowczewski, 'Returning Indigenous knowledge in central Australia: "This CD-ROM brings everybody to the mind"', in Graeme K. Ward & Adrian Muckle (eds), *'The Power of Knowledge, the Resonance of Tradition': Electronic Publication of Papers from the AIATSIS Indigenous Studies Conference, September 2001*, Australian Institute of Aboriginal and Torres Strait Islander Studies, 2005, viewed 4 June 2015, <http://aiatsis.gov.au/sites/default/files/docs/asp/Indigenous_studies_conf_2001.pdf>, p. 145.

20 Ibid., p. 146.

21 Roger Benjamin, 'The fetish for Papunya boards', in Roger Benjamin (ed.), *Icons of the Desert: Early Aboriginal Paintings from Papunya*, Herbert F. Johnson Museum, Cornell University, Ithaca, 2009, p. 37.

22 Fred Myers, 'Graceful transfigurations of person, place, and story: The stylistic evolution of Shorty Lungkarta Tjungurrayi', in Roger Benjamin (ed.), *Icons of the Desert: Early Aboriginal Paintings from Papunya*, Herbert F. Johnson Museum, Cornell University, Ithaca, 2009, p. 57.

23 On the spiritual significance of this, see Paul Carter, *The Lie of the Land*, Faber & Faber, London, 1996, p. 49

24 Ibid., p. 37.

25 Bardon & Bardon, *Papunya: A Place Made After The Story;* pp. 9, 23, 25.

12

LISTENING TO THE WATER UNDERGROUND

What kind of ground is evoked here? If the proposed meeting place in Alice Springs was not to treat the ground as a dead, blank canvas on which new infrastructure (paths, street furniture, public art) was to be imposed, it would need to take account of the fact that the ground was both deep and alive: it was flesh, like the body irrigated with flows, synaptically discharging energy, trembling regionally like a spider's web. Christine Watson points out that in the sand drawings of Kutjungka women from Balgo (a further four hundred kilometres north-west of Papunya), the technique Geoffrey Bardon refers to as 'stippling' retains a physical connection to the ground:

> The penetration when a traditional healer looks 'piercingly' at a patient and when a storyteller pokes the surface of the earth in sand drawing, are both suggestive to local people of entering a different realm of matter or experience. The poking of the ground involved in *walkala*, and the formalised beating of the ground with the *milpa* stick in *milpapungin*, is closely linked with this desire to penetrate the surface of the earth and to enter the realm of experience of the Ancestral beings – the Tjukurrpa – located geographically beneath the surface

of the ground, but experientially beneath the surface of waking reality.[1]

Just as the artists at Papunya adapted sand painting and body painting techniques to create original works on canvas, so the Balgo painters have carried over these symbolically invested techniques of poking and beating into new media. Stippling and poking are kinds of hand dancing. They have their counterpart in the stamping of feet during ceremony. At such times, it is not only the ground that is pierced; the mark-maker is also opened up. In *yawulyu* and initiation ceremonies, Watson states, Kutjungka 'women's bodies are opened...by the process of inscribing the nyirrtinin body painting designs within the flesh of the breasts and upper arms. In this process, women's torsos are penetrated by a volley of sound from the song cycle, while the forms made by the Ancestors as they metamorphosed into the fleshly features of their country are ingrained within the flesh of their own bodies. In this way, Ancestors and sites in country penetrate the bodies of living women'.[2]

Perhaps these place-making techniques are not commensurable with whitefella planning legislation: an Arrernte artist told me that when she looks across the centre of Alice Springs, she does not see the buildings, but only the old arrangements of trees and the relics of the passage of the Ancestors; for her the rest is invisible. Alice Springs resident and artist Dani Powell explained to me the title of her exhibition *Under Today* in this way: 'It comes from an Arrernte woman trying to emphasise the proximity of the past, in reference to a map she designed to demonstrate cultural practice pre-settlement. It is the last thing she says, as if she doesn't want to leave us with the clichéd sense of "traditional" being "past". She flattens her palm on the map. "This is just, you know, under today"'.[3] The Alice Springs CBD is a landscape of scars but also a field of buried pulses, caterpillar-like or comparable to the slow seepage down old water lines. But is this insight an exclusively Aboriginal Australian possession? An awareness of this energetic underlay influences planning, social behaviour and even habits of locomotion. 'Whites don't know their place, and so they have to find it, and they do that by making allegiances with Indigenous people', explained Dani. 'Footy matches' grandstands, hospital lawns, courthouse lawns, church lawns all have their cultural allegiances marking out the topography. These protocols on finding your place depend on the relationships between people, depend upon your relational identity. That's what determines where you are in a place. How you are in a place might also be culturally determined.' Dani noticed that white people move fast, 'on a mission'. Aboriginal people more often 'sit', 'just sitting' being the way to look out for people, see what's happening. Cars 'have primacy of movement throughout the CBD, even in the pedestrian mall, and [of course] the cars and car parks truncate pedestrian movement, and limit those places people can "spill out", slowly, or just sit'.[4]

Some efforts at symbolic rapprochement have been made – superficial perhaps, but indicative of an openness to a sense of place defined performatively and reciprocally. The Uniting Church's own founder-hero and the church that commemorates him are a case in point. In designing a church on Todd Street that would commemorate the vision of John Flynn, the pioneer of the Australian Inland Mission Aerial Medical Service, for 'a cathedral within central Australia where people of all faiths could worship',[5] architect Arthur Philpot proposed a symbolic hybrid. The sandstone north and south walls of the nave metamorphose a typical landscape feature found at Stanley Chasm or Emily Gap. The pool of fresh water at the entrance alludes to the kind of waterhole typical of the region: it recalls Flynn's saying 'In the Inland, water is life';[6] and it is noteworthy that Flynn personally compiled water maps which assisted the settlement of the 'Inland'. Such symbolic associations were, though, more picturesque than profound: Philpot's (unrealised) proposal for a 'sacred grove' outside the church's east end, for instance, was both sensitive and insensitive; the species proposed for the grove were cypresses, laurels and yews.[7] Looking back, it seems curious that the immediately adjacent red river gums of the Todd River, or for that matter the tenderly beautiful ghost gums so prominent in the watercolours of Albert Namatjira, were not preferred, or, indeed, the indigenously occurring cypresses.

And, while Flynn was a true son of the telegraph, using radio to pioneer the Flying Doctor Service, he and the Presbyterian Church he represents have rarely, it seems, taken Aboriginal Australian identifications with country seriously. Even the 2007 invitation to promote 'the heart of Alice [as] the meeting place of difference, where diversity is respected and something new emerges in its coming together', to create 'a place of welcome, connection and encounter',[8] invoked an idea of congregation predicated on the involuntary dislocation of families from their traditional estates and, with it, the elimination of the power to determine the rules of legitimate passage. Another act of historical amnesia was also involved: the alleged 'indifference' of the man for whom the Uniting Church was named to the plight of central Australian Aboriginal people and, connected with this, the ad hoc and decontextualised assimilation of Aboriginal Australian cultural motifs into the architect's symbolic scheme for the church. While Flynn developed the twin technologies of flying and radio transmission to service isolated communities, in this way building a networked region of care, his vision sidelined or ignored Aboriginal people, treating their laws, society and culture as a no-go zone – not, according to David Trudinger, out of respect but from 'indifference'.[9]

'Whatever happens in this place should be whimsical', Mike Gillam said to me when I discussed the manifestation of the Alice Springs meeting place, 'like a mapping that shows through here and there, like the stories do. So many of them aren't "seen" because they literally disappear into the ground. Many sacred expressions of the stories are actually buried to protect them, so maybe small elements of them surface – like the public level of the stories – or are uncovered if you just sweep a little sand away, and then put it back'. This observation was consistent with the way stories came to us, not as continuous narratives but as here-and-now verbal performances accompanied by gestures. The stories we heard in Alice Springs – stories understood broadly as anecdotes, conceptions, lines of induction, various kinds of ejaculations, apostrophes, exhortations and admonitions – were not best respected by a form of synthetic analysis. They reminded me of the phenomenon to which philosopher Jean-Luc Nancy refers as the 'interruption' of myth, where dialogue 'is made up only of the articulation of mouths: each one articulated upon itself or in itself, facing the other, at the limit of itself and of the other, in this place that is a place only in order to be the spacing of a singular being – spacing it from the self and from others – and constituting it from the very outset as a community being'.[10]

Could this performance of breakings off, where a turning towards (conversation) existed in partnership with a turning away (tergiversation), have a pattern? Geoffrey Bardon celebrates

Johnny Warrangkula Tjupurrula's simultaneous conversation with the ancestral Water Man and with Bardon himself, egging him on to greater clarities of articulation. Of his painting *Water Dreaming with Man in Cave*, Bardon writes, 'As a distillation of a life force, an ordered depiction of the creation, Warrangkula's suggestions of clouds, landscape, running water, and the Water Man himself are immaculate. The painting shows the painter's great vitality in 1972, the "dotting" more like a stippling and irregular "hard-force" over the board; Warrangkula uses the board to suggest an incisement of the paint strokes, seemingly letting them run in an emotional determinacy and force which in its unfinishedness seemed to be the antithesis of that stale and inert dotting and the suffocating stillness of that convention as it was later used'.[11] This is mark-making as dramaturgy, as haptic intelligence discovering the symbolic meeting place of natural event and human action.

> Johnny Warrangkula would work harder than anybody else with his nervous tremor and suppressed rapture. The vortex of the radiating circle was a dynamic outer movement of the travelling line from a place of rest... These hieroglyphs were a poetry, a heightened visual language making 'figures of sight', an approximation to figures of sound; they did not necessarily tell of a detailed place or time, but sometimes of a place or time by association, and in a subjective and heightened way; also they could tell of ordinary, or day to day matters, the dirt under the fingernails, and therein lying the importance of the forms, and the all-important matter of intelligibility between the painters and also amongst the Aboriginal people.[12]

In other words, any ground design will be echoic, an essential response to sound (the song). It will be a design on hearing, performative rather than passive, intended to encourage listening as much as the meeting of glances. The vortex in this context is not a modification of the ground plane that interrupts the direct line of walking; it represents the blossoming of self-awareness into a multisensory sense of place. The visitors imagined by the discourse of planning are goal directed, motivated by neediness and prone to infantile tantrums if their needs are not promptly met. Architects and landscape architects are obliged to respond with visually prominent signage that seeks to hold at bay any scope for misinterpretation. Where the lie of the land obliges some treatment of gradient, uniformity of slope, standard handrails and illuminated treads remove all power of measure from the walker: the informal metrication of the ground that occurs when steps are negotiated, irregularities of pavement navigated and the alternation of narrow apertures and ample openings threaded are wiped out. In contrast, the occupant of a meeting place conceived as a site of encounter may have no other business than that of coexistence. Such people exist in the echo of the other's voice, in the shadow of the other's passage. The vortex is like the experience of sound that encircles the hearer but never returns to its starting theme. The effect is access to the ambience of the place. The meeting place is, in this discursive construction, a figure of speech. It is speech materialised in the encounter with another.

Further, as the topic of discussion, the *reason* of the talking place, is the way in which the place came into being (the Water Dreamings, the history of the Overland Telegraph), what is said is the echo of this larger setting. The rhetoric of place-making is in its performance analogous to the character of the place. The discourse of choreotopography deploys what Thomas Rickert would call an 'ambient rhetoric', a way of denoting meaning that remains tied to the circumstance of its enunciation. As Rickert writes,

> an ambient approach no longer sees rhetoric as a direct extension of human will or human meaning making. Thus the commonplace understanding of rhetoric as a discursive exchange between contextually arranged but otherwise disparate rhetorical agents falters. Instead, we need to see that rhetoric emerges from the ambient environs, the in which and from which that give it its bearings and thrust it forward. If we retain rhetoric's traditional notion of context, it is stretched far beyond its delimitation as a social-discursive situation to include a vibrant materiality, such that rhetoric is not just played out in an environment but embedded complexly in and through it.[13]

The sense of dwelling that emerges from this awareness of context allows the actants, Rickert states, quoting Martin Heidegger, to '"receive directives" from and mutually sustain one another'.[14] This is an echoic inhabitation of place, a way of being together that is sonorously based or song-like: it does not presuppose the ground but produces it. Instead of arguing about ownership, reinforcing ego-led political divisions, the identifications fostered by the storytelling ways of choreotopography aim to create a space in-between. Here, the singularity of difference appears without being threatening. Here, different histories do not have to be reconciled, only echoed. 'The echo deconstructs the metaphysical projection of an "original ground"', David Levin writes, 'compelling us to recognize this "permanent ground", a "constant presence", as the deluded projection of a metaphysical reading of the field of perception'. The echo, he adds, 'teaches our hearing the presence of absence and the absence of presence'.[15]

The situation we encountered in Alice Springs bore many strong resemblances to the one we entered in Shepparton. The new designer is a dramaturg, equally concerned with the arrangement of objects and the spaces in-between them. But, in Shepparton at least, I was also a rhapsode, a particular kind of ambient orator. The master planning process I was being asked to undertake was *already happening* in the room as we spoke. It did not have a *representandum*, which (whether in the form of a museum exhibit or an architect's model) is a product of the future. The place being brought into being was the product of a performative process. The reunification of the Goulburn and Broken rivers country, its peoples and environments, occurred in my speaking that vision. Exactly like the ancient rhapsode taking the threads of different stories and weaving them into a new story flatteringly responsive to the occasion, I was producing a mental place that was fully historical. It is, of course, a fiction of place, but nonetheless real. Indeed, it is real as place because it is a fiction. For the places that master plans invoke are theatrical in nature. They are architectural sublimations that prevent anything unscripted from happening. In my rhapsodic weave, in the passage of the shuttle, something was happening, both unforeseen and true to the past. Those listening were being taken on a journey at once geographical and poetic in which a flattened out and silenced realm was given back its voices, its interconnections – its capacity to generate a sense of place. Such a place, simultaneously mental and physical, does not have cartographic coordinates, even if its rough location on the Earth's surface can be indicated. It is choreographically organised, and its geography is rhythmic. Such a place is like Arakawa and Madeline Gins's 'fiction of place', a chiasmatic zone, formed when and wherever a meeting occurs.¹⁶ Potentially, this meeting place – the place where the story gets told – is everywhere where it happens. Places do not simply come into being after their stories; they are produced wherever the right stories are told.

There were illuminating occasions in the four years of talking in Alice Springs when comparable breakthroughs occurred, and, in concluding the *Red Ways* story, I recall one episode, doubly interesting because it brings us back to the symbolic function played by trees. The diary of the exchange captures the drama of introducing a places-made-after-their-stories approach to place-making into a forum dominated by a planning mentality:

> Where there are no plans, no creationist myths, only stories of coming into being repeatedly through their enactment, how do new things come into being? If places are made after their stories, this question can be rephrased: what 'voice' guides the designer? What is it that allows him to find the way that opens up the sense of place? The word 'design' already presupposes a gestalt or emergent pattern either potentially or actually present. How is this made out? Here is an anecdote that in some way throws light on this. At last night's meeting with the Alice Springs Town Council I found myself at the beginning in tempestuous waters. The engineer wanted clarification of some 'conceptual designs' done by ——; S——, an Aboriginal-Afghan Alderman seemed keen to put a white interloper in his place, and others were finding it difficult to grasp where I was 'coming from'. They had expected the identification of a number of infrastructural initiatives that would bring about the CBD's revitalisation. Instead I was insisting on the

intangibles of story, arguing that, as these were invariably story ways or narratives accompanied by drawings, and their topographical counterparts, travelling ways and gathering places, the future revitalisation of the town could come out of their recollection and showing. I advocated this with some passion but the body language and the expressions in their faces indicated either resistance, suspicion or outright incomprehension.

Then – as I analysed the dynamic of the meeting afterwards – S—— tentatively proffered the observation that the palm trees outside the council chambers were precious to her because they recalled the cooperative relationship that had once existed here between Aboriginal people and Afghan cameleers. This remark had, as I now reflect, a decisive effect on the collective mood. It was as if an inhibition to dream had been removed, as if S——, whose heritage bestowed on her a particular authority, had decided – who knows why? – that she would initiate the game of initiation, assuming in this the role of guide or master. I don't think this was conscious, and talking to her afterwards there was no sense that she was aware of what had happened at this juncture. Nevertheless, her seemingly modest contribution licensed the aldermen and women to visualise, and from this moment onwards the 'stories' that had seemed abstract were suddenly concrete, composing themselves into recognisable patterns in the town.

What happened when S—— spoke of the palm trees? At that moment she ceased to speak for herself, as an independently willed ego, and allowed herself to be spoken through. She began to speak on behalf of the trees, erotically of her love for them and of their love for us. But hers was not a rote repetition of one amongst many items on the heritage wish list. The palm trees imaginatively engaged her because they embodied something that happened in the past. They were born of an encounter that a historicist vision of the past would have considered over and done with. Against the odds, Afghans and Arrernte found common cause.

The palm trees were not the silent sentinels of a history already told in a myriad of ways round town. They referred to something that had not found its way into the master narrative. They referred to a gap in the collective memory, and for this reason to a way through to a new psychic understanding of what it means to be in place. The palm trees let her speak of what otherwise could not be narrated. They guided her. Intuitively, she knew that they were what was needed in the present moment, an instance of the material imagination at its work of opening ways. And her example allowed the others to pass through, and in the process to change the place from which they spoke. Ceasing to be politicians, stubbornly and aridly defending an opinion, they became storytellers looking for further connections. The guide they intuitively followed was not one or another story, but these stories in their places, as meeting places or as travelling ways.

This experience led me to reflect on my own role: the designer as storyteller. With reference to the traditional oral bard, who, like an ambient orator, trimmed his poetic material to suit his audience, I concluded my narrative with the following reflection:

As a rhapsode, stitching together the vestments of an identity, I am not simply assembling parrot-fashion a miscellany of what I have heard. The playback I improvise is selective, critical, a poetic contraction of what I have picked up. It constantly forms itself into associative or conceptual clusters which are the emergent forms of ideas. Yesterday, for example, the emphasis on creativity, on the production of the scene of story-telling and its sustaining, grew stronger because of the responses it gained; in turn these served to compact, mould and materialise this first concept into the beginning notion of a production house, cultural centre or digital story-telling place. Such processes do not lead to contextual architecture or its inverse brutal functionalism. They are homologous with the process of dreaming new forms into beings, places that will be as astonishing as the created landscape. In any case, there is a subtle transference that occurs in these talking out of figures. Repeatedly, I have the sensation of the palm trees, that I am speaking to the memory, or in anticipation, of an environment that guides me. My own voice is strong here – it is not a collage of bits and pieces – but it does not embody any will to invent. In fact, despite the pressure to show conceptual designs, it reserves a Keatsian negative capacity to wait and see what turns out. It guides because it is guided, as the tracker tracks because she is tracked.[17]

There were many moments of listening like this when a symbolic breakthrough occurred, but it is difficult to sustain this willingness to receive directives where the culture of decision-making is based on the competition of wills. Our eventual formal response, in probably unpropitious circumstances, was the design proposal called *Red Ways*, which argued that urban and landscape interventions into the physical fabric and spaces of Alice Springs should be guided by a design options framework or creative template. Instead of place-making, we spoke of the lace-working of places that occurs after rain, a process in which channel and vessel continuously flow through one another. We drew a ground pattern, which was to be understood like an acupuncture chart, as a diagram of differentially connected centres or sites of association (in a human as well as a sacred sense). The aspiration was to translate the creative turbulence of water – understood here as the re-creative aspect of T. G. H. Strehlow's destructive 'primeval giant' – into the blueprint of a social choreography. Although our pattern referenced the physical floodplain and the salient springs and flow lines of the site, it simultaneously stretched and pulled the town's colonial grid and the envelope of the Todd River until, as it were, they found a shared topological ground. The pattern was a strange attractor drawing forms to the edge of their self-consistency and threatening to pull them apart – a disintegration undertaken in the confidence that the turbulent energy manifested in this way was self-organising at a higher level of complexity. Running through our swirling pattern were the energy vectors able to transform the spindly lines of the Overland Telegraph into the fat 'triglyph' of the north–south arrangements of red river gums in the bed of the Todd. But the pattern itself was a web of vortices or spirals that existed between circle and line: scores to be stepped and sounded, 'figures of sight' implying 'figures of sound' (see Figure 11).

Of course, in contrast with the master work of Johnny Warrangkula, the unfinish was not due to aesthetic restraint. It reflected the character of the talking place as we had found it over four years, a place composed of limits, overflowings and abruptly

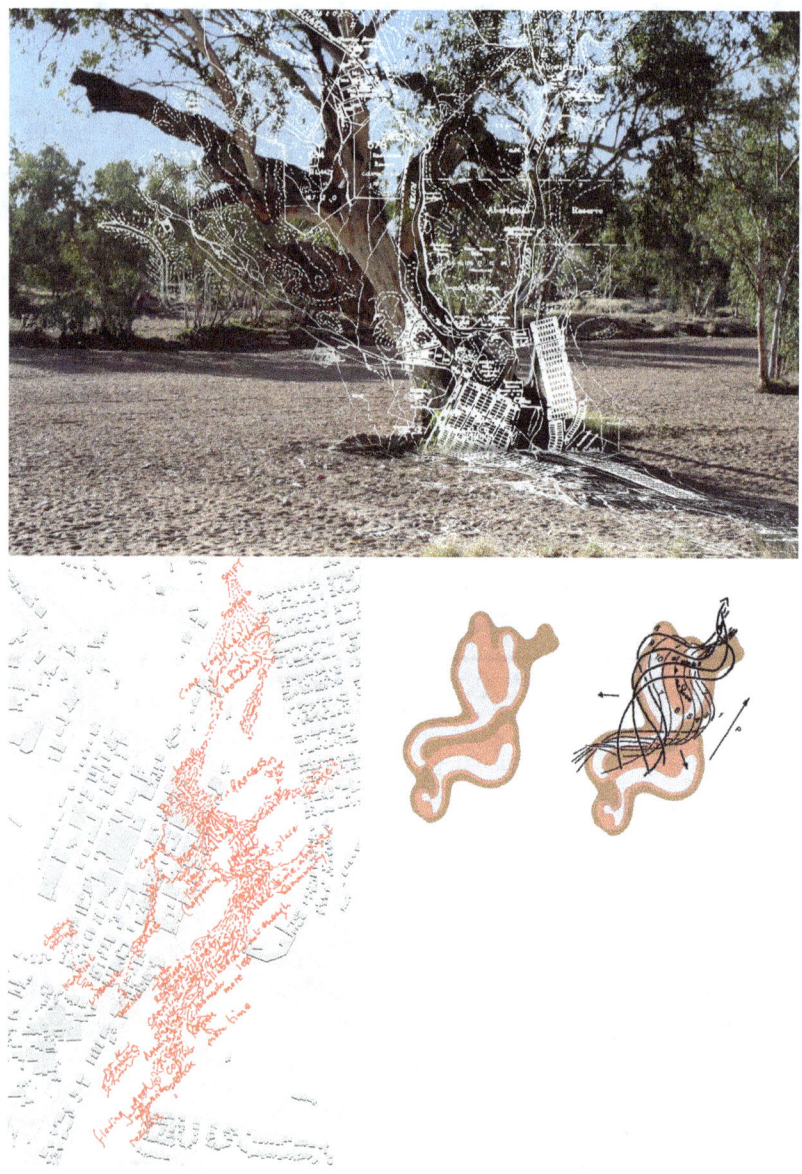

Figure 11 Material Thinking, 'Tree Drawings, Processes of Connection, Meander' in 'Red Ways: Alice Springs CBD Revitalisation, Design Options Framework', June 2008, pp. 1–70, p. 44, 46, 52.

changing emotional weather.[18] In Arrernte, the Todd River is called Lhere Mpantwe.[19] In Aboriginal Australian understanding, an analogy is perceived between the course of the river and the sparkling band of the Milky Way. This resemblance is found in other watercourses in Arrernte and related peoples' countries.[20] If interest had been shown in this proposal, one temporal expression of that transformed ground would have been the assembly of glances. The new look would not be penetrating and intrusive; it would look away out of respect. In the gesture of meeting would be secreted the expression of exile; protocols of approach, encouraged by the choreography of the ground, would allow meeting to contain within itself the rules of departure. The choreography of this would have been echoic and mimetic.

In *Meeting Place*, I quote a Delphic oracle:

Be ever watchful, wanderer,
For the eyes that gaze into yours at the bend of the road
May be those of the goddess herself.[21]

The goddess, I suggest, is Pallas Athene, the patron saint, we might say, of meeting places: 'She presides over the curvilinear space of the everyday, where genuine meetings occur that are both foreseen (designed) and unpredictable. She legislates for 'the difficult country of the everyday': 'where space is experienced parabolically as a folded ground projecting a labyrinth of convergences and departures, coincidences will constitute the normal reason of appearances'.[22]

Notes

1. Christine Watson, *Piercing the Ground: Balgo Women's Image Making and Relationship to Country*, Fremantle Arts Centre Press, Fremantle, 2003, pp. 107–8. *Walkala*: 'to spear, pierce, poke' (p. 380); *milpapungin*: 'type of sand drawing where the earth is beaten with a curved stick' (p. 379).
2. Ibid., p. 198. *Yawaulyu*: 'women's ceremony' (p. 381); *nyirrrntinin*: 'to smear paint, to paint the body' (p. 379).
3. Dani Powell, pers. comm., 1 September 2008. This story is reproduced in Spencer, 'Stories from the Street', p.15.
4. Spencer, 'Stories from the Street', p.15.
5. Tracy Spencer, for the Uniting Church in Alice Springs, 'The Heart of Alice: a place for welcoming, connecting and encountering,' draft statement 16 December 2006, 1–4, 1.
6. Arthur A. Philpot, *The John Flynn Memorial Church, Alice Springs, The Design and Its Significance*, The Uniting Church: Alice Springs, 1956, p. 4.
7. Ibid, p. 3.
8. Tracy Spencer, for the Uniting Church in Alice Springs, 'The Heart of Alice: a place for welcoming, connecting and encountering,' 1–4, 2.
9. David Trudinger classifies John Flynn's attitude to the Arrernte and other regional peoples as belonging to what W. E. H. Stanner calls 'the history of indifference' ('Demythologising Flynn, with love: Contesting missionaries in central Australia in the twentieth century', in Frances Peters-Little, Ann Curthoys & John Docker (eds), *Passionate Histories: Myth, Memory and Indigenous Australia*, ANU Press, 2010, viewed 4 June 2015, http://press.anu.edu.au/apps/bookworm/view/Passionate+Histories%3A+Myth,+Memory+and+Indigenous+Australia/8271/Text/ch07.html, citing W. E. H. Stanner, '"The History of Indifference Thus Begins"', in W. E. H. Stanner, *The Dreaming & Other Essays*, Black Inc Agenda, Melbourne, 2009, pp. 93–122. Originally published 1963.
10. Jean-Luc Nancy, *The Inoperative Community*, p. 76. In a comparable way, Mike Gillam understood meeting dialectically, his 'here and there' (Pers. comm., 19 July 2008) corresponding to Nancy's 'spacing'.
11. Geoffrey Bardon, 'A Place Made After the Story: The Hieroglyphic Representations of the Western Desert Painters, and their Cultural and Stylistic Significances, at Papunya, 1971–1973', typescript, 2001, pp. 147–8. The materials that eventually led to the publication *Papunya: A Place Made After the Story* went through many drafts. Some of the earlier writing preserves an 'emotional indeterminacy' and 'unfinishedness' reminiscent of the paintings under discussion, a stylistic idiosyncracy sometimes edited out in the published version. The 2001 text exists as a typescript in my

possession and can be consulted by arrangement with the Geoffrey Bardon Estate.
12 Ibid., pp. 147–8.
13 Thomas Rickert, *Ambient Rhetoric: The Attunements of Rhetorical Being*, University of Pittsburgh Press, Pittsburgh, 2013, p. 254.
14 Ibid., p. 254, citing Martin Heidegger, *Poetry, Language, Thought*, trans. A. Hofstadter, Harper & Row: New York, 1971, p. 158.
15 David Michael Levin, *The Listening Self: Personal Growth, Social Change and the Closure of Metaphysics*, Routledge, London, 1989, p. 238.
16 Arakawa/Madeline Gins, *Pour Ne Pas Mourir/ To Not To Die*, Edition de la Différence, Paris, 1987, p. 86.
17 Material Thinking, 'Care at a Distance project journal', 2007.
18 Perhaps the closest analogue to this approach outside of the urban design and place-making discourse is Tess de Quincey's *Bodyweather* project. See Mary Elizabeth Anderson, *Meeting Places: Desert Consciousness in Performance*, Editions Rodopi, Amsterdam, 2014, pp. 81–126.
19 The name of the Registered Native Title Body Corporate is Lhere Artepe, 'which can be glossed in Central Arrernte as *alhere* = river or creek and *artepe* = backbone' (Manuhuia Barcham, *Working with Indigenous and Western Corporate Structures – the Central Arrernte Case*, White Paper 2012/01, Synexe, 2012, viewed 4 June 2015, <http://static1.squarespace.com/static/53b85a6ce4b046129f33a042/t/547101cee4b0922a0c042990/1416692174333/001–2012-WP-Working+with+Indigenous+and+Western+Corporate+Structures%2C+the+Central+Arrente+case.pdf>, p. 1). Note that Dick Kimber spells it Lhere Mparntwe', explaining that 'Lhere means river or creek, and this is a local name derived from a sacred site, Mparntwe, several hundred metres north of Heavitree Gap.' (Dick Kimber, 'Cultural Values Associated With Alice Springs Water', 2011, p. 10. At http://lrm.nt.gov.au/__data/assets/pdf_file/0020/118181/Cultural-Values-of-Alice-Water-Kimber-2011.pdf).
20 See Dick Kimber, 'Placenames of central Australia: European records and recent experience', p. 292.
21 Ann Shearer, *Athene: Image and Energy*, Viking Arkana, London, 1996, p. xi.
22 Carter, *The Lie of the Land*, p. 293.

Part 3

13

THE SOCIETY OF TREES

Red Ways was an exercise in minor planning. Given the modest impact of the design proposals on the form and content of the 'revitalisation' initiatives eventually endorsed by the Alice Springs Town Council,[1] this statement could be interpreted as unintentionally ironic. We advocated minor planning but did not want the impact to be *that* minor! In these circumstances, there is a temptation to conclude that the practices of choreotopography and master planning are incommensurable: despite their apparently shared interest in place-making, their place-making discourses have too little in common to make dialogue possible. There is pressure to unravel the strands from which a choreotopographic approach is woven and to accede to the convenience of the status quo. Once again, the symbolic narrative is delegated to public art; once again, the crowd is classified as turbulent and subjected to surveillance; and once again, the new setting is detached both from its setting (topography) and from the ambient rhetoric that not only communicated its form but (in theory) provided its content. But this withdrawal into aestheticisation has to be resisted, if only because of the palpable failure of planned spaces to meet the simplest expectations of sociability. Most urban master planning briefs require consultants to deliver 'liveable places'. A key component of these is invariably the provision of 'opportunities for people to meet'. However, even the most socially and environmentally engaged definitions of master plans fail to indicate how master plans deliver these. In fact, the United Kingdom's Commission for Architecture and the Built Environment's guide *Creating Successful Masterplans* manages to define *well-designed places* without any reference to sociability at all.[2]

Planning historian Patsy Healey identifies three phases in recent planning ideology: the notion of a uniplex city extracted from chaos – seen these days as 'a relic of the "command and control" welfare state, and of the modernist conceptual equipment of positivist science and utilitarian rationalism which went with it'; the neoliberalist conception of the urban environment as a competition of interests – fragmented, divided, disorganised and market driven, in which 'planning systems [become] quasi-market regulatory mechanisms for dealing with conflict mediation over complex spatially manifest environmental disputes'; and a third, which Healey describes as a '"new" institutionalism', associated with environmentalism and driven by questions of sustainability, 'which emphasizes the importance of a politics of place-making', and which focuses on 'the active social construction of place-focused frameworks' and 'efforts to cultivate strategic imagination through which key attributes of a "place" can become identified and "owned" by the many stakeholders…"Permanences" are created in the dynamic relational dialectics of urban life'.[3]

In reality, the three phases of planning that Healey describes coexist. In Alice Springs, for example, the original grid layout of the centre corresponds to the 'command and control' idea of planning. (It was also apparent in the current expectation that the revitalisation of Alice Springs would involve an enhanced east–west connectivity.) The hangar-like shopping complexes and associated carparks, which suddenly dwarfed the grid in the 1980s, exemplified the delegation of planning authority to the forces of free-market competition. When we entered the fray, in 2007, a belated awareness of the role that 'permanences' play in making sense of place was emerging, but it was timorous and inarticulate, as this passage from a 2004 master plan indicates: 'While it is often difficult to define the "character" of a place, it is necessary to define those aspects that attribute [sic] to the character of Alice Springs, which allows the community to develop a sense of place'.[4] Evidently, the planners who wrote this had little idea what they were talking about, and little appetite for translating it into action.

Landscape architects and urban designers interested in the mysterious character of place have found the new institutionalism a more welcoming culture in which to work. However, the language of the new place-focused planning remains functionalist and bleak; and, probably for the same reason, the politics and the poetics of what counts as a place remain unexamined. Hence, the design brief for the 2013 Gold Coast Cultural Precinct Design Competition was not atypical in informing us that 'Council's Vision [sic] for the cultural precinct assumes a largely blank canvas, open to creative possibilities'.[5] This brief was in other respects committed to a constructionist ethic and aesthetic; it simply lacked the choreotopographic vocabulary to express this. A partial solution to the false equivalence of blankness and creativity – a coupling that surely disguises planning's bad conscience – is to emphasise the creativity already invested in the site. Even the most utopian eye cannot fail to see what the aerial photographs and local maps document: rows of houses, streets, abandoned factories, power lines, canals and so forth. The characterisation of the site to be redeveloped, revitalised, gentrified or whatever as a 'blank canvas' must be very frustrating to would-be designers (urbanists or landscapists). As a fair part of their training is aimed at developing a keen eye for local features – topographical, environmental, functional and cultural – whose analysis acts as a reference point for whatever new space syntax is proposed, to make a precondition of their engagement collusion in the obvious lie that there is nothing to see puts them in an invidious position.

The argument that what exists is itself the product of creativity, a jigsaw of future visions that jostle for attention and whose value unfolds towards the future, counters the impulse to clear everything away. But it is a perilous one, as planners tend to confuse it with the heritage defence when, in fact, an emphasis on the attributes of memory, imagination and inventiveness embedded in the site aims to redirect attention to less tangible characteristics of the site such as arrangement, orientation, distance, gradient and scale.[6] The new materialism advocated here is not an intensification (or broadening) of heritage interests and tastes but argues for the historical importance of such intangible properties as resonance, volume, dimension and interval. As I noted earlier, reflecting on the collaborative art practices described in my book *Material Thinking*, Cameron Tonkinwise asks how they would fare when transferred to the city.[7] Properties of this kind do not exactly map to the physical site: they pass through it, congregate and eddy and whirl away. Their residue may be subtle secondary effects registered in the human behaviour of shadows - I always recall Sir Walter Raleigh's observation 'No man can walk abroad save on his own shadow.'[8] When I quoted this remark in the final report prepared for the *Connecting Alice* project, I twinned it with the statement of distinguished Eastern Arrernte painter Kathleen Kemarre Wallace: 'If we had no living spirits, our life would be nothing to us. It is the spirit in us who makes us do things, move around and live life.'[9] Transposed to place-making, these insights signify that when the collaborative art practices advocated in *Material Thinking* move out into the streets, they posit a new human subject, who is constituted doubly, dyadically, interactively. In contrast with the billiard-ball model of human movement and motivation, which underpins master planning presumptions about sociability and its design, choreotopography incorporates the tracks of those who have gone before. It recognises that the design of traffic involves the recognition that places already possess coefficients of friction, resistances to free communication that serve, in fact, to make room to move about. But for these doubling passages, time would lack a horizon, meeting cease to be an event.

Shadows, of course, can also run behind – the ancient Greeks even had a special daimon denominated *synopados* – 'he who follows behind'. The shadow as accompanying spirit is much more than a physical phenomenon: he is a psychic mask, a figure of fatefulness, steering the subject into the thick of things, or life. If this intuition is multiplied, imagined as a shared characteristic of a multiplicity of singularities, then public space starts to look like a plot, a skein composed of possible pathways of propinquity. This is not simply a spatial impression: as the word plot implies, it proposes a new narrative of public space. Part of Tonkinwise's knowing discovered through the act of 'making-useful' consists in establishing this multifocal, collaboratively produced sense of place. The stories that correspond to this collective desire to open to the future are not the pious foundational myths commemorated in statues; they describe unfinished journeys and improvise between these new meeting places. This is the differential 'poetics' of public space in formation when it is the offspring of dyadically formed subjects partially inclined towards one another rather than standing stiffly apart.

But, as I say, the understanding on which this partial meeting of different interests lies is fragile. It suggests that, instead of the field of social interactions being yielded to planners and administrators, storytellers, choreographers – in fact all interested in spinning yarns to thread the labyrinth of the world – should be invited to play. And, if this is not threatening enough, the choreotopographical turn of material thinking further suggests that the public whose 'liveability' the local authorities undertake to secure is never given: it is, like democracy, a project. The achievement of civility is an event, perhaps a repeated event, that takes place. Generally, in Western modernity, *taking place* is understood on the model of colonisation, as a usurpation of existing land justified by the rhetoric of rational improvement. The alternative, a taking place that is modelled on the dance, the game, the *workmanlike play* of dialogue, and which, when it is done, incubates an understanding of give and take, is unknown in the powerful circuits of government policy-making, private enterprise and the mixed technocratic discourses of legalistic and instrumentalist project management. The rhapsode is revived as a stitcher of old stories into new patterns. The new public space is promoted as an arrangement, and its designer is cast as dramaturg.

It is a lot to take in, especially when design is associated with the figure of *becoming*, where the only constant is change, and unpredictable rearrangement at that. Rosalind Deutsche claims, 'Democratic public space [is] a phantom because while it appears, it has no substantive identity and is, as a consequence, enigmatic. It emerges when society is instituted as a society with no basis… With this mutation, the unity of society becomes purely social and susceptible to contestation. If the public sphere of debate appears with the disappearance of an absolute social basis, public space is where meaning continually appears and continuously fades'.[10] Translated into graphic terms, this is a vision of public space as a surface continually scribbled over. It has no metaphysical ground but is a constant collective act of repsencing. It builds absence into the scene of being together, the desire of encounter into the plan to meet. But what planning authority is likely to sign its own death warrant? Even when the canvas is not considered blank, the practical form of public space in the planned city is a square or regular quadrilateral. Even if it is not square, it is called a *square* – witness Federation Square in Melbourne – not simply because a better term is lacking but because the symbolic association of the public domain with the figure of stability is comforting to the authorities. The baroque piazzas, plazas or places, whose absence from Brasília, in Brazil, James Holston laments, are like a swelling in the street.[11] They are nerve cells in the urban body: around the nucleus of open space the cell body consists of outdoor cafes and arcades; informal laneways and passages infiltrate the surrounding building blocks, like dendrites; the axons are axial streets and boulevards synaptically joined to other cellular neighbourhoods. But the modernist square qua urban public space is not like this. It does not flow unpredictably or generate new forms. It is a device of arrest and direction. Even if remnants of former vitality are allowed to withstand the flood of new connections overwhelming the old order, the power to introduce turbulence into the even, laminar pace of planning must be suppressed.

Suppose instead that the origins and forms of practical public spaces were different: that public spaces began as discourse, as the to and fro of utterance, and that the pathways created between speaking positions (physical metaphors in transporting meaning from one place to another) literally spelled out the intervals, the directions and the patterns of convergences adding up to a meeting place. And imagine that the primary form of the emerging sociability were tree-like, a local reminiscence perhaps of the great world tree revolving on its axis. In this case, public space would grow out from the inside; it would be an expanding volume whose interior was increasingly complex, a developing labyrinth of passages scored into the stuff of the world. The genealogy of urban form would be inverted: before the grid, the generative trunk; instead of the charmless myth of uniform space, a cosmic evolution of constellations of communities. Instead of being a sterile void, the commons or *chora* of the new public order would be an opening out, an active zone of exploration and expanding shelter. Its double aspect would be captured in the idea of the hollow, which is at once a nest or refuge and (as a verb) a principle of place-making. The collectively excavated hollow is the sculpture formed by all the gestures of everyday life; it is the scored, pummelled cloud envelope of their continuous, expressive labour.

Talking about the derivation of the tree of life from the 'cube of space' in the Kabbalistic *Sefer Yetzirah*, or the *Book of Formation*, Christopher Benton speculates that the tree was created by the simple device of imagining the facets of the cube as hinged and laying them out on a two-dimensional ground: the resulting figure resembles the Christian cross but also a stylised tree (see Figure 12). Alternatively, the tree might be obtained by rotating the cube until it looked like a hexagon: by inscribing two additional triangles inside this, a hexagonal star is formed; finally, by the addition of a further triangle in the head of the figure, a tree is created.[12] These operations anticipate the way in which, in his study of the golden ratio, Euclid makes the leap from the linear to the exponential curve: the planner's square is not inevitably opposed to the organic principles of the Fibonacci series, and Le Corbusier's Modulor is a fusion of these historical proportional systems.[13] And the Kabbalah, at least, introduces the case study of this chapter – *Golden Grove*, an artwork integrated into the public domain of the University of Sydney – in yet another way,

The Society of Trees

for Benton reminds us that in rabbinical tradition, the world was created 'with 32 mystical paths', where the paths are understood to be decrees. These utterances or spellings out of the law were, the same text states, engraved: in contrast with the Western philosophical tradition, where writing and speaking are theorised oppositionally (most notably by Jacques Derrida[14]), in the Hebraic tradition, the word is stone: 'He engraved them with voice', one verse of the *Sefer Yetzirah* runs.[15]

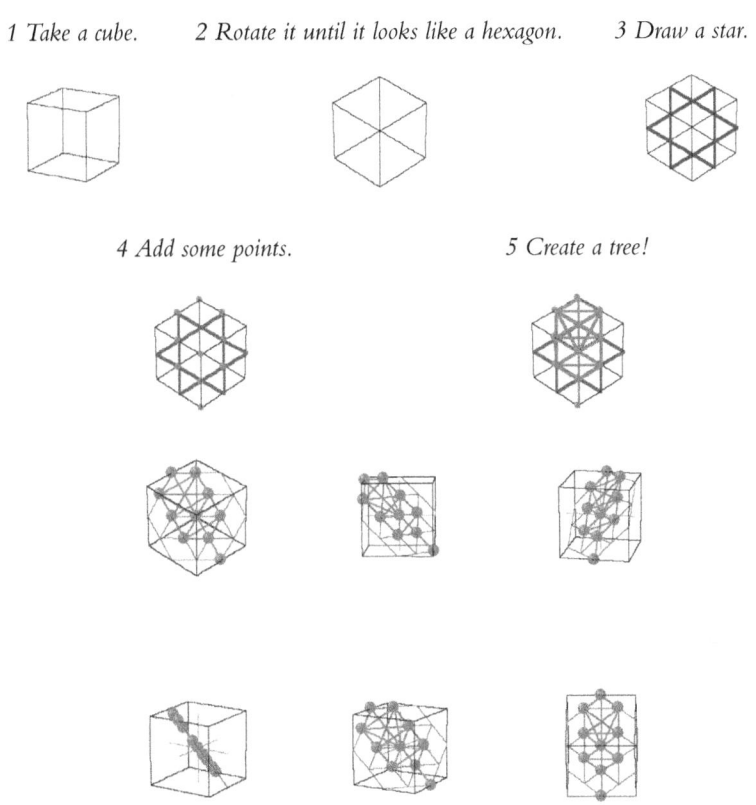

The Tree of Life *embedded in the Cube of Space*

Figure 12 'The Lurianic Tree', adapted from Christopher Benton, 'Sefer Yetzirah, the Cube of Space, and the Emergence of the Tree of Life,' n.d., pp. 43–4. On line at http://www.maqom.com/journal/paper33.pdf. Viewed 26 February 2011. Drawing: Edmund Carter.

Places Made After Their Stories

In 2004, the landscape architecture studio Taylor Cullity Lethlean entered a competition for the redesign of the public domain of the University of Sydney's Darlington campus, inviting me to join their team as a kind of hybrid cultural heritage consultant and public artist. 'Fertile Ground', the design concept for the campus was accepted and since then has been largely constructed. Our competition entry invoked the university's motto – 'The stars may change, the spirit remains the same' – and it was agreed that the mythopoetic turn implied by suggesting that the Darlington campus was in some sense made after the story (or at least after the motto) should also be developed. It was in this spirit that *Golden Grove* emerged, a distributed public artwork integrated, indeed hidden, within the landscape design. Because of its almost exclusive derivation from a name, *Golden Grove* is perhaps the purest example of a place made after its story (see Figure 13). In our case, the emergence of the design stemmed from the discovery that the phrase *golden grove* could be interpreted poetically or metaphorically in a number of different ways, and that each of the connotations attributable to the phrase could be shown to contain a site-specific reference. In the name of a former Redfern pub, swept away when the site was absorbed into the university domain in the 1960s, was discernible the uppermost stratum of a nominal Hill of Troy, whose strata were layers of cultural association rather than distinct periods of occupation.

In the event, *Golden Grove* became a strategy for reconceiving the 'square' of the brief as a tree; spelling out the stories associated with the site, we were able to transform the master plan's void into a generative site or (as our proposal was called) a *fertile ground*; installing the stories as pathways or filaments crisscrossing the public domain, we produced a geometrical web, a variation, if you like, on the Hebraic hexagon. And here, before I explain

The Society of Trees

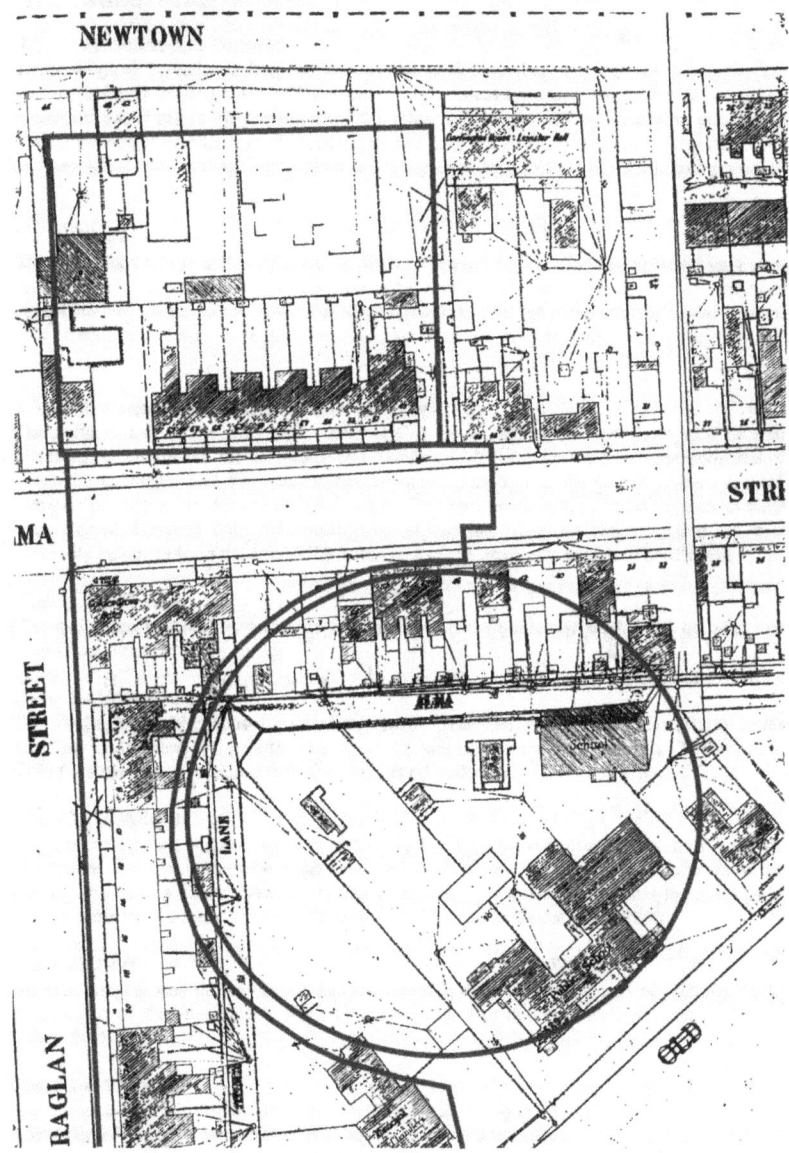

Figure 13 Material Thinking, 'Outline of University of Sydney Central (top) and Maze Green (circle) overlaid onto detail of Municipality of Darlington map (Sheet 28, 1884); Golden Grove Hotel cnr. Raglan and Alma Streets', 15 January 2006.

how this was done, another serendipitous nominal coincidence needs to be mentioned; for it was a curious fact that at the heart of the Darlington campus there existed an open space which rejoiced in the name Maze Green. On the face of it, here was a perfect pretext for reinterpreting the cube as a tree, transforming a bland expanse of lawn into a new labyrinth of encounter. Yet the name Maze was not only a misnomer in the sense that it had been applied to an entirely un-mazelike green; it was misleading because it did not, in fact, invoke a landscape design concept but commemorated one instead. W. H. Maze, the assistant principal responsible for a Camperdown campus master plan in 1961, aimed at expanding 'the potential of outdoor spaces created by grouping the buildings to form pleasant enclosed spaces that would be suitable for pedestrian movement'.[16]

It is ironic that the maze's name became attached to a default space subtracted from the wholesale demolition of pre-university educational buildings and adjacent terrace houses. But the irony is also verbal: anyone unaware of the provenance of the name might find in Maze Green a characteristically Australian oxymoron. A labyrinth as bare as a bowling green is a contradiction in terms. It recalls such coinages as Illusion Plains or Lake Disappointment,[17] but the point is that, oxymoron or not, such names are generative. The popular associations of the place called Maze Green exemplify the mythopoetic principle that places are made after their stories. Thus, Colin Bell, a Darlington resident interviewed in 1994, recalled that as a child he found the half-constructed Darlington campus 'like a huge playground'. Between the Seymour Centre and the engineering departments, he recalled, 'they used to have native Rosemary shrubs everywhere, and so we would go into those, and it would be like travelling around in an English hedge maze'.[18]

So, like so much else in poetic existence, *Golden Grove* was licensed by a pun: its intention to introduce a new complexity of association into the Darlington public domain depended on a kind of historical, self-interested mishearing of what was being articulated, comparable in its performative logic to the kind of communication improvised between Aboriginal and non-Aboriginal people in the early days of Sydney's white settlement.[19] And, in fact, the history of the application of the name '*Golden Grove*' to the site now occupied by the Darlington campus illustrates a kind of Chinese Whispers principle of analogical reasoning quite comparable to the logic of creative mishearing that characterises cross-cultural encounter. For the charm of the name resides precisely in its polysemous potential, the richness of its possible interpretations.

Notes

1   All mention of a meeting place disappeared from the final recommendations adopted by the council.
2   Commission for Architecture and the Built Environment, *Creating Successful Masterplans: A Guide for Clients*, CABE, 2008, viewed 15 June 2015, <http://webarchive.nationalarchives.gov.uk/20110118095356/http://www.cabe.org.uk/files/creating-successful-masterplans.pdf>, p. 18, citing Commission for Architecture and the Built Environment, *Design Review: Guidance on How CABE Evaluates Quality in Architecture and Urban Design*, CABE, March 2002, viewed 15 June 2015, <http://webarchive.nationalarchives.gov.uk/20110118095356/http://www.cabe.org.uk/files/design-review-original-guidance.pdf>, p. 10.
3   Patsy Healey, 'Planning in relational space and time: Responding to new urban realities', in Andrew Ballantyne (ed.), *Architecture Theory: A Reader in Philosophy and Culture*, Continuum, London, 2005, pp. 260–1, citing Michael Dear, 'Prolegomena for a post-modern urbanism', in Patsy Healey, Stuart Cameron, Simin Davoudi, Stephen Graham & Ali Madani-Pour (eds), *Managing Cities: The New Urban Context*, Wiley, London, 1995, pp. 27–44; Patsy Healey, 'Collaborative planning in a stakeholder society', *Town Planning Review*, vol. 69, no. 1, 1998, pp. 537–57; B. Gleeson & K. J.

Grundy, 'New Zealand's planning revolution five years on: A preliminary assessment', *Journal of Environmental Planning and Management*, vol. 40, no. 3, 1997, pp. 293–314; and David Harvey, *Justice, Nature and the Geography of Difference*, Blackwell, Oxford, 1996.

4   Northern Territory Government Department of Planning and Infrastructure, Cardno Willing, *Alice Springs Traffic Management and Parking Study*, Cardno Willing, Darwin, December 2004, p. 2.

5   City of Gold Coast, *Gold Coast Cultural Precinct Design Competition: Design Brief, Document 2*, Gold Coast Cultural Precinct, 26 March 2013, viewed 4 June 2015, <www.goldcoastculturalprecinct.info/sites/default/files/document_2_gold_coast_cultural_precinct_design_competition_design_brief_26_march_2013.pdf>, p. 13.

6   See Carter, *Dark Writing*, chap. 6.

7   Cameron Tonkinwise, 'Knowing by being-there making: Explicating the tacit post-subject in use'.

8   Sir Walter Raleigh, quoted by Sir Herbert Read, 'The Personality of the Poet', in *Selected Writings of Herbert Read*, Faber & Faber, London, 1963, p. 81.

9   Kathleen Kemarre Wallace, *Listen Deeply, Let these stories in*, IAD Press: Alice Springs, 2009, p. 22.

10 Deutsche, *Evictions: Art and Spatial Politics*, pp. 324–5.

11 James Holston, *The Modernist City: An Anthropological Critique of Brasília*, Chicago University Press, Chicago, 1989, p. 127.

12 Christopher P. Benton, '*Sefer Yetzirah*, the Cube of Space, and the Emergence of the Tree of Life', Paper 33, MAQOM, n.d., viewed 4 June 2015, <www.maqom.com/journal/paper33.pdf>, pp. 41–5.

13 See 'Riemann for Anti-Dummies Part 54, The Dramatic Power of Abelian Functions', for an accessible account of the emergence of 'exponential curves' 'from outside the domain of sense-perception.' Published online by The LaRouche Youth Movement. No author identified. At http://www.wlym.com/antidummies/part54.html. Viewed 14 March 2015.

14 Jacques Derrida, *Of Grammatology*, trans. Gayatri Chakravorty Spivak, The Johns Hopkins University Press, Baltimore, 1974.

15 Benton, '*Sefer Yetzirah*, the Cube of Space, and the Emergence of the Tree of Life', p. 5.

16 Rosemary Kerr et al., 'Appendix A: University of Sydney Overview History', in Michael Pearson, Duncan Marshall, Donald Ellsmore, Val Attenbrow, Sue Rosen, Rosemary Kerr & Chris Betteridge, *University of Sydney Grounds Conservation Plan*, University of Sydney, October 2002,

viewed 5 June 2015, <http://sydney.edu.au/documents/about/heritage/gcp_appendix1.pdf>, p. A83.
17 Carter, *The Road to Botany Bay*, p. 46.
18 Michael Pearson et al., *University of Sydney Grounds Conservation Plan*, vol. 1, University of Sydney, October 2002, p. 37, citing Colin Bell.
19 See Paul Carter, *The Calling to Come*, Historic Houses Trust of New South Wales, Sydney, 1995.

14

THE NAME OF THE GROVE

I had established the association of the site with education. When, in 1789, Governor Arthur Phillip reserved land around Petersham Hill (the 'Kangaroo Grounds') for church, school and Crown purposes, the eighty-hectare School Reserve was located south of the future City Road on the land now occupied by the Darlington campus. This means that, as ground projected as *intellectually* fertile, the Darlington campus predates the Camperdown campus, where the University of Sydney was established, in 1859. Two other educational associations predate the spread of the university to the Darlington campus, in the 1950s and early 1960s: the New South Wales Institution for the Deaf, Dumb and Blind, founded in 1860 and consolidated in 1870, with the erection of the Institute Building, at the south-western corner of our site, and the opening of Darlington Public School, in 1878 (also on the Old Newtown Road, now Darlington Road). Aerial photographs show that as recently as 1969 the triangle of land formed by Raglan Lane, Alma Lane and Darlington Street (now known as Maze Green) retained its full complement of school buildings, together with the Darlington Municipal Chambers.

On this reasonably firm historical foundation, the object of *Golden Grove* was to re-educate the site, to demonstrate the existence of a place-based knowledge that the pedagogical traditions of the place had overlooked; and the mechanism of this new education of leading out would be the retracing of the metaphorical pathways that lent the place its identity. The figure of this identity would not be a square container but a maze of knots, a radiating and radiant figure. For when the stories after which the Darlington campus was made were allowed to distil into their essential elements, a remarkable homogeneity emerged. Repeatedly, albeit by very different routes, their pathways led to intersections with a 'Golden Grove'. This happened because the phrase turned out on inspection to be like Walter Benjamin's bud, which, as it unfolds, discloses more and more folds.[1] The folds, or associations of the phrase, were local and cosmic, historical and mythological. They yielded useful topographical information about the structure of meeting places. They disclosed arrangements that modelled forms of cluster, group and aggregation. They also furnished symbols of exploration, discovery and invention. Last (and perhaps first), the topos of the 'Golden Grove' was always associated with the place of education, where the uninitiated are initiated and as a result become qualified to remember what is at risk of being forgotten. The 'Golden Grove' was, in this sense, the symbolic face of the university. It represented the changing stars constellated and stabilised by the spirit invoked in the university's motto.

During Governor Lachlan Macquarie's administration (1810-21), one William Hutchinson received twenty hectares of land, south-east of Newtown Road, known as 'Golden Grove'. This is the first historical association of the poetic trope with the site that later became the Darlington campus. 'The *Golden Grove Estate* was also known as the "Bullock Paddock" as it was used to pasture cows destined for the Sydney meat market.'[2] Presumably, the immediate allusion Hutchinson intended was to *The Golden Grove*, one of the four store ships of the First Fleet.[3] In adopting its name, Hutchinson may have indicated the comparable contribution he intended his land to make to the subsistence of the colony. In our context, it's also interesting that *The Golden Grove* had the distinction of carrying the Reverend Richard Johnson and his wife. Johnson was not only the first chaplain to the colony, but, arguably, the first educator: as early as 1789, he had a female child, Abaroo, living in his home; 'he taught her to speak a little English and to read The Lord's Prayer, and expressed the ambition that, as she came to understand him better, he could 'instruct her respecting a supreme being &c'.[4]

By 1884, when the network of streets and terrace houses forming the heart of the Darlington suburb was already well advanced, the name was attached to a street running south of Darlington Road[5] and, more intriguingly, to a hotel located on the corner of Raglan and Alma streets – a site which, in the 'Fertile Ground' design, was bordered by the proposed USYD Central, the north-west quadrant of Maze Green and the present Wentworth Building.

The origin of the name itself – and the poetic logic of its association with a ship – is harder to sort out. There is probably no single line of descent. Instead, a constellation of meanings attaches to *golden grove*. In fact, the concept, like the name, is a golden grove of poetic associations. For example, the earliest white settler names for our site already *cluster* golden grove associations, for, beside Hutchinson's *Golden Grove Estate*, there is also attached to the site the name Black Wattle Creek. When it flowers, in November, the black wattle *(Acacia mearnsii)* produces golden groves of sweetly scented blossoms. The species played an important role in the local ecology, in Aboriginal Australian culture and in the early white settler material economy. In all of these domains, it was associated with ideas of shelter, wellbeing and place-making. The *intellectual* cultivation of this species is another important site association: Thomas Shepherd, who established an experimental nursery on the Darlington campus site in the 1840s, was a pioneer conservationist. To advocate the tasteful arrangement of native trees in place of their 'indiscriminate destruction' was, in an Australian context, to use an aesthetic device to secure a regional identity. It was not to reproduce the appearance of an English park but through imitation to produce something new: the new country would 'present an exterior…such as no other country in the world I believe could furnish'.[6]

Working out from these concrete local associations towards the meaning of *golden grove* in world mythology, we found that it had both earthly and heavenly connotations. On earth, the golden grove is associated with the golden bough, whose function in ancient human fertility sacrifices was exhaustively explored by Sir James Frazer. The *golden grove* is not only where a primitive cultivation and ritual act of renewal occurs;[7] it is the Elysian Fields, in whose groves the happy reside after death, especially those who have rendered service to humanity.[8] As an object of worship, the golden bough stands in a synecdochical relation to the grove as a whole. It is associated with mistletoe, as well as the rays of the setting sun. As a golden cluster, it suggests a collection of stars. The constellation of the Pleiades is known as the 'Golden Grove'.[9] In Greek mythology, the golden grove is associated with the golden fleece, another solar symbol. It is interesting that the guardian of ancient wisdom, the Sun god, Apollo, is also known as a shepherd. In the same vein, the Moon is known in other traditions as the shepherd of the stars. In this sense, the golden grove is also a flock of heavenly sheep.

The general relevance of these mythological associations to the story of the place now occupied by the Darlington campus is obvious: located between Aries and Taurus, the Pleiades have pastoral associations, suggesting the early white settler uses of the land. They have navigational associations, their name coming from the verb *to sail*. They have the strongest educational associations, leading out the year when they rise (in the northern sky) in November:[10] in both Aboriginal and non-Aboriginal traditions, the appearance of the Pleiades is an occasion for dancing. Of the seven sisters forming the Pleiades, the most important, Maia, is said in the *Homeric Hymns* to be the mother of Hermes, the god of messages and hermetic wisdom.[11] From this welter of associations, I suggested that the last was most important. Any local application of a conceptual cluster derived from myths involves tact, restraint and flair[12]; that said, it is the *feminine* qualities of the central meeting place at Maze Green that the name *Golden Grove* evokes most strongly. The golden grove is the place where (in Aboriginal Australian culture) the women have responsibility for the outflowing (the education) of water. Among Eora peoples, Dennis Foley explains, 'women's law governed fresh water'. This determined a social relation: 'In the presence of women, men cannot take water straight from the stream. They must ask permission of their womenfolk first'.[13]

Leaping forward in time (and with the university motto still guiding us), I noted that Sydney University plays a leading role in every phase in the development of modern astronomy. Historically, this science has gone through three phases: optical observation using increasingly sophisticated telescopes; radio astronomy, enabling the detection of 'invisible' phenomena; and computer-assisted into-space surveys. Throughout, scientists based at the University of Sydney have been at the forefront, developing the conceptual maps needed to imagine the universe differently, devising and testing technologies to test the theories and leading the way in building computing programs capable of analysing an exponential growth in data.¹⁴ Since the 1960s, the laboratories where these star studies have been carried out have been located on the Darlington campus. It was intellectual leadership of this kind, I argued, at once local in its educational culture and cosmic in its intellectual outreach, that needed to characterise the university in the future. In any case, the association of the site with a concerted tradition of star study offered another site-specific story that found its poetically logical place in the mythos of the Golden Grove.

The palimpsest of stories associated with the Pleiades offered a poetic template, a ground or background against which the stories associated with our place could stand out or blaze forth (see Figure 14). We perceived two reasons for this. First, although the seasons, orientations and brightness of the Pleiades change from place to place around the world, the stories that geographically remote cultures tell about them are remarkably similar. This reminded us of the university's motto. Second, we were impressed by the *arrangement* of the stars. The important thing about the Pleiades as a constellation is not that they form nine isolated points but that they are a field of lights subtly joined by filaments. Perhaps for this reason Aboriginal Australian paintings show them as a solid field of twinkling spheres. Further, from Galileo onwards, the Pleiades have been drawn as if they were composed of two elements – a long curving path or tail and an uncoiling spiral. These facts suggested to us a *distributed* historical site marker, especially when we found that the physical shape of the Pleiades seems to articulate two of the Darlington campus public domain's main functional requirements: that the major movement way between Shepherd Street and USYD Central should be clearly, and attractively, defined; and that the identity of Maze Green as a gathering place – a place of repose – should be strengthened.

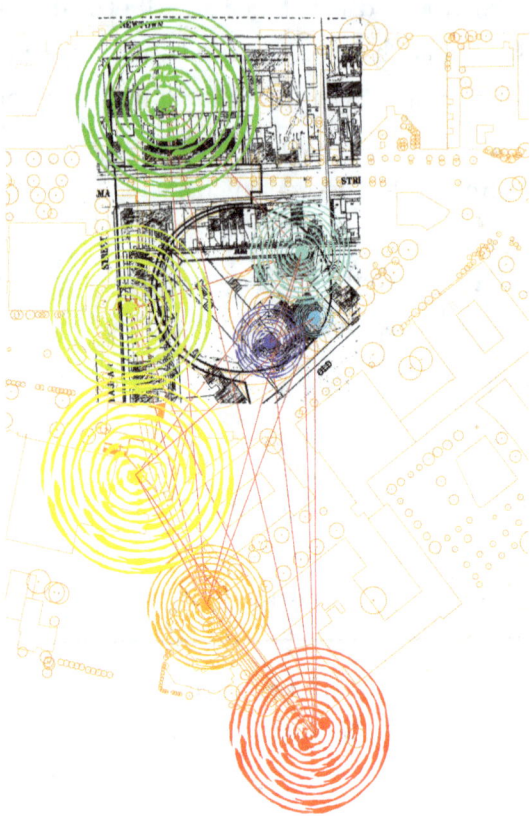

Figure 14 Material Thinking, '*Golden Grove* Template, University of Sydney, Darlington Campus historical map palimpsest with colour coded Pleiades overlay', 12 February 2006.

When we had located the nodal points of our design, we thought about the ways in which they were connected. The paths between them are for walking, so they should suggest a rhythm of passage, the harmony of many moving bodies. Therefore, we developed a ground pattern that calibrated the pathways, introducing a sense of rhythm, passage and arrival, subtly enriching the experience of crossing through the place. With a statement by the famous American artist Robert Smithson in mind, we imagined the ground pattern as formed of a spiral lightning bolt.[15] This figure refers to the path opened up between heaven and earth, between distant places. It suggests how the energy of the stars radiates in ever-widening circles. It also, of course, translates into a ground choreography recalling the force fields described in René Descartes's celestial mechanics – our ragged spirals being a typically informal, Australian interpretation of his tight vortices (see Figure 15). The resulting ground pattern not only articulated the two major zones of the Darlington campus public domain but related them to each other, in this way ensuring that 'Fertile Ground' fulfilled its intention to create a place of *simultaneous* repose and movement (see Figure 16).

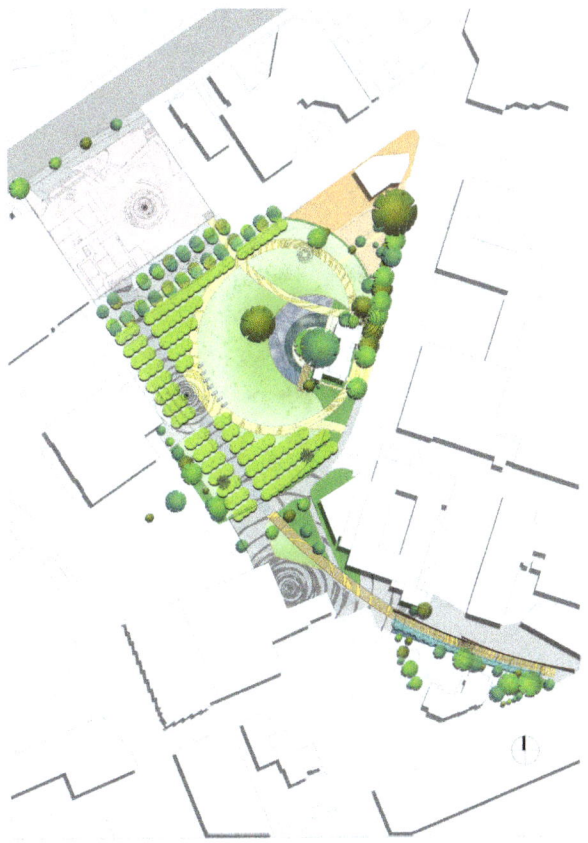

Figure 15 Taylor Cullity Lethlean, 'USYD Darlington masterplan, incorporating banded granite pavement', 31 March 2006. Reproduced by permission.

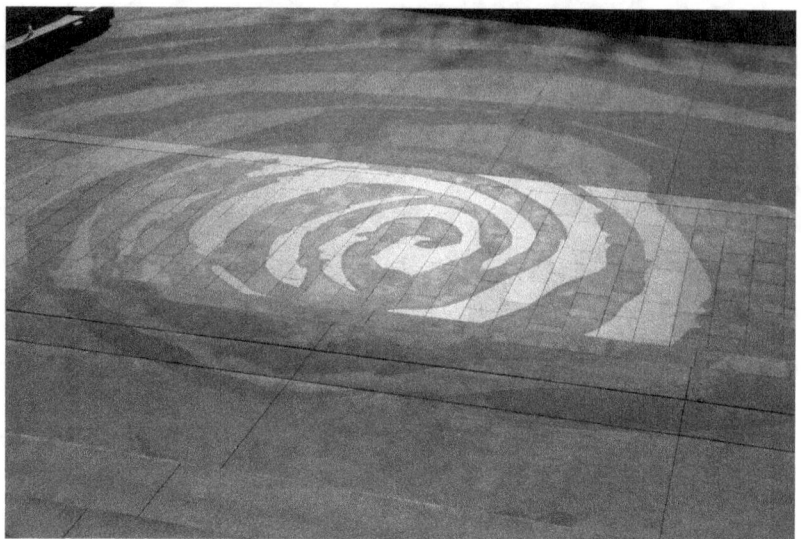

Figure 16 Taylor Cullity Lethlean/Material Thinking, 'Celeano, *Golden Grove* pavement spiral', detail. Photo: the author (18 July 2009).

Notes

1. Walter Benjamin, *Illuminations, Essays and Reflections*, ed. H. Arendt, trans. H. Zohn, Schocken Books, New York, 1969, p. 122. 'The word "Unfolding" has a double meaning. A bud unfolds into a blossom, but the boat one teaches children to make by folding paper unfolds into a flat sheet of paper.'
2. Rosemary Kerr et al., *Appendix A: University of Sydney Overview History*, p. A18.
3. Originally built at Whitby, in 1780, and weighing three hundred and seventy-five tons, after playing a lively role in a convict rebellion at Norfolk Island, the ship returned to England and worked the London–Jamaica run. She disappears from records after 1804.
4. See Jakelin Troy, *Australian Aboriginal Contact with the English Language in New South Wales: 1788 to 1845*, Pacific Linguistics, series B, no. 103, Australian National University, Canberra, 1990, p. 22.
5. Casey & Lowe, *Non-Indigenous Archaeological Assessment*, August 2004, in *University of Sydney Campus 2010*, Report to Capital Insight Ltd., Final Issue A, figs 6, 10.
6. Thomas Shepherd, quoted by J.M. Powell, *Environmental Management in Australia: 1788–1914*, Melbourne University Press, Melbourne, 1976, p. 29.

7   Sir James George Frazer, *The Golden Bough, a study in magic and religion*, 1922, chapter 68 'The Golden Bough' passim. See abridged 1922 edition on the Internet Sacred Text Archive. Accessed 14 October 2014.
8   See Virgil, *Aeneid*, in *Virgil*, trans H. Rushton Fairborough, W. Heinemann, London, 1947, 2 vols., vol. I, Book VI, ll.136–155, memorably illustrated in J. M.W. Turner's painting, *The Golden Bough* (1834), Tate Britain Collection, London.
9   The fact that mistletoe berries are silver in colour rather than golden doesn't seem to inhibit this identification. Similarly, Alfred Tennyson likens the 'Pleiads' to 'a swarm of fireflies tangled in a silver braid' (Alfred Tennyson, 'Locksley Hall,' *Poems and Plays*, Oxford University Press, Oxford, 1968, p. 91.).
10 In our southern skies, it is not the Pleiades that rise in November but the flowers of the black wattle: the spirit is the same but the stars change.
11 Interestingly, Richard Hinckley Allen, a mine of information about the poetic associations of the Pleiades, omits this connection (*Star-names and Their Meanings*, Dover Publications, New York, 1964, pp. 391–413). I found it at Jimmy Joe, *Genealogy: The Pleiades (The Atlantids)*, Timeless Myths, 1999, viewed 5 June 2015, <www.timelessmyths.com/classical/family14.html>.
12 However, it is important to point out that mythic thinking is constitutionally local and situational – and in this sense, mythic thinking isn't imposed but is always stimulated by the properties of the place.
13 Dennis Foley, *Repossession of Our Spirit*, Aboriginal History Inc, Canberra, 2001, p. 12.
14 The telescopes that mediate their enquiries have, of course, largely been built off-campus, but not entirely. To study high-energy cosmic ray particles and the direction of arrival of cosmic ray air-showers, in the early 1960s, Sydney University physicist Brian McCusker built a cosmic ray air-shower array at the rear of the Physics School. It consisted of '92 coffin-sized boxes each containing three Geiger counters and a power supply… laid out in rows' (Raymond Hanes et al., *Explorers of the Southern Sky: A History of Australian Astronomy*, Cambridge University Press, Cambridge, UK, 2010, p. 312).
15 'I took my chances on a perilous path, along which my footsteps zigzagged, resembling a spiral lightning bolt' (Robert Smithson, 'The Spiral Jetty (1972)', *The Collected Writings*, pp. 143–153, pp. 147–48.)

15

APPLYING THE ASTERISK PRINCIPLE

So much, then, for the derivation of a landscape design, a physical grove, from the mythological golden grove. The function of this poetic genealogy was to make available for recollection aspects of the site's human associations that a conventional public art program would not be able to communicate. The nodal points were stars shining out in the dark. More exactly, they illustrated a principle of site marking which we had first proposed in another project in Melbourne: there, we had applied what we called an *asterisk principle*, the idea that the asterisk or star sign signifies a place where an *absence* shines more brightly.[1] Just as the night sky suggests that memories illuminate the dark – perhaps with the idea that the constellations we imagine there assume their shape against a background of collective amnesia – so with the public memory incubated through *Golden Grove*: it would incorporate the structure of forgetting, making room for acts of re-creation that the design itself could not predict. In the meantime, its non-prescriptive openness acknowledged the many dark spots in the history of the site. In particular, for example, we were conscious of the violence done to the human and urban fabric of Redfern when, in the 1960s, the university unilaterally expanded its premises to form the Darlington campus.

In this context, *A Stone's Throw*, a short documentary film made in 1980, is significant. The film documents the reactions of

Darlington residents to the University of Sydney's destruction of houses, streets and public spaces as it spread into the Darlington campus and redeveloped it. An Aboriginal man describes his fear of being 'put out within twenty-four hours'; a white Australian woman reflects, not without irony, that the weak have 'to make way'. The film shows the interviewees not as victims but as agents, creating oppositional narratives. It also documents the protests of student artists against their own institution. To symbolise the violence of the evictions, the artists scattered household items along public paths that a few months earlier has been the sites of private dwellings. Art of this kind is not after history but embedded in it, actively engaged in its production and interpretation.[2] When, over twenty years later, the 2002 *University of Sydney Grounds Conservation Plan* at last recognised the wreckage of the former community, extensively recording working-class testimony from that period, it challenged the university to remember the past differently. One of the values of *A Stone's Throw* is to show that this involved a different technique, one of concomitant production, not belated piety.[3]

The notion of a public space as an arrangement of illuminations rather than a blank canvas imagined under a solar glare influenced the second expression of *Golden Grove*. The first expression was the distribution of nodal points; the second was a lighting or night-time wayfaring design. In a report commissioned by the University of Sydney, Sarkissian and Associates Planners had stated that female members of the university found the Darlington campus one of the most uncomfortable and threatening night-time environments that they had to negotiate on a regular basis. The client was explicit that 'Fertile Ground' should address this concern. With the poetic myth of the golden grove to hand, we were able to propose a lighting strategy that met this requirement in a way that celebrated female strength rather than vulnerability. As we noted at the time, 'The nine "illuminations" of *Golden Grove* do not respond with a blaze of light that "dumbs down" the character of the place. This is an approach, it can be argued, that simply puts women in their place by a different means. Conscious of the associations of the Darlington Campus with female power and enfranchisement, the *Golden Grove* lighting design instead aims to harness those associations, creating a suite of lighting installations that communicate the accumulated pride and collective strength of a larger female body'.[4] Hence, for example, the installation associated with the sister known as Pleione (a name signifying in Greek *flock of doves*) took the form of a spiralling swarm of twinkling points set into the boardwalk (see Figure 18).

It was important that the lighting design be integrated into the physical designs associated with the nodal points. The lighting should illuminate the way in a double sense, providing a functional strategy for navigating the public domain at night but also enlightening the passer-by as to the character of the place. The lighting should mediate between the path as thoroughfare and the path as *sentier*, one of a constellation of passages collectively creating a sense of place. Hence, the Smithson-inspired spirals used to indicate the nodal points were not an arbitrary import. They had a mythopoetic rationale derived from the story of the golden grove, as one of the Pleiades, Celeano, is said to have been struck by lightning! Little else seems to be known about her, but somehow this was connected in my mind with two aspects of locomotion – the dynamic and the errant – and, as I see now looking at the notes I made at the time, this thought was in turn associated with a reflection that was the precursor to the discussion of the cube–tree distinction with which part 3 of *Places Made After Their Stories* opened:

The streak fissures the ground, splits open its uniform face, destroys order and at the same time releases the buried Eros. Robert Smithson describes a similar intuition. When planning Spiral Jetty, he needed, he said, to descend from the digital state (associated with the logos of the line and square) into the 'surd state', an amorphous, colloid condition associated with the continuous curve of lived movement. When he achieved this the line turned into a path, and the path itself changed form and character: 'I took my chances on a perilous path, along which my footsteps zigzagged, resembling a spiral lightning bolt.'[5]

Informing this line of thought was a desire to 'circle the square', to develop a design language robust enough to withstand the linearism of conventional landscape architectural drawing. To rethink the linear path as a jagged lightning bolt was already to reconfigure the line as an episode in a drama of drawing out, to endow the metaphysical Cartesian line with a regional dynamism and sense of relational contingency. When this gesture was combined with the energy imagined as radiating concentrically from the light sources, the interference pattern that resulted was helical. This kind of thought, mediated by drawing, is rarely described, even though it supplies the subconscious environment informing the eventual design. I suppose, taking a cue from Smithson, I thought of this free graphic associationism as a kind of descent into the 'surd state'. I noticed that the irregular radiating rings we had produced recalled the diffraction rings caught in telephotography, but also the arcs produced by grass stalks in rock, or by other kinds of fossilised impact traumas. These patterns of radiating rings over a stippled ground reminded me of a style of etching with aquatint that the German artist Max Ernst was making in the early 1960s. In a work like 'Printemps du ciel', for example, one sensed a strange homology between the dark blots and ragged tracks and the kind of cosmic phenomena a radio telescope might pick up – negative stars, strange energy rifts and intergalactic dust (see Figure 17).[6] These designs were produced at the same time that Ernst was collaborating with master art book designer, Ilia Zdanevich (Iliazd) to produce *Maximiliana, or The Illegal Practice of Astronomy*, a strange homage in image and text to the largely forgotten nineteenth century German astronomer Guillaume Ernst Albrecht Tempel. Tempel, despite his remarkable discoveries, including a dozen or so comets and an asteroid or perhaps distant planet which he named Maximiliana, 'was not eligible to be a member of the National Society of Astronomers, who cruelly refused to credit him and renamed his cherished planet "Cybille".'[7]

Instead of becoming a star, Tempel faded into obscurity, a biographical trajectory that Ernst and Iliazd visualise graphically: 'Throughout the book, letters resemble stars in the night sky, at once random and again not random, goading you to see patterns where there are none. In a calligram visually playing out the astronomer's words, letters descend the page as if charting the course of a shooting star falling to earth.'[8] In a manner that anticipates our own overlays of celestial and terrestrial patterns (stars, local maps, line drawings), Ernst found a way to represent disappearance, to visualise a history of asterisks: referring to Ernst's blow-ups of details of lithographs, Rockel comments, 'These blow-ups are scattered throughout the book, the enlargement overlaying the original, creating an impression not only of perspective but, significantly, of shadows projected across vast areas of space. If *Maximiliana* is about one thing, it is distance, not only in the sense of physical space and time but also social distance, obscurity and ostracisation'.⁹

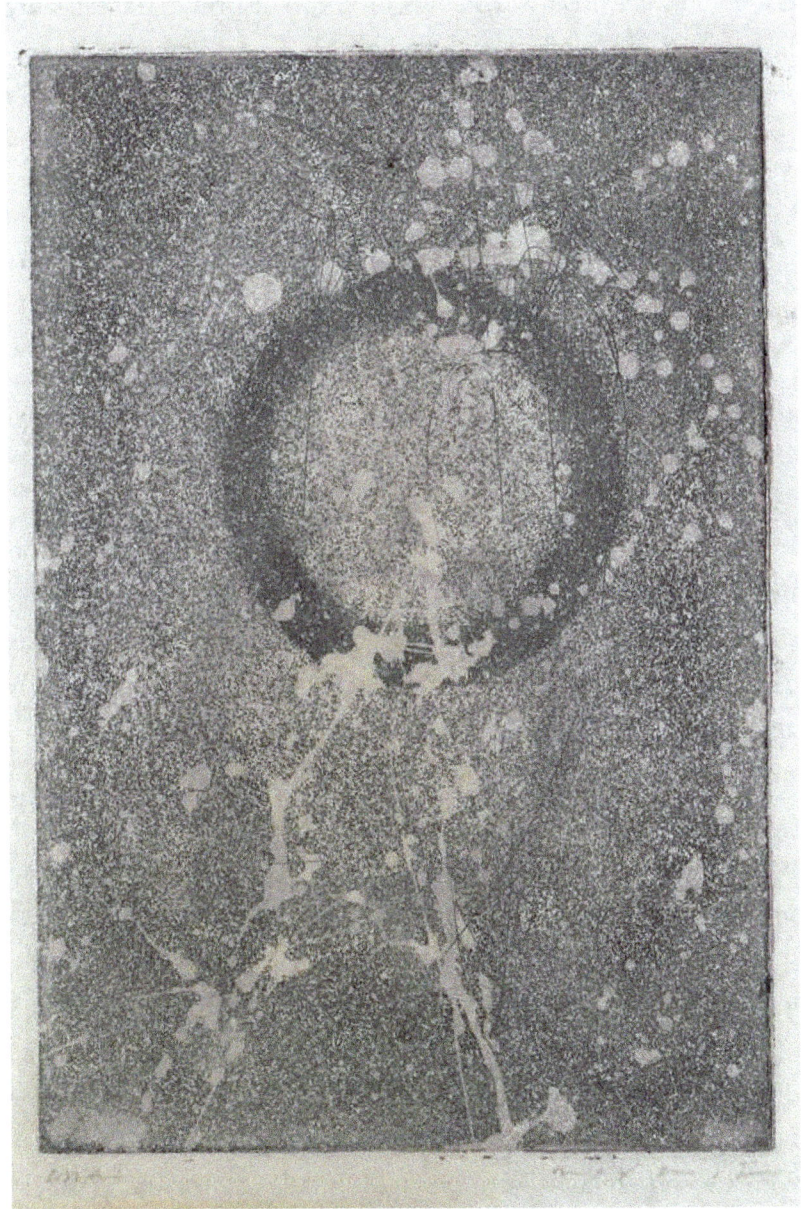

Figure 17 Max Ernst, 'Printemps du ciel', 1963. Aquatint-etching in two colours, 230 x 167 mm. Copyright: ADAGP. Reproduced by permission.

Conceived in a similar spirit, the drawing of *Golden Grove* is a pattern of ephemeral passages, a set of poetic traces attesting to the endless comings and goings of bodies, earthly and heavenly, human and meteorological. The lines corresponding to this experience of casual wandering are streaky, ragged, their light flimsy, filmy and apparitional – like the Pleiades themselves. Ernst's 1964 catalogue contains a Surrealist text which, in translation, reads:

> The wetnurse stars refuse to serve.
> Jacob's ladders break noiselessly, the comets of both
>   sexes growl and sulk in their hiding-place.
> Everything is upside-down.
> Everything becomes confused and blurred.[10]

In short, a principle of transformation operates at many scales: the helium spectrum invoked in 'Asterope' (see Figure 19) visualises the radioactive decay of elements one into another but the work as a whole imagines social transfiguration. Michel Maffesoli writes about 'transfiguration' in terms of a redrawn contract between individuals and their imaginal universe: 'by remaking the unity between "corpus" (the body, industrialised product, commercialised product, local community) and "spirit" (qualitatively, sense of beauty, disinterested caring, pleasure in the sensual, stress on the nearby and neighbouring), the image realises the stakes of the transfigurative tradition'.[11]

A work like *Golden Grove* conceives of this rearrangement negatively, or as a work of the chiaroscuro imagination creating new dark matter defined by a network of illuminations. Together with the provision of safe passages, it keeps alive the prospect of unimaginable futures and the inheritance of vanquished visions.

How, it might be asked, could a template derived from a constellation be expected to contribute to the functionality of a landscape design? I have indicated that the two main features of the Pleiades star cluster — the curving line and the spiral — corresponded to two major features of the site — its walkway connecting Shepherd Street to the new student services building and the oval to the east corresponding to Maze Green. But how, beyond this, could the location of the nine nodes be anything but arbitrary? What relevance could their arrangement have to the local lie of the land, to such vestiges of the older street pattern that still survived and to the present and future uses of the site? In replying to these questions, the first point to make is the one already alluded to: that the constellation is to be understood as a web of filaments in which the nodal points are embedded. This is the common Aboriginal Australian representation of the Pleiades, and it accurately reflects the way the constellation appears to the naked eye: as a bright swarm.[12] This means that in terms of plotting the exact locations of the nodes, there is ample licence to scale up or scale down the template until an intuitive fit is discovered between the salient landscape features or functions and the proposed locations of the lighting features and the spiralling ground patterns radiating from them (see Figure 18).

If this shifting of the overlay to establish a coincidence with the underlay is thought to be arbitrary, it is because the landscape design orthodoxy (derived from the blank canvas mentality of the master planning brief) is functionalist. That is, it attempts to design the new public space on the basis of typical behaviours. The theory of these typical activities — sitting, walking, playing — is behaviourist and individualist. The object (always unattainable) is to create an arrangement of formal and informal elements that can in principle predict, choreograph and satisfy

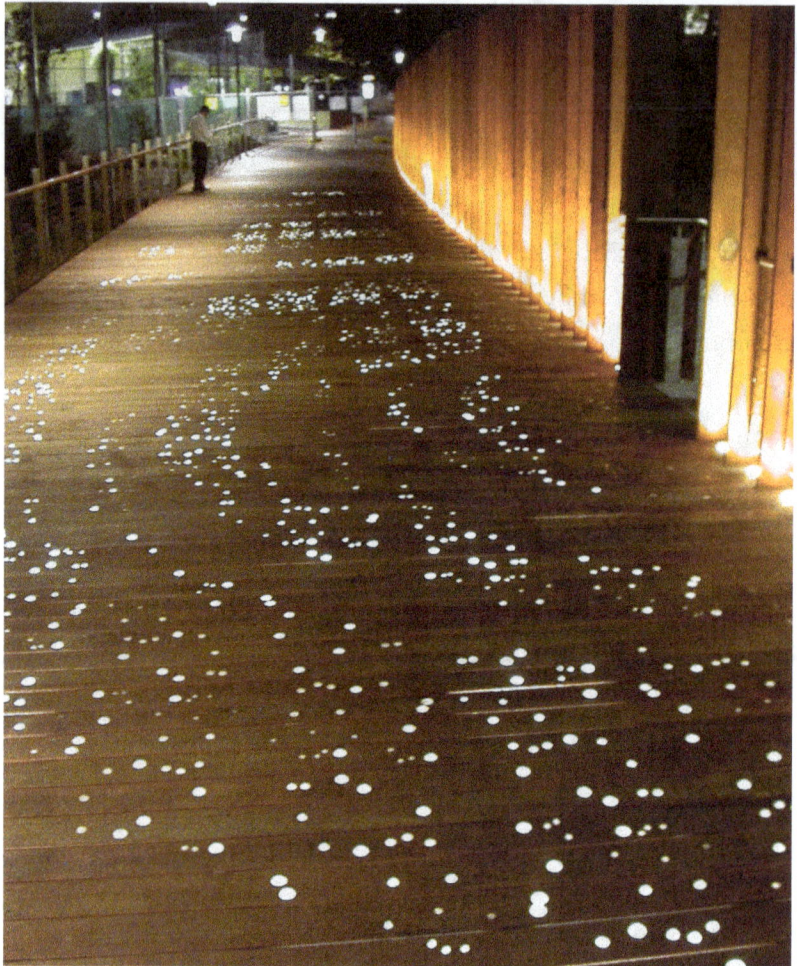

Figure 18 Taylor Cullity Lethlean/Material Thinking, 'Electra, *Golden Grove* boardwalk illumination spiral'. Photo: the author (2 February 2009).

every reasonable physical expectation that the public may have of the new park. However, this stimulus-based theory of sociability wholly overlooks the fact that people have an inherent interest in gathering and possess a sophisticated spatial praxis that enables them to meet (or not), to associate (or not) and to manage the complex field of interactions that comprise any active public space. From this perspective, the location of street furniture, for example, is non-critical; the fetishisation of certain patterns of regularity – aligned furniture, regularly spaced lighting poles – simply reflects the fact that no larger, overarching mythopoetic template is available to guide the design. In reality, the individuals who collectively form the public are not, psychologically and emotionally speaking, blank canvases; they are always already on their way somewhere. What they need is not a stimulus to stop (seat) or start (path) but environmental affordances that subtly endow their passage with meaning. The function of the nine-point lighting design in *Golden Grove* is to illuminate the ambience of the place, its potential to create new associations, convergences, departures and possibilities. By handing back the experience of coming across the place for the first time (the experience of discovery), a mythopoetically informed design of this kind encourages a kind of self-actualisation at that place. Someone inhabiting this new place does so not only with all their senses but with their accumulated habits of thought and their always unfulfilled expectations.

The nine elements of the lighting design are intended to fulfil three criteria: to stage the progressive metamorphosis of one topologically consistent form, to express in their physical design and lighting specifications features of the individual stars forming the Pleiades and to develop the formal potential of these considerations in relation to the physical and cultural characteristics of the localities they occupy. The extreme expressions of the form are a planar canopy and a column. Typical intermediate expressions of these extremes are a concave saucer recessed into the ground (alluding to the radio telescope's dish but functioning as a mini-amphitheatre); a tilted, umbrella-like structure, practically adapted to provide seating and weather protection; a loftier stem-and-flower structure, offering a flexible canopy; and finally what was described at the time as the gathering together of all of these evolutionary stages into a column whose capital displays the elemental geometry informing all of the structures. This scheme is, as we emphasised, indicative: it can and should be developed or modified in relation to other needs identified in the brief or through our own observations: these components 'will serve variously as entrance markers, lighting structures, pavilions, shelters, amphitheatres, and water basins'.[13]

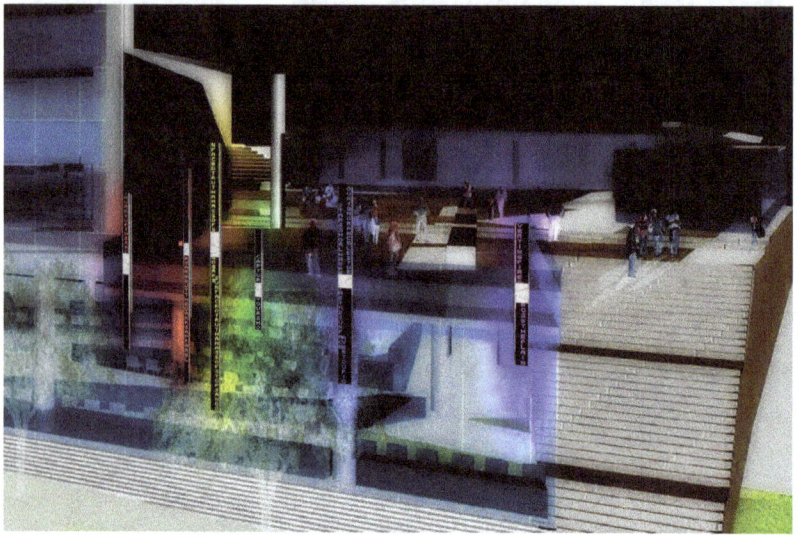

Figure 19 Taylor Cullity Lethlean/Material Thinking, 'Asterope, *Golden Grove*, proposed LED array', Student Services Building, University of Sydney, Darlington Campus. 21 February 2006.

Indications for the character of the lighting nodes were also derived from mythological information about the individual stars composing the Pleiades. Recognising that Atlas and Pleione were the parents of the Pleiades and cast their influence over the entire family of stars or lights, we suggested that they should be associated with the Shepherd Street entrance to *Fertile Ground*: 'They are the entrance to the constellation, and the exit from it. They are the twinned portals, standing at the entrance to *Golden Grove*. They are "twinned" but they are different. One is male, the other female, one father, the other mother. These archetypal complementarities are reflected in their stories'.[14] Functionally, we noted, the blade-like forms 'show the way; they are "message sticks"; or information nodes (see Figure 20). They are associated with site maps and other kinds of practical information'.[15] A particularly exciting but unrealised development of the scheme proposed that the Asterope node should be used to tie together the new public domain and the new University of Sydney student services building being designed by John Wardle Architects (see Figure 19).

To explain this variation on the original contract, which arose from the shared desire of the architects and the landscape architects to integrate their separately commissioned designs, we wrote,

> The 'Asterope' installation consists of 6 LED (light emitting diode) arrays, located at the Maze Green edge of the new University of Sydney Student Services Building. The LEDs carry information about the stories, associations, histories and meanings of the University site. The electronic lettering can be arranged vertically. It can ascend or descend: parallel vertical columns of text can flow in opposite directions. The texts can also be configured horizontally, across all six arrays. The selection of texts is triggered by either of two external determinants: user access to the website or pedestrian patterns in the proximity of the artwork. The combination of these creates a constantly changing selection and arrangement of texts.

And we explained the choice of colours for the six arrays as follows: 'The stars in the Pleiades are relatively "young", having been formed about 100 million years ago. They are relatively "hot", and their spectral type, according to the Henry Draper catalogue, is B, which manifests itself as neutral helium lines. When these lines are excited in a helium spectral tube they produce six chromatically-distinct rods – and it is these colours that form Asterope's "face"'.[16]

Notes
1 See Carter, *Dark Writing*, p. 187.
2 A Stone's Throw [video recording] a Department of Architecture Student's project, University of Sydney Television Service, 1980, University of Sydney Library, Schaeffer AV.
3 Heritage Management Consultants, *University of Sydney Grounds Conservation Plan*, October 2002, prepared for Facilities Management Office, University of Sydney, vol. 1, pp.1–100, p. 8.
4 Material Thinking, 'Golden Grove: Design concept for a public artwork integrated into the landscape design, Darlington Campus, university of Sydney, May 2005', 1–7, p. 4.
5 Paul Carter, '*Golden Grove* project diary', 22 March 2005, in author's possession, citing Smithson, 'The Spiral Jetty (1972)', p. 147.
6 Max Ernst, 'Printemps du ciel', 1963. Signed Max Ernst, essai. Printed on Vélin BFK Rives at Georges Visat, Paris. Aquatint-etching in two colours. Visible size 230 x 167 mm.
7 Rosie Rockel, 'A Mysterious Accord: 65 Maximiliana, or the Illegal Practice of Astronomy', http://rosierockel.com/2015/01/27/a-mysterious-accord-65-maximiliana-or-the-illegal-practice-of-astronomy/. Accessed 23 February 2015. Only sixty five copies of the book were printed: the Kandinsky Library, Paris, has a copy that can be viewed by the public.
8 Ibid.
9 Ibid.
10 Edward Quinn, *Max Ernst*, Éditions Cercle d'Art, Paris, 1976, p. 342.
11 Maffesoli, *The Contemplation of the World*, p. 120.
12 Interestingly, one of the Pleiades, Electra, is traditionally associated with amber – because of its colour – and, by extension, with honey, the swarm and the hive (Munya Andrews, *The Seven Sisters of the Pleiades*, Spinifex Press, Melbourne, 2004, p. 41).
13 Material Thinking, 'Golden Grove: Design concept for a public artwork integrated into the landscape design', Darlington Campus, University of Sydney, October 2004, pp. 1–15, p. 13.

14 Material Thinking, 'Notes for Fertile Ground feature/Functional Lighting Design,' 19 January 2005, pp. 1–5, p. 1.
15 Material Thinking, 'Notes for Fertile Ground feature/Functional Lighting Design', pp. 1–5, p. 2.
16 Material Thinking, 'Golden Grove: Design concept for a public artwork integrated into the landscape design, Darlington Campus, University of Sydney', October 2004, p. 9.

16

THE STRATEGY OF AMBIENCE

The reference to texts in the last chapter brings me to the third component of *Golden Grove*, the nine poetic texts designed to be inscribed into the landscape. The inscriptions are collectively called 'Contractions'. The allusion to childbirth and to the feminine experiences represented in the texts is obvious enough. But there was another sense in which 'Contractions' was adopted, which relates directly to the paradox of a place writing that trades in occasional illuminations rather than a steady enlightenment. The verb *contract* has a double meaning, which is useful in articulating the kind of drawing relevant to the purpose of *Golden Grove*:

> On the one hand it means to join up, literally to draw together. On the other hand, it means to shrink back – to draw together in the sense of withdrawing from contact. What kind of mark would meet both these conditions? A clue lies in the figure of traction and in its cognate terms, *tract*, *trait* and *track*. All of these terms refer in one way or another to a practice of tracking. The tracker/artist steps in the footsteps of the past with interest: she pays attention to the spatial disposition of the prints, deriving information from the depth and direction of the marks.[1]

The Strategy of Ambience

But this sensation of stepping in another's footsteps, of simultaneously drawing together and drawing apart, also applies to people navigating a public space — at least when that space has not had the ordinary Brownian motion of everyday life smoothed away. A design language that indicates passages rather than representing destinations is more likely to induce a social contract, a sense of identification with others' interests, than one that leaves behind no trace of its own act of drawing.

In the present context, *contract* is used in a different though related sense. Apart from its physical connotation, it describes the way the lines composing the inscriptions compress grammar and syntax and present the individual words of the text without gaps between them. This contraction is reinforced by the character of the texts themselves, which present a wide range of cultural information in an extremely concentrated and allusive form: the texts read more like clues to a crossword puzzle than fully self-explanatory statements. Because of this contraction, together with the way the inscriptions are presented sculpturally, comprehension of them involves the same double-take that the tracker experiences. On the one hand, coming across these letters in the public domain produces a shock of immediate encounter comparable to the impact urban graffiti can have — one feels confronted by the sudden appearance of a message seemingly addressed directly to oneself. On the other hand, the meaning of the inscription withdraws itself. A double contraction occurs: the materiality of the sign draws the would-be reader in, but it also stands as an obstacle to closer acquaintance and interpretation (see Figure 20). The double movement solicited here is not only cognitive but choreographic: turning towards this writing in the landscape — which, paradoxically, resists reading — implies a physical departure from the straight line. Unlike advertising, which carries the observer briefly into an associative fantasy, the Shepherd Street entrance blade inscriptions dissociate passers-by from the taken-for-granted line of flight up and down the public footpath. They propose a turning away from the received passage. Their inscrutability fosters introspection, puzzlement, irritation perhaps. In withholding information, they translate into design practice Thomas Rickert's notion of a rhetoric that 'emerges from the ambient environs' and, instead of being limited to a 'discursive exchange', includes a 'vibrant materiality'.[2]

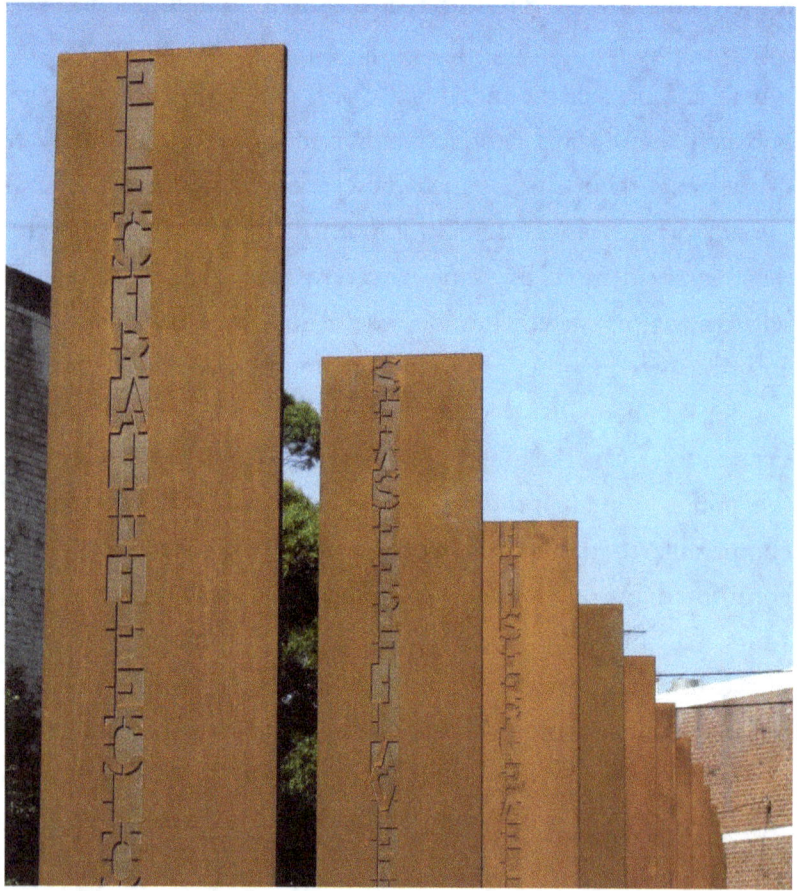

Figure 20 Taylor Cullity Lethlean/Material Thinking, 'Atlas, *Golden Grove*, stele text', 2008. Photo: the author (2 February 2009).

The Strategy of Ambience

The rhetorical expression of this attitude – the apostrophe, or turning away – is also a dance figure. A Shakespearean monologue in which the protagonist suddenly withdraws into himself and at the same time, ignoring his surroundings, addresses the audience is an example. In one sense, the speaker abstracts him- or her-self from his dramatic setting; in another, though, by addressing the audience directly, they make the situation of the action concrete. The 'Contractions' are characteristically written in the second person and in a public setting operate like the famous Boer War recruitment poster, appearing to address you directly. In another personification of ambience, a contraction may speak in the first person, as if the place itself seeks to communicate. Finally, sometimes the inscription can be addressed to the place or spirit of place. In this case it is in the third person, and it is you, the passer-by, who is placed in the role of speaker: reading the lines at that place, you have broken out of the everyday drama of the path and its usual conversations. If a conversation is a turning towards, you have, for a moment, turned away. By these means, the inscriptions introduce chance into the scene. They materialise the act of encounter. Instead of being immediate, their communication is mediate – that is, inseparable from their materialisation at that place, and at that time in the perception of the passer-by. It might be fairer to describe these sensible letters as kinds of markings in the landscape that suggest a previous history or heritage. They are like the traces of passage, impressions of time passing, perhaps. They suggest something deeper than the present organisation of space, a dissident remnant of something left over from the past. Equally, they could belong to the future. In any case, they communicate by way of physical association as well as conceptual coherence.

In Australia, it is not possible to promote the gestural qualities of mark-making without acknowledging their ubiquity in Aboriginal

Australian cultures. And, interestingly, many Aboriginal Australian societies rationalise writing as a form of marking, locating it within the same genealogy of scratching, sewing and painting that etymologies of writing words reveal in Indo-European languages. Penny van Hoorn summarises a number of such explanations: in the language of the Burarra and Gun-nartpa peoples of Arnhem Land, for example, the word *jurra* refers to 'tracks and footprints, as well as to books and marks made on paper'.[3] The enigma of the lettering has other genealogies, though. One of these in particular is relevant to the question of programming chance. In Western political thought, public space is associated with a particular way of speaking: our word *allegory* means literally the *other speech*, appropriate to the agora, or market or meeting place. Other speech is political speech; it used to be associated with formally composed and organised public speeches. The forensic eloquence of public speaking is not used in private: it is *other* in relation to the way we speak domestically or to friends. However, in more recent public discourse, allegory has fled the scene of public speaking; out of place in the functionalist and mediatised discourse of modern politics, it retains its political significance by concealing its meanings – or, by speaking indirectly, through allegory. The object of this is to hint at the existence of something outside the present order.

Those familiar with the interpretations placed on the paintings of Sandro Botticelli and other Renaissance artists by scholars such as Edgar Wind, Erwin Panofsky and Fritz Saxl will recognise in this formulation a neoplatonist inflection: as Philip Rollinson writes, 'Neoplatonic theorists emphasize the necessity of a text's hinting at the existence of its hidden meaning. The surface will point to added symbolic implications by means of…the "suggestive incompleteness" of its literal text'.[4] In his thesis on German baroque drama, Walter Benjamin gives this lost or effaced beauty a characteristically elegiac inflection. He associates what is hidden with history itself; it is the meaning of the past that is continuously effaced. 'The word "history" stands written on the countenance of nature in the characters of transience.'[5] In any case, the point is that allegorical writing of this kind turns away from the present in order to hint at a heritage that the present aims to erase. It alludes to the fact that the present is built on the ruination of the past: the regulation of social behaviour is engineered through a conscious decision to forget what has previously happened here.

In designing the alphabet for 'Contractions', we materialised the sign in another way. It is a little known fact, or at least it was unknown to me until I embarked on this project, that the word *stencil* literally means star writing – with the idea of light flashing or twinkling through the cut-out template of the stencil. What better typographical technique for *Golden Grove* could be imagined? Accordingly, we designed a *Golden Grove* typeface that exhibited the flashing cross of a distant star. In this way, the letters forming the inscriptions were a new kind of asterisk: shining out of the matrix, they formed part of a legible sequence but individually remained enigmatic, alluding to something beyond what could be read on the spot. In one sense, the star was a sign of radiation, or a palimpsest of occluded site associations: Cadigal or more broadly Eora people's associations of the site with women's custodianship of water; early colonial associations of the site with food production; a local tradition of education (the Darlington School, the Deaf, Dumb and Blind Institute and the University of Sydney) analogous to the rites of initiation performed on entering the classical Golden Grove; the Redfern community and the mapping of disappeared constellations of protest; the creative community of women artists and postermakers associated with the Tin Sheds adjacent to the Darlington Campus public domain; the site's astronomical associations through the university; and, first and last, the site's association with women's power, incarnated in the constellation of the Pleiades. In another sense, the star sign is a concentration of power, proposing a common site Gestalt – or 'hieroglyph', in Geoffrey Bardon's sense – that gives the university's motto a 'vibrant materiality'.[6]

Consistent with the desire to veil the sense, it should be acknowledged that the inscriptions are *intentionally* enigmatic, deliberately poetic condensations of images drawn from a variety of sources: while they make perfectly good sense, the significance of what they say is veiled, not least because of the *scriptio continua* manner of their presentation and the absence of punctuation.[7] Here, for example, is the script composed for the Pleiad known as Pleione, whose nine lines are etched vertically into nine steel louvres on the Shepherd Street entrance boardwalk:

GENEROUSDIVERSCATTERINGPEARLS
INCRANNIESDEEPASHUMANHUNGER
INVERTINGFIRESILLUMINATION
WITHOUTYOURPORTALMAKINGROOM
WHEREWOULDBECREATIONSCHAOS
YOUBREAKTHELINEUPINTOPATHS
FRETTINGWITHANCESTRALJOURNEYS
EVERYPASSAGETHATWETAKE
WITHDISTANCEDRAWUSTOTHEDANCE

To reassure both colleagues and client that this *did* make sense, I provided the following gloss: 'Pleione dives into the waters of matter, answering a human hunger for form. She counters the potentially self-destructive male principle, literally as well

The Strategy of Ambience

as figuratively "making room" for creation to happen in a way that is sustaining. Pleione carries within her a forming spirit that can be likened to the dance; for her the environment is from the beginning a potential place, inscribed with paths, journeys and meeting places'.[8] As this paraphrase indicates, the inscription does not strictly represent anything – the classical or the Aboriginal Australian stories associated with Pleione, for example. It is about the coming into being of the place itself; it is the translation of the creative place-making principles applied at this place into language; it is mythos bubbling up rejuvenated as poetry.

The adjoining script for Atlas, who shares guardianship of the Pleiades with Pleione (and who co-divides responsibilities for passage in and out of 'Fertile Ground' with Pleione), looks forward rather than back. Pleione plunges into matter, creating an opening (Creation's chaos); however, we know that in Western mythologies these beginnings are masculinised. Atlas represents this patriarchal trend, and in many traditions (including most Aboriginal Australian stories) Atlas is imagined in destructive pursuit of the Pleiades. In this context, the script for Atlas is a call to break with tradition and by imagining origins differently to enable a different future to come into being:

HEAVENAVIDMOUNTAINEER
YOUARENOTFALLINGMERELYSTAYED
INYOURPURSUITTHEGOLDENGROVE
ISATYOURFEETTHESISTERSSPREAD
ACROSSTHEPLAINARENOTWINKING
ELECTRAINTHECLOUDSBLACKROAD
SEWSHERFILAMENTSOFPOWER
ITISHERJEWELLEDFINGERSTHATFLY
THREADINGMEMORYSWAYBACKHOME

Atlas, like Orion and a number of Ancestral personages in Aboriginal Australian beliefs, is invoked here as the male pursuer of the Pleiades, who, in order to escape his ravishment, is lifted up to the heavens. However, in this 'contraction', Atlas is advised that the golden grove, the female principle of place-making, is not something to be hunted down and subjected to male will; it is the spread of places, the weaving of their jewels into the tapestry of the land. Electra is named because she is associated with concealed power and scintillations that shine through the dark. Like Pleione, Electra understands place-making as a form of recollection. There is a play on threading, treading and reading that conveys the threefold educative strategy of *Golden Grove*, to lead out into a new mazelike country, to do this through the reinstatement of the social contract involved in walking as tracking and to create a sense of ambience through the verbal-visual affordance of the inscriptions, which, bordering on sense without exposing it, contribute to the production of the enigmatic quality, the sense of place.

The educative justification of the inscriptions – the fact that they are appropriate in a place whose many stories converge on ideas of knowledge, initiation and growth – becomes the explicit message of Alcyone's contraction (see Figure 21).

BLUEBACKEDLIKETHEHALCYONWATER
DOYOUTHINKYOURMIRRORFOOLSME
STARSSHOALWHEREISTABTHESURFACE
LASTNIGHTSCHILDRENLATEFORSCHOOL
WHATTIMESWAVESDISPERSESCINTILLATIONS
SYLLABLESISAMPLEFORTHEIRSENSE
CENTREOFTHEKNOWINGUNIVERSE
TEACHERHUSBANDINGTHEPUBLICMIND
AVERTOURIGNORANCELESTWEDIE

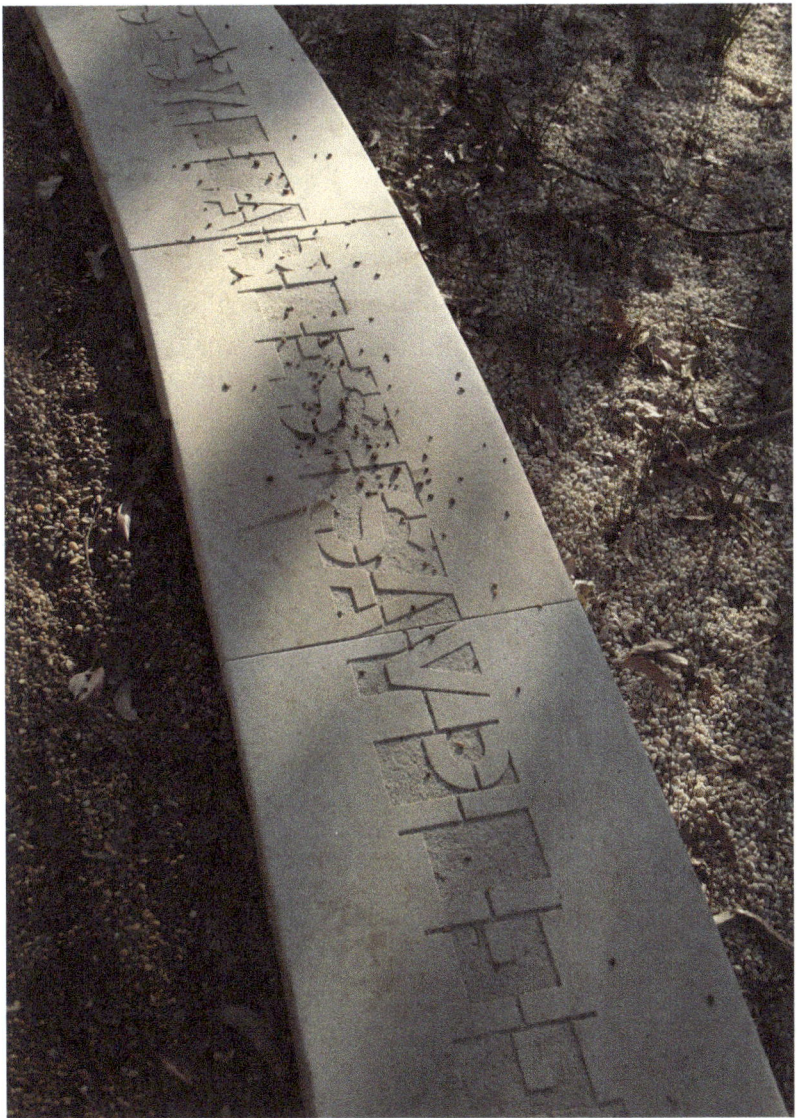

Figure 21 Taylor Cullity Lethlean/Material Thinking, 'Alcyone, *Golden Grove*, ground spiral with text', 2008. Photo: the author (18 July 2009).

Alcyone's inscription is located along a low wall abutting the Maze Green wetlands, and, as we explained on the Material Thinking website, it alludes to this amphibious site (one that agrees with her mythological character: 'Blue-backed, like the halcyon water'). Alcyone dives into the water, shattering its mirror. But in this momentary chaos of light, she sees shards symbolising the many, which she identifies both with the stars and with the former occupants of the site: 'Stars shoal where I stab the surface, last night's children late for school'. Alcyone is the first teacher, that archetypal instructress who looms so large in most infants' lives. This is not to belittle her importance. She begins the process of education, or leading out into the public sphere. Briefly, in the mid-nineteenth century, the stillness of Alcyone relative to other stars in her part of the sky led some to believe that she stood at the centre of the universe.

The three scales of *Golden Grove* (the spiral ground patterns, the nine illuminations and the nine 'Contractions') aim to produce an arrangement of affordances, a skein of sensory attachments and passages, that contributes to the emergence of that enigmatic site quality: ambience. In the context of the cube–tree, square–volume dialectic summarised above, the innovation of *Golden Grove* is to reconfigure the evolution of one into the other in terms of a plurality of increase sites, turning points or nodes. The cube is not a kind of geometrical glasshouse inside which the tree of life sprouts; trees sprout from every point, the square collapses, and the new space is composed of a wood, an arrangement of trees. What counts in this arrangement is the infinity of steps, paths and opportunities for adventure spelled out in the design. And the analogy between utterance – which when pluralised is the discourse of society – and engraving is taken literally, as we composed poetic inscriptions for each of the nine nodes with the intention that these would be engraved, displayed or otherwise materialised within, on or around the lighting structures themselves. But in concluding this investigation into the design of ambience, it is inevitable, and important, that the question of

The Strategy of Ambience

reception is raised. The poetic logic informing the design process has been set out in detail; the drawings from which the physical structures, ground signatures and typographical hieroglyphs emerged capture the characters of the stories informing them, and to the extent that the original *Golden Grove* proposal has been realised they are faithfully materialised. But what impact have they had? Is there any evidence that the intention of the work has been recognised? Or would the generally favourable response to the landscape architects' design have been the same without the integration of this (admittedly unusual) public artwork?

The question posed here is raised whenever 'good' design is challenged to demonstrate its superior functionality. There may, in fact, be a toxic feedback loop between the scepticism of the commissioning body and the inflation of the designer-artist's rhetoric. As the client (usually representing a combination of functionalist interests – planning, engineering, finance and the combination of these, a risk-averse project management culture) increasingly demands a one-to-one correspondence between each design element and a demonstrable contribution to 'liveability', so the landscape architect team is under growing pressure to inflate the claims for the *attention* their work will draw. Each object, each pathway, even each item of street furniture must be translatable; that is, it must answer a plausible social purpose. The objecthood of the objects is secondary to the regulation of social behaviour – the management of traffic. In this functionalist context, any tendency of the design to deregulate passage, to lengthen the stay of the passer-by or to induce errancy, reverie or inattention is regarded as introducing an element that should not be paid for and which, in fact, seems to involve a supplementary investment of resources on which any return in terms of improved site management is doubtful.

Notice that the point being made here is not the same as the argument for a minimalist intervention: when a landscape architect recommends editing the existing state of things (literally and figuratively weeding out undesirable accretions), the aim may be to return the site to its former state, but the criteria for defining the former state remain functionalist. The seeming withdrawal of the designer from any grand gesture does not reflect a commitment to complexity, ambiguity or the provocation of encounter. Simplification aims to improve connectivity, not to intensify the relatedness of things considered in terms of their proximity, orientation and sensuous properties. I see little evidence that these functionalist designs are ever subjected to rigorous performance evaluation. Nor is it clear that the tools of evaluation have been developed that can quantify the extent to which the public's sense of wellbeing has been improved or diminished by the redesign of a public space. Given the difficulty of assessing the functionality of even functionalist landscape and urban design, it is not clear why embedded artworks like *Nearamnew*, *Relay*[9] or *Golden Grove* (which avoid explicit communication) should have to meet more arduous criteria of success. However, it is indisputable that works of these kinds, which deliberately court *inattention*, find it much harder to overcome the first hurdle to acceptance: the client's pre-commissioning scepticism.

One thing is clear: the mimetic fallacy does not work as a defence. For example, I wrote the following in my notebook at the time when the first of the 'Contractions' was being engraved:

> The nine texts for *Golden Grove* are star hymns. They evoke the occluded histories of the site, those that the daylight of reason eclipses with its brightness. Unlike solar knowledge, the wisdom of the stars pulsates. It

suggests the rhythm of the dance. The great stars tread water, or hold their positions in the flux of space. The knowledge of the stars is catenary: the star is always a cross and a field of concentric circles. The Pleiades are shawled: they disclose their collective presence reflectively, through a veil of dust. The Heavenly Sisters associate with the Moon: their year dance is accelerated and made theatrical in the huge transformation of the Moon. When the stars are withdrawn from view, the explorer experiences homesickness. In a world of exiles, home is located above. The ground of being is the sky's upside down. To evoke the other histories of *Golden Grove* is not to rake the soil for sherds of neglected societies, but to turn the gaze towards the glimmering night sky. Women's wisdom, Indigenous tracks, the nocturnal reveries of the scientist and the dynamism of dreams discover their meeting place there.[10]

No doubt this captures something of the artist's aspiration. It illustrates the truth, perhaps, that any artist is driven by wholly impractical concerns and fantasies that it is unlikely the public can share. A desire to transcend anything possible inside the commission seems to inspire these lines. But, however deeply felt, this ecstatic impulse is no justification for making the poems obscure, for even what is occluded must shine forth clearly if it is to make any sense. Strictly speaking, my interest in the stars is irrelevant to their representation; what counts, and counts entirely, is the efficacy of the proposed lighting designs in illuminating the way.

My defence, at this point anyway, is different. It is, first, that the public for which this kind of design is intended is not composed of behaviourist robots, sensory and mental blank canvases whose behaviour is dependent on, and entirely dictated by, external stimuli. And, second, it is that the world we inhabit makes sense only because proto-patterns of sense are embedded in its phenomena. 'There exists a middle ground between the tendency of dynamical systems to grow more complex and the pattern-making propensity of human being. It is the existence of this middle ground that lends sense to what the senses vouchsafe us.'[11] This is pretty inexact; nevertheless, it represents a testable position. As mentioned above, Michael Tawa has written a book about the teaching of architectural design which utilises 'ana-materialistic thinking', the recovery from the materials of thinking of certain immanent structures or tendencies towards higher levels of self-organisation. These 'assemblages' are simultaneously associations of ideas and the 'existential infrastructure for life'.[12] They are disposed to join together in new ways that are conducive to producing the conditions where life is lived twice, constructively and reconstructively, actively and reflectively.[13] Such a world is not uniformly bright. It is not free of hollows and prominences, but navigates them: 'The research program capable of conceptualizing complexity in a way likely to foster the public good balances dejection and projection, skeptical withdrawal and joyous affirmation. It is idle to imagine that a knowledge lacking these parameters can deliver anything of human interest.'[14]

In contrast with the needs-led individual of late capitalist consumerism, my ideal subject is constituted relationally; just as Edmund Husserl claimed that consciousness is intentional (consciousness is always consciousness *of* something),[15] so with the whole human subject, it is born into and navigates a world whose interstices are organised vortically in terms of competing centripetal and centrifugal forces. Of course, this reduction is to be taken with a grain of salt, although I like the fact that the words *intention* and *tendril* are etymologically related.[16] The person already on their way – disposed to encounter and directed by inclinations – is not necessarily fired by a desire to keep to a straight line: like the arrow, they describe an arc; like the tendril, their successive exchanges with others may resemble climbing spirals. There is in this sense a direct connection between wayfinding and wellbeing.

As regards the second claim, it is perhaps a translation into landscape design of Paracelsus's doctrine of signatures, which 'rests not only on the ability of the believing doctor to see the significance of visual correspondences, but also on the premiss that the cures for human ailments are to be found in the localities where they occur'.[17] Applied to the typography of *Golden Grove*, for example, it claims that the physical marks – the specially designed letters physically engraved at a large scale into steel or stone – communicate *apart* from the concepts they express when read for their meaning. They communicate like patterns in nature: the zigzag in the butterfly's wing or the serpentine lip of the shell, the notch in the bark of a tree or the sudden columnar shadow in the hem of the storm cloud. They stand out from the general mottle of the visual field, and yet they stay on the border between indistinction and definite sense. As smaller versions of the great 'Know Thyself' at Delphi – which, above all, invited the reader to engage in an act of self-confrontation at that place – they are socially oriented public signatures rather than readerly signs to be absorbed in private meditation. They communicate an intention, a design on the public space and its public, some ordering principle or social contract, whose terms must necessarily remain enigmatic if the freedom of growth is to remain. They suggest perhaps the possibility of further illumination and revelation; at the same time, they are discreet; inviting touch or even an aesthetic appraisal for their purely formal properties, they decline to exhaust the scope of the place for further inventions, adventures in coming across significant things or oneself. They attune passers-by to the possibility that the place resonates with senses, but they do not deafen them to these by the over amplification of one meaning at the expense of all others. They aim to invite further exploration; they promote the endlessness of veils associated with ambience.

Ambience implies, at least etymologically, a trajectory that is curvilinear, perhaps like the reiterative spiral of the creative process. The root, *ambi*, seems to mean primarily both, on both sides, ambiguous. How does being on both sides acquire a front and a back and a rotation? The word *amble* implies a departure from the straight and narrow, a certain locomotory self-awareness: one might sway from side to side; one who ambles takes notice of things about them; they are the rural equivalent of D'Arcy Wentworth Thompson's individual in the marketplace who wanders around without any business of their own.[18] It is speculated that *amble* comes from a root that combines *ambi* (around) and a Proto-Indo-European root meaning to go (see the Greek *alaomai*, meaning to wander). Alternatively, the roundabout sense of *ambience* is experienced acoustically. In one etymology, *amplify* is derived from the same root as *ambience*: '*Ambi-pulus*, i.e. full on both sides; where *pulus* = *para*, full'.[19] There seems to be a direct connection between the adornment of walking about and the cosmetic improvement of the milieu. Brian Eno describes his ambient music 'treatments' as occurring on the cusp between 'melody and texture'.[20] Does he mean timbre? But texture applies to clothing, the adornment of walking about. Ambient music has a soothing effect: it clothes, immerses, surrounds. In short, the ambient qualities of a space seem to envelop the subject and induce a particular kind of errancy or lingering.

The Strategy of Ambience

Ambient design of this kind associates ambience with ambulation, and both with an ambiguity inherent in the experience of being in the midst of it all. The space theorised in this presentation of the self as one among many selves is not a prior ground or theatrical void; it is more like a dense forest through which the figures navigate their way. Public space in this conception of place-making is situated: it is wherever encounter is imagined or meeting fostered. It is never abstract, able to be contained in the outline of a plan. It is a movement towards conducted by a minimum of two parties. It is discursively produced in the physical sense of discourse as a running hither and thither. Its unit is the mobile body, understood always as an inclination towards or a potential relationship with another. It translates into spatial practice William Desmond's notion of a primary sociality driven by the desire to become other than one is; it is 'this affinity between the human self and the world of becoming', he says, 'which grounds the possibility of a two-way, that is, *metaxological* mediation between them'. And what applies to the inhabitants of this world also applies to its designer or dramaturg: 'We do not decipher the world by standing stiffly outside it, nor by lording over it in a domineering fashion, but by venturing into the thick of things and vigilantly moving through them'.[21]

The built environments that emerge from this process, in which the arrangements invite the re-enactment of primary senses of place, are educative. The place-making stories that inform them are made available to the public. Although the sources of the design may be veiled in the physical realisation of the design, in this way launching the adventurer into the thick of things, the information they are based on can be attractively presented through publications, websites and, of course, place-based apps. In this way, the delicate interplay between virtual and physical encounters with place characteristic of the headset age can be kept in play. However, the critical determinant of the design's exploratory character is the technique employed in the design itself. Just as the program of the new domain centres on the act of drawing out, so the drawing practice informing the design must similarly be indicative – score-like – rather than pre-emptively final and finalising. Lines drawn in this spirit are material, possessing width, depth and pressure. The use of digital drawing programs to create the three-dimensional arrangements proposed in *Red Ways*, *Golden Grove* or *Pearl* are not necessarily inimical to these materialist ambitions, as their capacity to draw bundles of lines close together, to multiply superfluous and redundant trajectories and to draw these into new non-functionalist but intuitively sociable figures (the arabesque, the vortex, the swerve) offers a kind of hyper-representation of the potential for meeting that lines drawn out and drawn together can model.

The drawing practice associated with the application of material thinking to making something useful recalls Kostas Terzidis's account of design. The Greek equivalent of the Latinate word *design* is, he points out, the word *schedio* (*schedule* in English), derived from a root, *schedon*, 'which means nearly, almost, about, or approximately'. Terzidis extrapolates from this that design 'signifies not only the vague, intangible, or ambiguous, but also the striving to capture the elusive'.[22] In other words, design is a design on time as well as on space. It not only locates points and draws lines through them; it draws together moments in time. It not only indicates a direction; it leaves behind the material trace of passage – the physical mark that, Jacques Derrida reminds us, is exactly what is not carried over and absorbed into the future but is the sign of difference.[23] In this context, Terzidis explains that *schedon* is in turn related to a verb meaning 'to have had in the past'; hence, 'design is linked indirectly to a loss of possession and a search into an oblivious state of memory'.[24]

In this way, design is not a departure from the old but its active recollection. It is invention only when invention is understood in its etymological sense of coming across something: 'Discovery is the act of encountering, for the first time, something that already existed. In contrast, invention is defined as the act of causing something to exist by the use of ingenuity or imagination'.[25] In a comparable fashion, the place-making stories discovered and retraced in the process of making the spatial arrangements of *Golden Grove* and *Red Ways* are mythopoetic in nature. They are not formed out of picturesquely represented myths; they preserve the creative potential of stories that secular modernity and its cult of the master plan have consigned to the realm of superstition. They recuperate poetic fertility in a time of crisis.

Another way to understand ambient design is to say that in the context of planning it is *strategic*. It is a sign of the cultural power and prestige planning enjoys that it has managed to appropriate strategy, with the result that most master plans these days are described as 'strategic master plans'. This phrase is, though, a contradiction in terms. John S. Nelson points out that 'strategies are easily but disastrously misunderstood as plans, particularly in times when universities [but we might add municipalities] strive to follow firms into the business of "strategic planning"'. As he elaborates, 'Plans are blueprints for execution on selected sites or applications to distinct situations…Plans are not especially porous, and their tiniest details can command application because they face knowable situations…Strategies are especially flexible, loose, porous'.[26] When planners claim to be strategic, they either confuse strategy with a militaristic campaign to eliminate obstacles to progress or seek to address the fact that a plan by itself is immobile, offering no critical prioritisation of opportunities. The militaristic connotations of the term have overshadowed its profounder association with concepts of spread. The cognate Latin term *sternere* means to spread, extend, stretch out and cover. The term *stratum* describes the result of this process. But the root is active as well, as the related term *strew* indicates. As a territorial phenomenon, spreading out is obviously an ambiguous and ethically charged process. It can be the erotic mechanism of sociality or the means of military domination. *Stratum* is connected with the Latin *strata* – hence, indeed, our *street*. In any case, the act of spreading out implies a porous environment; it presupposes a humid medium, disposed to spreading.

Strategy is essentially a movement form circumscribed by specific durations and environments. It is determined and shaped by the intelligence – the scope for growth, amalgamation, transformation – of matter. It is a critical process of making, equally evident in mythopoiesis and design. *Golden Grove* is strategic in this sense. It is not a ground plan but a network. As Nelson writes, 'Strategies and plans do not cohere in the same way. Plans are fabrics, with the elements woven tight into cloths ready for cutting and sewing. Strategies are networks, with the webbings left loose to catch or otherwise direct to their purposes what passes near. The components of plans are specific rules and measures that define and dictate particular deeds. The aspects of strategies are prudential principles and moves that might be made, depending on the emerging circumstances. Plans are pre-determined; strategies are opportunistic'.[27] Evidently, Nelson's notion of strategy is very similar to Terzidis's sense of design. Both seek to give back to planning an evolutionary creative sense. They reject the creationist predetermination of the future in favour of a postmodern openness to the contingency of making (and place-making in particular).

As Nelson comments, 'Strategy becomes the postmodern counterpart of classical poiesis. It is how we make-to-do: rhythming our words and deeds in pervasively uncertain times'.[28] The performance of the rhapsode-designer evoked earlier is strategic in this sense: it discovers a pattern in stories that were formerly considered separate from one another, and by sewing together the loose threads between them creates a new plot. However, the new pattern is not like the completion of a jigsaw; it is simply another way through the labyrinth of possible places, another provisional pattern with new edges, folds, passages and gates.

Notes

1 Carter, *Dark Writing*, p. 93.
2 Rickert, *Ambient Rhetoric*, 254.
3 Penny van Toorn, *Writing Never Arrives Naked: Early Aboriginal Cultures of Writing in Australia*, Aboriginal Studies Press, Canberra, 2006, p. 226.
4 Philip Rollinson, *Classical Theories of Allegory and Christian Culture*, Duquesne University Press, Pittsburgh, 1985, p. 9.
5 Walter Benjamin, *The Origin of German Tragic Drama*, trans. J. Osborne, Verso, New York, 1977, p.177.
6 Bardon and Bardon, *Papunya – A Place Made After The Story*, p. 124. Bardon envisaged the 'hieroglyphs' or recurrent motifs of early painting done at Papunya in 1971–72 as the coming together of 'archetypal forms' (p. 124) that made the visual telling of a story possible: 'Western Desert hieroglyphs of my experience in 1971 sought to write the landscape they enacted, by and through the formalisation of pictograms as hieroglyphic representations.' (Quoted from typescript in my possession in Carter, *Dark Writing*, p. 124.)
7 For the psychological and physical impact of *scriptio continua*, see Carter, *Dark Writing*, pp. 217–19.
8 Material Thinking, 'Golden Grove at Darlington Campus: Celebrating heritage through design', August 2006, pp. 1–15, p. 7.
9 Ruark Lewis and I designed the public artwork *Relay* for the Sydney Olympics in 2000 (see Carter, *Dark Writing*, pp. 203–27).
10 Paul Carter, '"*Golden Grove*" project workbook', 2004–2008, 23 March 2005, in author's possession.

11 Paul Carter, *Turbulence: Climate Change and the Design of Complexity*, Puncher & Wattman, Sydney, 2015, p. 69.
12 Tawa, *Theorising the Project*, p. 235.
13 For a discussion of the phenomenon of recognition, see Carter, *Turbulence: Climate Change and the Design of Complexity*, p. 71.
14 Ibid, p. 71.
15 Ronald McIntyre and David Woodruff Smith, 'Theory of Intentionality,' in J. N. Mohanty and W. R. McKenna, eds., *Husserl's Phenomenology: A Textbook*, Center for Advanced Research in Phenomenology and University Press of America, Washington D.C., 1989, pp. 147–79, p. 147.
16 See Levin, *The Listening Self*, p. 69.
17 Ian Maclean, *Logic, Signs and Nature in the Renaissance: The Case of Learned Medicine*, Cambridge University Press, Cambridge: 2002, p. 324.
18 Thompson, *On Growth and Form*, vol. 1, p. 76.
19 Walter W. Skeat, *An Etymological Dictionary of the English Language*, Clarendon Press, Oxford, 1888, p. 22.
20 Michael Jarrett, *Sound Tracks: A Musical ABC*, Temple University Press, Philadelphia, 1988, p. 11.
21 James McGuirk, 'Eros, Power and Justice: William Desmond and his Others,' in T. A. F. Kelly, ed., *Between System and Poetics: William Desmond and Philosophy after Dialectic*, Ashgate, Farnham, Surrey, 2007, pp. 163–74, 174.
22 Kostas Terzidas, *Algorithmic Architecture*, Architectural Press, London, 2006, p. 1.
23 Gayatri Chakravorty Spivak 'Translator's Preface', Jacques Derrida, *Of Grammatology*, The Johns Hopkins Press, Baltimore, 1976, p. xvii.
24 Terzidis, *Algorithmic Architecture*, p. 1.
25 Ibid., pp. 6–9.
26 John S. Nelson, 'Strategy studies: Explications of rhetorical performance', *Poroi*, Essays on Poroi's Set of Occasional Features, Iowa Digital Library, August 2003, viewed 5 June 2015, <http://digital.lib.uiowa.edu/poroi/poroifeaturetypes.htm#strategystudies>.
27 Ibid.
28 Ibid.

Part 4

17

THE LAWS OF CHANCE MEETING

One lesson of *Red Ways* is that meeting involves pulling away; turning towards and turning away are joined, like the eddies that form in a vortex tree. Although tied to the space-time of the larger dance, the individuals performing the figures of conversation and tergiversation experience coming and going rhythmically. The constant rearrangement of figures is essential in producing and reproducing spaces in-between that retain the possibility of encounter. *Red Ways* indicates 'that a third kind of meeting [is] possible, provisional, situated and capable of inscribing the act of meeting into future protocols of coexistence'.[1] In the passage between others, an encounter with the self becomes possible. While the ego examining itself in the mirror is subject to an infinite regression of selves questioning selves, the person entering into the thick of things and vigilantly moving through them captures, almost with a sense of deja vu, former complexes of feeling that have eluded them in therapy. Distraction is not necessarily an obstacle to self-awareness: to be drawn away from one's conscious direction may make the construction of that line apparent. The double origin of self-consciousness becomes manageable, and the echoic, mimetic nature of social behaviour no longer masks an emptiness but springs, as it were, from the cymatic foundation of social relations. People bunch and vibrate according to complex eido-kinetically mediated choreographies. When the curators of the 2007 exhibition *Seduced: Art and Sex from Antiquity to Now*, at the Barbican, in London, wrote in their catalogue introduction – 'Inherent in the Latin meaning of "seduced" is the concept of "bringing close to oneself"' – they not only offered a questionable etymology but appropriated a term that more properly characterises the operations of Eros, the Public Worker.[2] Seduction, like distraction, is an act of leading away, of departing from some fixed position. It leads not to the bedroom but to the hollows of public space.

From a choreotopographical perspective, seduction is the action of the setting on sociability. The pleasures Søren Kierkegaard describes in 'The Seducer's Diary' presuppose a separation between the practical-sexual and the aesthetic-erotic. One object of the Barbican show was, no doubt, to avoid this sociopathic split: while the exhibition aimed to 'engage everyone in a special way with the beauty and emotion of "intimate relations" as vitally enriching human experiences', the curators explained, their business was exclusively with 'sexual images', with 'depictions of the sexual act – whether before, during or after'.[3] But if the theme was seduction, an entirely different field of images might have been selected. 'There is something shocking about a person's directing a hiker, uncertain of his way, to the wrong path and then abandoning him in his error; but what is that compared with causing a person to go astray within himself?'[4] Of such a man it can be said 'that his journey through life was undetectable (for his feet were formed in such a way that he retained the footprints under them – this is how I best picture to myself his infinite reflectedness into himself)'.[5] But this brilliant image of the solipsistic dangers of self-absorption also indicates an alternative: the man who *does* leave behind a trace of passage and who could, if he looked back, see not only where he had been but, in all probability, the scribble of all the footprints that had traversed that region. Images of this seduction would comprise ground patterns, histories of tracks that, by demonstrating significant distributions, intensities, flows and catchments, captured the ordinary parameters of sociability: rhythm or non-selfsame repetition.

As noted in the discussion of *Opening*, choreotopographical phenomena cannot be studied from the outside. They have an interiority that is invisible from the external viewpoint of the observer. Accordingly, they cannot be registered in the plans, elevations and cross-sections that provide the graphic lexicon of master planning. The space perception they embody has resonances with Aboriginal Australian protocols of inclusion and exclusion. In her article 'Excluded Spaces: The figure in the Australian Aboriginal landscape', Nancy Munn discusses the performative spaces of everyday life in the Central and Western deserts, where people are 'spatially and temporally situated' and engage in dynamic exchanges across 'spatial regions and moving spatial fields'. This active notion of presencing makes it possible to materialise counter-zones of non-presencing or sites of 'spatial exclusion'. The interdictions associated with these sites 'create a partially shifting range of excluded or restricted regions for each person throughout his or her life. A specific kind of spatial form is being produced: a space of deletions or of delimitations constraining one's presence at particular locales'. In these communities, the individual's life-world is, spatially speaking, a 'patchwork of regions', and Munn notes that such 'particular spatiotemporal formations produced out of the interactions of actors' moving spatial fields...cannot automatically refer to limits marked out on pieces of land (or in architectural forms); nor can bodily boundaries be dealt with as body surfaces apart from the body's spatiality, actions and locatedness'.[6]

But this is not simply an anthropological observation: from the inside, as it were, it illuminates the subjective perception that social space is dappled, composed of alternating troughs and crests, convergent and divergent spaces that bunch or stretch. These impressions are not derivable from the setting; nor are they solely the projections of the lonely individual. They seem to register characteristics of the space in-between, which, in the choreo-topographical design, is imagined as a place where things happen, unpredicted coincidences occur and mimetically engineered novel arrangements. In 1919, the Viennese intellectual and Neo-Lamarckist biologist Paul Kammerer published *Das Gesetz der Serie* (The Law of Seriality). His typology of serial events was designed to explain the phenomenon of the mere coincidence. When understood in relation to a theory of seriality, he suggested, mere chance proves to be the manifestation of a higher organisational principle characteristic of complex systems; the anticipation of cybernetic models of systems-level self-organisation and growth is obvious.[7] Kammerer is intriguing to us because he draws some of his examples of unexplained coincidence from human behaviour in the public domain.

> Kammerer conducted many (rather naive) experiments, spending hours in parks noting occurrences of pedestrians with certain features (glasses, umbrellas, etc.) or in shops, noting precise times of arrivals of clients, and the like. Kammerer 'discovered', that the number of time intervals (of a fixed length) in which the number of objects under observation agrees with the average is by much smaller than the number of intervals, where that number is either zero or larger than the average. This, he argued, provided evidence for clustering. From

today's perspective, Kammerer merely noted the perfectly normal spontaneous clustering of signals in the Poisson process.[8]

But perhaps not: Kammerer was not a disinterested observer (he was not studying probabilities); he was looking for exceptional series or clusters – self-forming patterns that might even defy the logic of the Poisson distribution, where the number of observed occurrences fluctuates about a mean with a standard deviation. What is relevant to the topic of programming chance encounters in public space is not whether or not these spontaneous clusterings were real or reproducible (or even, within limits, predictable); it is the fact that Kammerer *perceived* these coincidences. Whether or not they could survive mathematical scrutiny as something unusual and distinctive, they appeared to Kammerer to pattern his environment.[9] As Koestler puts it, Kammerer's law of seriality governed the 'lawful recurrence of the same or similar things and events – a recurrence, or clustering, in time or space whereby the individual members in the sequence – as far as can be ascertained by careful analysis – are not connected by the same active cause'.[10] Applied to the phenomena observed from a park bench, a downtown pavement or a busy shop, the laws suggest that public space is governed by rules of attraction that are neither objective (inherent in the urban design) nor subjective (a function, for example, of what German sociologist Georg Simmel identified as the heightened eroticism of life in the modern city), but organisational, growing up in a creative feedback loop between individuals (forming non-causally related groupings) and between individuals and their surroundings. For it is reasonable to assume that the urban milieux where Kammerer conducted his surveys produced interesting results precisely because they cultivated 'the metropolitan type of individuality' whose psychology, according to Simmel, 'consists in the *intensification of nervous stimulation* which results from the swift and uninterrupted change of outer and inner stimuli'.[11]

These rules operate in-between and perhaps across biology, psychology and social behaviour; at their heart is a principle of imitation or mimetically based attraction that tends to the evolution of ever more complex feedback loops and systems of regional self-organisation, whether at the scale of individuation or species mutation.[12] In this sense, Kammerer was not only a biological Neo-Lamarckist who contributed to probability theory and systems theory. In a simpler fashion, he catalogued the phenomenon of chance in the public domain, aiming to demonstrate that seeming mere coincidences follow laws. Applied to social behaviour, the proposition is that people unconsciously copy one another. They sense affinities and act these out in various forms of mimetic behaviour: the crowd is not a random Brownian motion of people-particles; it is composed of forming vortices, bunches of collective mind matter that tend to incorporate whatever coincides with their interests or lines of expansion. In this theory, which finds a counterpart in René Girard's notion of mimetic desire – the principle that people can desire pretty much anything as long as other people seem to desire it too[13] – people are inherently needy and desirous, propelled by mimetic instincts to make sense of the world *performatively.* We may think we are acting independently; in fact, our behaviour is subject to the laws of seriality. Even seemingly random gestures or signs become, when mirrored in the behaviour of another, something more than a mere coincidence. In certain circumstances, they can generate performative protocols that turn the chance encounter into something more complex and enduring, a principle of coexistence or sociability.[14]

What are the design implications of redefining chance in this way? The schism between everyday life and urban design seems to be so deep that no resuturing of space-time is practicable. Through their access to virtual spaces and the magnification of opportunities for sociability off the street, contemporary urban dwellers cease to inhabit Planet Earth (in its inherited urban incarnation, which is resolutely defined in terms of theatrically installed immobile infrastructure). The mimetic ecologies of social desire that the contemporary city intensifies flourish despite any official attempts to channel or regulate them, or even to lend them enduring symbolic form. The notion of the meeting place, for example, as an ideal crucible of democratic growth and transformation has long ceased to have any political significance; and the meeting places qua civic squares and the like, which regional and local public authorities continue to commission, may seem to belong, geologically speaking, to the Jurassic period. Meeting, whether defined in terms of a turning away from the prescribed or as a mere coincidence subject to laws of which we are unconscious, recovers its etymological association with the older term *moot*: the meeting place is a moot point, an undecidable place in discourse or space where the meaning, the direction and the outcome remain undecided. A moot point is a state of suspense, where being and becoming are entangled; here, meeting recovers its fatness, its potential for associations or exchanges that have yet to be fully formulated and decided. Agreeing to differ, the actors withdraw temporarily, in the process preserving room for something to happen.

At a macro level, the discovery of a logic of encounter foreshadows an ending to master planning: if people are not programmable monads but beings that possess the ability to strategise, gathering and ungathering according to rules that, while inscrutable to linearist thinking, conform well to the way nonlinear feedback systems maintain themselves, then master planning is either supererogatory or impertinent. The useful function that design might play is to encourage these cultures of self-organisation and transformation. Instead of discouraging eventfulness (in the agoraphobic theory of modernism always associated with the emergence of the murderous mob), design might work to make public spaces feel propitious – that is, especially ready for the materialisation of desires. In one interpretation, the literal sense of the Latin word *propitiatio* is *a falling or rushing forward*. In this sense, it signifies an intensification of chance (in the sense of something falling out), a recasting of it as an environment imagined in terms of affinities, histories and laws. To propitiate is also to make atonement to the gods, a function that a number of *Golden Grove*'s 'Contractions' recognise. For the gods are the dramaturgs of the collective spirit, the stirrers of the public mind, producing in its sluggish flow the vortices of grouping, individuation and growth. They oversee the turbulence through which the *turba* becomes self-aware and generates more complex algorithms of sociability: Alcyone, 'centre of the knowing universe, / teacher husbanding the public mind'; Maia, 'expectant…wise as many…conduct the turmoil of the mind'; Celeano, 'let footsteps be for all outsiders, / a way of light that outruns dark'.[15]

Notes
1   Carter, *Meeting Place*, p. 105.
2   Marina Wallace, Martin Kemp, Joanne Bernstein, *Seduced: Art and Sex from Antiquity to Now* (Merrell, in association with Barbican Art Gallery, London, 2007, p. 11.
3   Wallace, Kemp & Bernstein, *Seduced: Art and Sex from Antiquity to Now*, p. 17.
4   Søren Kierkegaard, *The Seducer's Diary*, trans. H. V. Hong and E. H. Hong, Princeton University Press, Princeton, 1997, NJ., p. 10.
5   Ibid., p. 9.

6   Nancy Munn, 'Excluded Spaces: The figure in the Australian Aboriginal landscape', *Critical Inquiry*, vol. 22, no. 3, 1996, pp. 448, 449, 462, 465.
7   For the influence of these ideas on the development of Carl Jung's notion of synchronicity, see John Townley & Robert Schmidt, 'Paul Kammerer and the Law of Seriality', in Stephen Moore (ed.), *Fortean Studies*, vol. 1, John Brown Publishing, London, 1994, pp. 251–60. Both meditations occur in the context of the discoveries being made by physicists like Wolfgang Pauli which suggested that at the subatomic scale at least the position and the direction of a particle could not both be known at once: what you knew was inseparable from what you chose to know. See also Elena Nechita, 'Some Considerations on Seriality and Synchronicity', *Brain*, Issue 1, January 2010, pp. 49–54.
8   Tomasz Downarowicz, *Law of Series*, Scholarpedia, vol. 3, no. 11, 2008, p. 3922, viewed 3 June 2015, <www.scholarpedia.org/article/Law_of_series>.
9   Where Carl Jung's synchronicity deals with the relationship between subjectivity and the external world, Paul Kammerer's seriality is more concerned with patterns and groupings of objects that occur in the environment. (See Nechita, 'Some Considerations on Seriality and Synchronicity', p. 50.)
10 Arthur Koestler, *The Roots of Coincidence*, Random House, New York, 1972, p. 85.
11 Georg Simmel, *Simmel on Culture: Selected Writings*, ed. David Frisby & Mike Featherstone, Sage, London, 1997, p. 175. Emphasis in original.
12 See Townley & Schmidt, 'Paul Kammerer and the Law of Seriality'.
13 See Paisley Livingston, *Models of Desire: René Girard and the Psychology of Mimesis*, Johns Hopkins Press, Baltimore, 1992, p. 1.
14 See Carter, *Meeting Place*, p. 56.
15 Material Thinking, 'Golden Grove at Darlington Campus: Celebrating heritage through design, August 2006,' 1–15, p. 7–9.

18

COLLECTIVE ATTUNEMENTS

To turn to *Alterations*, a public space design project carried out for a new civic square in Dandenong, Melbourne, is easy after a discussion of the sociability of chance (see Figure 22). The opportunities to find out from people living in Dandenong what they expected or wanted of their new civic square were limited, for reasons it appeared directly attributable to the master planning habit of thinking top-down, reflected in this case in a local government politico-administrative alliance that seemed nervous about engaging with communities able to self-organise and transform. Nevertheless, among those we were able to speak to informally without council surveillance, there was, on one or two themes, a surprising uniformity of view. There was, for example, a widespread opinion that the ideal community to which 'multicultural' Dandenong should aspire, whose values the new square should embody, was not any longer multicultural but cosmopolitan. As regards the character of the place, there was agreement that, whatever its physical attributes, it should possess *ambience*. And, as Thomas Rickert argues, ambience is an essential component of chance and its corollary social innovation. Adapting Eric Charles White's definition of *kairos* as a 'radical principle of occasionality establishing the living present as a point of departure for rhetorical invention', Rickert disputes that such moments of breakthrough are 'irrational'. According to Rickert, it all depends on context: the orator or, in our day, the media that returns the public domain to its political (democratic) function depends on the emergence of an audience disposed to listen (and act). When *kairos* is attached to 'a rich, material sense of place, with place thought beyond the subject/object dichotomy', the 'situational environs can be a "willing" and inventive agent'. In such a situation, rhetoric, the public speech act, is ambient or diffused, and *kairos* 'is not about mastery but instead concerns attunement to a situation'. *Attunement* means 'an ambient catalysis within what is most material or concrete, a gathering that springs forward'.[1]

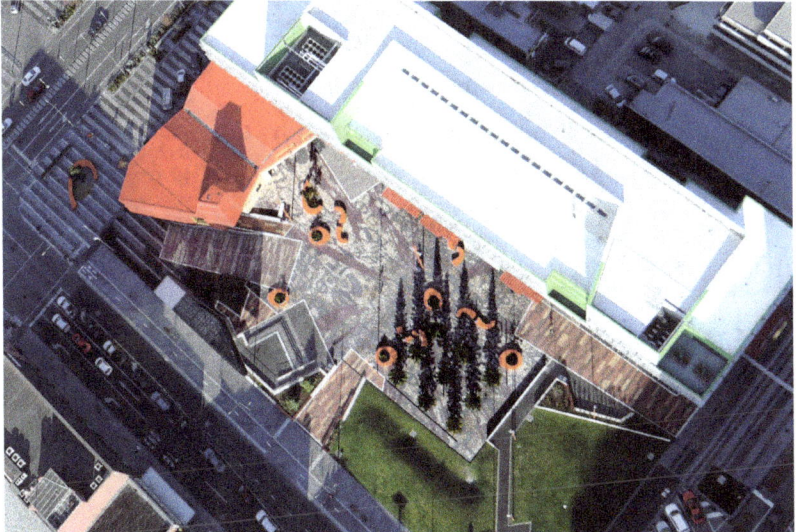

Figure 22 'Dandenong Municipal Building, Library and Civic Plaza', May 2014. Photo: Rush\Wright Associates. Reproduced by permission.

The key point about the Dandenong discussions was that they occurred before the urban block marked for redevelopment had been cleared. The people we spoke to were predominantly business owners whose shops, cafes, agencies and residences occupied the site about to be demolished. Having already been served with eviction orders, they were not empowered to resist the imminent destruction of the street, back lanes, sheds, carparks and informal services clinging to the walls. They accepted the pragmatic fact that they stood in the path of the master planning tornado and had no choice but to adapt. Nor was it necessarily the case that they would not benefit commercially from the clearance: the blank canvas from which the new civic square, municipal buildings and library would arise might well offer improved business opportunities. But this was not the point: the point was that in this concrete situation ambience was associated with destruction and change. Further, it was associated with access to something new. In particular, it was the attribute of a space that had (or might) become at last public. For the new civic square or meeting place that flowered from the implosion of buildings caused by the demolition was entirely new. At least from the point of view of recent immigrants, it could not avoid being read as revolutionary, as a collective act of place-making that incubated a new community ready to spring forward.

Of course, many different ethnic and cultural traditions were represented in the neighbourhood of the proposed civic square. But it soon became clear that the relevant tradition of public space being invoked in the call to ambience was not Anglo-Saxon. As Sandi Hilal and Alessandro Petti write,

> In Western political thought, the notion of public space is often associated with the 'collective interest,' and the 'common good.' However, in other cultural contexts, such as in the Arab countries, the notion of public space is seen as suspicious. During the years of direct colonial domination, the public space never denoted the 'collective interest' of the local population; rather, it expressed the arrogant, violent, and exploitative power of the white

European élite. In the name of the public good, state colonial authorities frequently expropriated that which people shared in common. For instance, the expropriation of land by the colonial authorities in the name of the 'public interest' illustrates how public interest does not necessarily coincide with the common good.[2]

Hence, they emphasise the importance of the act of cleaning Tahrir Square, Cairo, which followed the resignation of the Egyptian president Hosni Mubarak on 11 February 2011: 'The space was no longer perceived as public – the space of authority – but rather, the space of the people. Owning the space implied owning the future of the country. Cleaning the square was a gesture of re-appropriation, ownership, and care. In fact, this apparently banal act demonstrated a sense of reconstituted community and collective ownership'. The act of cleaning was a performance that demonstrated the land was, again, held in common. The Latin word *communis* (from which the Anglo-Saxon *commons* comes) means obliged to participate and has its counterpart in 'the Arabic term *al mashaa'*, which refers to communal land that is equally distributed among farmers....*Al-Mashaa'* is shared land, which was recognized through practice in the Islamic world. It emerged as a combination of conceptions of Islamic property and customary practices of communal or tribal land. *Al-Mashaa'* could only exist if people decided to cultivate the land together; and the moment they stopped cultivating it, they lost possession. Thus as the term denotes possession through common use, what appears to be fundamental is that in order for this category to exist it must be activated by *common uses*'.[3]

The leap forward, then, that the new civic square in Dandenong might enable was not into a novel postcolonial reality. It might, on the contrary, harbour a precolonial nostalgia. In this case, its federal distribution of responsibilities and obligations might mimic the way in which Aboriginal Australian societies occupied the land. In any case, ambience is tied here to performance, which, in a theatrical sense, may be defined as '"a tangible, bounded event that involves the presentation of rehearsed artistic action" for a specific audience in a particular time-and-space bound continuum, as in "a performance of a play, a dance or a symphony"'.[4] In relation to this notion of performativity, architecture plays a background role: it is, if you like, the theatrical setting for theatre. However, as Rustom Bharucha discusses in *Terror and Performance*, a broader definition of *performance* is possible – one that offers scope to extend the part that architecture, landscape architecture and public space programming can play in producing performative places. In this extra-theatrical performativity, J. L. Austin claims, 'performative utterances are understood to be crucial to the construction of reality, a construction that is sociotechnically *ordered*'. Or, as Judith Butler puts it, 'Performativity [is] the power of discourse to produce what it names'.[5]

Performativity, then, is the power to make things happen in the real world. There is an ironic sense in which theatre performances fail this test: they do not make anything happen. By contrast, public spaces that produce changes in the construction of reality clearly succeed: the mass 'performance' at Tahrir Square, integral to the 25 January revolution, is iconic in this regard. Mohamed Samir El-Khatib suggests that the identification of 'spectacle' and 'revolution' there might be linked to the Arabic word *farag*, meaning 'relief from distress, the dispelling of gloom and sadness, or watching something that amuses and diverts the mind'. Then, what took place at Tahrir Square was, according to El-Khatib, a renewal of discursive performativity: 'a group of signs within an integrated system' was undergoing 'restructuring'. 'The system's theatricalisation of the place and the city' was overthrown by 'a different theatricalisation of the place by creative bodies responsive to the latest technological developments and armed with a contemporary technological culture'.[6] In Rickert's terms, a collective attunement occurred, an ambient catalysis.[7]

Notes

1. Rickert, *Ambient Rhetoric*, pp. 95 (citing Eric Charles White, *Kaironomia, On the Will-to-Invent*, Cornell University Press, Ithaca, N.Y., 1987, p. 161), 97, 98.
2. Sandi Hilal & Alessandro Petti, *Al-mashaa' or the Space of the Common*, Haus der Kulteren de Welt, n.d., viewed 3 June 2015, www.hkw.de/en/programm/projekte/2013/edward_said_konferenz/multimedia_edward_said/text_workshop.php.
3. Ibid.
4. Rustom Bharucha, *Terror and Performance*, Routledge, Abingdon and New York, 2014, p. 19, citing Henry Bial (ed.), *The Performance Studies Reader*, 2nd edn, Routledge, London and New York, 2007, p. 59.
5. Bharucha, *Terror and Performance*, p. 20, citing J. L. Austin, *How To Do Things With Words*, as discussed in Jon McKenzie, *Perform or Else: From Discipline to Performance*, Psychology Press, New York, 2001, p. 208; and Judith Butler, 'Critically queer', *GLQ: A Journal of Lesbian and Queer Studies*, vol. 1, no. 1, 1993, pp. 17–32, p. 17.
6. Mohamed Samir El-Khatib, 'Tahrir Square as spectacle: Some exploratory remarks on place, body and power', *Theatre Research International*, vol. 38, no. 2, 2013, pp. 104–115, p. 113.
7. Rickert, *Ambient Rhetoric*, p. 98.

19

COSMETIC PRODUCTION

If public space is discursively produced, different styles of speech will produce it differently. In the choreotopographically conceived meeting place, talking is not a preliminary to silent action; it is fostered as a catalyst of discovering something in common. In contrast with the goal of administrative logic (and its self-disguise of power as a language stripped of imagination), the art of conversation is to open up a space of hearing: echoically measured and vortically structured, it builds ambience rhetorically. To understand the performance at Tahrir Square, or, indeed, any social performance tending to reorder sociability, the clothing of speech must be acknowledged as a critical vehicle of meaning. Authenticity is recognised in the fit of ornament to its purpose, not in flowery language or gestures for their own sakes. However, the meaning of the structured ebb and flow of people, walking, talking, passing by, is interior to the turbulent figure continually springing up and dying away in their motion. In a sense, the meeting place comes into being when its arrangements are seen to fit together, but the optimal fit is also the least substantial or governable. Suppose we watch a cloud for a while: 'if we look carefully, we shall see that at one end it is continually dissolving, while at the other end it is continually forming again. Thus it is not a fixed, unchanging object that we are looking at, but rather a process. What persists is the activity, as it were, of the "cloud." The constant cloud, as it appears to be does not exist...With its convections and vortices the cloud is in a state of constant change and atmospheric flux'.[1] So with the ambience of the crowd: it is a constantly ravelling and unravelling veil.

So, too, with ordinary conversation conducted in the right circumstances. In 2011, the architecture firm Lyons and landscape architects Rush\Wright Associates won a competition to design and deliver a new public library, council offices and civic square in the heart of Dandenong. Material Thinking was invited to develop a *programming strategy* for the new civic square. A programming strategy is planners' speak for defining the new facility's community uses. It might be assumed that departments of the Council responsible for community development, community arts, multicultural services and the like would already have established a community interest in an addition of public space. But this, it appeared, had not happened. Consequently, in soliciting support for the project, we were in the invidious position of renarrating a formulaic planning fantasy – every major place-making plan features a civic square – as an opportunity for democratic participation. In reality, the Council project managers had advised against public consultation, offering access instead solely to Council employees of different cultural backgrounds. Such a planning ideology, reflected in the risk-averse tactics of its officers, hardly exhibits interest in what Patsy Healey calls the 'dynamic relational dialectics of urban life'.[2] In these circumstances, there really was no alternative but to go undercover, as it were, into the shopping streets, and informally to sit down and watch, to have a coffee and to observe what was happening. But such flâneurship is narcissistic if unaccompanied by occasional speech and the ordinary courtesies of passing the time; and when such trespasses into sociability occurred, the results were revelatory.

Speaking off the record or in the immersive environment of their own shops, cafes and businesses, our interlocutors outlined views about future community far in advance of the Council's rote appeal to multicultural diversity. Substituting talking for asking questions, letting the conversation unfold in real time (subject to the interruptions of people coming and going) and letting topics arise spontaneously as little vortices spinning out of the situation itself, produced very different insights into what would constitute a future community and its spaces. Looking back, these precious conversations were inspired by the clothing of the interiors where we sat and drank coffee – that is, by the functional decoration of walls, shelves, furniture, posters and other elements producing the sense of place. The aim was not to unveil information that was private; it was to riff on the public interface of the subject's interests, the surface of signs recovering in this process their potency to initiate new forms of exchange. Below is an extract from the diary I kept at the time, which perhaps gives the flavour of the talk:

> Wandered into A——'s African Village Kitchen, a small sparsely fitted-out shop on the north (Walker Street) flank of the enormous cliff-high Social Services block (one of the first offspring of the master planning strategy). A corpulent Maori guy with a sports bag stuffed with women's tops, wrap-around skirts from West Africa, and a youngish Sudanese man, who talked about working the Wonthaggi abattoir, who showed me photos of his wedding, and who was anxious to prove his powerful connections back in Sudan; then an African woman

coming in, and haggling for ages over two items of clothing and some DVDs – music CDs, A—— insisted, and among them a Bob Marley ('Jamaican') CD. And while they talked I was wondering about the 'authentic' Africa in this, in A——'s forty year peregrination between Nigeria (presumably), England, the US and now Dandenong. A—— said that his interactions with the Council repeatedly failed because Council officers, while happy to take his ideas, and even to invite him to 'perform' or provide services at different 'multicultural' functions, failed to include him in decision-making or policy-development. We associated this with the tendency of 'multiculturalist' approaches to cultural and social management to stereotype different ethnicities or cultures. A—— gestured to the Maori guy sitting against the wall listening to music through the headphones: 'I am African, these are my community.'

We talked about the alternative approach to place-making and active citizenship, which, we agreed, could go by the name of cosmopolitanism. For us, cosmopolitanism referred to the possibility that different communities self-organised to support the larger community. Instead of being guaranteed certain freedoms to protect, promote and represent their own cultures, the cultures themselves were acknowledged as potentially cosmopolitan; any culture has the capacity and skills to reach out to the communities and to live alongside them. This is a political skill, a moral responsibility – and, in a 'multicultural' society, a creative opportunity for discovering common ground. Ironically, the focus on cultural difference, with the pressure to treat one's culture and identity as fixed and enduring, undermines the equally authentic dimension of cultural literacy, the capacity to lead, to negotiate across difference and to educate. In local terms cosmopolitanism translates into a different form of public space management and governance where creative individuals show initiative, and through this self-empowerment, build trust, respect and opportunity. A—— cited the little gesture of planting a temporary barbecue outside his shop in the street and the touching offer of a passing African kid to help him mend the food stall glass window.

In contrast with the 'multicultural' the 'cosmopolitan' is (as A—— said with regard to the people and the conversations and transactions that pass through his shop) 'without boundaries'. A temporary food stall acts more 'authentically' in this regard than the 'authentic' African song and dance performance, for in the former an African identity is seen in action forming new social connections across communities, whereas in the latter it tends to be exoticised and (ultimately) disempowered. A—— made the point that the 'authentic' has to include in its definition the journey to Dandenong from other countries: 'In Africa', he said, 'I am not considered "African"'; hence, the authentic African community in Dandenong is in part 'non-African', and there is a kind of inauthenticity about pretending otherwise. In any case, to build an emotionally and economically engaging Civic Space it is necessary to focus on the mechanisms that allow difference to construct a shared cosmopolitan personality, for it is in the exercise of the power to promote social innovation of this kind that different communities are continually reaffirmed and strengthened.

This theory is an original variation on, or departure from, conventional cosmopolitanism, that promotes a placeless network of disinterested parties, whereas the focus of this approach is to bring an un-masterplanned common place into being. The formula a cosmopolitan, post-multicultural approach to place-making offered was: opportunity, responsibility, creativity. Opportunity arises as soon as local government invites the communities to take leadership (and not simply to be consulted); responsibility follows from the opportunity to create a better social and physical environment; and creativity is the name of all the social forms that emerge from the social transactions needed to materialise the new cosmopolitan sensibility. Instead of multiculturalist virtues, inherently conservative and resistant – and which conform to the share house model (where the absent landlord controls the scope of the transactions) – cosmopolitan design focuses on the creative strengths of the different cultures and cultivates the themes, techniques and services that join the different communities together.

In contrast with the landlord model of multicultural difference, the cosmopolitan common place is without 'precincts', encouraging instead a continuous flow and interchange. In other words cosmopolitanism encourages trade across difference as a means of preserving difference, for this process of finding common ground builds respect for difference, mutual understanding – and, of course, an enlarged market (of goods, of sociability and of ideas). This enlarged market-place of exchange is, I reflect, very different from the passive cosmopolitanism of the Stoics or even the planned universal tolerance of Kant: it is an active citizenship focused on the emergence of something like N——'s witty adaptation (proffered during an earlier visit to the central business district) of the Australian national anthem – a market culture known as 'Australia Fair'!

A distributed model of civic engagement has another benefit: it allows potentially marginalized or smaller communities to avoid further fossilization or marginalization. A—— made the point that well-entrenched cultures in Dandenong – he cited the Afghani, Pakistani, Indian, Sri Lankan groups, all in his view broadly related culturally, linguistically – have less interest in reaching out. For them, the multicultural agenda serves to increase their influence as multicultural power brokers. It tends to reinforce inward-looking hierarchies, agendas and programs. By contrast, the seeding of different communities to develop outreach programs that demonstrate what cultures can bring to a shared project places the emphasis on creativity, exchange and the emergence of a new culture of exchange.

This emergent trade does not compromise difference, rather it builds a new resilience into the partnering groups as they are now operating as fully-emancipated citizenship advocates or community activists, a vocation that paves the way for intra-community education, knowledge transfer and cultural engagement as well as inter-community platforms. In any case, the focus of creative citizenship is on the harnessing of mechanisms for cross-cultural exchange, using these to build a new model of meeting, a new discourse of exchange. If you could define this, you would have the program of a new Civic Space suited to, because emerging from, the unique Dandenong 'community'. Suited because it 'fits out' a new environment, one that is defined by the alteration of existing costumes (inherited modes of self-presentation) rather than their simple reproduction and display.

A——, it will be said, was an exceptional individual. As this diary entry illustrates, socially progressive, politically astute, he is a natural community leader. However, this was by no means the only conversation I had which demonstrated the existence of a vigorous self-organising community ignored by the social and urban planners. When I spoke to M—— in her Mason Street shop, another establishment that is being affected by the new municipal development, she suggested that the consolidation of the 'Little India' precinct would help her business. This sounded like endorsement of the council initiative; in fact, though, the congregation of Indian retail businesses along the adjoining street and through the block where M——'s business is means that this council initiative mainly signposts what already exists. Even so the 'Little India' signs seem odd, give that the streets of Indian businesses do not constitute a closed precinct of any kind but a thoroughfare en route to the station.

Suppose the Indian precinct was developed, I said, what would happen in the event that a member of the group wanted to sell goods sourced from outside India? Logically, she replied, they would need to open another shop. I tried another tack: wouldn't the intensification of the India brand simply intensify intracultural trade and competition without significantly enlarging the customer base? M—— responded that her customers included non-Indian visitors but conceded that the main market was 'traditional'; however, she explained, she did have a wide non-Indian business through the tailoring and alteration service she offers. People of all backgrounds come to her to have their clothes fitted, refitted, altered and adapted. In other words, in addition to the business that conforms to the multicultural conception of identity, culture and social role, M—— has another business that doesn't conform to the multicultural stereotype, one where she is employed because her skills are not culture-specific but, on the contrary, are presumed to be valuable to any woman whatever her background.

The sophistication of these cultural, multicultural and cross-cultural practices was replicated elsewhere:

> A third model of commerce as community, which also transcends the multicultural ideology, is offered in H——'s Qaran Variety Shop and Money Transfer. The 'variety' refers to the diversity of countries from which he sources cheap goods of practical utility to his (small) Somali community. In this case, he draws together cosmopolitan goods – Chinese blankets etc – to service a multicultural community. Through his other business activity, however, he acts as transmitter rather than receiver, disbursing funds back to different places in Somalia. As H—— points out, even the more powerful multicultural communities effectively service more than

Cosmetic Production

one community. Just as his shop attracts people from all communities – besides providing a specialist Somali service – so the neighbouring Afghan supermarket supplies him with many of the basic food items he needs, besides offering him additional goods that he would not otherwise try. H—— emphasised the importance of continuity at one address in achieving this double function. Continuity is important in stitching together the overlapping functions. He pointed to the laybys (piles of clear plastic packaged blankets) as evidence of a trust that underwrote individual transactions. It is his own continuity in place that provides what he described as 'the bridge' between members of his community and between his customers and new customers. The bridge is a cosmopolitan metaphor, not a precinct-style multicultural figure of speech. It is interesting that what counts in this business practice is not a valuable stock-in-trade but an intangible service. Despite his modest interior *décor*, H—— is understood to put people in touch with articles and families at a distance. In a sense he lays up rewards elsewhere. The modesty of the appearance disguises the ambition of the investments he facilitates.

This distinction is not simply functional – a matter of professional opportunism: it articulates a fundamental dimension or aspiration of work, which is the labour of cosmetic production. From a multicultural perspective, the costumes, jewellery and other appurtenances of cultural distinctiveness belong to a closed economy, one that aims to preserve the distinctiveness of a particular ethnic group. Skills such as tailoring and alteration are ancillary and serve solely to intensify the singular appearance of individuals in relation to their prescribed social settings. However, as the 'cosmopolitan' character of M——'s other customers illustrates, the deeper commercial value of her skills leads in a quite different direction, towards the art of disguisement or transformation. In the broader community, skills in creating clothes that fit also enable people to fit in; they enable people to appear in styles and forms that conceal individual deformities or perceived differences. The result is not homogeneity because the tailor or seamstress employs styles, patterns, fashions and materials that circulate in the collective imaginary as archetypes of desirable personas. In other words, in this other office, the tailor works to improve the cosmetic appeal of the public domain, *the ambience*; she works to connect people through a shared discourse of adornment, attraction and affect. The act of 'alteration' corresponds exactly to the cosmopolitan goal of producing a shared otherness through the medium of shared styles. Those who participate in or support alteration identify themselves with certain social and sartorial performances. They assume that the public space is not given but is the potential site of co-appearance. Style in this context is as fundamental as the organization of streets and facades into a reasonably coherent visual and spatial experience. Yet, as in the case of M——, possession of the skill to alter is also a proud indication of cultural identity, strength and pride.[3']

I have quoted these conversations and the reflections they stimulated at length to show how an idea forms out of a multitude of opinions, interests and interpretations. In this passage, only three conversations are recorded; however, they occurred at a generative moment in the enquiry, one pivoted between a substantial exploration of the background literature (covering such topics as cultural heritage, community services, environmental sustainability and other reports, strategies and proposals) and a growing awareness of the sterility of the officially convened project environment. At a moment of breakout, on the verge of wanting to channel first impressions, ideas picked up from reading in-between the lines of the reports and intuitions of what the future place could be (drawn from earlier story-into-design public space design projects), I was motivated to discover creative mechanisms that brokered communication between the actual and the ideal – between two ideologically ossified formations, the organic multicultural community composed of a myriad of non-communicating, egocentric groups and the 'Australian community' of nationalist sentiment, itself incompetent to recognise, let alone evaluate, difference. However, the orientation of the questions towards models of societal organisation that avoided these extremes was without guile: the transition from the fragile hypothesis of a revived cosmopolitanism to an embodiment of the cosmos in the cosmetic could hardly have been foreseen.

This was a finding that had a practical, operational value. It resolved the localist–universalist, ethnocentric–Western (implicitly white) normative dichotomy by a kind of intensification of both (in which both were significantly transformed). What we called at this time a *cosmopolitan* vision for the new civic space was connected to a cultivation of highly situated and context-dependent artisan skills. In the old sense, the cosmetic is the adornment, the visible face of the cosmos: it is cosmetic because Nature is beautiful. So with the cosmopolitan labour of alteration: it fits out the places of the world to be fit to be lived in. In contrast with the essentialism of the multicultural rhetoric of identity, the cosmopolitan labour of world adornment aims at equipping people to enter a new common world, in which acquired characteristics and impure ensembles of physical self-adornment signify a readiness to engage in new forms of sociability. This is not the same as Westernisation, even if the cosmetic and sartorial lexicon is predominantly 'Asian' or 'American': in the context of extreme multicultural diversity, it represents a specific strategy for maintaining the otherness of different communities through a process of self-othering.

Self-altered, self-othered: the new public persona created in this way is not stripped of cultural equipment and attachments but, on the contrary, is able to wear these layers of identity more openly, more tactically and more creatively. It was intriguing in this respect that so many of the shops in the older, internal, bazaar-like passages of the city arcades offered cosmetic services – manicure, pedicure, coiffeur, make-up – and if you looked at the patronage, it was young women of many different cultural and ethnic backgrounds who were paying to look different. There was no sign of multicultural nostalgia here but every evidence of cosmopolitan aspiration, and yet it would be a kind of ethnic correctness to criticise these women for jettisoning their cultural and racial identities. But there was no evidence of this. On the contrary, to judge from the employment of these same women in the local businesses, a stronger face to the shared world increased their confidence in identifying with their own inherited culture. The doubleness of identity implied here was, in fact, the essential mechanism of trade across difference. And it is, of course, the migrant praxis par excellence: as A—— said, in Africa he was not considered 'African'. The cosmopolitan *semblable* manufactured in this way is not identified by their difference; it is a subtly modified new society of alter egos that comes into play.

The insight afforded by the cosmetic praxis of the seamstresses, tailors, repairers, recyclers, refitters and others involved in the industries of adornment was that any attempt to *strip back* the appearance of what was happening in order to arrive at an essential characterisation was mistaken. In other words, the social work of disguisement was not simply a cross-cultural phenomenon characteristic of a new society in formation; it also had a methodological implication – *implication* in the revived sense of infolding. In other words, the anatomical approach to knowledge, in which future plans are erected on the basis of essential, stable concepts, does not work in this context: to know how social life is being produced, it is necessary to abandon the epistemological obsession with stripping away and revelation, and to proceed in an antithetical manner, towards the reveiling of appearances. Like conversation, alteration produces infolding rather than unfolding meanings. Taking advantage of an intriguing pun, you could say that, in contrast with the architectural *fane* dedicated to the memory of the departed, the fane appropriate to the society of continuous self-production is one cognate with the Latin *fana*, the flag or banner, continuously folding and unfolding as it streams in the wind. Turning to the foundational question for any theory of sociability – How do people face each other? – the practice of alteration provides a ready answer: they do it through a disguise which, while it may make them strangers to themselves, fits them to meet others similarly fitted out and to be recognised on their own terms.

This is not, after all, so astonishing. It is perhaps only the reductionist insistence on nakedness, characteristic of the master planning mentality and the positivist identification of truth with nuclearised facts, that makes dressing up suspect. After all, few societies emulate the brazenness with which we interrogate the face of the stranger. Even within the Greco-Roman cultures of public life, it was well understood that access to the agora or forum involved initiation and self-othering. The act of appearing should not be confused with exposing oneself: on the contrary, in public, one covers up. Interestingly, Hannah Arendt identifies this transition from private to public explicitly with discourse – conversation and all the arts of storytelling: 'Each time we talk about things that can be experienced only in privacy or intimacy, we bring them out into a sphere where they will assume a kind of reality which, their intensity notwithstanding, they never could have had before'.[4] That reality is rhetorical: the good work of discourse is to *publicise* the common ground we share – 'the common world [that] gathers us together and yet prevents our falling over each other, so to speak'.[5] And the reason we don't stumble against one another is that the 'transfiguration' of the private produces (or names) a 'world of things…between those who have it in common'.[6]

In this case, to make public is not to expose what was formerly private; it is to dress it up in terms that fit it to circulate in society. The reworking of the intimate that occurs in talking about private things in public clothes uses figures of speech to clothe the naked truth. For this reason, the Greeks called the language proper to the agora *allegory*: allegory is the other speak proper to the public domain. 'Whereas the symbol postulates the possibility of an identity or identification', allegory, viewed positively, 'designates primarily a distance in relation to its own origin, and, renouncing the nostalgia and the desire to coincide, it establishes its language in the void of this temporal difference'.[7] If public space is understood as creating the distance that allows an approach to the other that does *not* lead to enslavement, the collapse of cultural difference, then allegory's recognition of the limits of what can be represented and communicated becomes its greatest political and poetic virtue.[8] The sartorial or behavioural counterpart of allegory is the alteration described earlier. It allows for a self-transformation that is not humiliating, that fits the individual for the changed conditions of public intercourse. The one who remains unaltered upon entering a novel environment risks exposure. The strong French connotation of *expose* is to displace, to throw out, to evict. In this case, to foster a space that is hospitable – the definition, according to Jacques Derrida, of the social – involves neither deposing nor exposing, but a kind of *reposing*, a resettling in a new way, one that, like a question reposed, both unsettles and allows for a fit.[9] What enters the public is what is fitting there, what has been altered and, what is more, what has shown itself fit to be refitted.

Notes

1 Hans Jenny, *Cymatics: A Study of Wave Phenomena and Vibrations*, rev. edn, trans. D. Q. Stephenson, Macromedia Publishing, Newmarket, NH, 2001, p. 255.
2 Healey, 'Planning in relational space and time: Responding to new urban realities', pp. 260–1.
3 Material Thinking, 'Eumemerring: Aspects of Atmosphere, Dandenong Civic Square, Visioning Notes', 1–16, pp. 8–10. Interviews occurred in October 2011.
4 Hannah Arendt, *The Portable Hannah Arendt*, ed. Peter Baehr, Penguin, London, 2000, p. 199.
5 Hannah Arendt, *The Human Condition*, Chicago University Press, Chicago, 1958, p. 52.
6 Arendt, *The Portable Hannah Arendt*, p. 201.
7 Murray Krieger, '"A waking dream": The symbolic alternative to allegory', in Morton W. Bloomfield (ed.), *Allegory, Myth, and Symbol*, Harvard University Press, Cambridge, MA, 1981, pp. 14–15.
8 Maurice Merleau-Ponty describes the distance between the seer and the thing thus: 'It is not an obstacle between them, it is their means of communication' (*The Visible and the Invisible*, ed. Claude Lefort, trans. Alphonso Lingis, Northwestern University Press, Evanston, 1968, p. 135).
9 Jacques Derrida and Anne Dufourmantelle, *Of Hospitality: Anne Dufourmantelle invites Jacques Derrida to Respond*, trans. by R. Bowlby, Stanford University Press, Stanford, Calif., 2000.

20

FABRICATING TOPOGRAPHIES

In Dandenong, we reached the conclusion that themes of hybridisation and appearance merged in the phenomenon of *alteration* (see Figure 23). Alteration might refer to the impact of migration on social, cultural and psychological senses of self, self-becoming and sense of place. It did not imply homogenisation; on the contrary, it might imply the emergence of a new alterity made possible by the relatively benign identity politics found in Australia's secular society. Alteration recommended itself because it was a prominently discernible social practice, evident in the number of tailors, seamstresses and dressmakers associated with a variety of clothes, fabrics and ethnically defined style outlets. The fact that the alteration service on offer in one business attracted local people from outside the ethnic group obviously identified with the business was a further recommendation, as it suggested a concrete practice for the cultivation of intercultural exchanges (rather than the reinscription of Little India–style multicultural precincts). In this context, we understood the proposed civic space as a vehicle for the encouragement of locally related identifications rather than the intensification of inherited identities.[1]

Emerging from this phase of the project, we could see that associations of place with adornment had considerable potential in informing the initial landscape design proposals. But how? How were vernacular practices for fitting out bodies for an emancipated post-traditional secularist public space to be translated into place-making practices? Given that landscape designers derive their vocabulary from functionalist models of social behaviour, wasn't their psychological reductionism, however picturesquely disguised, inimical to the social environment envisaged? What Dandenong's various centres (malls, retail complexes, streets) lacked, one member of the civic space consultative group told us, was 'ambience'; and without this, she said, no program of events, however inclusive, representative or well managed, would work.

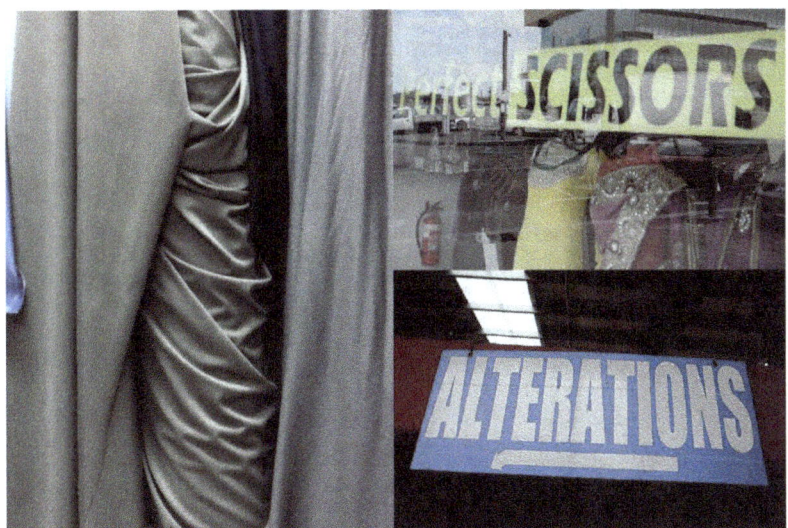

Figure 23 Material Thinking, '*Alterations 4*, programming Dandenong's new civic square', 4 March, 2013, 1–17, p. 2 (detail).

At the time I was brought into the project, the landscape architects had been exploring the notion of the civic square's public domain as a kind of carpet woven from multiple threads, a rendering in brick of Joseph's many-coloured coat, a weaving together of diversely originating threads – and, in relation to the communities in Dandenong, prominently represented in the local businesses in the neighbourhood of the proposed square, broadly relevant to the local focus on apparel. That the carpet could be a sitting down place, a meeting place, a microcosm of the common world that gathers us together, made it an interesting image. However, by itself, the idea lacked critical or creative mass. It bore evidence of a certain multicultural bias; it risked being generic, as most Australian metropolitan suburban shopping streets display carpets with derived Islamic patterning. It seemed to ignore the difference of the public domain from the private one; and, in the context of the push to reconnect landscape design to environmental sustainability, it underplayed any residual claim the ground or genius loci might have on the character of the new place. Could general ideas of pattern and crossweave, multicultural associations of (temporary) place-making and improvised sociability, be developed into a stronger rationale for pattern-making at this place and time? Leaving aside the lie of the land, what relationship could such a device have with Aboriginal Australian descriptions of this place? In their background research, the landscape team had referred to Aboriginal Australian possum-skin cloaks (documenting examples from Victoria's Western District), in whose linings designs are drawn said to represent estates, but no analogy could be claimed between the abstract patterns of the Middle Eastern carpet and any sense of place (topographical, cultural or associational) recoverable from the Dandenong site.

Another non–Aboriginal Australian analogy, we thought, offered a better way forward. In its ancient sense, a map, or *mappa*, was a cloth laid over the table of the Earth. The idea, perhaps, was that the lineaments of geography were indexically traced in its folds: the map exposed the underlay. Or if this 1:1 Borgesian impossibility is rejected, the map was a kind of tablecloth laid over a miniaturised model of the Earth's surface. In any case, in this original version, the value of the map as a description of geographical reality was related to the material from which it was made: the cross-ply linen, from which it would have been difficult to excise all folds, suggested an interest in an earth that could be cultivated, in a complex, cross-ply ground understood practically as earth and water providing the necessities of life (see Figure 24). Here was a notion of the public domain developed in terms of economy rather than politics. The map plotted that part of the world that sustained us: it comprehended, for example, all the parts of the world from which Dandenong's migrant peoples had come.

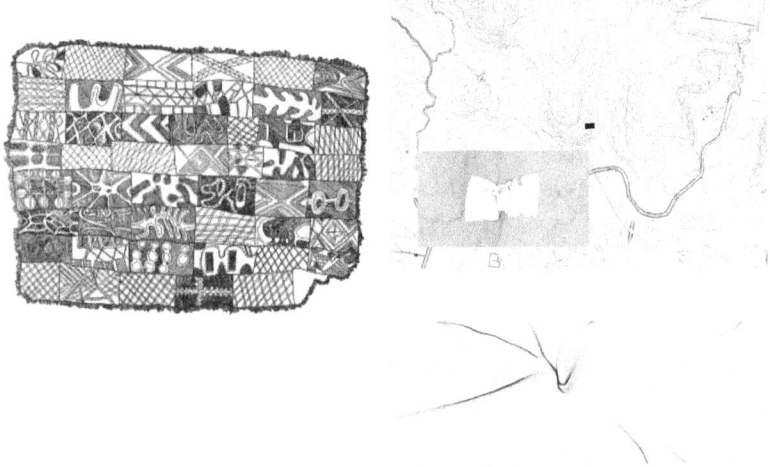

Figure 24 Material Thinking, '*Alterations 4*, programming Dandenong's new civic square', 4 March, 2013, 1–17, p. 3.

This line of reflection was strengthened, or at least found mythopoetic confirmation, when we discovered a similar set of associations in the Greek thinker Eratosthenes, who invented the term *geo-graphy* (probably by analogy with *geo-metry*) and who likened the inhabited world to a rectangle of cloth. This notion was suggestive for another reason: as pointed out before, *Alterations* had shown pretty conclusively that Dandenong's 'multicultural' communities aspired to occupy a shared public space where multicultural differences were transcended rather than reinscribed, but we had struggled to find a term to describe this aspiration. In this context, *ecumene*, the Greek term for inhabited (or inhabitable) earth, was suggestive. When the carpet was reconceptualised as a map-cloth that denoted the inhabited Earth, it acquired a certain specificity in relation to the character of the Dandenong site. Here, at least, was a ground pattern, or earth material, that most people could occupy, an ecumenical estate that transcended origins but also had inscribed into it values common to all cultures: notions of civility, respect and brokered coexistence (being together).

One reason why the comparison of the ground to a *mappa*, or cloth, was creatively stimulating was that Eratosthenes himself had understood the simile as a tool of heuristic investigation. In particular, the idea of a cloth laid over the natural surface of the Earth suggested that the lie of the land (the Earth's irregular topography) could be explained by reference to the behaviour of a rectangle of cloth when it is subjected to various kinds of deformation. Hence, the geographer Strabo reports that Eratosthenes also likened the inhabited world to a *chlamys*, an item of Classical clothing formed when a rectangle of cloth is pinned at two corners on the right shoulder and allowed to fall over the torso (Classical statues of Hermes show this item of clothing).[2] This idea appealed, because it indicated a way to recuperate the natural contours of the site that the landscape design had erased. At the same time, by imagining the slopes and bulges of the site as parts of a giant anatomy (outworks of a buried *macro-anthropos*, perhaps, which in Friedrich von Hardenberg's literary anthropology is to be identified with the political and social order[3]), we had a poetic device to connect the physical site to the cultural determination of its design. In a similar vein, William Blake imagines a transformed London, a revived Albion as a giant man:

> I behold London, A Human awful wonder of God!
> He says: 'Return, Albion, return! I give myself for thee.
> My Streets are my Ideas of Imagination...
> My Houses are Thoughts: my Inhabitants, Affections,
> The children of my thoughts walking within my blood-vessels ...'

And these 'Visions of Albion...Seen only by Emanations, by vegetations viewless' Blake attributes directly to the creative imagination of the artist:

> I write in South Molton Street, what I both see and hear
> In regions of Humanity, in London's opening streets.[4]

What would happen if the ironed-out cloth of the site were reconfigured as a *chlamys*? We would fabricate folds that in some way indicated the body of the Earth. Or – another permutation – what would happen if we inverted this process and, taking the remnant outlines of the giant body secreted in the local topography (within which the site was a 'patch'), drew it up into the figure of the *chlamys*? To explore the design potential of these ideas, we purchased metres of fine, broad cloth, cut them into pieces and draped these over various vertical objects, including me. We spray-painted the draped or shoulder-clasped figures, attending especially to the overlaps created by the scalloping of the folds, and laid the resulting figures on the ground (see Figure 25). The Rorschach-style patterns produced in this way were fairly crude, and it was clear that a *chlamys*-like treatment of the hemline – we had overlaid some googled Classical imagery onto the site with surprisingly good results – required a very precise pinning of the cloth if it were to be satisfactorily imitated. We also found it hard to reproduce the horizontal, crescent-shaped folds characteristic of the lower regions of the *chlamys* when it incorporates the differential fall from the shoulder and the stomach.

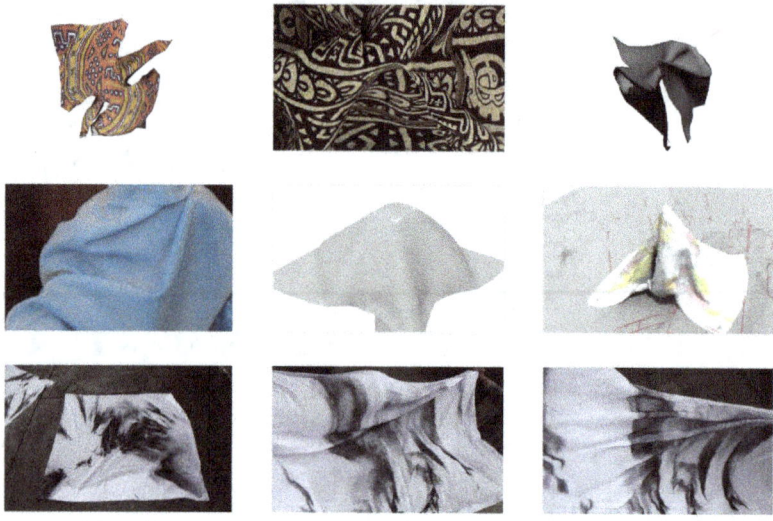

Figure 25 Material Thinking, '*Alterations 4*, programming Dandenong's new civic square', 4 March, 2013, 1–17, p. 4.

At the same time, however, our experiments produced another striking local connection: our draped figures surprisingly resembled the displays of cloth found in Dandenong's fabric shops, where bales are planted vertically on rods and the final metres of the material are wound around the top of the cylinder to create an elegant figure that these days might suggest a doll wearing a burqa and a foot-length robe. We could imagine fields of these forms, perhaps stitched into the fold lines of the resulting ground figure.

Fabricating Topographies

Our first attempts to create intuitive alliances between these drawn-together fields of cloth and the program for the site were not promising. The rationale for entertaining the idea of creating a unified field or informing framework was retrospective: it was recognised that the proposed ground patterns were functional, in the sense of offering playfully suggestive figuration, but they were themselves arbitrarily selected and repetitively deployed. The object of our proposed underlay was to create the kind of interactive network, the relationship of different materially formed knots and nodes, and intermediate striations, that allowed the choreography of the site to be grasped across space and time. Such a ground pattern is influenced by a combination of poetic geography, cultural eidetics and functional programming. In theory, it replaces the necessity for a ground pattern as such. Our approach is deductive: after a set of inductive generalisations from different data has been formed, the resulting Gestalt is applied, and subsequent (non-critical) locations of landscape elements are deduced from it. All of these operations are subject to aesthetic and other criteria, but in principle the underlay removes the need for additional surface decoration. In this case, though, our first iterations of possible fold forms across the site met with considerable resistance. This was expressed as a scepticism about our method – as a doubt that the double gathering up or extrusion of the ground plane and its subsequent resettling with the newly discovered fold lines inscribed into it could provide the kind of patterning that would be apprehensible to the public and likely to induce a sense of place.

On investigation, however, the scepticism arose from the failure of our method to produce *images* that the landscape architects could recognise as functional. While we repeated that a method was being demonstrated, not a design, the resulting discussion was fruitful, as it made explicit what had been a tension, or aesthetic friction, present in the collaboration from the start. The unresolved issue turned on the meaning, function and application of pattern: what is its function in paving, in the distribution of landscape elements and in the façade design of public buildings? What is the relationship between first-order patterns prescribed by the designer and second-order patterns (shadows, congregations of people, the residue of rainfall)? Should patterns concentrate (repetition, figuration) or dissipate (fractal complexification, flow and drift patterns, even random pixelation)? It was suggested that the 'abstract' field of folds would have little appeal to Dandenong communities, who, it was speculated, would be more likely to respond to patterns that were immediately pleasing, intriguing – representing or suggesting unambiguously recognisable styles of marking. The analogy was offered again of the civic space as an outside living room, a playful and eye-catching mosaic of bright patterns from wall to wall that focused the attention of the visitor on the local detail rather than the grand plan.

At this point, we had a minor breakthrough: when the fold images were magnified, they disclosed the crossweave of the material; that is, the large fold blots contained within them a tile-like local detail that possessed all manner of patterning influenced by the quality of the material itself. If the material was already patterned in its constitution, why not extend this principle to the pattern printed onto it: why not think of this patterned overlay and the material together as a single material to be folded and resolved? In other words, the danger of excessive figuration (local detail at the expense of the urban scale) might be avoided if the pattern itself were subjected to the *chlamys* deformation. To test this, we used a number of generic patterns derived from a mixture of African and Asian textiles and extruded them, documenting

Fabricating Topographies

the way they fell back into place: the folded figures thus produced created intriguingly geographically suggestive outlines that might have a strange attractor effect on the extant 'patchwork' of functional spaces. But, more importantly, they transformed the locally repetitive patterns into the building blocks of larger abstract folds, or crests and troughs, running through the field of the plaza. The overlaid pattern was now read as the expression of the underlay; and figuration (or its temptation) was transformed into a set of kinaesthetic cues for inhabiting a dynamic space experienced through the varying scales of its eidetic units as composed of approaches and releases, convergences and divergences – much as the folds falling from the shoulder of the *chlamys* move over the contours of the model (see Figure 26).

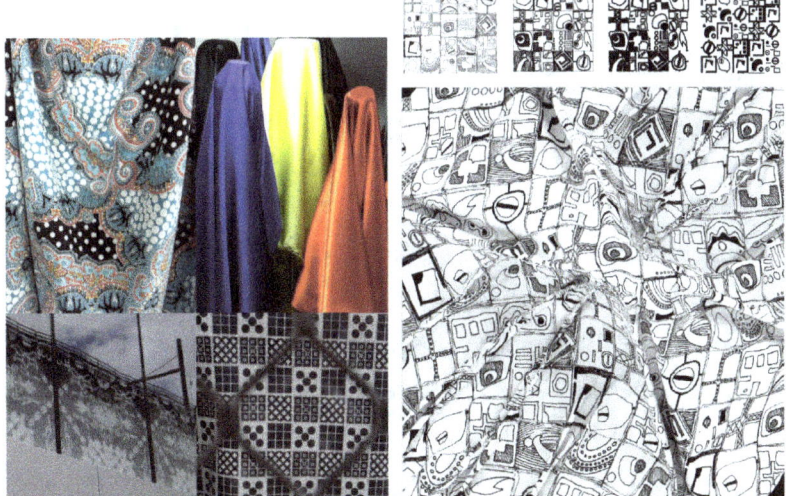

Figure 26 Material Thinking, '*Alterations 4*, programming Dandenong's new civic square', 4 March, 2013, 1–17, p. 5.

Experimentation with various patterns to produce folded topographies was promising – but also limitless. Evidently, there is no end to the variations that can be played on the simple device of the draped figure: for every patterned cloth an infinity of interference patterns can be generated. By the same token, no particular significance any longer attaches to the pattern. For a pattern to be retained in the folding of the surface, it is necessary that the eidetic units of the pattern have a certain regularity. If the surface is to be deformed, a certain ranging of graphemes or pictograms or other eidetic units is needed to indicate a formation. In endowing the ground pattern with a certain legibility, one could be said to stage a transition from textile to text, or at least from weave to script. The procedure for creating a set of eidetic units was – taking a cue from the seeming visual logic of the patterns – to create an icon set across a spectrum between the square and the circle and to populate this ideal sequence with motifs derived from the fabrics collected in Dandenong. The second step was to 'edit' these found icons to produce something like a family resemblance or style. Finally, the icons were arranged chequerboard fashion, in direct allusion to the way the Aboriginal Australian possum-skin cloak was constructed. As a result, the ecumenical pattern could be said to lie within the larger care of Aboriginal Australian space, whose connections to country provide its sinews and joints: without representing Aboriginal Australian patterns, the resulting pattern respectfully paid tribute to the prior organisation of space whose stitching together offers the historical, conceptual, political and poetic underlay of our pattern, the forming ground of the print.

Notes

1. A cosmopolitanism based on identifications echoes, of course, Richard Sennett's preferred model of civility, and one wonders whether Sennett had to be forgotten in order to be absorbed into popular wisdom or whether he was merely prescient. Organicist notions of community, Sennett argues, are predicated on an idea of self-disclosure that, far from securing social relations, is destructive. Or, as he puts it, 'A society in

which liberation of the self replaces liberation from the self as an ideal has obliterated any possibilities of self-transcendence from its moral life' ('Destructive Gemeinschaft', in Alan Soble (ed.), *The Philosophy of Sex*, Rowman and Littlefield, Totowa, 1980, pp. 302, 319).

2 A number of etymologies group the Latin words *pannus*, meaning a piece of cloth, and *pendere*, with the sense of to weigh or weigh down. The association of expansiveness with downward weight – material as drape – is exactly what we sought to investigate. (See, for example, Ernest Weekley, *An Etymological Dictionary of Modern English*, Dover, New York, 1967, entries for *pendant* and *pennon*, pp. 1066–7.)

3 The German Romantic poet Novalis (Friedrich von Hardenberg's pseudonym) held ' a wholly anthropomorphic image of organism': 'The State, said Novalis, was a macro-anthropos, the anatomy of which was composed of the different social orders that formed a polity.' (F. M. Barnard, 'Introduction', *Herder on Social and Political Culture: A Selection of Texts*, Cambridge University Press, Cambridge, 1969, p. 54.

4 William Blake, *Jerusalem: The Emanation of the Giant Albion*, in *Blake: Complete Writings*, ed. G. Keynes, Oxford University Press, Oxford, 1969, p. 665.

21

FITTING THE GROUND

Generally, attempts to derive scripts from movement forms in nature assume a condition similar to that found in writing. The pen inscribes the page, or the chisel grooves the stone. The third dimension of the matrix is disregarded: it may be essential to the production of lines – classical derivations of writing from the serpentine line of the snake, for example, presuppose this – but it is taken to be inert, without any formative intent of its own. Our experiments overturned this assumption, as the patterned surface itself – folded, bunched, evolving catenaries where it hung off the shoulder – started to produce interference patterns whose possibility depended on the three-dimensional mobility of the surface. As the cloth slid over itself, the units of the pattern were progressively deformed, bisected, eclipsed, while along the fold lines they appeared to collide and slip through one another. There was a further interesting development: where the folding of the material was provoked, roughly Euclidean figures (squares, diamonds and circles) started to grow curvilinear: minor anamorphic distortions of the outlines generated elastic arabesques and in some cases graphemes that recalled Arabic script (see Figure 27).

In this way, the tectonics of the surface, the formation and deformation of its topography, provided the mechanism of generating script from ground. A striking parallel existed between the findings of these simple experiments – experiments which reproduced the everyday phenomenon of the 'liquefaction' of flowing 'clothes' described by the poet Robert Herrick[1] – and the process said to have given birth to the first map: a cloth is laid over the body of the Earth, and as a result the topography emerges as a pattern in the cloth. The 'writing' of the map is the inscription of the Earth, neither a representation nor a symbolic equivalent (phonetic, say), but the active, forming trace of its anatomy – much as a dress discloses the movement of limbs beneath it. The writing thus elicited describes the movement form of the ground, the history of folding, uplift and downreach. It is a writing that expresses the depth as well as the width of the ground.[2]

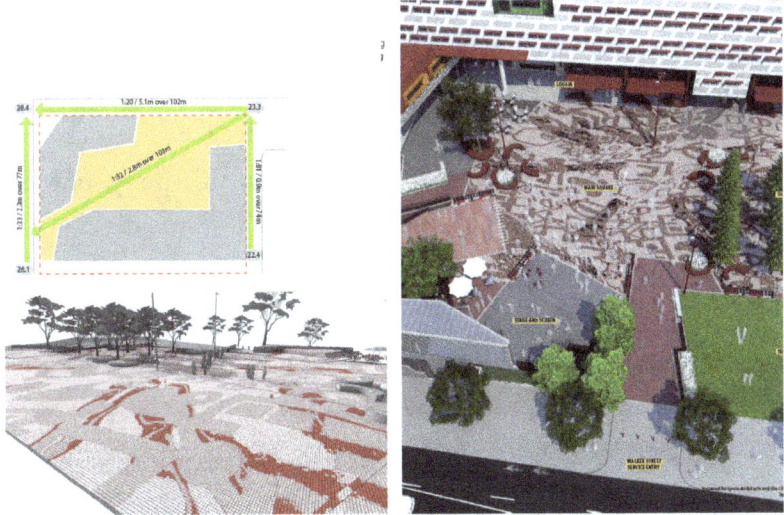

Figure 27 Material Thinking, '*Alterations 4*, programming Dandenong's new civic square', 4 March, 2013, 1–17, p. 6.

The textile into text experiment suggested some interesting reverse inferences. It was noticeable that as the extracted units of the pattern were arranged in the possum-skin cloak chequerboard, they resembled Mayan glyphs; that is, they suggested a writing system composed of logograms, in which individual symbols might represent a word or a syllable. In Mayan, this flexibility or ambiguity is said to reflect the adaptation of the script to new languages. It is intriguing to speculate that the third dimension of script, the unconscious writing of the fold, plays its part in the formation of legible scripts. In the Dandenong context, the indeterminacy of the resulting 'logograms' was consistent with the desire to produce a script of the common place, an ecumenical writing that spoke to all without articulating any distinct, or potentially divisive, message. In the absence of a system of equivalences, the resulting pattern remained tied to the movement forms that had generated it. There appears to be an intuitive, imitative resemblance between handwritten signatures or monogram flourishes and the signature gaits, passages and poses of their authors in public space.[3]

To scale up the chequerboard and apply it to the common place of the public domain was not, from this point of view, either arbitrary or a lapse into the figurative (the eidetic picturesque where the pattern units were justified by their cartoonish evocation of an object). It reconnected the extracted pattern to its topographical matrix at a scale that acted as a choreographic catalyst, an invitation to the public to perform the lineaments of the underlying body through the rituals of sociability. In fact, it is a mistake to talk about scale. The applied ground pattern resists the picturesque expectations of perspectivism. Its arrangement of lines, curves, rings, hooks and doubled figures has no other scale than the one that the *passenger* determines – the one who *weaves* their way through the chiaroscuro labyrinth. The pattern is a net, like the perspective grid, a frame for intrigue, with the proviso that it is moving, shifting, expanding and contracting in relation to the courses steered through it.

Fitting the Ground

Alberto Giacometti insists that the space between people has no scale: the distance is the dimension of approach: therefore, one on the edge of sight is no larger or smaller than the same figure close up; paradoxically, the same figure stands on the verge of infinity when furthest away, disappearance lending appearance its greatest power. Equally, the walking subject is not the puppet of space, having to measure up to their surroundings. Like Giacometti's groups of statues, they are life-sized to their own periplum, and in this sense have no scale at all. This accords with Giacometti's own statement that 'lifesize does not exist. It is a meaningless concept. Lifesize is at most your own size – but you don't see yourself'.[4] Hence, the key to the effect made by the patterned underlay lies in the movement form it evokes, the sense it communicates of coming into one's own being, wherever you are. The pattern is without destination or determination: an encouragement to enjoy the Brownian motion of everyday life. Its appeal comes from the fact that it adjusts to the invisible body of the walker, the peripatetic movement form which the eido-kinetic sense of neighbourhood makes tangible. The pattern works in the way that Maurice Merleau-Ponty's projective imagination works, throwing you out of yourself to be where you want to be already. The pattern is chiasmatic temporally and spatially, capturing the expanded present of co-presencing where the meeting is always occurring and about to occur.

As a result of these experiments we were able to produce a ground pattern for the proposed new public space that met aesthetic and functional expectations. However, the alterations to the *Alterations* pattern involved in fitting it to the existing body of the design raised (again) questions of genealogy and deductive logic: how did the ground pattern derive from an environmental movement form? And how was the leap from a multicultural economy of stitching to a ground design for ecumenical sociability to be explained? Another way to phrase the first question is: how is a moment in the unfolding selected? Digital representations of the *chlamys* had rationalised, or simplified, the fall of the cloth. Instead of trying to copy the complex folds created when a sheet is knotted and allowed to fall naturally from the shoulder, we built a digital model of a square sheet of cloth descending over a centrally located column. The modelling of the cloth's descent, the progressive gathering of the material around the central column, produced a movement form, a simulacrum of the analogue event ready for sectioning or freeze-framing and documentation. The folding pattern we extracted from this experiment – the instant in the folding sequence selected – was chosen on aesthetic grounds: it articulated a radiating set of fold lines and exhibited a knotting at the heart, both these qualities mapping well to the characterisation of the public space as one of gathering and passage.

Post Le Corbusier and Adolf Loos, public space is stripped of its clothing – its habit of encouraging errancy and its facades. The psychological and sartorial expression of the new functionalism is the new identification of authenticity with the face and the suit. The subtraction of adornment leaves people alone with one another, looking for a face in the crowd. Claustrophobia comes from the pressure to respond to every face, the new injunction to interact functionally with those around (an intolerable pressure that in its other expression produces petrification and the sense of an impassable void opening up between oneself and any emotionally satisfying destination). The agoraphobia that modern, pre-planned public spaces create is twinned with a claustrophobia produced by the extreme pressure to present oneself, to be face-to-face. Agoraphobia is due to the withering away of the interstitial nervature of sociability, the meander, the detour – but also, of course, the attenuation of fashion, the drying up, if you will, of the 'liquefaction' of clothes, as Herrick puts it.

In an essay about the psychiatrist Gaëtan Gatian de Clérambault, Joan Copjec relates his interest in drapery to the stripping away of façade ornament and the rationalisation of public space[5] – developments I associated with the intensification of agoraphobia as a symptom of urban unease.[6] Against these modalities of public exposure, de Clérambault clung to an art nouveau sensibility of flowing, semi-transparent garments: in relation to his huge and notorious collection of Moroccan photographs of draped women (but also men), Copjec makes an elegant case for a kind of sublimation, the head of the Police Infirmary for the Insane putting himself (with his camera) in the position of the male Moroccan other. But in my view, this (psycho-)analysis, although acknowledging the epistemological potential de Clérambault gave to the study of clothes, still assumes it lacks ontological value: drapery may make an interesting study, but it cannot supply a grounding framework for the project of knowing the other. A theory and practice of covering up is a direct affront to the totalising gaze of Western science, with its peremptory command to undress and stand naked in the bare light of truth.[7] How, then, can truth reside in folds and pleats, in the fall of the *chlamys* or, for that matter, the lie of the land? And, in the context of present attempts to legislate against the public wearing of the hijab, how can a figure who appears *allegorically*, disguised as another, not be a liar?

However, in the choreotopography of the spaces in-between, it appears to be clothing, folding and unfolding, all the way down and up and round about. 'We have pointed out the schematic flexion of thick cloth, the transparency and limpid tones of thin cloth, the back-lighting seen in interiors or outdoors, the effects of wind, the association of spiral forms to the large movements of the human body, and finally the gestures, unconsciously regulated, of the construction of drapery, as inexhaustible themes of art', writes de Clérambault.[8] And what he writes is not only true for art. These dispositions of cloth make manifest the character of public space, a zone of turbulent complexity or folding together. The body that produces, inhabits and choreographs this zone of constant appearing and disappearing, folding and unfolding, is not the self-conscious Ego, always challenged by the longing to step off the plinth of identity into the swarm of the crowd; it is not the arrows of the others approaching the self across public space; nor is it the fixed subject of social or urban analysis. Rather, it is perhaps something like Paul Valéry's 'Fourth Body', a concept that is admittedly hard to pin down, but which Valéry seems to have imagined as the form human consciousness takes when, to borrow Marina Warner's phrase, it is attuned 'with phenomena according to deep symmetries that remain invisible and impalpable in the ordinary order of things'.[9]

For Valéry's Fourth Body (the other three are the body we inhabit, the body others perceive and the body of science, defined by its exposure to analysis) seems to be a premonition of the human counterpart of quantum physics' hypothesis of packets, bundles or energy elements. Hence, according to one commentator, Valéry's '"indifferently called Real Body or Imaginary Body"…is ungraspable, unknowable and unseen. It is the sort of reality that physicists describe as a thing made of forces, of atoms, of movement, of energy'.[10] At the same time, to describe its appearance, Valéry coins the term *implexe*, which suggests the materialisation of relationality. One might think here of forms of clothing that exist beyond the need of personal protection or adornment: bed clothes, for instance, or curtains. Another commentator interprets Valéry's *implexe* as 'the body that is both real and imaginary. In today's terminology, this is the virtual body: the totality of the body that we own/experience yet can never grasp at this or that moment, by this or that system of thought. This is the complex of all bodies we own/experience as a being-in-the world'.[11]

The Fourth Body endows the natural body with a reflective aspect. The natural body appears only because it is veiled in something larger and invisible. 'According to the philosopher Hiroshi Ichikawa, the body as a realistic synthesis is possible only thanks to the potential of the *implexe*, though it is realized, in a sense, only by deterring (sic) and going beyond the *implexe*. For this reason, the body as a realistic synthesis is deemed both revealing and veiling. Upon the accomplishment of the synthesis, however, the implexe is buried under the subconscious. This fourth body – inasmuch as it is neither a realistically synthesized nor revealed object – is beyond phenomenological description.'[12] The potential of the Fourth Body is to give a face to the environmental unconscious (the world that lies about us beyond grasp but in which we are primordially involved). The derivation of the Fourth Body from de Clérambault's fascination with draping suggests that it is also the figure of choreotopography, the implicating angel that drapes space with the figures of fleeting, desirable passage.

As for the divinities that oversee life in the new society, one thing is certain: they will be in motion and – recalling de Clérambault's employment in the Louvre, where by the examination of the way the draperies were carved he could date the collections of classical statues – we will know they are in movement by the way their garments stretch and bunch, cling to the flesh or billow out. The patron saint of this country is not a Pallas Athene who has been immobilised and rendered statuesque. It is the other Pallas Athene, wedded to the lance rather than the shield. As Ann Shearer reminds us, 'There is another temple of Athene on the Acropolis of Athens, set between the Erechtheum in which she is worshipped together with Poseidon and her own maiden chamber of the Parthenon'. Here, Athene is depicted very differently, as a hunter or runner: 'She has thrown her weight on to her left foot; her knee is slightly bent and her right leg is extended behind her under the folds of her robe; she is all readiness for movement'. Indeed, this 'image of balanced power, remote attentiveness and flowing energy' is not *about* to move but is caught mid-stride.[13]

We do not need to go to Europe to see a landscape inseparable from the dignity of the human pose. Many Victorian photographs exist of Aboriginal Australian men and women wearing the kind of possum-skin cloak illustrated earlier, and whose patchwork of estates, represented as patterns, hieroglyphs or logograms, is inscribed into the lining. Here also exist paintings, notably by William Barak, elder of Melbourne's Wurundjeri people and an outstanding social justice leader, as well as artist. All these materials are well known, but the significance of the contrast between the statuesque poses adopted by the Wurundjeri elders in Fred Kruger's well-known Coranderrk photographs, for example, and the concertina-like animation of Barak's roughly contemporary *Figures in Possum Skin Cloaks* of 1898 (see Figure 28) has not been appreciated. The conga-like processions that Barak draws might be the animation of caterpillar spirits; whatever the case, his concern to depict the fall of the cloaks is notable. Represented is a society where the *implexe*, understood as a principle of folding the self and the setting together into a single and singular movement form, already operates, where a choreotopographical attunement is second nature (see Figure 29).

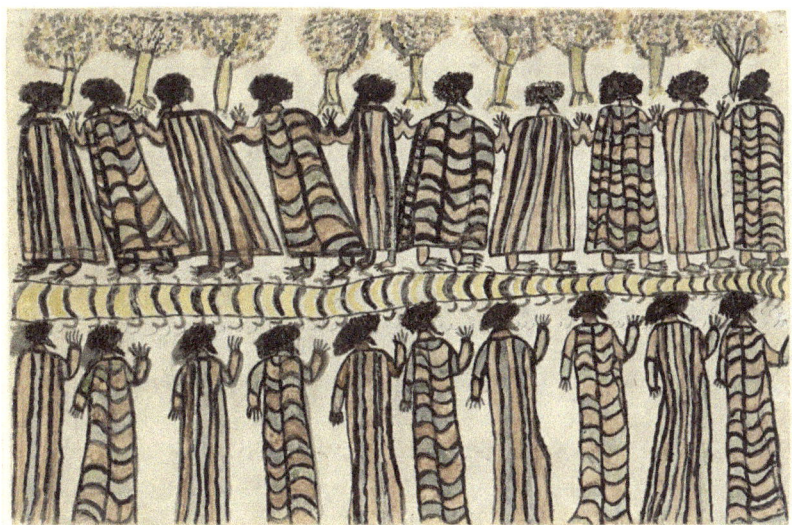

Figure 28 William Barak Wurundjeri, *Figures in Possum Skin Cloaks*, pencil, wash, charcoal solution, gouache and earth pigments on paper, 1280 x 820 mm, 1898, National Gallery of Victoria, accession number 1215A-5. Reproduced by permission.

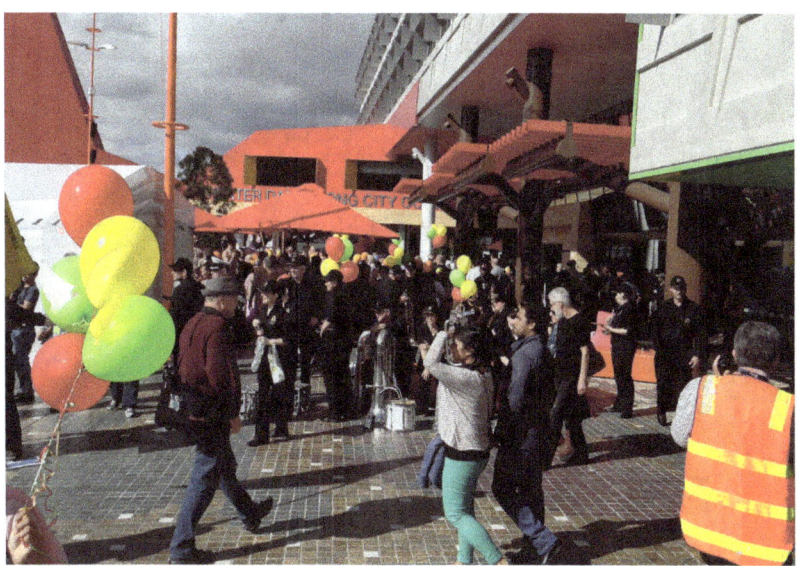

Figure 29 'Dandenong Civic Centre and Square opening', 17 March 2014. Photo: Michael Wright. Reproduced by permission.

Notes

1. Robert Herrick, 'Upon Julia's Clothes', *The Poems of Robert Herrick*, Oxford University Press: Oxford 1924, p. 248.
2. And also, of course, of the sea, which can be described as the effect of liquefaction in the moving parts of the Earth. The sea, like the land, can be thought of as a suit of clothes: 'Did he hold his course/ mid-sleeve/ where, at the wide gusset/ it's thirty five-leagues?' (David Jones, *The Anathemata*, Faber & Faber, London, 1972, p. 97).
3. Carter, *Dark Writing*, pp. 210–11.
4. Reinhold Hohl, *Alberto Giacometti*, H. N. Abrams, New York, 1972, p. 133. For discussion of the implications of this for public space design, see Carter, *Repressed Spaces*, pp. 195ff.
5. Joan Copjec, 'The Sartorial SuperEgo', *October*, vol. 50 (Autumn 1989): pp. 56–95.
6. Carter, *Repressed Spaces*, p. 23.
7. Carter, *Meeting Place*, pp. 33–7.
8. Gen Doy, *Drapery: Classicism and Barbarism in Visual Culture*, I. B. Tauris, London, 2002, p. 120.
9. Marina Warner, 'The Writing of Stones', *Cabinet*, no. 29, 2008, viewed 5 June 2015, http://cabinetmagazine.org/issues/29/warner.php. For his description of the four bodies, see Paul Valéry, 'Analecta', *Selected Writings of Paul Valéry*, New Directions, New York, 1950, pp. 228–235.
10. Frank González-Crussí, 'On my Mind', *Seed*, 16 May 2006, viewed 5 June 2015, http://seedmagazine.com/content/article/on_my_mind_frank_gonzlez-cruss.
11. Sabu Kosho, *On Seiko Mikami's* World, Membrane and the Dismembered Body, V2_, n.d., viewed 5 June 2015, http://v2.nl/archive/articles/on-seiko-mikamis-world-membrane-and-the-dismembered-body.
12. Ibid.
13. Shearer, *Athene, Image and Energy*, pp. 21–2.

Part 5

22

IMPROVISING THE PROGRAM

Alterations was a deviation from the original plan. The invitation had been to develop the 'program' for the new civic square. Instead, our community consultation had led to a ground pattern, a hybrid design that could be classified either as a public artwork or as an integral component of the landscape design. The *Alterations* ground pattern was strategic, in the etymological sense of spreading out, blurring distinct outlines – both in disciplinary and in urban design terms – to create a more complex sense of place. In relation to the 'program', *Alterations* was a creative template, a flexible diagram, score or spatial gesture that had the potential to draw together a variety of cultural and social activities to produce a shared, cosmetically articulated, or adorned, public domain. True to the choreotopographical impulse, we understood our own activities as occurring inside the creative region we were finding. Instead of regarding the ground pattern as foundational – a ground on which figures would be arranged in the future – we took it as the accompaniment of concurrent creative activity, which, in return, was mimetically influenced by its formalisation of a folded space.

Dirk de Bruyn, Soo Yeun You and I reconvened in Dandenong to undertake new movement improvisations. These were broadly of two kinds: daytime pavement performances using fabrics purchased at local textile retail shops and night-time light graffiti performances (see Figures 30 and 31). Both of these activities were located around the perimeter of the civic square site and occurred during the time that the site was being cleared for redevelopment. Both were filmed, using the dynamic in-the-round techniques we had developed in making *Opening*, and we therefore had a record not only of our creative constructions but of the destruction of the old buildings on the site as they were cleared to make a 'blank canvas'[1] for urban redevelopment.[2] (see Figure 32).

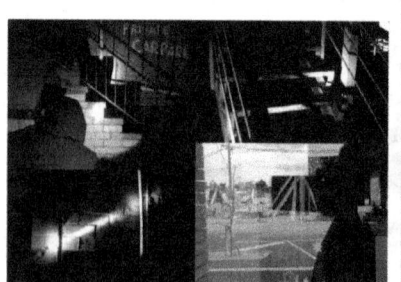
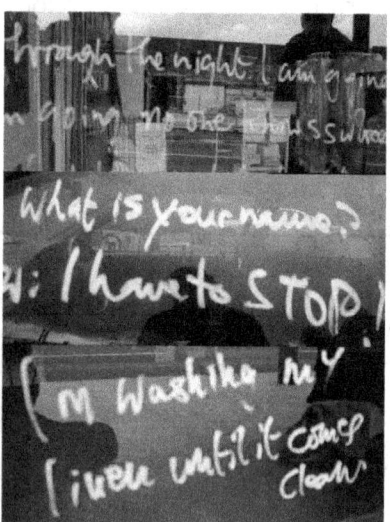

Figure 30 Material Thinking, '*Alterations 4*, programming Dandenong's new civic square', 4 March, 2013, 1–17, p. 8.

It is important to emphasise the interiority of the process and, further, the conviction we had that the process not only *was* the reality but was a reality that displayed structure (to recall A.N. Whitehead). The program that we were materialising through our improvisations and their video documentation was not retrofitted onto a place already defined by liveability criteria. It was an analogue of the destruction–construction dialectic bringing the

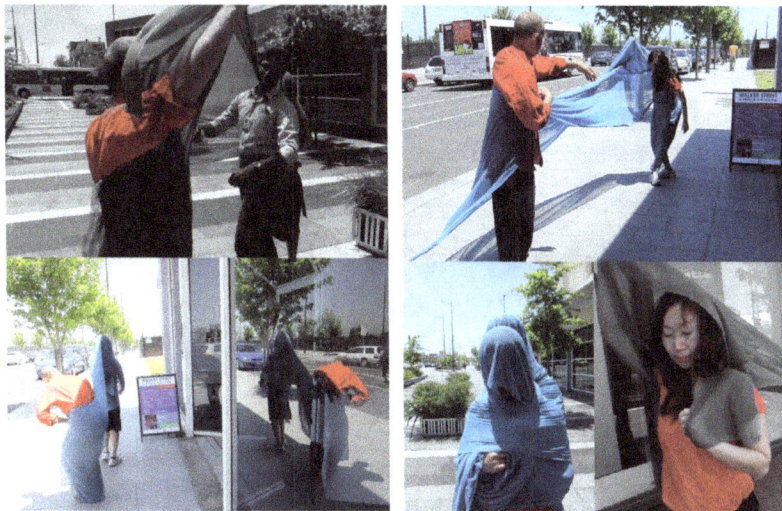

Figure 31 Material Thinking, '*Alterations 4*, programming Dandenong's new civic square', 4 March, 2013, 1–17, p. 9.

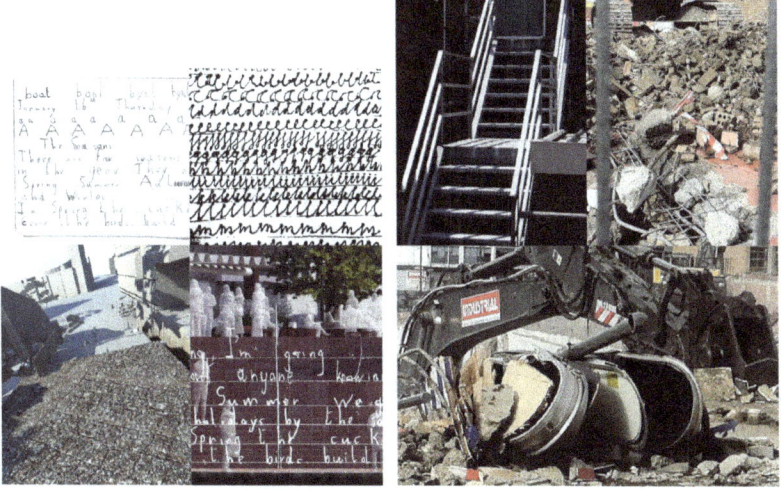

Figure 32 Material Thinking, '*Alterations 4*, programming Dandenong's new civic square', 4 March, 2013, 1–17, p. 7.

new place into being. If our actions traced out passages, they did so in relation to the transformation of the site. They were, in this sense, mimetically inspired. They followed the ruin of the buildings through lines of flight that could be construed as emotional arabesques or vortices of mingled defiance and grief. In these actions, we were locating the future program of creative activity at this place in the character of the passage (which we undertook to witness and re-create).[3] The eido-kinetic intuition mentioned elsewhere is an intuition of the fit between the mobile body and its surroundings. It refers to our ability to judge distance, to calibrate intervals, to throw ourselves into space and land safely. Exponents of parkour typically excel in this kind of rhythmic space navigation. In the improvisations with streaming cloth and the nocturnal inscription of windows and façades, we were invoking this sense of fit aesthetically: like the conductor whose baton inscribes in air the rhythmic architecture of music, we were outlining the ghosts of runs, buildings – that is, in a state of falling. And, as the field diary from that time indicates, we had the impression that these passages also altered us, returning us to our different, but shared, migrant destinies.

> With Dirk I grafittied windows in which the oblique reflection of the Dandenong demolition site was visible: it felt like I was using the cursive writing to stitch a healing sentiment into the rubble and across the exposed walls. A certain illegality associated with this window work curtailed the length of the phrases and shaped the speed of the writing. The line of the continuous writing becomes in the filming magnified, overlaying the reflected image like a road, a cloud trail or a mist. I was sad that the site was already reduced to one central shed (internally wrecked and hollowed out) surrounded by levelled concrete platforms. The outlines of the demolished shops could be seen and there were

two great low pyramidal piles of bricks. The shops are swept away; the stock, the community connections, the talk — even the imaginal interflow created by the front window. The result does not feel like an exposure: it is a more complete erasure that feels to me filled with anger. Why is such resentment associated with transformation? What would a minor transformation be? In a way this is the purpose of our improvisations: to create an archive of minor transformations that rebuild rather than dismember. This approach is neither prospective nor retrospective (the approach associated with documenting the site ahead of destruction and afterwards producing an exhibition, work of public art, etc)…

We use torches to transform the steps that form the exoskeleton of the interior of the site. In this exercise the geometry of the railings is projected onto the adjacent walls. In this way the movement of the eye/light/observer is turned into a transformation or analysis of the site. The shapes stretch, broaden, climb up the wall or suddenly shrink in a way that can be controlled so that an animation occurs. The line, the angle, the cross come alive, acquiring the vitality of insect legs or crab legs. The exoskeleton starts to walk, as if alive. This is one iteration of choreotopography, where the choreography consists of the artist's manipulation (or dramaturgy) of the built forms. In this instance, the animation produces an infrastructure, a movement scaffolding that shelters (or could shelter) the passers-by wherever they go. The eido-kinetic intuition is the cognitive mechanism that recognises the human affordances these projective geometries and overlaid arabesques create. In another game we play at light writing. The illumination seems important where the buildings are no longer lit up…

The period of transition is affecting: a man approaches us, distressed to find that the emporium he remembered from the 1970s is boarded up, fenced off and in a state of progressive wreckage. He is talking about the escalator, the Aladdin's Cave feel of the old shop. It is the second occasion that he has visited the site to photograph it. What is he photographing? The exposed parts of the interior that he recognises? Or something like the widening void? His anxiety makes the disappearance appear. When the row of street shops can no longer be taken for granted (as a kind of subliminal affordance), it becomes visible; that is, its invisibility is noticed. As the witness of absence, the man suddenly finds a vocation: he is photographing the void. Only, the void is strangely animated. While cordoned off from public access, it resembles a public stage where novel rituals are performed: further demolition, the consolidation of rubbish hills, further excavations and, strangest of all, an excrescence of temporary worksheds. These architectural weeds clothe the site the bulldozers have stripped…

Is the appeal – the ambiguous fascination – of the site due to the historical experience of the multicultural collectivity? How broadly can the ritual of redevelopment be interpreted? Is migration in general an act of destruction/reconstruction? Is there a historical sensibility attuned to scenes of violent destruction, haunted by memories of panic-stricken flight, temporary shelter and reclamation? If there is, the guerrilla activities we perform are concomitant acts, materially and psychologically aligned with a collective experience of displacement. Classified as transgressive, they protest against loss. However, their mimicry of lost buildings and the manner of their collapse is therapeutic. Rehearsing what has happened, and what goes on happening (even where the country is said not to be at war) they find and outline the reason of its going: the animation of destruction reincorporates it into the living body. When it does this, the double condition of the migrant is felt. The rooms exposed and gouged, progressively reduced to rubble, are the places we came from. They are cliffs, coastlines. They are our parents. These actions are moulds of shells, they are gestures of the hollows we no longer occupy…

These performances are not 'site-specific'. They are not fitted *to* the site but spring from the concrete materiality of the situation, which includes not only the vanished forms of the buildings and their negatives (the carparks) and frames (the external staircases, the lanes, the friezes of cyclone fencing), but also 'those things that would seem to be laughable, such as Hair and Mud and Dirt or any different thing that's very worthless and lowly.' Instead of representing destroyed solids, as an artist might reproduce from memory an urban view, our arabesques spring from the room of the place, from the volumes that always existed in addition to the masonry enclosures. These volumes (exterior to the former buildings and interior to them when they existed) belong to a higher topological order – call it the hollow – where things appear. It feels appropriate that the fenced off building site is 'plunged into darkness'. Our torches stitching loops of light into the abandoned laneways do not offer a simulacrum of natural light. They illuminate the dark. They suggest the presence of ghosts.[4]

Soo Yeun You's pavement divagations with flowing sheets of silk were ably complemented by Shaun McLeod, a dancer colleague from Deakin University. Their joint manipulation of the materials mediated what Michael Jackson refers to as the 'intersubjective experience', their mimetic response to each other illustrating the point that identity is '"mutually arising" – as relational and variable'.[5] This is an insight with peculiar application to the migrant, whose identity is mimetically formed, usually in relation to a phantom of the other, so that frequently one has the sensation of dancing with ghosts. However, the difference of these rituals laid out along the edges of the site – where they acted as modest ceremonies of deconsecration, returning a special place to general use – lay in their exchange with the physical environment. The wind, for example, determined the wave patterns formed in the flowing cloth, as well as the direction and amplitude of the billowing. The adjacent building site provided stage sets, inviting temporary adornments, or an *arte povera*, of street-edge scenography.

As the origins of these windings and unwindings were the alterations observed in the collective life of the community, they not only illustrated Michel de Certeau's contention that stories are 'spatial practices' but inverted the genealogy of forms. If it is true that stories 'bear within them ghostly reminders of our quotidian journeying to and fro in our constructed environments', then, we showed, it is also true that stories can provide choreotopographical cues. If stories can 'convey in words a sense of the body-subject occupying, inhabiting, and moving through space, thus transforming it into places embued with particular meaning and specific presence',[6] then, equally, gestures born of the materiality of the situation can perform the same role, serving to give what has been stripped of affect and rendered a blank canvas once again a history, expressed in the passage of wind-streaming cloth or pencilled arabesques of light.

In other words, *Alterations* not only provided the creative template of the program; it embodied that program in the action research performed to discover the meaning of the place – a meaning we identified with the historical transformation occurring. Late in 2013, we presented some of the outcomes of our work, including the four screen video work called *Loops*, in an exhibition at the Walker Street Gallery and Arts Centre, in Dandenong, explaining:

> The ground pattern of the new Civic Square is inspired by the culture of 'alterations', understood as a service for the alteration of clothes but also as a social aspiration: in the new Dandenong the new public self involves self-alteration, the remaking of identity. New forms of sociability are associated with the resewing of traditional materials into new garments. The cinematic equivalent of this is the camera moving through the urban fabric like a needle, sewing together images into a new understanding of place. Loops occur in film, in urban transportation, in acrobatics and are essential in all forms of stitching, knotting and knitting. When a trajectory returns to its point of origin after making a detour, it exhibits the phenomenon of feedback. The repetition of a passage produces something new: attention is drawn to a site of production – and elements are suddenly drawn

together, recognised, and a relationship between them established. In skating or sewing the loop has a temporal significance. Looping doubles a gesture, introduces a habit: excessive looping is baroque and can be a sign of disorientation, distress or turbulence. Eddies in fast-flowing water, arabesques forming at the edge of clouds: these are also loops – open loops that continuously break into spirals.

In this work loops are studied in public space. The gesture of writing is interpreted as a way of conjuring up space. Many of the scenes in *Loops* are like graffiti in air: they show lines growing out of glass or walls that could easily be diagrams or histories of flight. Laid over urban scenes – very often mirrored in street glass – they mimic the ways in which people produce the passages they need. They are like forces of attraction scratched into the urban atmosphere. In Dirk de Bruyn's work, the camera is inside the process, grooving the physical environment with its own wandering line of desire. The effect of his restless return to certain points of departure is to sew together fragments in a way that suggests a public space that is turbulent, woven out of surfaces that reflect other surfaces and which together trace the local history of time.[7]

Notes

1. See Chapter 13, note 5 above.
2. The destruction of the old buildings and the construction of the new ones was also documented from an adjacent building. The time lapse record was later incorporated into *Loops*, the video work and exhibition composed from these materials (Dirk de Bruyn, *Loops*, video installation for four screens, first shown at Walker Street Art Gallery and Arts Centre

as part of Paul Carter, Edmund Carter, Soo Yeun You, Dirk de Bruyn, Glenn d'Cruz, Shaun McLeod, 'Alterations: the Exhibition' (17 October–2 November 2013).

3   After all, this is not such a radical proposal: while a work of art is situated in space, 'it will not do to say it simply exists in space; a work of art treats space according to its own need, defines space and even creates such space as may be necessary to it'. Henri Focillon, *The Life of Forms in Art*, trans. C. B. Hogan and G. Kubler, Zone Books, New York, 1989, p. 65. Projects like *Alterations* merely extend Henri Focillon's observation to the design of public space: considered as an artwork, public space also 'treats space according to its own need'.

4   Material Thinking, '*Alterations 3*, project notebook, 2011–2012, pp. 1–30, p. 26', June 2013, quotations from Carter, *Material Thinking*, pp. 57–8.

5   Michael Jackson, *Minima Ethnographica: Intersubjectivity and the Anthropological Project*, Chicago University Press, Chicago, 1998, p. 7.

6   Ibid., p. 32, citing Michel de Certeau, *The Practice of Everyday Life*, 1984, trans. S. Rendall, University of California Press, Berkeley, Calif., p. 118.

7   Material Thinking, '*Alterations 3*, project notebook, p. 28.' August 2013.

23

THE HAUNT OF GHOSTS

These activities give a new meaning to the idea of fit. Fitting in is, in this scenario, a matter of continuous self-alteration. Such flexibility may be a feature of successful social adaptation and growth. The essence of a feedback loop is the flexibility of its components: parts must be able to flex in relation to one another. If 'flexibility may be defined as uncommitted potentiality for change',[1] then fitting in cannot be pre-planned or programmed. In contrast with the 'human planners and engineers' – represented in this case by the state government agencies and local government officers charged to 'deliver the project' – *Alterations* was committed to the proposition that 'the pathways of change would be governed only by equality of probability'.[2] Fitting in may be, as Constantin Doxiadis suggests, a basic condition of sociability – intersubjectivity is 'a force field of human interaction in which contending needs, modes of consciousness and values are forever being adjusted, one to the other, without any final resolution'.[3] Focusing on the forces shaping external structures, Doxiadis envisages a continuous feedback between humans and their settings that allows for the development of new modes of living together. However, evolutionary, interactive, mutually arrived at articulations of fit such as these are remote from planning definitions of fitting in.

Many terms or points of reference in master planning documents tacitly acknowledge the authority of ecological theory. Indeed, the current fashion for naming master planning *place-making* unconsciously revives the old sense of ecology as the study of the house or dwelling place, the idea in both cases being that human life is an interaction between human and non-human systems at that place or within that habitat. A term like *resilience*, for example, which is very popular with politicians attempting to boost community optimism in the wake of a disaster, implies not only bouncing back after disturbance but a richness of cultural identity comparable to the biodiversity needed to underpin environmental resilience. The notion that planning should be *holistic* invokes another ecological proposition, that systems are more than the sum of their parts and organise themselves in ways that cannot be fully predicted (or broken down). However, the translation of ecological ideas into the design of the *oikos* (understood broadly here as the meeting place or home of a community) remains problematic. Perhaps it has to remain this way: if a planning culture is to encourage holism, then, logically, it must resist holistic gestures. Only by leaving things to chance, or creative community self-organisation, can something vital emerge. The enthusiasm of planners for *revitalisation* – another nod in the direction of ecological metaphors – is, as we have seen, usually a belated reaction to the fact that functionalist, interventionist planning from a former era has killed the very community it was intended to build.

In other words, ecological metaphors are used without any serious reciprocity with the environment being considered. 'Judgement about quality can be made in several ways in terms of the relation of every individual to his environment – that is, his relation to nature, society, shells, and networks – and the benefit that he gets from these contacts. We can measure his relations to air and to its quality; to water in his home, in the river or lake, and at sea (its quality and his access to it); and to land resources (their beauty and accessibility) and the recreational and functional facilities provided by them'.[4] These criteria exemplify the 'judgement about quality' that planners understand when they talk about place-making, but it is obviously very dated. Its chief problem is its failure to factor in a cybernetic awareness of the mutual modification involved in the exchange between society and setting. Instead of developing techniques for designing change, for marking and navigating complex processes of alteration, it perpetuates a figure–ground model of sustainable human activity: 'Human cultures are strongly influenced by ecosystems, and ecosystem change can have a significant impact on cultural identity and social stability. Human cultures, knowledge systems, religions, heritage values, social interactions, and the linked amenity services (such as aesthetic enjoyment, recreation, artistic and spiritual fulfilment, and intellectual development) have always been influenced and shaped by the nature of the ecosystem and ecosystem condition'.[5] This is no doubt indisputable, but the implicitly normative condition that underwrites these statements – that, ideally, society exists in a state of being in which forces of becoming represent a risk to rationality – is obviously unsustainable.

These interpretations represent an ossified idea of ecological systems, which, in fact, are characterised by the kind of complexity that fosters emergence, transformation and growth. Amy Kulper points to this distinction when she asks why architectural discourse on morphological change (key figures here are D'Arcy Wentworth Thompson, Rudolf Arnheim and Henri Bergson) is 'so consistently forgetful of its ecological origins? Why is a formalist monologue embraced at the expense of a situated dialogue between morphology and ecology?' Morphology might be characterised as the discourse of development: 'Morphology is a relational and situational field attentive to the small changes that constitute development; second, this attentiveness to change privileges communicative exchanges between the organism and its environment'. Morphology finds its counterpart in 'contemporary interests in parametrics, versioning and digital form', but, as Kulper notes, these interests adapt 'the representational conventions of morphology' without any epistemological rigour. In particular, they ignore the concrete situation and conditions of morphological change or, as Kulper puts it, 'a version of ecology without the oikos'.[6] But the attachment of architecture, or any place-making activity, to place is delicate, especially when the place in question is associated with dereliction, homelessness and the blank canvas of planned amnesia. In these circumstances, the transformation of an inhospitable site into one of hospitality involves confronting the demons of destruction. It may entail negotiating the double aspect of the host, simultaneously hospitable and hostile. The *oikos* in this situation is not defined as the ties to place but as the process of tethering. The object remains the pursuit of sociability through the shaping of the dwelling place, but the place, or network of relations, signifying home, is constantly morphing. Further, the development of new social relations may need to have the hollowness of homelessness at its heart.

An interesting study University of Melbourne colleagues and I conducted in 2006–08 of the experience of transnational and temporary residents in inner Melbourne inadvertently cast light on these negative place-making mechanisms. I say inadvertently because the study's goals were framed in entirely positive terms: by interviewing overseas students about their experience of studying in Melbourne, it was hoped we could identify improvements that could be made – to residential services, to public facilities and above all to mechanisms assisting them to fit in. As a particularly ephemeral form of migrant, living in parenthesis, as it were, while obtaining a professional training, students predominantly from South-East Asia make no mark on the symbolic apparatus of the city: at right angles to the longitudinal history of nationhood, their fleeting presences leave no permanent trace, whether in the form of public monuments, new institutions or even modified academic curricula. They pass through like gingerly welcomed ghosts, tolerated, and nominally embraced on the understanding that, in due course, they will obediently go away or assimilate.[7]

The assumptions of the study were perhaps questionable: in the light of what happened, it could be argued that the researchers brought a ghost community into the room. While it was clear that temporary and transnational students did not fit into a community conceived in organicist terms as homogeneous and geographically delimited, it was also obvious that the category *transnational and temporary* was an invention of our own. Our interview-based methodology was also open to question, as it granted no epistemological value to the performativity of the situation. Participants in the interviews were treated as neutral subjects whose testimony could be taken as empirically reliable. A collusion between research techniques and research subjects was likely, especially as the two hundred students who dutifully drew their personal maps and offered extensive commentary on their perception of the relative welcome afforded by different parts of the neighbourhood were guests of the very institutions (University of Melbourne and Royal Melbourne Institute of Technology) auspicing the transnational and temporary study. Quite apart from the ordinary protocols of politeness (it is unseemly to criticise the manners of one's host), criticism could expose individual students to retribution (not in Australia, but in their home countries, where a vigilant eye was kept on any sign of political activism or dissent). Finally, there was a discursive double bind that, in my estimate, we were reluctant to acknowledge: the majority of the students interviewed shared the educational culture of the interviewers; in addition, many of them were studying in place-making disciplines (architecture, landscape architecture, planning and so on), in which they were acquiring critical vocabularies that were functionalist, positivist and rationalist.

The results of the study have been published. The key point here is that, despite the desire to fit in – politically, but also as a goal of good urban design – there emerged in the students' responses a surprising projection that could not have been anticipated. Despite the researchers' conscientious focus on the measurable, the representable and the discernible, there emerged in the students' accounts of their experience of the city a ghost community, an invisible but vigilant troop of strangers, characteristically inhabiting the derelict land of the old Carlton and United Brewery, located midway between the two campuses. We had noticed initially a negative fact about the hand-drawn or hand-annotated maps that the students executed. As obvious as the scoring of habitual routes were the unscored areas lying in-between. Perhaps to call them negative was too strong, because, in an analogous exercise designed to measure the affect of different locations, we also seemed to find that these same zones bore neither negative nor positive connotations: they were simply places without qualities, or non-places. One of these was the aforementioned brewery site. As a derelict and fenced-off space partially bordered by disused factories, it may not have counted as a place in the sense the students imagined we meant. Either it was genuinely unknown, which, given the site's central location within our study area, would have been a curious instance of environmental editing; or it was not unknown, but simply ignored for the purposes of our enquiry. Alternatively, it was known in the negative sense that it was consciously avoided. Either way, in a second exercise, we put the site on the map and asked directly for any physical observations, emotional associations or other reflections that our study group might care to share.

It was here that something curious emerged. Beside the kinds of responses already alluded to – positive suggestions covering a range of options for the future reuse of the site and its environs – we also found that some of our students considered that the site already possessed a community. It was not an empty site awaiting development; it had a territorial charge, a cultural identity and an urban significance, all of which impacted directly on the everyday lives of the respondents. Unknown, unmarked and indifferently regarded within one frame of reference, within another it seemed to occupy a pivotal position – quite literally as it caused daily flight lines to hinge and split. No one crossed it, but many were obliged to go along one side of it or another. One student remarked, 'I don't particularly enjoy going anywhere near that area. I've been there once at night – very late at night, after the last trams – and it was the hang-out of a lot of scary types'. Another (who had taken part in a film project on the site) said, 'It was a bit scary as well because there could've been any [sic] homeless people inside'.

Yet another, querying the description of it as an empty site, speculated that 'maybe it was just one of those places…there's always smokers down there. They hang out the front out here…I think they work in here – in the bit behind'. These testimonies can be multiplied. Another student commented on the wire fence and the 'No Entry' signs: 'Seems to have a bit of a druggie feel, like there'd be homeless people there', and added, candidly enough, 'I don't know why I have that image'. In any case, that image was replicated in many of the map annotations, where phrases such as 'abandoned, empty', 'haunted place: it looks scary', 'quite a few people thought it was a prison' were reasonably typical.[8]

As far as we could tell from our enquiries, this impression of a ghost community secretly occupying the ruined site is fanciful. The individual testimonies appeared to extrapolate from single observations – of unruly behaviour at a public house on the north-east corner of the site and of illegally dumped rubbish (including mattresses) on the site itself. The site was difficult to access and, while it might occasionally have harboured drug users, was essentially unoccupied. The ghost community projected onto the site was not a sociological datum but a symptom of the uncomfortable recognition that the brewery site, far from being a non-place, was, in fact, a place in a far stronger sense than any of the places currently available for meeting or congregation. These latter places, the interviews showed, were not perceived as powerfully attractive. The shopping plazas and associated eating places were more or less welcoming, in the sense that they were not considered unfriendly. Although representing positive places from a planning point of view, they were from these users' perspective negative places, places without communities, empty of collective cultural attachments, socially, ethnically and behaviourally unmarked. From this point of view, the brewery site, far from being empty, was strongly marked. It was perceived as having a history ('very historical', as one respondent put it) and a character that did not include these students. If it was empty, it was because at some point it had been abandoned. But the residue of this history of prior occupation persisted and cast a shadow over the way it was interpreted. It was a non-place, out of bounds, precisely because it was occupied, haunted.

The haunting could be interpreted another way, as a freedom to develop its own program: where nothing is planned, anything might happen. The positive aspect of this haunting emerged in the observation of another student:

> It's on the fringe of the city and all the perfectness [sic] of the city. When you go in and out of the city, you always go past it and I love it because it [is] so run down and just really abandoned and empty. You walk in there and you see people have got their mattresses and stuff like that. You think a few people are crashing there. It's free from this perfect organization in the city. It seems to be the first encounter with this sort of roughness. You feel like if you went in there, there would be no hassles, there would be nothing, you could just do anything, because it's unkempt.

On the margins, it engages the imagination. As a fat margin, a weed-bound labyrinth of fallen masonry, abandoned girders, threaded with an informal network of trails, such ruined sites share the characteristics of the 'space on the side of the road' explored by Kathleen Stewart, 'a place that insists on the necessity of gaps in the meaning of signs and creates a place for story – for narrativising a local cultural real. Here a prolific narrative space interrupts the search for the gist of things and the quick conclusion with a poetics of deferral and displacement, a ruminative re-entrenchment in the particularity of local forms and epistemologies, a dwelling in and on the cultural poetics contingent on a place and a time and in-filled with palpable desire'.[9]

Stewart's 'cramped, intimate *hollers* tucked into the steep hillsides like the hollow of a cheek and these winding, dizzying roads that seem somehow tentative, as if always threatening to break off on the edges or collapse and fall to ruins among the weeds' are tenanted and traversed by the marginalised. In contrast, our decommissioned space was also depopulated. But this, perhaps, was only an incitement to fantasy. Stewart asks the reader to 'picture how it oscillates wildly between dreams of order and its prolific excesses, how it drifts in the flux of desire and condenses under its weight and force'.[10] Presumably, this temptation is amplified in the absence of inhabitants. Perceived in the shadows of the destroyed brewery were aliens, not a ghost community (in any organicist sense), but the always alienated or homeless. Since the period of the study, redevelopment has gone ahead: a bluestone facade has been preserved, now signifying tasteful gentrification. There was, as there always is, discussion about how the old history of the site should be represented in the new compound of high-rise apartments and mixed business outlets. But nowhere in the visual and literary documentation of nineteenth-century working conditions did a ghost community appear. In a curious way, the ghost community that the students had discerned, which persisted through the present period of abandonment, ahead of further destruction in the interests of redevelopment, was erased again, confusingly identified with the hapless figures staring out at us from faded Victorian photographs.

The character of this phantom society suggests an important variation on the usual, and no doubt sincere, lament heard among social commentators who ascribe moral authority to the collective memory. For what kind of community is or was the Carlton and United Brewery? To illuminate this point, consider the argument put forward by Mari Paz Balibrea in the context of the recent urban and cultural transformations in Barcelona, in Spain. She points out that the massive overhaul of formerly industrial suburbs has produced a new urban landscape in which relics of the place's working-class history change their meaning. The chimneys preserved as monuments, for example, may be intended to 'become symbols of bygone socio-economic activity', but 'their spatial recontextualisation, the new syntax of space, disconnects them from the local history in which they originated'. Isolated in now predominantly middle-class areas, 'they are rendered increasingly unable to convey a sense of their own historicity to those ignorant of local history'. Indeed, rebranded as landmarks, these fragments conceal 'the complexity of an industrial past characterized by social struggles and human relationships that were lived out on that spot'.[11] But, without wishing to deny that the people who formerly occupied that 'spot' constituted an identifiable community, how sustainable is this metonymic elision of their interests with the morphology of their workplaces? Except in the eye of the nostalgic revenant, it is hard to see how the once belching chimneys of textile factories would elicit much affection. They are from any Marxian perspective powerful expressions of an environmentally onerous and humanly destructive phase of capitalism. They quite naturally (and seamlessly) survive into the tertiarisation of Barcelona's urban fabric.

No doubt Balibrea intends a broader point – that these new industrial monuments are ironic because they appear to license the comprehensive erasure of whole suburbs of collective memory. But my point is simply that, within these disappeared estates, we need to distinguish between the organicist working class and the counter-community of alienation embodied in the architectural forms and functions of the factories. There may have been tight-knit communities outside the factory walls. But inside, there were rows of human automata. Inside, as Henry Mayhew's many descriptions of London's factories remind us, the picturesque image of the domestic sphere was replaced by the terrible sublimity of men and women sacrificed to the deities of capital. These were places where life in any ordinary sense was placed on hold. They were environments where one lived beyond the grave, buried alive in a kind of suspension of routine.[12] To return to the brewery site, considered in isolation from the residential streets around it, it has been from the beginning of its existence, in 1866, unoccupied. Generations of workers may have filed through its doors, but they became something else while they occupied it. Accordingly, there is no lost community in the ordinary sense that can be metonymically invoked through, for example, the preservation of the original Bouverie Street bluestone wall.[13] The brewery has a ghost community, as our temporary and transnational students intuited, but it is composed of aliens, of figures charged with the rehumanisation of places where they (and we) have been dehumanised.

This is our point of contact with the past. There may be limited interest in the archaeology of nineteenth-century working-class Melbourne, but there is an immediate identification with the potentiality of spaces to incubate meeting. We are drawn to places not as historical events but because they suggest the spatio-temporal conditions for things happening or taking place. Far from admiring their stability in time and space, we are drawn in by their power to mobilise space and time, to induce a sense of the possibility of change. These projections are not inconsistent with the preservation of ageing structures; they simply shift the emphasis from the aesthetic to the creative, from the attempt to locate the affective properties of places in certain supposedly objective qualities to a recognition of the role the desire for sociality plays in the production of places and their meanings. Piety has its limits, but the desire to realise the blocked potentialities of the past is limitless and continuous. In a way, we are emotional archaeologists. As cryptographers, archaeologists clear away what is in full view in order to expose what has gone missing. In the field of affect, our study group performed a comparable operation. They saw through the clarities of the emptiness to make out another, vanished anti-community, defined not sociologically but by a shared experience of passage, temporary and transient.

These ghosts *other* the place because they refuse to let its desire to incubate community die down. They insist on an intensity of hope that cannot be driven out or incorporated into a program. They are signatories to the passionate paradox expressed by one of Austrian writer Ingeborg Bachmann's characters: 'Hope: I hope that nothing happens as I hope it will'.[14] Or, as one student put it, 'It is interesting when you go by because why would there be a space in the middle of a very popular place where everyone is and everything's built on, and then there's this random, falling-apart building and a bit of paddock and it's interesting'. For this contributor, the interest of the brewery site resided in the gap that had opened up between facticity and functionality. Here was a place that, in terms of the usual functional requirements of inner urban living, failed to signify. It had no immediately legible social meaning or function. For the same reason, though, it automatically acquired a symbolic value. As an anomaly in the urban fabric, it resisted being assigned a prescribed use-value. And this symbolises something: the possibility of unpredictability in the midst of predictability. If the choreotopography of places denotes the feedback between sociability and setting, then such ruined sites are the memory places from which the negative choreography of the new society derives. As sites making historical absences present, they are the environmental consciences that the artwork alludes to when it adopts the asterisk principle.

Notes

1. Gregory Bateson, *Steps to an Ecology of Mind: Collected Essays in Anthropology, Psychiatry, Evolution, and Epistemology*, University of Chicago Press, Chicago, 2000, p. 505.
2. Ibid., p. 405. We did not mean to be subversive, but we were: it was a striking fact that not a single council officer or councillor visited the *Loops* exhibition. Invitations were issued, prior briefings given, but the five-minute walk between the gallery and the council offices proved an impenetrable barrier.
3. Jackson, *Minima Ethnographica*, p. 14.
4. Constantinos A. Doxiadis, 'Ekistics, the Science of Human Settlements', *Science*, vol. 170, no. 3956, 1970, pp. 393–404. <www.doxiadis.org/Downloads/ecistics_the_science_of_human_settlements.pdf> Accessed 15 June 2014.
5. Millennium Ecosystem Assessment, *Ecosystems and Human Well-being: Synthesis*, Island Press, Washington, DC, 2005, p. 46.
6. Amy Kulper, 'Ecology without the oikos: Banham, Dallegret and the Morphological Context of Environmental Architecture', *Field Journal*, vol. 4, no. 1, 2011, pp. 69, 70, 84.
7. For a summary of the project, see Ruth Fincher & Kate Shaw, 'Transnational and Temporary: Place-making, Students and Community in Central Melbourne', *Planning News*, vol. 32, no. 3, 2006, pp. 12–13.
8. Ruth Fincher, Paul Carter, Paolo Tombesi, Kate Shaw, Andrew Martel, *Transnational and Temporary: Students, Community and Place-making in Central Melbourne; Final Report*, University of Melbourne, Melbourne, 2009, pp. 1–144, p. 96.
9. Kathleen Stewart, *A Space on the Side of the Road*, Princeton University Press, Princeton, NJ., 1996, pp. 3–4.
10. Ibid., pp. 13, 17.
11. Mari Paz Balibrea, 'Urbanism, Culture and the Post-industrial City: Challenging the "Barcelona Model"', in Tim Marshall (ed.), *Transforming Barcelona*, Routledge, London, 2004, p. 209.
12. See Humphrey Jennings, *Pandaemonium, 1660–1886, The Coming of the Machine Age as Seen by Contemporary Observers*, eds. M.-J. L. Jennings and C. Madge, Picador, London, 1987, pp. 274–6.

13 And, of course, the organised labour within the Victorian brewing industry both on this site and elsewhere was almost exclusively male and, it seems, 'exclusively of Anglo-Saxon or European descent' (Louise Walker, *Gender, Age and Class in the Hospitality Industry, Victoria, 1900–1914*, Australian National University, n.d., viewed 5 June 2015, <www.anu.edu.au/polsci/marx/interventions/wagesboards.htm.>

14 Ingeborg Bachmann, *The Thirtieth Year*, trans. Michael Bullock, Holmes & Meier, New York, 1987, p. 25.

24

EXCEPTIONAL PASSAGES

The choreotopographical approach to place-making unfixes familiar terms and puts them into play again. The idea of place, for example, is dissociated from its master planning connotations of stable location, defined dimensions and planned program. Likewise, the public ceases being an audience of change and starts to produce its own senses of place. Both setting and sociability mobilise themselves and conceptually enter into a vortical relationship. In general, this turn in design inverts or reverses the standard associations the term *place* carries. The Melbourne study showed, for example, that non-places (abandoned factory sites) possess a stronger sense of place than those places designed for conviviality and exchange (shopping malls and associated sitting places). Similarly, terms like *fit* and *ambience* cease to be the bland desiderata of welcoming civic plazas and the like: they recover a historical sense of passage and alteration, which are effects of displacement. In this reversed optic, the dialectical relationship between places and non-places emerges. Ruins exist in relation to an ideology of development that, like Walter Benjamin's 'destructive character', clears away obstacles for the simple reason that they stand in the way, and which even destroys the signs of its own destructiveness.[1]

Reviving the dialectic, the choreotopographical turn finds that the category of non-place is an artifact of master planning. It is the projection of the planner's program onto the territory about to be claimed. Further, it mirrors the master plan's concealment of the place from which it claims to speak with authority. For the paradox of the master plan is that its authority to legislate for places depends on its claim to apply universal principles of good social and spatial organisation. In this sense, the new place always springs *ex nihilo*, a rational creation of the rational mind.

Nigel Taylor differentiates between two approaches to urban planning: a '"systems view"…derived from a theory of the *object* that town planning seeks to plan, namely, the environment (towns, cities, regions, etc.), now seen as a system of interconnected parts' and a '"rational process" view of planning…a theory about the *process* of planning and, in particular, of planning as a rational process of decision-making'. Taylor's differentiation of these approaches serves to show how they recapitulate the creationist–Darwinian divide in the realm of morphology, but, as he acknowledges, despite their contrasting emphases on substance (environment) and process (procedure), both presuppose the intrinsic value of planning, assuming the merits of a cybernetic model of control. Both in this sense embody a distinctively modernist optimism about the historical realisation of utopias, whether conceived socially, politically, materially or as a combination of all three. Whether mastering the plan is conceived in terms of harnessing the laws inherent in the organisation of the environment or in terms of a sociopolitical process of rational persuasion, it is creationist in that it presupposes that 'the world could be made better by casting aside tradition and constructing things anew from "first principles" based on "pure reason"'.[2] For the new world to come into being, the homology between community and place has to be retained, but only on condition that any sentimental connection between them is left behind. In future, people will enjoy wellbeing, because the places where they live will have been designed to provide it. In the same way, presumably, Adam felt at home in Eden.

The point here is that these provisions have to be promoted and protected. Planned cities do not occur by chance. For something to be included, something else must be excluded: utopias are constructed from the rubble of war, as the 'rubbish hills' of Berlin, with their amusement parks and lookouts, demonstrate. The inside of conviviality depends on an outside called history. Fitting in cannot be left to chance: those unfit to enter the new society must be identified and turned away. To rationalise the choices, passage from one place to another must be controlled and monitored, mechanisms for quarantining new arrivals put in place. Free access to public space depends on techniques for detecting threats to the public order. When these mechanisms take architectural form – as happened with the institution of the quarantine station – it becomes clear that our formally anointed places of congregation are ringed with a protective barrier of non-places whose function is to perpetuate the illusion of a freedom immune to exceptional circumstances. The exceptional must be kept out. As Giorgio Agamben explains, in creating exceptions, the law does not consign these to a realm of primordial freedom; it locates them outside what is *inside* the law.

> The exception is a kind of exclusion. What is excluded from the general rule is an individual case. But the most proper characteristic of the exception is that what is excluded in it is not, on account of being excluded, absolutely without relation to the rule. On the contrary, what is excluded in the exception maintains itself in the form of the rule's suspension. *The rule applies to the exception in no long applying, in withdrawing from it.* The

state of exception is thus not the chaos that precedes order but rather the situation that results from its suspension. In this sense, the exception is truly, according to its etymological root, taken outside (*ex-capere*), and not simply excluded.[3]

What, then, in the light of the dialectic between inside and outside, fit and non-fit, is the correct response to the invitation that came our way in 2008 to develop a strategy for the future management of the Point Nepean Quarantine Station, a ninety-hectare heritage property and associated grounds located south of Melbourne on Port Phillip Bay, just inside The Heads? (See Figure 33) The Commonwealth, which had assumed control of the site in 1910, was planning to hand the property back to the state of Victoria, and ahead of this the Point Nepean Community Trust, the body appointed to manage the transfer, had

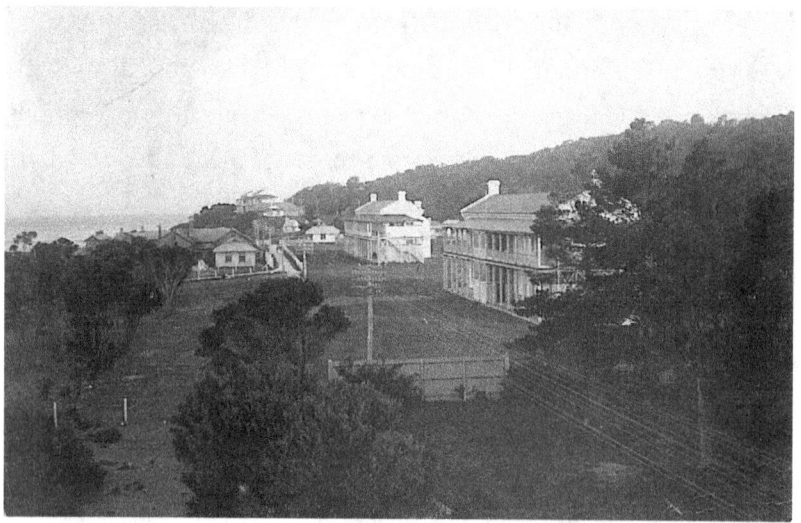

Figure 33 'Point Nepean Quarantine Station, looking north'. Photo: Deveraux-Gray Oral History Collection, provided by Point Nepean Community Trust. Reproduced by permission.

commissioned a master plan intended to assist the state of Victoria in protecting and promoting this rather exceptional cultural and environmental asset. The Trust was concerned that the master plan offered a smorgasbord of possible tourism, educational and recreational opportunities but failed to integrate these organically into the physical experience of the place. But what was the place?

In the light of what I have just said, the judgement of a heritage historian – that the quarantine station was 'a public place but a mysterious place because of its forbidden past, its former inaccessibility and its fragility anchoring the peninsula to the mainland between the roaring southern ocean and the quieter waters of the bay' and that it had 'a very distinct sense of place' – must be questioned.[4] No one who has visited the station would deny its affective qualities, but these do not derive from any well-developed sense of place in the conventional meaning of the phrase. The station is not 'a public place'; it is a public non-place, as its public value has depended on inaccessibility. It is not a place valuable for a distinctive ambience or atmosphere, born, say, of deep, abiding human associations. On the contrary, throughout its various institutional incarnations, it has lacked a permanent population; instead, it has been dedicated to passage migrants, whether these have been nineteenth-century immigrants or trainee naval cadets (see Figure 33). And, environmentally, as Jane Lennon indicates, it is an architectural janitor, filtering passage between outside and inside – a function that is far from neutral, as the 'noise' of the ocean is, as Giorgio Agamben explains, really a chaotic projection of law and order themselves.[5]

Our response was to define the future program of the station in terms of its non- or meta-place status. It was a hinge place, a pivot on which the doors of legal ingress and egress swung. It was not a non-place but a *place of places*, an essential monitor of passage. It damped down the noise of becoming in the interests of preserving the quietude of colonial cohesion. It was like the governor in the old steam engine, which regulated the build-up of pressure in the system to ensure the machine worked efficiently and constantly. It was a turbulence curb, a cybernetic mechanism that preserved the illusion of linear progress and linear planning. As a zone of regulated transfer, its culture resembled that of an arrested vessel; it was a journey on hold. More ominously, it was an examination: it staged what was potentially a life-and-death bifurcation in the paths of life. The turning circles in the railway track leading to and from the fumigation chamber were the functional expression of this. The rhetorical authority of the station resided in the fact that its design punctuated passage, turning passage into a series of choices (see Figure 34). Passage was calibrated down to the scale of one footstep, or *pas*, made in front of another. Because of the possibility that inmates might harbour cholera or typhoid, the isolation of the dormitories, the degrees of separation enforced in the exercise areas, the ritual purification of personal belongings and the medical examinations inmates suffered turned the experience of passage into the enactment of a personal *passion*. Potentially surrounding the living was a fatal aura or nebula: according to the miasmatic theory of infection,

> if any person will take the trouble to stand in the sun and look at his own shadow on a white-plastered wall, he will easily perceive that his whole body is a smoking dunghill, with a vapour exhaling from every part of it. This vapour is subtle, acrid, and offensive to the smell; if retained by the body it becomes morbid; but if re-absorbed, highly deleterious. If a number of persons, therefore, are confined in any one place, not properly

ventilated so as to inspire and swallow with their own spittle, the vapours of each other, they must soon feel its bad effects.[6]

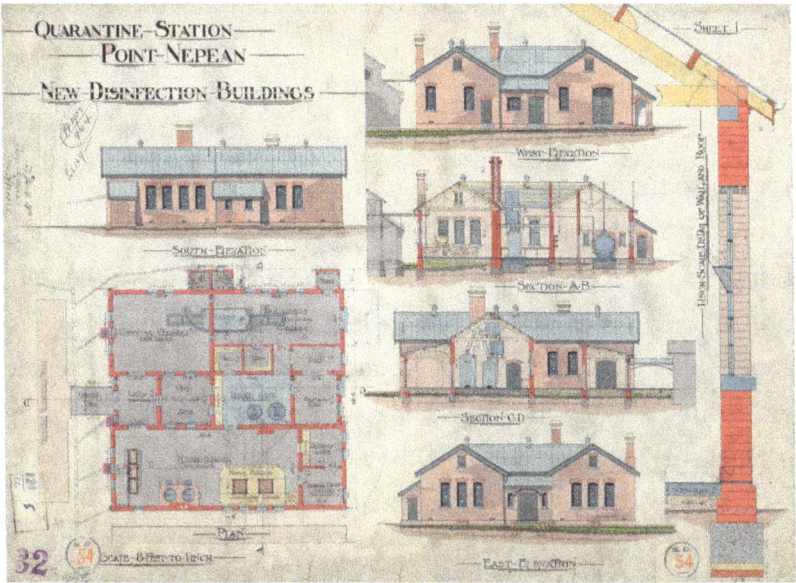

Figure 34 'Quarantine Station Point Nepean, New Disinfection Buildings', architect's drawing, c.1900, National Archives, B84_Folder 12.4. Provided by Point Nepean Community Trust. Reproduced by permission.

Here is atmosphere with a vengeance, an ambient rhetoric fit for ghosts. Post 9/11, Slavoj Žižek writes, what awaits us is something 'much more uncanny' than spectacular warfare: 'the spectre of an "immaterial" war where the attack is invisible – viruses, poisons which can be anywhere and nowhere. On the level of visible material reality, nothing happens, no big explosions, yet the known universe starts to collapse, life disintegrates'.[7] But this is not so new: the spectre of the immaterial is coeval with the idea of the quarantine station. The station materialises an anxiety about invisible enemies. Its plan is designed to eliminate wandering, to suffocate the danger of the subject's free will. It is not a destination so much as a force field, an institutional network of checks, prohibitions and tests. Among the items on display at the station museum in 2008 were board games such as snakes and ladders, and chequers (see Figure 35). These not only served to pass the time; they mimicked the administrative labyrinth would-be immigrants had to navigate. Curiously, the word *plan* seems to contain two contrasted meanings. Associated with such words as *planet* (from the Greek for wandering), *plant* and *plantation*, a plan is both immobile and mobile. It fixes things in place so that new things can be planted there. In its darkest manifestation, the pure plan is a template where 'everything is possible'. The plan can include everything, but only on condition that it can also exclude everything. As Agamben elucidates, it embodies the law (the general rule) only because it is above the law.[8]

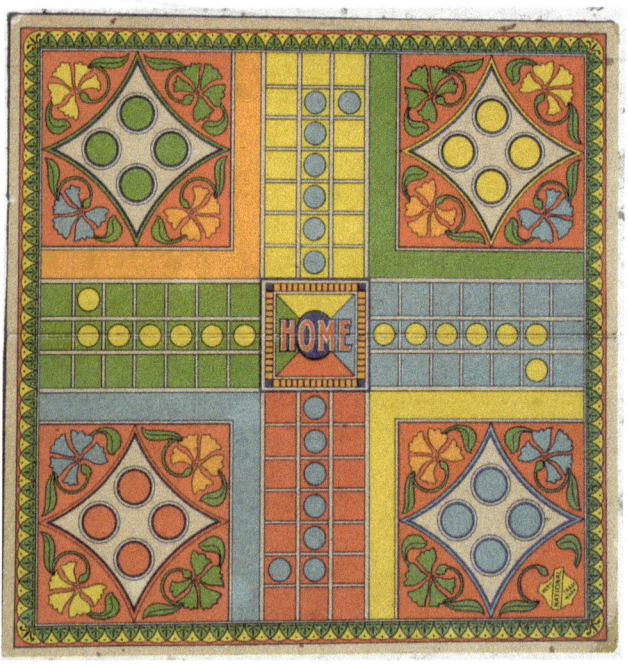

Figure 35 'Board Game', late nineteenth century, Point Nepean Quarantine Station Museum. Photo: the author (March 2008).

Translated into design terms, *the general rule* is the mechanism of an architecture of exceptions. The constitutive feature of this environment – at once discursive, political and physical – is that it cannot be negated. In negating its own exceptions, it suspends the ethical in favour of the aesthetic. This is why it is hardly possible to tell the ground plan of Auschwitz apart from the ground plan of the quarantine station at Point Nepean – and why both are generically similar to any late twentieth-century institution of social engineering, whether the mission of the place is charitable or coercive. Hence, the bland conclusion that the Point Nepean Quarantine Station's sense of place was characterised by its 'isolation' really would not do.[9] Its identity as an exceptional place emerges dialectically in relation to the places of order where sovereign power is exercised (the entire public realm of the state of Victoria). It is a place where the rules governing civil life are suspended. It is a place outside the law in this sense. But it is not, on this account, an *other* place. It does not offer an emancipatory, Bakhtinesque zone of spontaneous play freed from the usual inhibiting social customs. On the contrary, it mirrors the logic of the general rule to which it forms an exception. And this, as I say, is because the public space governed by general rules is itself an exceptional state, as it operationalises both socially and environmentally 'a kind of exclusion'.

Our response had two aspects: an operational strategy, or program, and a design proposal that materialised the strategy in the form of a site modification. The operational strategy aimed to give the familiar rhetoric of 'place-based knowledge' a new inflection. As we explained,

> Mitchell Thomashow maintains that the kind of knowledge place-based education aspires to provide entails

the creation of '[an] extraordinary synthesis [that] transcends disciplines, connects local and global ecologies.'[10] He describes the 'three pillars of place-based perceptual ecology' as 'analysis, imagination and compassion'.[11] Underlying this aspiration is the desire to establish the concept of 'the sense of place' at the core of the educational experience. A 'sense of place' is incidental to scientific and other narrowly empirical disciplines. Ironically, it is also ignored in master planning processes. To elevate the multisensory experience associated with the 'sense of place' is itself the basis of a research program. It is agreed that a key medium through which the 'sense of place' is created, incubated, communicated and used to create value is storytelling – 'our relationship to place is communicated in stories and other representations'.[12] This fact makes a new dialogue between the empirical and interpretative disciplines essential. The rationale for brokering this new dialogue is the place itself – for, as D. A. Gruenewald has argued, 'places are constitutionally real world laboratories'. As they cause diverse species to live together, they represent an act of *placing together* that deserves study. It deserves study because from that process springs our stories, our identities, our scientific and poetic understandings of our place in the world.[13]

We suggested that the program had distinct implications for the future governance of the quarantine station:

> The place-based learning movement springs from a recognition of the value of empowering communities to assume greater custodianship over the environments

they inhabit...Discipline-bound environmental scientists, government planning departments and national park management policies have routinely failed to acknowledge the fundamentally qualitative experiential significance of people's 'sense of place'. The 'sense of place' resides in the relationships (cultural, ecological and personal) or stories that bring places alive.[14] Place-based knowledge recognises that, when these meanings are leached out of places, they die. Consequently, place-based knowledge is not only knowledge that leads out into the world – Thomashow and others show in great detail how developing a 'place-based perceptual ecology' is the basis of learning 'how to move beyond that place and explore the relationship between places', and the same principle informs place-based learning strategies both here and in the US.[15] Place-based knowledge is also local knowledge about how to run the place where you live, work and dream. In short, to secure the PNQS site and its environs as a place-based knowledge centre involves developing a governance model that reflects place-based knowledge values. Thomashow suggests that 'you practice biospheric perception by virtue of three interconnected pathways – natural history and local ecology, the life of the imagination, and spiritual deliberation.'[16] And the same inter-related pathways of research, recreation and respite would shape the place-based knowledge program at the Point Nepean Quarantine Station.

As these proposals were overtaken by political events and did not come to fruition,[17] they do not deserve further development here. The point to make is that the application of place-based knowledge models of education and conservation to the station came with the proviso that the term *place* itself was under scrutiny. It was not simply a question of developing an economically viable program of educational, cultural and community activities broadly inspired by the stories of the place. It was important to materialise the overarching ideological program informing the site, to confront the paradox of a site that has to disappear (or remain *hors de court*) for civil life to function. Any program that treated the quarantine station as simply another place whose history fitted in to the narrative of progressive democratic self-realisation would effectively aestheticise its political meaning. To adopt this stance was not to dismiss the governance model that sought to connect local knowledge to a creative region; on the contrary, the object was to provide this new governance model with a firm base. To do this, it was necessary to grasp that the 'no-man's-land' of the quarantine station represented a suspension of the law that could go either way. It could not be taken as given but had to be articulated as the (non-) place where the juridical had traditionally taken precedence over the political. The task of any self-aware governance model inspired by the character of the place needed to take account of this.

It is not only dictatorships that, as Agamben argues, identify the juridical with the political: in post-9/11 Western democracies, declarations of states of emergency in which the ordinary protections of the rule of law are suspended increasingly blur the boundaries between democracy and absolutism. As a result of this identification of political measures with the proliferation of juridico-constitutionally based exceptions, there opens up a 'no-man's-land between public law and political fact, between the juridical order and life'.[18] Agamben's point is that any investigation of this growing discrepancy between 'life and law, anomie and *nomos, auctoritas* and *potestas*' involves the investigator not simply in assuming a political interest or stance, but in bringing into question what is normally regarded as the political. Where politics has been contaminated by the law, seeing itself as a constituent power – violence that makes law – the only truly political action is one that severs the nexus between violence and law: 'to show law in its non-relation to life and life in its non-relation to law means to open a space between them for human action, which once claimed for itself the name of "politics"'.[19] The same applies to public space. Where public space has become the locus of legally sanctioned activities – and where, indeed, the design of public space (its master plan, its redevelopment of infrastructure and proposed program of cultural events) is intended to exclude all 'illegal' elements, thus making of the citizens who occupy it agents of power – it seems that any intervention on the side of 'life' will involve a process of recognising the no-man's land – the space between law and life – that is not where politics occurs but is political space as such.

Corresponding to this rematerialisation of the quarantine station as a no-man's-land was a proposal to develop a public artwork that materialised the experience of crossing a no-man's land. *Turning Point* was a maze of posts hosting an infinity of passages according to the different ways in which they were linked to one another – to create through ways, offcuts of labyrinths or simple dead ends (see Figure 36). The program, or storyboard, for the place was the information discovered by attempting to thread the maze. Just as our response sought to demystify the master planning definition of *place*, so our program aimed to rematerialise communication – for, when traced back to its origins, a program is a written notice posted in a public place. In this way,

Places Made After Their Stories

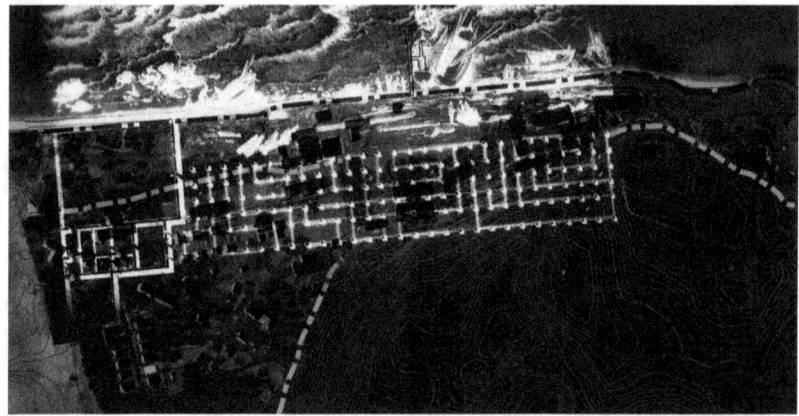

Figure 36 Material Thinking, '*Turning Point* concept sketch', overlay of Jean Houël, 'Plan de la Barrière de la Santé' (from *Voyage pittoresque des Îles de Sicile, de Malte et de Lipari*, Edizione per il Banco di Sicilia realizzata dalla 'Storia di Napoli et della Sicilia', Società Editrice, Palermo, 1977; orig. pub. Paris, 1782) on to Point Nepean Quarantine Station site plan, 28 January 2008.

Turning Point mediated between choreography and topography, an economical instance of a choreotopographical design. Our inspirations included a representation of an eighteenth-century quarantine station in Malta by French engraver and topographical artist, Jean Houël. We had already discussed the minimalist groundplan he depicted as an archetype of the modern institution.[20] And now, particularly in the context of the Point Nepean Quaratine Station's double function, as a filter of immigrants as well as illnesses, it seemed to us to capture the spatial logic of detention with chilling economy. Anticipating the way queues are organised in any administrative environment where the public has to be processed, double rows of roped-together posts were arranged to create corridors down which the new arrivals would proceed. An inverse proportion would exist between the time spent in the queue and the progress made. We also thought of Andrey Tarkovsky's description of the nameless Zone in his film *Stalker*, which 'doesn't symbolize anything, any more than anything else does in my films: the zone is a zone, it's life, and as he makes his way across it a man may break down or he may come through. Whether he comes through or not depends on his self-respect, and his capacity to distinguish between what matters and what is merely passing…In the end everything can be reduced to the one simple element which is all a person can count upon in his existence: the capacity to love'.[21]

The maze of turning points not only created the stage set for a kind of *ballet mécanique*, where simple flows would be regularly stopped and redirected; it aimed at a conceptual reorientation. We wanted to turn people away from the dominant conceptualisation of the Quarantine Station as a place (sequestered, no doubt, but essentially like any other bounded spatial figure comprising public spaces and buildings) and to introduce an alternative. In this, the Station was a passage or, rather, a filtration system for the identification and regulation of flows. It was like the coastline where it stood: tidal, a device for the registration of regional pressures associated with the migration of forces from one place to another. In other words, we took literally the meaning of the term *trope*: a figure or turn of speech – etymologically, a turning. Our turning points were not simply story posts; they aimed at materialising a new trope, or figure of speech, for the character of the Quarantine Station and its environs as a whole. They would have invited the public to turn away from the dominant trope (the place with its related normative ideas of centre, edge, territory and population) and to embrace – indeed perform – another figure of speech, which, we considered, offered an operationally more efficient and productive description of the place, its historical function, political significance and relation to the law.

Invited to thread a storied and interactive maze, the public, we imagined, would change into something else. For *the public* is another trope, which, like *place*, reinforces the impression that public planning is a matter of containment and regulation. In practical terms, the management of public expectations becomes an exercise in crowd regulation, a question of determining an optimal visitation rate, which balances economic return and environmental wear and tear. This approach, which perpetuates the administrative mindset evident in the physical design and program of the quarantine station from its inception, regards the public as a potentially turbulent irruption from outside, an exceptional (noisy) circumstance to be calmed (quietened) and coordinated; the rectilinear serpentine in which the queues of immigrants are arranged spatialises the linearist logic of bureaucratic cultures. Creating obstacles to the flow, drawing attention to the regulation of passage inscribed into the arrangement of spaces and functions, we would have invited the public to become aware of its juridical construction.

Then, in theory at least, the crowd might have become political, something like the 'multitude' which, in Antonio Negri's formulation, is a mobilisation of the masses that, while tumultuous, is also progressive and self-realising.[22] In Plato, perhaps in social theory more generally, the emergence of the many is associated with the city in motion.[23] The agency of the people coincides with political instability. 'The masses and the mob are most often used to name an irrational and passive social force, dangerous and violent precisely because so easily manipulated. The multitude, in contrast, is an active social agent – a multiplicity that acts. The multitude is not a unity, as is the people, but, in contrast to the masses and the mob, we can see that it is organised. It is an active, self-organising agent.'[24]

Notes

1. Walter Benjamin, *One Way Street and Other Writings*, trans. Edmund Jephcott & Kingsley Shorter, Verso, London, 1985, pp.157–9.
2. Nigel Taylor, Urban Planning Theory since 1945, Sage, London and Thousand Oaks, 1998, p. 61 (emphasis in original), p.75.
3. Giorgio Agamben, *Homo Sacer: Sovereign Power and Bare Life*, trans. Daniel Heller-Roazen, Stanford University Press, Stanford, Calif., 1998, pp. 17–18.
4. Jane Lennon, *Point Nepean: Assessment of Its Sense of Place*, Lovell Chen, Melbourne, 2002, p. 15. <http://www.lovellchen.com.au/superintendentsHouse.aspx.> Viewed 10 May 2010.
5. Giorgio Agamben, *State of Exception*, trans. Kevin Attell, University of Chicago Press, Chicago, 2005, p. 46.
6. C. E. A. Winslow, *The Conquest of Epidemic Disease*, Princeton University Press, Princeton, NJ., 1943, p. 239 footnote.
7. Slavoj Žižek, *Welcome to the Desert of the Real*, Verso, London, 2002, p. 37.
8. Agamben, *Homo Sacer*, pp. 170–1. It is no accident that the cover of this English translation of *Homo Sacer* bears an image of the masterplan for Auschwitz, for the paradox of the general rule is that, translated into blueprints for rationalised place design, it produces buildings and environments that are excepted from the normal rules governing everyday life.
9. Lennon, *Point Nepean, Assessment of Its Sense of Place*, p. 15.
10. Mitchell Thomashow, *Bringing the Biosphere Home: Learning to Perceive Global Environmental Change*, MIT Press, Cambridge MA., 2003, p. 105.
11. Ibid, p. 117.
12. Maffesoli, *The Contemplation of the World*, p. 98.
13. Material Thinking, 'Place-Based Learning at Point Nepean: Vehicle for a Vision in Context', August 2008, 1–11, p. 8; see also Material Thinking, 'The Point Nepean Spiral: Place-based Knowledge for the Whole Community,' July 2008, pp. 1–14, for further discussion of place-based learning values. See also David A. Gruenewald, 'Foundations of place: A Multidisciplinary Framework for Place-conscious education', *American Educational Research Journal*, vol. 40, no. 3, 2003, pp. 619–54, who on the basis of the argument that 'places themselves have something to say' (p. 624) advocates 'the pedagogical power of places (p. 641). An important catalyst for promoting this approach was a University of Melbourne proposal to establish a national centre for coasts and climate research at the Quarantine Station.
14. 'Until recently, the importance individuals attach to places was not considered directly relevant to management of public lands'. (Jennifer

Farnum, Troy Hall, Linda E. Kruger, 'Sense of Place In Natural Resource Recreation and Tourism: An Evaluation and Assessment of Research Findings', General Technical Report, PNW-GTR-660, Forest Service of the U.S. Department of Agriculture, Washington D.C., November 2005, p. 1.
15 Thomashow, *Bringing the Biosphere Home*, pp. 76–7.
16 Thomashow, *Bringing the Biosphere Home*, p. 5.
17 After another round of master planning, a newly elected Victorian Government decided to lease the property to commercial interests, a decision that at the time of writing continues to be contested by community groups.
18 Agamben, *State of Exception*, p. 1.
19 Ibid., p. 88.
20 Carter, *Dark Writing*, pp. 65–9.
21 Andrey Tarkovsky, *Sculpting in Time: Reflections on the Cinema*, trans. Kitty Hunter-Blair, Faber & Faber, London, 1994, p. 199.
22 Antonio Negri, *Reflections on Empire*, Polity, Cambridge, UK, 2008, p. 87.
23 Plato, *Timaeus*, 19B, in *Plato in Twelve Volumes*, trans. W. R. M. Lamb, W. Heinemann, London, 1925, vol. 9.
24 Negri, *Reflections on Empire*, p. 87.

Part 6

25

THE MISSION OF IMAGES

As a design practice, choreotopography operates at the crossing place of human time and space. To assert the existence and value of a feedback loop between human behaviour and the character of the setting is not revolutionary, although its implications for urban design remain under-theorised: while Constantinos Doxiadis's ekistics can be described as a cybernetic model of human dwelling where fit is creatively established and renewed, its connection with design remains, at best, implicit. The achievement of ambience, for example, through design remains mysterious and, quite possibly, if detached from the self-forming creativity of crowds, meaningless. The novelty of choreotopography is to insist on the discursive formation of public space which is not the raw product of built spatial arrangements and voiceless human instincts but an outcome of symbolic communication. At the heart of choreotopography is a revival of the symbolic mode leached out of the communicative logic of master planning and its associated administrative lexicon. The power of symbolic forms (stories, images) to engage the imagination overcomes the divisionist rhetoric of regulation; it enables new arrangements to be visualised and, above all, translated into the common property of the community. The new post-communitarian community may be identified by its symbolic attachments rather than such traditional identifiers of communities as longevity of residence, racial homogeneity or cultural alikeness.

Over half a century ago, Mircea Eliade was claiming that the European rediscovery of the cognitive value of the symbol was paving the way towards a deeper understanding of non-European values. The inherently polysemous nature of symbols, he said, facilitated the identification of cross-cultural interests and commonalities that eluded a narrowly exercised communicative reason.[1] These claims have particular relevance to cross-cultural place-making in contemporary Australia and, perhaps, to any environment where the ontological and epistemological claims of Indigenous peoples are at last taken seriously. The proposition is that the recognition of the role symbolic economies play in creating senses of place offers a practical tool for resisting the generally dispiriting and destructive techniques of urban renewal associated with conventional planning authority. Symbolic forms, especially when embedded in mythopoetic accounts of coming into being at that place, describe traditions in their generative aspect (under the aegis of change). As templates for analogous inventions, they make possible the emergence of meeting places whose governance is inscribed in their performativity.[2] It is acknowledged that a rhapsodic technique of eliciting these mental and emotional commons is not easily transferable (although storytelling as a group activity has a performative potential when it is not 'planned' away); at the same time, the hybrid artist-scientist subject position of the investigator should not be dismissed as merely aesthetic. Beside having important precedents in Australian anthropological practice, it invokes a constitutive reasoning that may be genuinely radical.

The importance of symbolic thought outside the realm of anthropological understanding or philosophical speculation resides in the fact that its discourse is performative: it makes things happen, like the artwork in Henri Focillon's remark, making a space of its own.³ In the context of planned change in the urban domain, it offers a different way of talking about things, where change is removed from its planning association with the dialectic of destruction/construction and recast as the renewal and recomplexification of the sign. Eliade emphasises that symbolic thinking is not an aesthetic choice. It is a way of gaining access to truths that signs cannot communicate: 'The function of a symbol is precisely that of revealing a whole reality, inaccessible to other means of knowledge: the coincidence of opposites, for example, which is so abundantly and simply expressed by symbols, is not given anywhere in the Cosmos, nor is it accessible to man's immediate experience, nor to discursive thinking'.⁴ Symbolic logic of this kind is not simply a way of revealing certain truths; it is a way of communicating. In other words, it implies different political, social and economic arrangements.

Naturally, Eliade's writing position may look to us now somewhat dated and Eurocentric, but this should not obscure the relevance of his key insight that symbolic thought is historically significant. It does not belong to the past but, in Eliade's estimate, is poised for a new career, a renaissance brought about precisely by Europe's new encounter with other cultures. Writing at the end of the 1950s, Eliade considered the historical emergence (in Western consciousness) of non-Western peoples as a

> fortunate conjunction in time…[that] has enabled Western Europe to rediscover the cognitive value of the symbol at the moment when Europeans are no longer the only peoples to 'make history', and when European culture, unless it shuts itself off into a

sterilising provincialism, will be obliged to reckon with other ways of knowing and other scales of value than its own. In this respect, all the discoveries and successive fashions concerned with the irrational, with the unconscious, with symbolisms, poetic experience, exotic and non-representational art, etc., have been, indirectly, of service to the West as preparations for a more living and therefore a deeper understanding of non-European values.[5]

The viewpoint here may seem classically Eurocentric, but, as we know, concealed within it is a creative identification with the indigenous culture of Eliade's home country. In other words, the new dialogue made possible by the modernist sensibility is imagined as intra-European as well as international. Eliade explicitly rejects any identification of the symbolic with the archaic or primitive. Rather, where 'everything is held together by a compact system of correspondences and likenesses', human beings become conscious of themselves 'in an "open world" that is rich in meaning'.[6]

According to Seymour Cain, as 'an example par excellence of the co-working of the two modes' of 'literature (art) and scholarship (science)',[7] Eliade goes a step further in defence of the imagination: the historian of religions, he writes, seeks 'general patterns of meaning, spiritual realities that are to be discerned in the facticity of historical and ethnological documents through the shaping imagination of the inquiring interpreter. Knowledge... is not a matter of photographic verisimilitude or logical analysis, but of *poiesis*, of a making and shaping that in certain ways is analogous to that of the writer or artist'.[8] The relevance of this consideration to the European encounter with Aboriginal Australian culture and art should be obvious. To mention two figures with whom I have some familiarity, T. G. H. Strehlow and Geoffrey Bardon, the merging or interweaving of 'facticity' – represented respectively by the hyper-real annotation of the Arrernte song texts and the encyclopaedic documentation of the paintings being done at Papunya in 1970–71 – takes place in both cases in the context of their making and shaping as writers and artists.[9] In synthesising his extensive field notes and recordings of Arrernte song, ceremony and associated place-based knowledge, to produce his monumental work of scholarship, *Songs of Central Australia*, Strehlow made the extraordinary decision to frame his thematic narrative of central Australian ceremony inside a Teutonic epic cycle celebrating the labours of Odin. In short, the fusion of knowledge and poiesis is far more than a framing device: it embodies a sense of the scholar-writer's active or collaborative standing in the transaction and interpretation of stories and images. Far from being disinterested, the searcher after meaning is interested, identifying the cultural shapes and forms under discussion with certain directions in a creative life. The initiatory cycle of 'The Twins' at Ntarea, to which Strehlow gives so much weight,[10] has its emotional, if not structural, counterpart in Eliade's interest in the initiation myth of Zalmoxis, as both materialise a metaphysical stance in a concrete physical site or story. Like the story of 'The Twins', whose struggle not only embodies an idea of archetypal power relations but also explains the birth of a place in one's own life, 'The myth of Zalmoxis is also exemplary for the historian of religions' theory, according to which the popular creations are "found somewhere between the level of pure principles (symbol, metaphysics, magic, which are the origin of any popular product) and that of immediate historical reality (happenings and men, the memory of which is stored by popular memory and projected into mythological categories"'.[11]

Bardon was a modernist of a more conventional type, but he shared with Eliade a belief in chronophanies, irruptions of sacred time into the duration of the profane; the apprehension of a conjunction of mythic time and historical time at Papunya was a powerful spiritual incentive to his work. And, again, this was not simply a conceptual framework applied to foreign material: it stimulated the emergence of a new lexicon of terms to describe the painting produced at Papunya that were operational and transformative inside the movement. Finally, it licensed Bardon to believe that he had experienced an act of self-realisation at the place, a mythopoetically-mediated sense of *being placed*. As he wrote in an unpublished note explaining his interest in the children's art at Papunya, 'I wanted to be a painter and poetically artistic person for my nation'. In a similarly impure way, *Red Ways* infolded chronology, space and culture to discover analogies that might inform a new crosscultural symbolic economy.

Eliade's account throws light on two features of the choreo-topographical approach: the character of the designer and the nature of the stories. The designer-dramaturg who adapts some of the skills of the rhapsode to the rearrangement of space according to the intuition of certain movement forms undertakes a kind of poiesis 'analogous to that of the writer or artist'. Inevitably, the dramaturg of that new imagined dramatic society is making a personal investment. The principle common to both is a strategic capacity to respond to what is already in movement in the neighbourhood, to catch on to it and to redirect its energy. The classical rhapsode had a basic repertoire of plots, themes and episodes that was adapted – re-collected, re-imagined, re-invented – to the concrete situation of the performance. Poiesis has always had this opportunistic cast, because it occurs at a certain time and place – or brings these axes together crucially. Besides, change is not necessarily uncertain; opportunism may be about continuity, as it was in the rhapsode's improvisatory art, and (as Jenny Green has described) it is in the sand-drawing practice of the central Australian Arrernte women, where wiping out the ideogram and drawing another is coeval with the telling of a story that is not fixed in a scheme (however approximate) but incorporates adventitiously whatever has happened that might stand in need of narration and rationalisation.[11] Rhapsody is the riff on the facticity of history narrated through the poetics of myth. The hybrid expression of this is a mythopoetic event that discovers a new crossing of the archetypal and the political, a new fiction of place. The new covenant or symbolic ecology is contingent on a performative contract. The dialogue enacts the inauguration of a new relationship, score or grammar of gestures.

The potential of this to offer an alternative practice of place-making is a theme of my earlier book *Meeting Place*. Insofar as the performance is interactive, it produces interest, a supplement of engagement, surprise or admiration, that cannot be divorced from the immersive experience of being there, whether *there* is the scene of the original enactment or the occasion on which the performance is related and passed on. 'One could exhaust the signs and yet know that there is an "over-and-above". When they succeed, performances communicate directly.'[12] The design challenge is to reverse the evolution of gesture into contract and write the emergent forms of communication back into the physical setting. On the loom of ideation, it weaves choreography and topography into a new pattern. Here, the dramaturgy of the encounter means eliciting its symbolic design. The rearguard action fought by mythopoetic thought is to insist on certain homologies across scales, fields and regimes. In finding 'mere coincidences' between Arrernte and non–Aboriginal Australian place-making, a creative commonality is asserted (not a historical reality or even some principle of cultural convergence). The homologies that metaphorical thinking identifies add up to a kind of imaginal embryology – as if the anatomical homologies Ernst Haeckel claimed to show between the embryos of different species could be transferred to the realm of concept formation or logical pattern recognition, thus furnishing the object of mythopoetic thought. These homologies are inherent not in the phenomena but in the framework brought to bear on their analysis. A metaphorical mode of analysis will discover homologies across scales, fields and regimes not because these are inherent in nature but because they embody the work of the living or plastic imagination.[13] We breathe life back into nature through the mythopoetic engagement with it.

The designer who is analogous to the artist or writer contests the language of the master plan. This is not simply an aesthetic preference; it represents a view of history and asserts the role of the imagination in navigating change. From a symbolic perspective, the stage is not empty; it is a string figure of potentialities. In contrast, in a symbolically stripped-out scientific culture, what Philip Rieff calls 'an assured relationship between the everyday and the transcendental' evaporates. Symbols yield to signs, which, in turn, come to be regarded merely as 'symptoms'. 'The gesture, the environment, and certainly any sense of being addressed from the beyond could no longer be trusted. In a culture where everything is a sign of something else (something repressed), what counts is the possibility that something means something else'. Rieff sees the legitimation of this libertarian doctrine, in which every limit must be passed in the interests of knowing the reality, as the death warrant that western culture has handed itself. In a sign culture, he suggests, hunger is inscribed in the act of communication; instead of materialising its meaning, the sign always points beyond the present. The sign dematerialises or brackets off the encounter. Symbolic communication, by contrast, focuses on the discovery of meaning in the performance.[14]

In a psychoanalytic context, it does what Sigmund Freud was reluctant to do: acknowledge the therapeutic role of the transference. Transposed to the realm of mythopoiesis, a talking cure occurs when the participants' symbolic thought processes are liberated. The transference effected here does not require a theory of sexual causation; it depends on the power of language itself to generate new psychologically appealing meanings: 'Symbolic meanings can grow autonomous and independent from their primary reference; they can turn into "complexes." They can reflect upon one another and multiply into the "meaning of meaning" and transcend into the infinite. The understanding of meaning supposes a common ground, a degree of sympathy between the speaker and listener, thus supposing "transference"'.[15] Theodore Thass-Thienemann refers here to the creative dynamics of the dreamwork, but his observation applies equally to the activities of the designer-dramaturg when they seek to elicit the stories after which places can be made. As Thass-Thienemann implies, it is not *any* image, sign or symbol that stimulates the discursive feedback necessary to produce symbolic identifications. In cross-cultural dialogue around place-making, the stories that intertwine to disclose something new are those that display structural homologies as well as thematic resonances. Symbolic morphogenesis occurs when a mere coincidence serves to illuminate the meaning of a meaning, to recontextualise and revivify a received story (a creation story, a historical narrative). The scientist-writer who advocates the recovery of symbolic narratives engages the plastic or primary imagination, that '*imitates* the exemplary models – the Images – reproduces, reactualises and repeats them without end'.[16]

These 'Images' are not the usual records of personal events found in most oral historical collections. In most community consultations associated with the development of a master plan (or with its implementation), participants are invited to say what they expect of the new precinct. As this approach obliges the audience to make a choice they did not wish to make – to endorse the new order or to resist it – the conversation that results is characterised by resentment. This may be addressed towards the existing order or towards the proposed changes. Either way, a threatened identity is at stake. The designer-planner's conventional response to this anxiety is to commit the project to a public art program that ensures sense of place is woven into the new fabric. Almost certainly, an oral history (or comparable) project will be commissioned, which, later, finds its way into the public art brief. Such consultation techniques as these invest in identity rather than identification; they nuclearise experience and trivialise the collective experience. In particular, they use the smokescreen of photography-like anecdote to conceal the existence of overarching elemental orders.

An ability to think outside the rationalist planning paradigm occurs when participants are invited to reimagine the stories, to explore the new meanings, interpretations and associations their symbolic economy makes possible. In contrast with the 'degraded' images of a visualist administration, where visualisation is identified with the coercive programs of linearist accounting, the images conjured up in this way give scope to the primary imagination to imitate, to incorporate and to extend. To imitate 'the exemplary models' is to reactualise them. It is not to copy but reimagine them: it is, like the relationship of mythopoiesis to myth, imitation with interest.[17] Critically, it brings into question the reduction of such narrative complexes to fixed plans or rigidly repeated scenarios. The act of relating precisely makes room for the incommensurable: 'To have imagination is to be able to see the world in its totality, for the power and the mission of Images is to *show* all that remains refractory to the concept; hence', Eliade adds, 'the disfavour and failure of the man "without imagination"'.[18]

Notes
1 Mircea Eliade, *Images and Symbols: Studies in Religious Symbolism*, trans. Philip Mairet, Princeton University Press, Princeton, NJ., 1991, p. 177.
2 Carter, *Meeting Place*, pp. 55–6.
3 See Chapter 23, endnote 3 above.
4 Eliade, *Images and Symbols*, p. 177.
5 Ibid., pp. 10–11.
6 Ibid., p. 178.
7 Seymour Cain, 'Poetry and Truth: the Double Vocation in Eliade's Journals and Other Autobiographical Writings', *Imagination and Meaning*, eds. N. J. Girardot and M. L. Ricketts, Seabury Press, New York, 1982, 87–103, p.100.
8 Seymour Cain, 'Poetry and Truth: the Double Vocation in Eliade's Journals and Other Autobiographical Writings,' p. 98. For broader discussion, see Anca Popoaca-Giuran, 'Mircea Eliade: Meanings (the apparent dichotomy: scientist/writer)', PhD thesis, King's College London, London, 1998, p. 336.
9 See Carter, *The Lie of the Land*, pp. 21–114. Carter, *Dark Writing*, pp. 103–139.
10 Carter, *The Lie of the Land*, p. 29: 'Evidently, Strehlow's invocation of Ntarea as his own conception site was not another instance of naively Modern primitivism, or a latter-day flirtation with the Dionysiac Nietzsche. Strehlow was affiliating himself to a place from which the spirit had fled'.
11 Popoaca-Giuran, 'Mircea Eliade', p. 139, quoting Mircea Eliade, *Myths and Symbols*, University of Chicago Press, Chicago, 1971, p. 89.
12 'Jenny Green has watched and filmed Arrernte women performing sand drawings in the Todd, rhythmically clearing and re-clearing the sand as stories are layered on top of each other, none of them erased, but always existing in the sand. "Stories persist in the country: once cleared, the residue of stories remains," Jenny explained, "they finish the stories like a ceremony, closing the ground, burying the leaves to reuse later." It's a narrative structure that assumes the ongoing life of story in the rhythm of

clearing the ground.' (Tracy Spencer, 'Stories from the Street: Todd Mall/ Todd Street, At the heart of Alice, July 2008', p. 14.) See also Jennifer Green, 'Signs and Space in Arandic Sand Narratives', in M. Seyfeddinipur and M. Gullberg, eds, *From Gesture in Conversation to Visible Action as Utterance: Essays in Honor of Adam Kendon*, John Benjamins Publishing, Amsterdam, 2014, pp. 219–43.

13 Carter, *Meeting Place*, p. 44, citing John von Sturmer, '*Aboriginal Singing and Notions of Power*', in *Songs of Aboriginal Australia*, eds. M. Clunies Ross, T. Donaldson, S.A. Wild, University of Sydney Press, Sydney, 1987, p. 74.

14 See, for example, Carter, *Mythform* (p. 84) where plates from Haeckel's *The Evolution of Man*, which show foetuses of different species in an evolutionary series, suggested to me 'sleeping worms…shapes of time awaiting our awakening.' (Ernst, Haeckel, *The Evolution of Man*, 2 vols, G. P. Putnam's Sons, New York, 1905.) Haeckel has been accused of fabricating cross-species resemblances to justify a theory of evolution; more charitably, he exhibited 'artistic leanings towards ideal symmetries.' (see www.britannica.com/biography/Ernst-Haeckel. Viewed 18 January 2015.)

15 Philip Rieff, *The Feeling Intellect: Selected Writings*, ed. Jonathan B. Imber, University of Chicago Press, Chicago, 1990, p. 349.

16 Theodore Thass-Thienemann, *Symbolic Behavior*, Washington Square Press, New York, 1968, p. 6.

17 Eliade, *Images and Symbols*, p. 20 (original emphasis).

18 For a discussion of this paradox through which the eternal forms (or Images) undergo continuous reinvention, see Carter, *Dark Writing*, pp. 84–8.

19 Ibid., p. 20.

26

OPTIONS, FRAMEWORKS, TEMPLATES

Although the critique of master planning has been assertive – and has, no doubt, essentialised an executive technique that retains flexibility in the hands of flexible practitioners – it has not been intended as wholly negative. As has been indicated, invitations for Material Thinking to become involved in place-making processes have regularly morphed into invitations to develop master plans. Therefore, the convening authorities must discern a significant resemblance between the goals of the mythopoetic place-making approach and their own ambitions for societal improvement. If the action research methods advocated in response to these requests were not to fall back (and contract) into the kind of data collection and treatment characteristic of public art, it was important to formalise a vocabulary that could capture the resemblance with master planning while, at the same time, differentiating what we offered. An early iteration of this alternative methodology was called the *design options framework*. Later, this morphed into a more cinematic description that foregrounded the discursive basis of the design process; we called this *storyboarding*.[1] More recently still, we have settled on the phrase *creative template* to evoke a middle ground between the conventional master plan and the conventionally commissioned public artwork. None of these designations may be entirely satisfactory, but a brief discussion of them serves to illustrate the tension that exists between plan and program, between, if you like, the discourse of being and becoming. For a work such as the proposed *Turning Point*, at Point Nepean Quarantine Station, was perhaps taking too much upon itself when it proposed translating a highly intellectualist redefinition of the 'exceptional' place in one step into a public artwork. Surely, something in-between was needed, a translator, a kind of algorithm that allowed the conceptual homologies to be transferred across scale, media and sense.

The design options framework, as its name might imply, recommended a planning approach that accommodated emergence. Speculation was encouraged as well as criteria for prioritisation. The approach was strategic in the flexible, elastic sense given to that term earlier. Further, the framework implicated architects and landscape architects quite as much as urban planners. It aimed to insert an additional step into the process of translating the master planning brief into a developed design. The reason for this was the observation that much design in the computer aided design epoch shared the utopianist fantasy of planning and was, as Amy Kulper puts it, forgetful of the *oikos*.[2] As early as 1981, French philosopher Jean Baudrillard recognised that with the digitisation of the image, the old representational contract had been broken; but the same, it could be argued, was true of digital design. Distinguishing three orders of simulacra – the naturalistic, the productionist and the simulation – Baudrillard wondered whether the last of these yet existed in the field of science fiction writing. Certainly, it now exists in the world of digital design, where, for a generation, 'models no longer constitute an imaginary domain with reference to the real; they are, themselves, an apprehension of the real, and thus leave no room for any fictional extrapolation – they are immanent, and therefore leave no room for any kind of transcendentalism'.[3]

The stage Baudrillard regarded as imminent is now well and truly built, 'set for simulation, in the cybernetic sense of the word – that is to say, for all kinds of manipulation of these models (hypothetical scenarios, the creation of simulated situations, etc.), but now *nothing distinguishes this management-manipulation from the real itself: there is no more fiction*'. The corollary Baudrillard draws is that the relationship between reality and fiction is reversed: 'Today, it is the real which has become the pretext of the model in a world governed by the principle of simulation. And, paradoxically, it is the real which has become our true utopia – but a utopia that is no longer a possibility, a utopia we can do no more than dream about, like a lost object'. There are questions that this scenario raises. Baudrillard's thesis presupposes a utopian period when fictional worlds are based on 'image, imitation, and counterfeiting'.[4] They generally have a transcendental or nostalgic paradisal inspiration.

But isn't this to mistake these schemata for 'mere literature' when their motivation was to make appear at once a world different from the one determined to be true and immutable by the dominant order of things? Isn't it precisely the calumny of the dominant order (whose discourse is the public history of events) to pass off the balances of conversations about the real (about what it might be, can be and is) as mere speculation? Similarly, the 'lost object' of the real that Baudrillard laments is only lost from this same historicist perspective: as something that simply resists modelling of any kind, it belongs neither to the past nor to the future but to what Stanley Rosen, writing about the unfolding experience of Eros, describes as an extensive present.[5] We breathe life back into nature through the mythopoetic engagement with it. We never copied nature but, rather, derived master drawings from it – essential 'Images' in Mircea Eliade's sense,[6] or forms possessing morphogenetic potential.

Gregory Bateson reports that his father taught him to expect 'to find the same sort of laws at work in the structure of a crystal as in the structure of society, or that the segmentation of an earthworm might really be comparable to the process by which basalt pillars are formed'. Bateson's innovation was to transfer this intuition of biological patterning to the realm of reason: '[I] would rather say that I believe that the types of mental operation which are usual in analysing one field may be equally useful in another – that the framework (the *eidos*) of science, rather than the framework of Nature, is the same in all fields'.[7] Something similar applies to the design options framework: the framework is not like a master plan, a relatively inflexible blueprint or set of rules, but a way of looking at diverse things together. It is an ordering principle that lends the act of design a certain direction or set of foci, propitious sites of analogy disclosed through metaphorical thinking.

It is evident that the discoveries made in this way do not have strictly linear outcomes (either from a project management perspective or in terms of the field of the design): their end is in the recollection of the relational infrastructure that informs the separateness of things. The structural analogies found through this approach would have their discursive equivalent in Thomas Rickert's 'ambient rhetoric', a mode of relating that eschewed the habit of Walter Benjamin's 'destructive character' and, instead of removing all obstacles in its path, flexibly deviated. According to Michael Tawa, the speech of readiness, rhetoric, possesses these characteristics in its etymological roots: 'The notion of whirling and swerving are inherent in the idea of rhetorical speech'.[8] The constant feedback between performance and context finds its scientific equivalent in a *minor science* that is qualitative rather than quantitative in its interests.

To go back to the writing of Paulo and Alexandra Correa, from this ethical view, 'what matters is not the motion/non-motion antithesis but the "which motion"'.[9] Bateson sees this project as profoundly democratic, contrasting it with science's 'instrumentality', its interpretation of 'the whole structure of life' in terms of 'blueprints'. He sees that the transfer of this worldview that separates means from ends, from science to technological innovation and the master planning of society leads to anti-democratic outcomes: 'Are we to reserve the techniques and the right to manipulate people as the privilege of a few planning, goal-oriented, and power-hungry individuals, to whom the instrumentality of science makes a natural appeal?'[10] The counter-proposition, which Bateson derives from his and Margaret Mead's studies of Balinese culture, is that the human scientist must recognise (and resist) the separation of ends and means: 'Only by working in terms of values which are limited to defining a *direction* is it possible for us to use scientific methods in the control of the process'.[11]

In Correa and Correa's terminology, the 'thing-event' and the 'sense-event' have to coincide. An artwork fulfils this condition when the 'intrinsic logic of the composition' conveys 'the logic of sensation'. Here,

> the sense of a sensation is a function, as is the sense of a concept; the senses of things, artwork or natural things – the senses of sensations, perceptions – and the senses of ideas are, like the senses of forces or values (axiology), their functions, their intrinsic articulations that inevitably call forth a context (the context that alone confers sense)...An idea is wrong if it cannot account for the relationships it seeks to establish, explain and condense; if it decontextualises the relation. And an idea is stupid

if it seeks to establish no account of relation, or denies the existence of a relation so as not to have to account for it.[12]

The etymology of *delirium* suggests that a person is mad if they step out of the furrow. But the opposite may be true. It is the orator who monitors where they are going who is wise, whose 'motion with intrinsic measures, that occupies Space as it generates it',[13] is not linear but curvilinear. A self-reflexive or self-aware 'direction' of this kind would be comparable to a framework or eidos, a way of understanding concepts analogically, in terms of the multivalent relationships they subtend rather than the univocal concepts they communicate. In semiotic terms, it would favour the indexical or iconic over the arbitrary sign, or approach the problem of communication with this bias.

According to Bateson, in Bertrand Russell's theory of logical types, a means and ends separation in scientific method corresponds to a digital conception of signs and communication. The critical distinction made is between on and off states; negation is the precondition of affirmation. However, most ideas are communicated contextually and depend for their meaning in varying degrees on analogous or habitually associated other actions or signs. The idea of *going for a walk* is given where it is impossible to communicate a *not going for a walk* state. 'Sometimes, as in the matter of context markers, there is a continuous gradation from the ostensive through the iconic to the purely digital. At the digital end of this scale all the theories of information theory have their full force, but at the ostensive and analogic end they are meaningless.'[14] Communication that is analogue can stretch from the gesture whose meaning is defined by context to the

Options, Frameworks, Templates

symbolic form (the metaphor or figure of speech) that suggests polysemous possibilities.

Communication of this kind does not look beyond the present forming situation; its directions integrate 'thing-event' and 'sense-event'. In the context of the design options framework, it defines options in terms of related but as yet undetermined pathways within the framework. The options are not arbitrary; they already coexist as potentialities of the framework. Design consists in drawing out the connections, but when this is done, a new state (cut off from what has gone before and a negation of it) does not come into being; there exists instead a re-drawing out of relations shared across the spheres of separation but faded from recognition or previously unrealised.

As we were trying to clarify the relationship between this flexibly conceived patterning of a spot in time and space and the master plan, someone compared the design options framework to master *drawing*. In intention, if not proficiency, the design options framework *is* conceived in an analogous fashion. The great drawings of the human figure by Michelangelo or Pontormo leave much to the imagination. The passages of paper in-between the chalk strokes convey as much information as the lines themselves. The paper is skin-like, existing in a strange feedback loop with the subject matter of the drawing. A passage of the nude human form is presented, flexed and poised – a movement form caught in the lapse of motion – and the viewer is left to visualise the rest of the body, the completion of the (usually) controposto action and, by implication, to connect the torsion, the vortical drift, to the character of the setting. Whether executed in chalk or charcoal, master drawings bear the trace of the medium and the material with which they are executed. Charcoal is in detail a cloud of black particles held in place with a fixative. Chalk smudges, a fact turned into an expressive technique; chalk is responsive to the pressure of the hand – the line can be thin or broad according to the character of the flesh the artist wants to portray.

In an analogous fashion, the graphic expression of the design options framework communicates the *passages* from which the sense of place emerges. In one derivation, *sense* is associated with French *sentier*: mobile, where place is static, *sense of place* emphasises qualities of orientation and path-making. In this dynamic interpretation, 'a social-experiential orientation emphasizes meanings that are created as people interact with a place and with each other in a place, developing connections to the place'.[15] A critical sense of place is one that develops tools for calibrating the *sentiers* said to lend places their experiential drag. The pathways may be physical grooves, representable in plans, but they signify because they bear poetic associations, rhythmic, kinaesthetic, metrical and ultimately poetic dimensions. They are discursive in the etymological sense. In this case, what is called *place* emerges where *sentiers* meet, intersect, interfere with one another or cancel each other out. Place is not a meeting place of stories – themes that the heritage lobby can restore and reinterpret – but an arrest, or filtering, of passage.

A place of this kind is a chiaroscuro construction, imaginable as a contrast of light and shadow. To draw it, much has to be withdrawn: the holistic temptation to predict every relation has to be resisted. As Kostas Terzidis reminds us, design understood in this fashion precedes planning.[16] It can be described as the initial drawing out of certain connections or *sentiers*, a retracing rather than an inscription of something new. An environmental unconscious is assumed; the ideal plan is not a plain but a forest,

Options, Frameworks, Templates

a topography, and perhaps all of these, viewed from the point of view of the choreographer of meeting.

The additional description of this hybrid place-making approach – somewhere between the public artwork and the master plan – as a form of storyboarding was a crude attempt to highlight the fact that bringing new places into being is a mythopoetic process. Storyboarding as developed in the Walt Disney studios is a way of pre-visualising movement forms; its counterpart outside the animation studio is Sergei Eisenstein's notion of the *mise-en-scène*: 'a graphic flourish in space. It is like handwriting on paper, or the impression made by feet on a sandy path. It is so in all its plenitude and incompleteness…Character appears through actions…Specific appearance of action is movement (here we include in "action" words, voice etc). The path of movement is *mise-en-scène*', and so on.[17] Such visualisation practices successfully fuse motive and motion, story and action, into a single compelling image set, but, of course, the purity of the aesthetic effect depends on eliminating environmental considerations and interactions.

In contrast, our interpretation placed equal emphasis on *story* and *board*. The word *board* was associated with *border*, and both in my mind recalled the meaning that the philosopher of culture Giambattista Vico gave to the term *contorno*: 'The verb *contornare* not only means to give a new turn, but also "to surround; to go round; to outline; to border"'. According to Vico, the faculty of invention (*ingegno*) or symbolic thinking connects disparate and diverse things by going round them and drawing them into a relationship.[18] The act of drawing together, then, turns the board (the surface on which a story is written or engraved) into the passage itself, the border that, in the act of going round, becomes a graphic flourish or arabesque drawn through all the points. The resulting line might in principle be the passage of all the passages, an algorithm of sociability.

The remade myth in this theory is one that is replaced or properly placed, re-enacted as a passage (in the double sense of a stretch of story and a length to be walked). There is a quaint anticipation of this idea in the memoir of the great late eighteenth century Northumbrian engraver Thomas Bewick. Pondering the ephemerality of most churchyard monuments, and the confinement of their epitaphs to more or less private histories, Bewick imagines a system of public monuments, calling it 'a debt of gratitude – due from the public to the Author of our being for the loan of departed worth'. Inspired by the 'great projecting Rocks' of the Scottish Highlands, he proposes that names of national heroes should be inscribed upon them. One thought leads to another: why not 'fill up' 'the bare rocks in other parts of our Islands' with famous names? And why confine the inscriptions to names? 'Maxims, or quotations from their works would fill up many of these Rocks (which are waiting for them).' In addition, passages of the Bible might 'be added to fill up every vacant spot'. Finally, Bewick imagines texts chosen to be read at that place. 'Imagine the effect on the traveller of coming across Cunningham's lines ("as the river runs, time wings his trackless way") as he stoops to quench his thirst!'[19] Bewick's fantasy is a variation on the classical identification of *topic* (theme) with *topos* (place). Its novelty is to imagine a conjunction of choreography and topography in the human utterance. But none of this would be news to Aboriginal elders charged with keeping themselves and their country alive: 'One has not succeeded in "thinking black" until one's mind can, without intellectual struggle, enfold into some kind of oneness the notions of body, spirit, ghost, shadow, name, spirit-site, and totem'.[20]

And this segue introduces another consideration. The framework, or, as we came to call it, the creative template, scores historical ground. Its stories are mythopoetic reinventions of primary place-making stories. They are not exercises in place-branding. Their chiaroscuro refers to collective memories as well as differential emotional attachments. They allow for the co-presencing of what is present and what is absent; imagining time as composed of openings, they make room for comings and goings (daily but also mortal). They mark the no-man's-land as, alternatively, a place of self-becoming or a no-go zone. In Aboriginal Australia, the stories not only operate to put everything and everyone in their place – and hence to regulate passage; they also identify places that are selectively out of bounds.

> Some parts of this country are not to be lived on. In our culture we recognize that there are places we can't go to because of a powerful event, places that are so powerful that you can become cursed by the land, you get sick from it. It is recognized as sickness country for all time… They have a mystical power and if you venture too close something will happen. That's why we don't go to these places. We always go around them, asking permission first from the people who know that country. Spirits talk to you. You can hear the land talk to you. People feel it.[21]

These 'powerful events' may be ancient or modern. They include murders, massacres and other forms of violence. How can a terrain associated with apartheid, sexual exploitation and theft become a place to frequent? At the very least, it has to incorporate rules of avoidance.

In fact, the ordinary perception of places as choreotopographies, as flexibly ordered systems of passing, dovetails easily with Aboriginal Australian place-making stories. In a way, places imagined in this way are microcosms of the arrangements said to order the region as a whole. Further, recognition of this creates common mythopoetic ground. It is possible, without great difficulty, to reinterpret Aboriginal Australian understandings of place and ecological insights coming from place-based knowledge. In relation to *Turning Point*, at the Point Nepean Quarantine Station, for instance, we noted that that under the aegis of *passage*, one might incorporate the local Boon Wurrung myths ('Orion was Karakorak, the crow that brought a firestick in his beak from the sun to the first inhabitants of the world'), the appearance of the landscape ('Fires were mainly lit to maintain pathways through dense scrub, to increase the fertility of the land, to drive game and quite probably as a smoke screen to hide behind'), certain food avoidances, the physical journeying from one place to another (the government-appointed Aboriginal Protector William Thomas noted, 'When they go in large bodies, two or three seniors direct their movements from encampment to encampment' – sometimes by a 'whole circuitous route'; also, 'Visitors who did not have kin or moiety entitlements could ask for access, the guiding principle for these relationships was reciprocity'), the management of the passage of the soul, and the explanation for the arrival of the whites (the *ngamajet*, or revenants – deceased black people who came back in a white body).[22]

Where passage is understood to entail ethical responsibilities, the post-contact exposures to infection, forcible removal, incarceration and property-based relations must be seen as a kind of cultural arteriosclerosis, an illness that is registered in the landscape. 'Boon wurrung tradition has it that the flooding of Port Phillip occurred at a time when the people were neglecting their children and fighting other Kulin people. Bunjil told the people to change their ways and, when they did, he raised a spear and the flow of water ceased'.[23] Hence, the choreotopographical myth invoked in the context of making *Nearamnew*, at Federation Square, is also a description of the intimate relationship between environmental change and human wellbeing. It is believed that the ongoing tension between people of Boon Wurrung descent and people to the north-east who identify as Ganai stems from the pressure the flooding of Bass Strait put on the Boon Wurrung to retreat onto neighbours' land: 'It is possible that the long-standing hostility between Boon Wurrung and Ganai had its origins in rising sea levels'.[24] Places in this sense are socially and politically propitious when they constitute the reason of passage. The Kulin *tanderrum* ceremony conferred temporary rights of passage or residence. Typically, white colonists failed to understand this, taking acquiescence to passage as a sign the land was ceded.[25] In a contemporary context, the increasingly popular custom of opening public events with a Welcome to Country is meaningless if no responsibilities, reciprocities or benefits flow from it.

Notes

1 Carter, *Dark Writing*, pp. 182–7.
2 Kulper, 'Ecology without the oikos: Banham, Dallegret and the morphological context of environmental architecture', p. 84.
3 Jean Baudrillard, 'Two essays', essay 1, 'Simulacra and Science Fiction', trans. Arthur B. Evans, *Science Fiction Studies*, #55, vol. 18, part 3, November 1991, viewed 5 June 2015, <www.depauw.edu/sfs/backissues/55/baudrillard55art.htm>, para. 9.
4 Ibid., paras 2, 9 (original emphasis), 11.
5 Stanley Rosen, *Metaphysics in Ordinary Language*, Yale University Press, New Haven, Conn., 1999, p. 31: 'We produce the lived present, not as a synthesis of temporal points, but as the self-orientation of erotic striving', a condition, Rosen states, that is only possible through "being by or next to"'.

6   Eliade, *Images and Symbols,* p. 20.
7   Bateson, *Steps to an Ecology of Mind,* p. 74.
8   Michael Tawa, *Agencies of the Frame,* Cambridge Scholars Publishing, Newcastle upon Tyne, 2010, p. 312 n. 22.
9   Correa & Correa, 'Whither Science?, p. 37.
10 Bateson, *Steps to an Ecology of Mind,* pp. 160, 162.
11 Ibid., p. 159, citing Margaret Mead, 'The Comparative Study of Culture and the Purposive Cultivation of Democratic values', in, *Science, Philosophy and Religion, Second Symposium,* Columbia University Press, New York, 1942, pp. 56–97, p. 64 (original emphasis).
12 Correa & Correa, 'Whither Science?', p. 41.
13 Ibid., p. 37.
14 Bateson, *Steps to an Ecology of Mind,* pp. 251, 291.
15 Linda E. Kruger, Rhonda Mazza & Kelly Lawrence (eds), *Proceedings: National Workshop on Recreation Research and Management,* General Technical Report PNW-GTR-698, Forest Service, US Department of Agriculture, Washington, D.C., June 2007, viewed 8 June 2015, <www.fs.fed.us/pnw/pubs/pnw_gtr698.pdf>, p. 84.
16 Terzidis, *Algorithmic Architecture,* p. 1.
17 Arun Khopkar, 'Graphic Flourish: Aspects of the Art of *Mise-en-scène*' in Ian Christie & Richard Taylor, *Eisenstein Rediscovered,* Routledge, London, 1993, pp.151–64, 152. The questionable derivation of Eisenstein's notion of *mise-en-scène* from descriptions of Arrernte painting is discussed in Carter, *Dark Writing,* pp. 263–4.
18 James Robert Goetsch, *Vico's Axioms: The Geometry of the Human World,* Yale University Press: New Haven, Conn., 1995, pp. 42–3.
19 Thomas Bewick, *A Memoir of Thomas Bewick, Written by Himself,* Robert Ward, Newcastle upon Tyne, 1862, pp. 251–2.
20 Stanner, *The Dreaming and Other Essays,* p. 59.
21 Andrew McMillan, *An Intruder's Guide to East Arnhem Land,* Niblock Publishing, Nightcliff, 2007, p. 19, citing Gumatj elder Mandawuy.
22 Christine Williamson Heritage Consultants, *Point Nepean Quarantine Station Draft Management Plan,* Christine Williamson Heritage Consultants, Melbourne, 2008, pp. 50, 51, 52, 56, 57.
23 Richard Cotter, *Boon Wurrung: People of the Port Phillip District,* Lavender Hill Multimedia, Melbourne, 2001, p. 7.
24 Ibid., p. 9.
25 See Ian D. Clark & David A. Cahir, *Tanderrum, 'Freedom of the Bush': The Djadjawurrung Presence on the Goldfields of Central Victoria,* Friends of Mount Alexander Diggings, Castlemaine, 2004.

27

BICULTURAL SENSES OF PLACE

In 2014, invited to propose a public art strategy for the new Perth City Link City Square project,[1] we recommended an approach where the public art should be 'generative in the design': 'It does not stand outside the City Square design process. It does not precede the project and have to be accommodated. It does not come after the design process and have to be accommodated. It is the art of making the new City Square authentically public. It does not occupy the space: it helps to create it'.[2] We noted that

> integration does not mean: reduction, homogenization or sameness. It means restoration of authenticity and renewal of meaning. It means 'to make whole or one'. But an integer stands apart and is untouched. Do we want a collection of integers? No, we want the operation that multiplies them. This operator is good design: it makes things clear but it also combines them with a new logic and power. a whole number only makes sense as part of a set: wholeness is inseparable from many: convergence (community, meeting) and diversity depend on each other for their human appeal. The operator creates a set of authentic elements. In the City Square we achieve integration when the authentic elements are arranged in a coherent way. The coherent arrangement

is a 'template': the template is the design equivalent of the set.³

'A creative template', we asserted, 'is a way of translating across different scales of the design: at the scale of the site as a whole, it is subtly imprinted on the site's multisensory appeal, producing ambience; at a middle scale, it influences specific features of the landscape and, particularly, the successful development of an integrated landscape and architectural vision; at a local scale, it creates a rich setting that supports the public art program, ensuring that individual works are in dialogue with their surroundings – and with one another.'⁴ Not only did this cease to be a rhetorical claim when our team was awarded the contract; in the period between our tendering for the job and winning it, the premier of Western Australia decided that the new Perth City Square due for completion in 2017 should be known as Yagan Square. Yagan was a Noongar man who in the early days of white colonisation led resistance to the invasion. He was what would today be called a freedom fighter. He was treacherously murdered by white 'friends'.⁵ In contrast with the situation in Alice Springs, where a bicultural approach to place-making was resisted, an opening was being created in Perth, on the highest political authority, to envisage a bicultural place of meeting and reconciliation.

In explaining the character of the creative template, we drew on the etymology of the word *template*. The creative template establishes a symbolic lexicon, a constellation of cross-cultural convergences or likenesses. They are visual forms, physical gestures, narrative structures, metaphoric associations and shared economic interests. The lexicon has a grammar in the sense that it is derived from the 'Images' in Mircea Eliade's sense and articulates a particular myth of place.⁶ The template does not presume commensurability or translatability. The word *template* is interpreted in the older, dynamic sense of tension, stretch and measure. The Sanskrit root may have the idea of stretching space or introducing time. Space imagined in this way is a string figure, and the string figure became an important symbol of the meeting place that the symbolic encounter might open up. As I wrote in the interim report,

> A creative template is a technique for holding things apart together: in an urban context it enables us to see the public space as immanent, self-organising. In terms of heritage, it isolates the through lines or principles of change that materialize at certain times and places. The cultural, educational and symbolic significance of string figures in Australian Aboriginal cultures is widely documented: they are spatial mnemonics for the fundamental relationship between sky and earth; they can model family relations. They translate social laws into a lasting physical gesture: the sinews of the body are transformed into the 'tension' that tunes the good society.[7]

These are positive associations, but the value of reinvigorating the symbolic lexicon is that it allows things to lie apart: to be drawn together because they lie apart. The metaphorical association does not cancel out the difference (as happens when it is seen as illustrating a concept) but goes beyond the concept to map what lies irreducibly in-between. It is 'dark writing' in relation to the light writing of the computer aided urban design concept. This discretion addresses, incidentally, the question of intellectual or cultural appropriation – the challenge of translating local knowledge either cross-culturally or geographically. For, in effect, it allows the distinction between the inner story and the outer story to survive. If any 'Image' (story or symbolic form) is a Russian doll of meanings, it can never be reduced to a sign. An imaginative identification with its purposes protects the inner meanings, which belong exclusively to knowledge-holders within communities, and whose proper circulation is dictated internally but peels off, as it were, the outer layers that can be secularised, transported and exchanged successfully.

The myth is treated mythopoetically, but at the heart of the discovery of convergent meanings is the resistance of the symbol to full translation or exposure. 'Mythic fictions have the advantage that they can simultaneously carry several different meanings. They also veil those meanings, which is an advantage since "familiarity breeds contempt"'.[8] Because the symbolic form is constitutionally polysemous, it allows a multiplicity of identifications. It is not exhausted by the proposed equivalences but can build new associations, significances and recognitions.

It is worth pointing out that the key terms *passage* and *template* are related; and, further, both contribute to a dynamic definition of *fit*. This emerges in Georges Didi-Huberman's book-length study of flamenco in its relation to bullfighting. The bullfighting term *templar* is, broadly, the technique of maintaining the space between the toreador and the bull through the manipulation of the coat.[9] In this temporary, temporising or making timely moment, the instant seems to contain the whole of eternity. Space is similarly contracted and unfolded: an extreme potential approach or rapidity of movement is balanced with a virtual immobility (comparable with the way the flamenco dancer revolves on the spot). To create this kind of *templum* is to control a spaciousness, which is essentially a stretching out of the moment. The toreador tempers the impulses of the animal and is himself well tempered – flexible, supple, strong. To be bad tempered is to lose this sense of time as the pass, the materialisation of the space in-between. Both bullfighter and flamenco dancer temporise; that is, they create space, finding pretexts not to converge on the conclusion. Their evasion is artful because it is confined to such a narrow template, which maximises the chance of violent meeting (the *temporale* of the lightning strike) and therefore the skill required to temper the bull's behaviour. For the bull may be substituted the conversion of eros into a conventional pas de deux or the clockwork time of imperial routine.

The aesthetic of *templar* combines stillness (contemplation) and turbulence (the tempest). It is where *fit* recovers its etymological sense of *struggle*, when the fitful conflict that haunts meeting is played out. Its other side is the *pass*, the avoidance of the bull's attack. Pass, like passage, is a middle voice concept. You pass someone, but you also pass the ball. You make a pass, a flirtatious move, like the toreador shaking the red coat, perhaps. Or you pass, staying out of the game. If you have a pass, you have either free entry or permission not to take part. Similarly, a passage both implicates and liberates: a dead end is a passage that has lost its potential to discover a new beginning in the ending. A pass is not only in time; it has timing or tempo. The most modest dance is always polyrhythmic, just as the least ambitious of poems is polysemous.[10] The transition from stop to start is, in reality, from a suspended movement with its own inner time to a movement that externalises time. Thus, the poses do not succeed each other according to a formula: the different modalities exist simultaneously as possibilities. That is, they fit. It may be that this is a way to explain the efficacy of Aboriginal Australian rain-making ceremonies.

Carl Jung discusses metaphors 'in which time appears as a river, a wind, or a storm – "the stream of the hours that pass" – or "Tempestas horarum"', explaining that the Latin *tempestas* can mean '"space of time", "passing stream of time", as well as "weather" and "storm"'.[11] This use of 'weather' corresponds to the Australian-English identification of 'weather' with 'change', rain and so on. In any case, the template is a choreotopographical device when it opens up a space ready for something to happen: what happens is not a synthesis of earlier movements but the amplification of passing. Endless crisscrossing preserves the double movement of sociability. What Rodolphe Gasché describes as one of the earliest forms of thought, the *chiasm*, reclaims its function in public space as one of the primordial forms of sociability: allowing 'the drawing apart and bringing together of opposite functions or terms,' it becomes, transposed to public space design, a meeting place conceived in terms of borders, passages and the coexistence of mobile, undecidable differences.[12]

These reflections gave us a clue to the kind of mythopoetic data that might be looked for in the context of developing a bicultural sense of place at Yagan Square. The pre-emptive decision to name the new civic square for Yagan was a bold move politically, but what did it mean culturally? What kind of identification was imagined? Yagan was a charismatic figure, but the white settlers' treatment of him (and his people) was disgraceful, and his commemoration, while it provided long-overdue public recognition of Perth's Aboriginal peoples and a history of territorial dispossession and cultural injustice, offered little basis for walking together into the future. As Yagan said to the Irish-born settler and lawyer George Fletcher Moore, 'As we walk in our own country we are fired upon by the white men; why should the white men treat us so?'[13] The techniques might have changed over the last one hundred and eighty years, but not the treatment. The impact of the *Aborigines Act 1905* (WA) continues to be felt. On the recommendation of the notorious Chief Protector of Aborigines A. O. Neville, Noongar people were from 1927 forbidden to enter the city – a prohibition that lasted until 1954.[14] In effect, Noongar have lived and to some extent continue to live in what is for them a police state. While it may not be the function of a civic square to write a new social, cultural and political script, it was inescapable that the dramaturgy the Perth square proposed under the name of Yagan had to take account of this 'state of exception'.

One hopeful precedent for finding common ground was, in fact, Yagan's already quoted statement. Although placed in quotation marks, they were not Yagan's words. They were a translation of what Moore *thought* Yagan might have said. The full passage runs, 'Yagan stepped forward and leaning with his left hand on my shoulder while he gesticulated with the right, delivered a sort of recitation, looking earnestly in my face. I regret I could not understand it, I thought from the tone and manner that the purport was this: "You came to our country – you have driven us from our haunts, and disturbed us in our occupations. As we walk in our own country we are fired upon by the white men; why should the white men treat us so?"'[15] Moore *identifies* with Yagan, remarking of the speech he had just himself improvised, 'This reminded me of a chorus in Greek tragedy.' Understanding that Yagan's step forward, the hand on the shoulder and the gesticulations are forms of solicitation, Moore acknowledges the suffering that Aboriginal people experience. He recognises that the co-presencing Yagan attempts when he looks Moore in the eye is a moral injunction. Recognition of a contract based on mutuality is sought, one that can never be divorced from its physical performance. Moore appreciates intuitively the point that, as already stated, most ideas are communicated contextually and depend for their meaning in varying degrees on analogous or habitually associated other actions or signs. Moore appreciates intuitively Bateson's point that the idea of *going for a walk* cannot communicate an alternative way of going forward; there is, as it were, no going back. He understands immediately that Yagan's rhetoric is ambient, embedded complexly in the terror of the moment.

Such gestures were not only expressive; they could be imitated. In his *Descriptive Vocabulary* of the Noongar language, Moore lists the word *Ăbba*, defining it as 'a word of friendly salutation with the natives about Augusta, accompanied by the act of rubbing the breast with the hand, and spitting at the same time'. He notes that 'there does not appear to be any established mode of salutation customary among themselves [but] to hold up the open hands is used now by the white and black people as a sign of amity', adding 'but this is chiefly to show that the hand is unarmed, or the disposition friendly'.[16] Moore's observation offers an exact historical precedent for the method of the creative template. A convergence is discovered between Noongar people and white settlers through the medium of a hand sign; however, in being adopted as a general 'mode of salutation', the gesture changes its meaning. In a context of mutual suspicion and dread, it becomes a peacemaking gesture, a positive 'sign of amity'.

On the same principle of contingent convergence, a gesture that posed the question of admission was given to us by a Noongar custom: 'When Noongar people visit a river or water body, we throw a handful of sand into the water. We use language to let the Waugul know of our presence. Noongar people see the condition of the rivers and waterways as directly related to the wellbeing of Waugul. It is part of our caring for country and the cultural landscape to ensure that Waugul is not disturbed'.[17] The Noongar gesture informs the creative spirit of place of an intention to visit. Like the hand on the shoulder, it invites reciprocity. It implies a mutually sustaining contract. Therefore, in the context of a cross-cultural interweaving of movement forms, the obvious resemblance of the sand throwing to the action of the sower, that archetype of post-Sumerian agriculture, who bends forward to cast seed into the soil, was a priori worth investigating (see Figure 37).

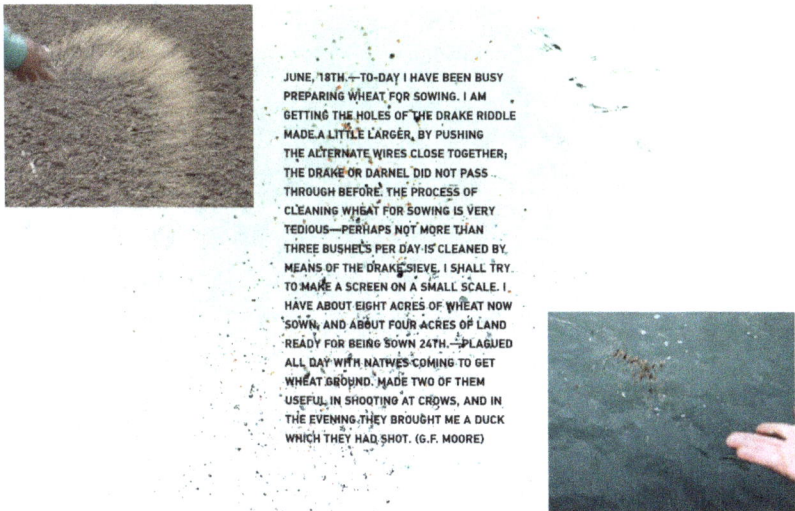

Figure 37 Material Thinking, 'A New Body: Creative Template at Yagan Square', 7 November 2014, 1–11, p. 4.

But we did not have to go the ancient Middle East, as, in Perth, in the early colonial period, these different cultural practices became entangled. Moore occupied Noongar land and began to cultivate it. The country's traditional owners visited him and observed him sieving grain preparatory to sowing; on 18 June 1834, Moore wrote, 'To-day I have been busy preparing wheat for sowing. I am getting the holes of the drake riddle made a little larger, by pushing the alternate wires close together; the drake or darnel did not pass through before', Moore writes, adding, two days later, that 'the process of cleaning wheat for sowing is very tedious'. Keen to have some of the grain ground to make flour, his Noongar visitors offered him ducks and swans' eggs, procured, one presumes, in their legitimate hunting grounds (where approach had been announced in the appropriate way).[18]

In other words, across different economies, common gestures spread. The fact that Noongar people were coming 'to get wheat ground' indicates that they were familiar with this food source – the idea that Noongar and other Aboriginal peoples were exclusively hunter-gatherers is another oppositionalist myth. The identification of cultivation with fixed property rights and exclusive ownership made it difficult for the settlers to classify Noongar passage as anything other than trespass. However, the ambivalence of ordinary gestures and their potential symbolic fertility suggested a different way of relating. The gesture of scattering, at once an act of Dionysian *sparagmos*, or fragmentation, and of renewed identification with the country, materialised an economy of care in anybody's language. It did not do this directly: throwing sand and scattering seed fulfil different functions; but, gathered like this, their different economic and cultural meanings brought into ironic juxtaposition, they could (through the mutual recognition of difference) generate an experience in common, one likely to promote 'amity'. In this sense it humanised a gesture met before in the discussion of Federation Square, where, as we saw in the account of the second creation, Bunjil not only cut up people and scattered them, but also, through this act of fragmentation, arranged them in their proper places, in this way placing undecidable difference at the heart of the new socio-political order.[19] As cultural or missionised Christians, white settlers and Aboriginal

Australians alike may have found such analogies easy to grasp: the Parable of the Sower was told, Jesus explained, because people approached understanding through the senses — and their senses had lost touch with the truth ('Though seeing, they do not see').[20] In another register, the newcomers heard but did not listen. Either way, the outward sweep of the hand and exposure of the palm communicated a meeting across difference outlawed by the law.

Place myths are given because they are histories. Places are made after their stories, and the designer dramaturg is, historically speaking, an 'archaeologist of the morning', as the poet Charles Olson says of himself.[21] As a choreotopographical catalyst, the template has no value if it is imagined as an inflexible overlay. Its sole value is to vibrate like a tympanum and make visible the spatial histories that ephemerally score the site, and whose retracking (amplification and relaying) can serve the double purpose of recollection and invention, a mythopoetic action directed towards cross-cultural identification. Just as the name *Golden Grove* was given at the Darlington campus of the University of Sydney, so, at Yagan Square, the story of Balbuk is given. While Yagan may have had only visiting rights to the country where Yagan Square will stand – in backing the premier's choice of name, strict historical accuracy has, it seems, to be weighed against the opportunity for long-overdue public recognition – the claims of Balbuk on the site are uncontroversial. On the other hand, her recorded behaviour there remains the best documented instance of civil disobedience on the (white) record.

In *The Passing of the Aborigines*, a book whose title is in this context doubly ironic, Daisy Bates writes,

> Balbuk had been born on Huiroson Island at the Causeway, and from there a straight track had led to

the place where once she gathered *jilgies* and vegetable food with the women, in the swamp where the Perth railway station now stands. Through fences and over them, Balbuk took the straight track to the end. When a house was built in the way, she broke its fence palings with her digging stick and charged up the steps and through the rooms. Time and again she was arrested.[22]

Here, in advance, as it were, was the antithesis of the situationist *dérive*. While Guy Debord advocated attending to 'the path of least resistance', and supported individuals setting aside 'all work and leisure activities, clearing their minds of all their usual motives for movement and action, then let[ting] themselves be drawn by the attractions of the terrain and the encounters they find there', Balbuk selected the path of most resistance.[23] If Debord advocated the *dérive*, she enacted the *arrive*.[24] There can be no doubt that this was a symbolic act of political resistance. We cannot know how precisely her track was 'straight', but in any case, it was followed in reaction to the occupation of the new urban grid with buildings. Her line was an antilinearist protest.[25] Again, in advance of Gordon Matta-Clark's architectural interventions, Balbuk undertook something far more radical: instead of punching holes through buildings earmarked for demolition, she took on buildings at the beginning of their life cycle. Looking for passages through them, she insisted on the existence of a negative architecture of communicating paths. She satirised the spatial schizophrenia that informed the favoured template of colonial planning, a grid that rationalised communication and regulating passage by multiplying obstacles to movement.

Balbuk put her body on the line. The spatial gesture (the *arrive*) pitted walking against building. She did not take *any* path.

Writing of another Australian Aboriginal people, the Gurindji, anthropologist Minoru Hokari explains that their concept of the *right way* is to be taken literally: the organisation of the landscape rightly orients people, teaching them 'how to look after this created world'.[26] Balbuk took a direction, the right direction, and 'her motion with intrinsic measures' occupied 'space as it generate[d] it'.[27] In this sense, the description of her path as a *track* is significant: in retracing the route, she remarked the track afresh each time. The authorities could follow her track and find evidence of trespass, but this she made no attempt to conceal. What mattered was the performative utterance and its ambient context. Reiterated in this way was a passage that remained unceded. In blocking her passage, the colonial property developers blocked their own access to country. Although straight and direct, Balbuk's path-making involved a reciprocity between her mobile body and the flesh of the land. Another Noongar word, *bidi*, is defined by George Moore as 'a vein; the main path, or track, pursued by the natives in passing from one part of the country to the other, and which leads by the best watering-places; also a sinew'.[28] Anthropomorphic interpretations of topography may be found in every culture. The novelty of this analogy is to identify a landscape feature with human locomotion. Passing from one place to another is imagined as muscular. Or else, the path is like a channel of recurrent movement, a vein of the regional heart.

Notes

1. Managed by the Metropolitan Redevelopment Authority on behalf of the West Australian Government, Yagan Square is a project of architects Lyons, and Iredale Pedersen Hook, landscape architects ASPECT Studios, and Material Thinking. Note that the name change, initiated by the Western Australian premier, occurred midway through the tendering process.
2. Material Thinking, 'The Challenge of Integration: Statement of Vision for

Public Art', 5 March 2014, pp. 1–7, p. 5.
3   Ibid.
4   Ibid.
5   For a well-informed account of his life and of the posthumous history of his severed head, its transport to England and its rediscovery and repatriation, see http://en.wikipedia.org/wiki/Yagan.
6   Eliade, *Images and Symbols*, p. 20.
7   Material Thinking, 'A New Body: Creative Template @ Yagan Square', Melbourne, 4 November 2014, p. 11.
8   Bucklow, *The Alchemy of Paint*, p. 168.
9   Georges Didi-Huberman, *Le Danseur des Solitudes*, Éditions de Minuit, Paris, 2006, p. 132.
10 Ibid., p. 94.
11 C. J. Jung, *The Seminars*, vol. 1, *Dream Analysis: Notes of the Seminar Given in 1928–30*, ed. William McGuire, Princeton University Press, Princeton NJ., 1984, p. 428, n. 2.
12 Carter, *Meeting Place*, pp.84–5, quoting Rodolphe Gasché, (Chap 9, endnote 20 above).
13 George Fletcher Moore, *Diary of Ten Years Eventful Life of an Early Settler in Western Australia; and also a Descriptive Vocabulary of the Language of the Aborigines*, M. Walbrook, London, 1884, p. 191.
14 Jo Darbyshire, *The Coolbaroo Club, 1947–1960*, City of Perth, 2010, viewed 8 June 2015, <www.perth.wa.gov.au/sites/default/files/Catalogue%20Coolbaroo%20Club.pdf>.
15 Moore, *Diary of Ten Years Eventful Life of an Early Settler in Western Australia*, p. 191.
16 Ibid., *Descriptive Vocabulary*, p.1.
17 *Spirituality*, Kaartdijin Noongar – Noogar Knowledge, n.d., viewed 8 June 2015, www.noongarculture.org.au/spirituality/Spirituality.
18 Moore, *Diary of Ten Years Eventful Life of an Early Settler in Western Australia*, pp. 221, 222.
19 See Chapter 9, endnote 1 above.
20 *Matthew* 13:13.
21 Charles Olson, *Collected Prose*, University of California Press, Berkeley, Calif. 1970, p. 206.
22 Daisy Bates, *The Passing of the Aborigines*, John Murray, London, 1957, p. 70.
23 Guy Debord, 'Theory of the Dérive,' trans. and ed., Ken Knabb, *Situationist International Anthology*, Bureau of Public Secrets, Berkeley, Calif: 1981, p. 50.
24 Literally, as she aimed to '*put ashore*' twice, crossing to the city site from Huiroson Island and traversing the city to the edge of the swamp.

25 In another publication, where the relationship between Daisy Bates and Balbuk is greatly fleshed out, Bates notes that the kind of 'road' Balbuk took was not straight but 'swerved to right or left according to the facilities (food, water, etc.) for camping or hunting, which certain places afforded – names were applied, either indicative of the natural product to be found in the vicinity, or marking some peculiarity or commemorative of some circumstance attached to a particular locality' (*Aboriginal Perth: Bibbulmun Biographies and Legends*, ed. P. J. Bridge, Hesperian Press, Perth, 1992, p. 23). In other words, names refer to passage and calibrate movement. They refer to encounter and have an order (like the peeling back of a wave or any other traverse of country).
26 Minoru Hokari, 'Gurindji Mode of Historical Practice', in Luke Taylor, Graeme K. Ward, Graham Henderson, Richard Davis & Lynley A. Wallis (eds), *The Power of Knowledge: The Resonance of Tradition*, Aboriginal Studies Press for the Australian Institute of Aboriginal and Torres Strait Islander Studies, Canberra, 2005, pp. 216–17.
27 Correa & Correa, 'Whither Science?, p. 37.
28 Moore, *Descriptive Vocabulary*, p. 8. Daisy Bates notes that Bibbulmun groups along the coast between Augusta and Jurien Bay called themselves *Bida-kal*, where *kal* meant fire, and the word signified 'members of the same fire, hearth, home, town, country, one and the same people, of the same sinew etc., or as we would term them, a kindred people' (*The Native Tribes of Western Australia*, ed. Isobel White, National Library of Australia, Canberra, 1985, p. 48).

28

PHYSICAL GESTURES, ENERGY PATTERNS

In string figure or fibrecultures, this mode of symbolic thinking may be commonplace,[1] but it is obviously attenuated in Western planning, where the language of connectivity is relentlessly Newtonian and functionalist. At issue is a poetic as well as a political impasse. The hand on the shoulder, the *arrive* of Balbuk, the gesture of scattering are commonsense choreotopographical graphemes: in the hands of the designer attuned to their symbolic potential, they can inform the dramaturgy of the new place. They point to the possibility of a new cross-cultural aesthetic habituated to the in-between, where passage is timed and meeting spaced. George Moore's *Descriptive Vocabulary* seems to lend support to this view. Take the term *wallu*, evocatively glossed as meaning 'an interval or open space between two points or objects; the division of the hair when parted on the top of the head; partial baldness; morning twilight; the interval between night and day'.[2] Here, the anthropomorphic cast of thought is allied to an aesthetics of the interval. The *sentier* is not simply a back-and-forth passage, like the arabesque of the needle; it is a parting, a score in time. A tradition of such openings would be a general understanding of the *right way*. But this analogical way of being in the world was not shared by the colonial authorities. The effort to reopen an old way in the new (dis-)order was regarded by the local magistrate as an act of trespass.

Although the black swan is native to the Perth region – the Swan River that flows through Perth is named for it – Balbuk was positioned as 'the black swan of trespass' – that is, as a foreigner in her own country. Australian poets Harold Stewart and James McAuley coined the phrase 'the black swan of trespass on alien waters' in 1943, in a series of hoax poems (ascribed to one 'Ern Malley') originally designed to satirise the pretensions of Australian literary modernists.[3] However, these ironically intended attacks on writers who attempted to 'go native' by incorporating Aboriginal Australian words proved more memorable than anything Stewart and McAuley wrote under their own names. Satirising facile and unhistorical efforts to build a cross- or bi-cultural literature, they confronted a cultural limitation of their own – the trespass of English in Australia, which continually risks self-contradiction when it attempts to forge poetic connections. Had the poets written 'white swan of trespass', they would have invented an apt, if conventional, metaphor of colonisation: the sailing ships of the early colonists probed the coastlines in exactly the same vaguely menacing way that the white swan haunts riverside picnickers in England. Instead, though, 'the black swan of trespass' is invoked, a spuriously impressive symbol. But what is satirised? The bird does not float on 'alien waters', but a poetic lexicon borrowed from England does.

As Mircea Eliade says, knowledge is not simply 'a matter of photographic similitude of logical analysis' but involves poiesis, 'a making and shaping that in certain ways is analogous to that of the writer or artist'.[4] In the designer-dramaturg, this takes the form of heeding mythopoetic intuitions, however they arise. For, after reflecting on these themes, I had a dream in which, indeed, the gesture of throwing or scattering became fused with the image of the black swan:

I have a dream in which the constellation of sand grains – like a field of raindrops on the water – turns into swan's feathers. They are the tiny down feathers, black and white, moulted when the black swan stands flightless in the estuary. The down feathers float on the tide and in this picture form a distribution pattern which bobs on the waves, contracting and widening like the knots of a string figure. These tiny vessels could be canoes or coracles. They could be a fleet of cirrus clouds strangely bruised and dark; they could be the 'dabs' of a Japanese brush master; they could be musical notes. They seem to be strung together by the water's elastic movement.[5]

Dreams are not only propitious or otherwise: in the context of mediating a new sense of place, they offer a primary medium of symbolic communication that is direct because pre-rational and unthreatening because (seemingly) innocent of intention. They may have little historical value, but the very ingenuity of the connections they suggest makes for an interesting talking point. They introduce a topic where the symbolic imagination can safely roam.

This, indeed, proved the case when discussions with the appointed Noongar representatives, the Whadjuk Working Group, were opened. These discussions followed earlier ones with Noongar artist and Metropolitan Redevelopment Authority consultant Richard Walley, which had found both of us independently arriving at the black swan as a singularly fertile symbolic form. We had agreed that there is a repression at the core of the black swan–white swan antithesis so integral to the trope of Antipodean inversion. The black swan is partly white; although its plumage appears largely black at rest, when it spreads its wings and takes flight, its primary feathers and the trailing edges of its secondary feathers are revealed to be white. Why – in public signage, in heraldic devices and in graphic design convention generally – has this obvious symbol of black–white entanglement been repressed? When our ideas were introduced to the Whadjuk Working Group as a joint proposal, our advocacy of the black swan as an 'Image' in Eliade's sense was not controversial (see Figure 38).[6] The challenge was one of translation. How was a species of bird to inform the programming of Yagan Square? To assemble its cultural and ecological associations might provide a useful educational curriculum, but where was the connection to design?

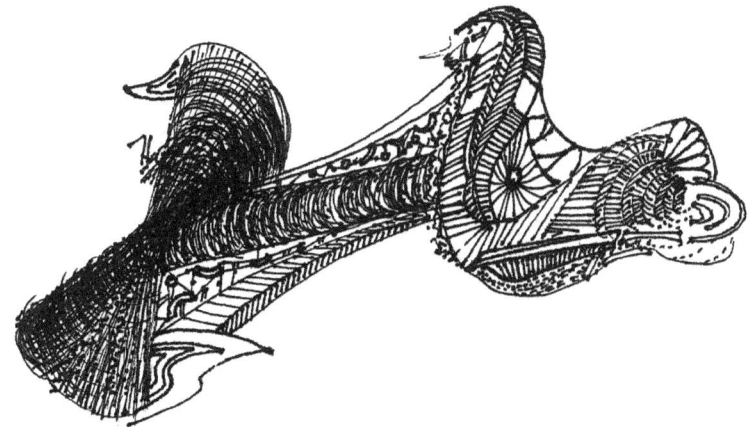

Figure 38 Material Thinking, 'A New Body: Creative Template at Yagan Square', 7 November 2014, 1–11, front cover.

In this context, the dream proved useful: it suggested structural analogies or homologies across scale, technique and purpose, and it implied a unifying field, a centripetal energy counterbalancing the centrifugal force of the *sparagmos*, or fragmentation. In the context of a mythopoetic enquiry, the dream had a heuristic value: it enabled us to discover an elastic principle informing the fragmentation. The critical point was that the transformation of the thrown sand into an interference pattern on the water's surface depended on a minimum of two energy sources. The English physicist Thomas Young's wave theory of light is said to have been inspired by watching the interference patterns two swans created in the surface of the water as they swam side by side. This is not only an uncanny poetic precedent for my dream association of the black swan with the water pattern; it establishes the physical principle that an interference pattern synthesises two sources of radiating energy, which do not cancel each other but combine to produce a new complexity. In my dream, as in any ordinary observation, the water surface agitated in this way appeared to expand and contract; troughs or hollows formed between competing crests. Although wave fronts pulsed through the medium, the distribution of nodes and antinodes remained stable. The dynamic redistribution of the swan – sown into the waves in the form of moulted feathers – was the consequence of turbulence created when two forces met and passed through each other.

As a parable about Aboriginal and non-Aboriginal relations, this phenomenon seemed irresistible. It suggested that the new public space should be thought of as an elastic medium that held the many together in an arrangement that remained topologically constant however much it was stretched or squeezed. The minimum condition of this dynamic movement form was a couple of poles: set opposite each other or side by side, they generated radiating circles of energy which, when they met, produced a new stability. This was not only a physical fact; transposed to the polarised social relations in Perth, it suggested how a new sociability might emerge.

In this thought process, an analogy is found between a physical gesture and an energy pattern. The gesture of scattering finds its counterpart in an interference pattern visible in the water's surface. When these are put together, the body of the sower or thrower is, as it were, pluralised, and the environmental dynamic is humanised as a pattern of sociability. In another analogy, the collective movement form that weaves together the passages through the space, holding them in a state of tension, is the string figure. The familiar cat's cradle resembles an interference pattern where the cords can be imagined as crests and the spaces in-between as troughs. In water, the medium itself holds the waves in place; in the cat's cradle, the outstretched left and right hands fulfil the same office: pulling apart, they create the tension needed to produce the figure that holds together. There are endless regional variants of the basic cat's cradle, including one in which the repeated looping and crossing of strings yields the figure of a swan. But whatever figure emerges, it is the outline and trace of all the interweavings that have gone before. The more complex it becomes, the more stable it is, even though the final form it may assume is increasingly unpredictable. Similarly, it can be imagined that the cumulative behaviour of a crowd is the outcome of all the passages that have led up to it.

In this case, the function of the choreotopographical gesture is to induce a kind of social *hysteresis*, 'the dependence of the output of a system not only on its current input, but also on its history of past inputs'.[7] In dramaturgical terms, it is the recollection of individual memories of passage in a new, collective movement form. The dramaturgical gesture contributes to the public space design when it scatters the fixed forms of the new civic square (the equipment of passing and dwelling, steps, walls, passages) to their proper places so that the right way is taken. As an algorithm of sociability, it can be expected to meet the conditions that the philosopher Emmanuel Levinas found fulfilled in artist Charles Lapicque's *Figures entrelacées*: 'Destroying perspective in its function as the order of walking and of approach, Lapicque creates a space that is mainly the order of simultaneity…It is not space that houses things, but things, by their deletion, that delineate space. The space of each object sheds its volume. From behind the rigid line there emerges the line as ambiguity. Lines rid themselves of their role as skeletons to become the infinity of possible paths of propinquity'.[8] Allowing for differences of context and medium, this formulation might describe the mythopoetic reinvention of Balbuk's walk.

In Perth, though, it will acquire a new body and a new feminist inflection. In her short story 'A last lesson in geography', the American poet Laura Riding declares, 'They say that the earth is round, but we know that it is not'.[9] She is not expressing a flat earth conviction. The story describes 'the beginning of the sixth sense, the sense of speech [as] a sense suffered rather than enjoyed, a sense of the impossible, which in the weak people had meant stuttering notions of immortality, and in the strong people, up to now, only a terrible crying out sometimes with pain they didn't feel'. Riding's 'earth' is the body: 'She was the body now, and the body had but one sense now, the sense of speech'. This sense of speech no longer 'scares away failure' with 'aesthetic success'. It recognises the inarticulateness of the flesh as its horizon. Representing the 'pain' of the body, poetic 'truth' is constitutionally 'inexact': 'The words [the body] spoke were only broken meanings of the word that she spoke…a word not to say but to know'.[10]

Riding's embodied sense of speech, with its curtailed powers of reference, anticipates Maurice Merleau-Ponty's argument set out in *The Prose of the World*: 'We shall completely understand this trespass of things upon their meaning, this discontinuity of knowledge which is at its highest point in speech, only when we understand it as the trespass of oneself upon the other and the other upon me'. And, just as the world of things trespasses on language, so language, the body of speech with its established significations, is imagined as containing 'the new signification only as a trace or a horizon'.¹¹ This is also a good description of the impression Balbuk's trespass might make when re-embodied in Yagan Square's sense of place.

Notes
1 See Carter, *Dark Writing*, pp. 160–4.
2 Moore, *Descriptive Vocabulary*, p.72.
3 See Michael Heyward, *The Ern Malley Affair*, Queensland University Press, St Lucia, Queensland, 1993, p. 243.
4 See Chapter 25, endnote 8 above.
5 Material Thinking, 'A New Body: Creative Template @ Yagan Square', p. 12.
6 Eliade, *Images and Symbols*, p. 20.
7 The BACC II Author Team (eds), *Second Assessment of Climate Change for the Baltic Sea Basin*, Springer International Publishing, London, 2015, p. 485. For the application of this concept to the history of crowd behaviour, see Christian DuComb & Jessica Benman, 'Flash Mobs, Violence and the Turbulent Crowd', *Performance Research*, vol. 19, no. 5, 2014, pp. 34–40.
8 Emmanuel Levinas, *Outside the Subject*, trans. Alphonso Lingis, Martinus Nijhoff Publishers, Dordrecht, 1990, p. 145. For illustration and discussion of the application of these figures to the choreography of public space, see Paul Carter, *Repressed Spaces*, pp. 190–2. Lapicque worked on his interlaced figures in the period 1946–48. Levinas emphasizes their spatial revisionism: other commentators were impressed by their musicalisation of line. For instance, in his introduction to Dessins de Lapicque, La Figure (Paris: Éditions Galanis, 1959), Charles Estienne compared them to the art of J.S. Bach: *'ainsi dans l'art de la Fugue après le sujet il y a le contre sujet et, après le point, le contre-point.'* (p. 2)
9 Laura Riding, 'A Last Lesson in Geography,' *Art and Literature* (Autumn 1965): 28–43, p. 28.
10 Philip Rowland, '"Celebration of failure": The influence of Laura Riding on John Ashbery', *Flashpoint*, no. 6, 2004, viewed 8 June 2015, <www.flashpointmag.com/riding.htm.>
11 Maurice Merleau-Ponty, *The Prose of the World: Studies in Philosophy and Existential Philosophy*, trans. John O'Neill, Northwestern University Press, Evanston, 1973, pp. 132, 133.

Part 7

29

PRESSURE CULTURES/VACUUM CULTURES

Choreotopography encourages performative learning. It returns education to its physical roots in the idea of leading out. The citizen who ventures into the thick of it all is caught up in the to-and-fro of discourse. Stories are found that narrate passage: in acts of analogical naming that create a new pathway between formerly remote concepts, in gestures that express elemental rhythms and periodicities and in images that score essential relations. The position of the designer-dramaturg in this is like that of the migrant in a new country: the passage advocated as the creative principle of the new place is an insight derived from their own situation. The migrant knows there is no end to arriving, that any promise of home security is an illusion. The key to admission is to keep in play the different forces at work, opposing, communing, buffeting, seducing. It is to hold in mind and bodily memory a double movement, towards and away. It is to be able to visualise all the paths to propinquity without any expectation of producing a map. The various iterations of the method – the design options framework, the creative template or even the installed public artwork – are essays, trials in a double sense: they are experiments to keep open the possibility of a meeting across difference and, of course, in encountering the resistance of formally trained planners and the agencies they represent, they are also obliged to defend their intentional incompleteness against the charge of operational indefiniteness.

This view of learning as a collaborative venture explains the style and structure of *Places Made After Their Stories*. Writing of situations characterised by the abandonment of any claim to understand the totality of what is happening, *Places Made After Their Stories* obeys what Theodor Adorno calls in his essay on the essay 'an epistemological motive'. It is 'open' because it eschews all pretension to create its subject. Its subject, in this case the places referred to throughout the book, exists outside it. The essay is, in this sense, a passage or traverse: 'Its form follows the critical thought that man is no creator, that nothing human is creation. The essay, always directed towards artifacts, does not present itself as a creation; nor does it long for something all-embracing, the totality of which would resemble creation. Its totality, the unity of a form thoroughly constructed in itself, is that of non-totality'. In contrast with the 'master work', which (like the master plan) persists in 'theoretically outmoded claims of totality and continuity', the essay can acknowledge the existence of something beyond its control, what Adorno calls the 'unremittingly natural essence of culture itself', whose 'blind natural connectedness' he identifies with 'myth'. Just as the Noongar language can give a positive connotation to the idea of *parting*, so the essay gives value to discontinuity. It thinks in fragments, just as reality is fragmented and gains its unity only by moving through the fissures, rather than by smoothing them over. Adorno writes,

> The way in which the essay appropriates concepts is most easily comparable to the behaviour of a man who is obliged, in a foreign country, to speak that country's language instead of patching it together from its

elements, as he did in school. He will read without a dictionary. If he has looked at the same word thirty times, in constantly changing contexts, he has a clearer grasp of it than he would if he looked up all the word's meanings; meanings that are generally too narrow, considering they change depending on the context, and too vague in view of the nuances that the context establishes in every individual case. Just as such learning remains exposed to error, so does the essay as form.[1]

It is easier to learn a language through the process of echoic mimicry exercised in the midst of a hosting group than to master it via repetitions at night of rote sentences found in a language grammar. Mastery at a formal level does not enable the migrant to fit in. Access to the ambient meaning of rhetorical performances can be acquired only through participation. Some recent writers prefer to talk about atmosphere rather than ambience. Writers like the German scientist Gernot Böhme and the Italian philosopher Tonino Griffero define *atmosphere* as the medium of experiencing the world. It is claimed that atmospheres are spaces insofar as they are 'tinged by the presence of things, people, or the surrounding constellations'.[2] In Böhme's ecological aesthetics of atmospheres, 'atmospheres are neither something objective, that is, qualities possessed by things, and yet they are something thinglike, belonging to the thing in that things articulate the spheres of their presence through qualities – conceived as ecstacies. Nor are atmospheres something subjective, for example, determinations of a psychic state. And yet they are subjectlike, belonging to subjects in that they are sensed in bodily presence by human beings'.[3] Put like this, atmosphere is scarcely distinguishable from ambience: as I write this, a lady on the radio recommends visiting her outback country town because of its 'ambience'. She could just as well have said its 'welcoming atmosphere'. However, this is the point: Griffero also makes a bigger claim, that atmosphere constitutes the original form of communication between human beings and the world. It is the world apprehended from a bodily perspective: it is not a metaphor for anything (an externalised inner state, for example), but is, as it were, an absolute metaphor, the primary carrier of sense, mediating between the senses and the sense of the world.[4] On this argument, learning is impossible unless the atmosphere is conducive to it.

If a distinction can be made between atmosphere and ambience, it is probably along sensory lines. Ambience is associated with locomotion, with the aesthetics of passage. Atmosphere, on the other hand, may be a primarily auditory experience. I doubt if Brian Eno's ambient music disproves this thesis: in the round, it provides a screen memory of place but not an inducement to move. Construed as the supplement of sonic information that contextualises communication but refuses encoding, noise, for example, is the choreotopography of air. Noise foregrounds the texture of sound; it evades translation, communicating a presence without purpose. In an architectonic sense, it is related to the shimmer of resonance and the quality of volume. Echoes are perhaps the most obvious symptoms of ambience: they create whisperings emerging from the tumult of noise, and as they are invisible but suggest presences, they can equally well be said to communicate an atmosphere, distinguishing where the listener is (creating a milieu).

Frances Dyson argues that 'the body has given way to the atmosphere – the resonant, information-filled atmosphere as the site for technological deployment. Like the aural, the atmospheric suggests a relationship not only with the body in its immediate space but with a permeable body integrated within, and subject to, a global system: one that combines the air we breathe, the weather we feel, the pulses and waves of the electromagnetic spectrum that subtends and enables technologies'. Atmosphere, she claims, is 'evocative of affective states within social situations…Thinking of atmospheres also returns us to the breath, the continuous and necessary exchange between subject and environment, a movement that forms a multiplicity existing within the space necessary for sound to sound, and for Being, in whatever form, to resonate'.[5]

Learning in this environment is readiness for change. To be aware of what is happening is, inevitably, to be more prepared for it. To put it another way: beside the incessant production of islands of reason out of the ocean of noise, there is always something more, the power of reflection. There is the constant emergence of information – but only in relationship to our capacity to read it. The ability to read is not simply measured by the accuracy – or ingenuity – of one's interpretation of the text. A good reader is prepared, ready to take care. To be ready is to be forearmed to resist, but it is also to be disposed to embark upon an adventure. Michael Tawa describes this 'being in potential' as gathering 'at the point of acting and assuming that point as a pivot of action', and he makes the additional point that the English words *read* and *readiness* appear to be etymologically connected. If this poetic association means anything, it is that 'reading is not therefore for information or communication. It is essentially a provisional and preparatory practice'.[6] Reading is a provisional orientation towards the future. It is an act of steersmanship whose goal is not necessarily the safe harbour of islands (of reason) but the prudent negotiation of turbulence itself.

In this context, the so-called action research involved in making the video installation *Loops* can be described more precisely as an act of learning through performance. In dissolving the figure–ground distinction, it asserts the existence of an ambience – a feedback loop between performer and place – that is unmappable by other means. It recalls Finnish choreographer Riikka Theresa Innanen's expanded definition of *dance* as an 'ecology of creativity, constituted by the body-mind in motion, interacting with the world through a visceral, aesthetic and kinesthetic interface'. The difference is that in the *Loops* experiment the feedback between people and place is mediated by the artist as dramaturg, and the video image that documents these vortical exchanges is integral to the production of the new social awareness.[7] Perhaps these days such an interaction can occur only through digital mediation. As Ava Fatah gen. Schieck and others point out, the co-presence of urban space and digital space does away with the notion that public space is a stage and replaces it with an environment that regains its exploratory charge: 'With the advent of mobile pervasive technologies (always and everywhere present) and the rapid adoption of bluetooth-enabled mobile devices [where a short-range electromagnetic field surrounds the mobile device to form a digital body], devices can emit a digital field that enables them to interact with nearby devices, and could create a new digital stage for potential new interactions that could give different meanings to our activities'.[8]

In situations like this, an interaction occurs between digital technology, imaginal space and a physical place: some of the observers will have headphones or be talking into mobile phones – or even taking digitally delivered walking tours that cocoon them acoustically from the ambient sound. Sociability is not only a product of mimetic desire but a triangulation between physical perambulation, the architectural milieu and digital technology. Occupants of these virtual or real spaces and interfaces are not the subjects of the master plan and the surveillance camera; able to locate these silent monitors of public behaviour, they can 'act back, self-consciously performing the space against the grain of the patternings and flows desired by the authorities'.[9] Ava Fatah gen. Schieck and Chiron Mottram describe thought experiments in which movement sensors detect people's movements in public space and reconstruct them as compositions of light and sound projected onto large screens. The people entering the field covered by the sensors are imagined as equipped with bluetooth-enabled devices that generate events that 'affect the projected composition; creating a kind of real-time choreography'. Observing their own influence on the composition, the passers-by would become self-conscious participants, invited 'to embody different representational narratives, which generate an emergent collective experience'. The feedback loop between 'the visual composition', 'constantly changing and evolving', and the 'movement throughout the city in real time' would produce 'a collective choreography defined by the structure of space itself'.[10] Permutations on this digital approach to public dramaturgy can be multiplied. It is not clear that the results would be socially emancipatory: instead of licensing hitherto repressed gestures of intimacy, the capacity to manipulate public projections might encourage physical movements that had the maximum effect on the changing image regardless of their efficacy in fostering social interactions. Instead of producing ambience, it might further fragment the social fabric, exacerbating the alienation between self and self-image.

By contrast, the sousveillance artist or counter-performance urban guerilla responds to surveillance technology critically and appears to be heir to Guy Debord's legacy of tactics designed to preserve the realm of the *anti-spectaculaire*. Steve Mann, Jason

Nolan and Barry Wellman classify sousveillance as a form of 'reflectionism', using technology to mirror and confront bureaucratic organisations. Its enquiry-in-performance aims to uncover the panopticon, 'undercutting its primacy and privilege', and to relocate 'the relationship of the surveillance society within a more traditional commons notion of observability'. They emphasise its continuity with Situationism, suggesting that reflectionism or sousveillance 'extends the concept of *détournement* by using the tools against the organization, holding a mirror up to the establishment, and creating a symmetrical self-bureaucratization of the wearer. In this manner, reflectionism is related to the Theater of the Absurd and the Situationist movement in art'. Mann, Nolan and Wellman describe performances that 'engage, challenge and invert the power structure of networked surveillance. The role reversal between the surveilled individual and the act of surveillance allows for the exploration of the social interactions that are generated by these performances'.[11]

However, they remain sceptical about the capacity of such interventions to recuperate the realm of collective sociability associated with the realm of the *anti-spectaculaire*: 'The social aspect of self-empowerment suggests that sousveillance is an act of liberation, of staking our public territory, and a leveling of the surveillance playing field. Yet, the ubiquitous total surveillance that sousveillance now affords is an ultimate act of acquiescence on the part of the individual. Universal surveillance/sousveillance may, in the end, only serve the ends of the existing dominant power structure'.[12] Or, to put it another way, the attempt to build a 'pressure culture', one alive to 'the atmosphere created by things, people and their surroundings', may be ineffectual so long as the performances occur inside the larger envelope of a 'vacuum culture'. 'The elimination of air from epistemological consideration characterises a vacuum culture, one that seeks to neutralize or exclude all human and environmental phenomena produced by the application of pressure',[13] and, interestingly, this technicist mindset (which, I suggest, is also embedded in the conventions of architectural drawing) also eliminates the possibility of a choreo-topographical pedagogy: Griffero argues that the best evidence of atmosphere is found in the 'first impression' a place or person makes on us. Atmosphere is, first of all, experienced as a kind of pressure pressing in from the environment. If for no other reason than the logic of breathing, the corollary of such a psycho-physical feeling is surely expression: the modal appearance of the situation – the design it may be said to have on us – demands a response. In this case, atmosphere is not so much produced as managed: springing up spontaneously between subjects and between subjects and their surroundings, atmosphere is a turbulent modality of air (air with attitude) that solicits a careful response. Transposed to a theory of sociability, Griffero's 'first impression' corresponds to the concept of encounter put forward in my book *Meeting Place*.[14]

Without pressure, the encounter that brings the meeting place to life is impossible. The meeting place slumps back into a square drawn on a blank page.

Notes

1   T. W. Adorno, 'The Essay as Form', trans. Bob Hullot-Kentor & Frederic Will, *New German Critique*, no. 32, 1984, pp. 161, 164, 165, 167.
2   Gernot Böhme, *Atmosphere. Essays zur ein Neuen Ästhetik*, Suhrkamp Verlag, Frankfurt, 1995, 33, trans Peter Dalsgaard & Karen J. Kortbek, 'Staging Urban Atmospheres in Interaction Design,' *Nordes – Nordic Design Research* No.3, Engaging Artifacts (2009), pp. 1–10, p. 2.
3   Kate Rigby, 'Gernot Böhme's Ecological Aesthetics of Atmospheres,' in A. Goodbody and Kate Rigby, eds., *Ecocritical Theory: New European Approaches*, University of Virginia Press, Charlottesville, 2011, p. 139–152, 144. Quoting Gernot Böhme, 'Atmosphere as the Fundamental Concept

of the New Aesthetics, *Thesis Eleven* 36 (1), 1993:113–126, p. 122. These references are found in Mark Deggan, '"Not such an empty space": Cinematic Ecocriticism and the Performative Landscape of Damon Galgut's Fiction', in 'Litterature, Paysage et Écologie', special issue, *TRANS – Revue de Littérature Générale et Comparée*, no. 16, 2013, viewed 8 June 2015, <http://trans.revues.org/835?lang=en.>

4   Paolo Caloni, review of Tonino Griffero's *Atmosferologia: Estetica deli Spazi Emozionali*, in 'Art, Objects', ed. Alessandra Galbusera & Pietro Kobau, special issue, *Methode*, vol. 1, no. 1, 2012, pp. 122–6.

5   Frances Dyson, *Sounding New Media: Immersion and Embodiment in the Arts and Culture*, University of California Press, Berkeley, 2009, pp. 16–17.

6   Tawa, *Agencies of the Frame*, p. 312 n. 22.

7   Riikka Theresa Innanen, *The Ecology of Creativity and Evolution of Choreographic Strategies*, Helsinki Meeting Point, 2011, viewed 3 June 2015, <www.helsinkimeetingpoint.com/riikka/paper2.pdf>, paras 1, 5.

8   Ava Fatah gen. Schieck & Chiron Mottram, 'Collective Choreography of Space: Modelling Digital Co-presence in a Public Arena', in George E. Lasker & Ana Luz (eds), *Systems Research in the Arts and Humanities*, vol. 1, *On Choreographies in Music, Visual and Performing Arts, and Environmental Design*, International Institute for Advanced Studies in Systems Research and Cybernetics, Tecumseh, Canada, 2007, pp. 59–63, viewed 8 June 2015, <http://discovery.ucl.ac.uk/7487/1/7487.pdf>, p. 1 (web version).

9   Ibid., p. 1.

10 Ibid., p. 2 (web version).

11 Steve Mann, Jason Nolan & Barry Wellman, 'Sousveillance: Inventing and Using Wearable Computing Devices for Data Collection in Surveillance Environments', in 'Foucault and Panopticism revisited', special issue, *Surveillance & Society*, vol. 1, no. 3, 2003, pp. 331–55, viewed 8 June 2015, <http://library.queensu.ca/ojs/index.php/surveillance-and-society/article/view/3344/3306>, pp. 333, 347.

12 Ibid., p. 347.

13 Carter, 'Pressure: The Political Economy of Air', p. 176.

14 Carter, *Meeting Place*, pp. 10–11. See also Tonino Griffero, 'The atmospheric "skin" of the city', *Ambiances, Enjeux-Arguments – Positions*, mis en ligne le 20 novembre 2013. URL : http://ambiances.revues.org/399. Accessed 14 Feb 2015.

30

INTERWEAVING BODIES INTO PLACE

Any advance, then, from the talking place to the meeting place must take account of the institutional and cultural forces ranged against it. However, in a community that understands 'the sense of speech [as] a sense suffered rather than enjoyed, a sense of the impossible',[1] the poetic discourse of place-making described here offers a promising route. When the repression of pressure is exposed, it suggests new approaches to urban design. In particular, it refocuses attention on sociability. Instead of conceptualising human interactions as an after-effect of functionally organised spaces, a pressure-responsive design practice conceives the city like a constantly changing weather system, where differential pressure is the driver of constant self-reorganisation. The same simile, it is suggested, can be applied to historical experiences: colonisation, for example, can be narrated in terms of differential pressures whose interaction produces a spectrum of traumatic symptoms, described in terms of the pressure metaphor. Hence, after oppression and repression, contemporary Aboriginal Australian communities characterise the revival of ceremony and storytelling as an act of *decompression*. In any case, to return to Yagan Square, as an emotional and political safety valve putting creative energy to productive use, the creative template served an educative purpose.

The creative template uses analogical thinking. It invites participants to encounter familiar concepts and images afresh. It perceives a resemblance between human gestures, movements and even anatomy and the 'giant body' of the urban space. It extrapolates from humanly scaled evidence of convergence distribution patterns relevant to the arrangement of objects and bodies in space. In symbolic logic, signs are polysemous. They do not stand in for something but are related indexically to the phenomena they represent. The gestures of throwing and scattering are not interpreted as the fixed, closed and distinctive signatures of different cultures. Instead, they are recognised as similar forms of design on place. They are the expressions of techniques invested in hand, eye and muscle coordination. Exactly the same 'real world' familiarity with embodied energy marks the way we walk, meet and relate in ordinary life. The dramaturgy of public space is not the intellectualist imposition of a new vocabulary of reconciliation. It understands the meeting place as a medium, elemental, like water, patterned with perceptions of the other and corresponding actions.

Once the non-intellectualist, poetic logic of the creative template is grasped, it releases participants to embrace creativity in the process of developing and interpreting it. Instead of reducing stories, symbols and practices to fixed cultural landmarks (inevitably presented defensively or defiantly), these can be mobilised, reconnected to one another and reinvested with the creative power that, after all, explains their cultural significance. Once, for example, we had located the black swan within an interference pattern of convergent practices, we were free to 'see it everywhere'. The serpentine form of the Swan River, as it turns southward and then west again around the city grid, uncannily suggests the graceful arc of the swan's neck. A similar kind of Rorschach test psychology found the sleeping swan, its neck reclining on its back, in the plan view of the architecture proposed for Yagan Square. Similarly, once we were in this identificatory frame of mind, my dream feathers began to appear everywhere, as shadows under clouds, as intense crosshatching in an artist's drawing, as suspended networks of trembling matter sensed throughout the physical site, like the shadows of people walking to and fro, stretching, alighting, then sailing on.

After the image of the black swan had been accepted by all parties as an appropriate vehicle of thinking about the place, many less esoteric and obviously educational stories emerged. The black swan's cultural and environmental significance could now be explored. The creative template had established the parameters of any anthropological or ecological narratives that might inform the project; they needed to be consistent with the primary function of the creative template, the discovery of the movement forms that would inform the dramaturgy of Yagan Square. Within this frame of reference, many telling data could flow into the program. For instance, Noongar social life was directly correlated with the black swan's nesting. Neville Green notes that the months in which 'swans and ducks [were] nesting in swamps' (September–November, or *jilba* and *kambarang*) coincided with 'family groups merging for collective hunting and gathering nearer the coast. Forming large groups'.[2] Swan behaviour was correlated with human behaviour. In the context of designing a new public meeting place in Perth, the fact that the swan's breeding cycle was associated with the formation of large groups was obviously important. Any educational program or artwork at Yagan Square that invoked the black swan had to be informed by the back story of seasonal sociability.

Swans are associated with large gatherings, but Daisy Bates explains that these meetings were governed by strict rules of resource maintenance. Equally significantly, these periodic assemblies provided opportunities to negotiate legitimate access to country normally out of bounds. Like the water, bunching and stretching, Noongar people alternately gathered together and spread out. According to Daisy Bates, the Noongar word for *totem* was *borungur*. In country immediately to the north-west of Perth, the black swan was a local totem: 'Swan *borungur* in the Gingin district sang for the increase of swans and swans' eggs'. She quotes two *kuljak* (swan) songs, in one of which the nest-making function of swan's down is mentioned:

> swans' down middle don't touch
> eggs sitting or lying around
> swans' down middle feathers lying
> swans' down middle cover up lying.

After the performance of the increase song, the men would invite the different camps to come to the feast. 'When the people came there were many, many swans for them, and eggs, and young swans.' After the feast, the visitors would disperse, 'probably to repeat the performance with some other district totem food of their own locality to which the *kuljaq borungur* [swan totem people] would be invited'.[3]

Yagan Square is heir to a brutal history. Yagan was murdered by settlers who betrayed his trust. His body was flayed for its markings; his head was cut off and preserved, eventually making its way into a museum collection held in Liverpool, England. It is difficult to find much that is redemptive about this story. It offers few grounds for optimism about present or future reconciliation between Aboriginal and non-Aboriginal peoples in Western Australia. On the other hand, the recalcitrance of this legacy, its refusal to contemplate any myth of social progress, may be the point. It forces us to confront history as a narrative of violent interruptions, which, at best, records successive cycles of destruction and reconstruction. It obliges a recognition that the past cannot be papered over and that the present is a parting. When Yagan's head was eventually tracked down, in a mass grave in Everton, and repatriated, Noongar elder Ken Colbung expressed the view that 'the spirit of Yagan would now be able to join the continuum and could perhaps live on in a new body'. And, he added, 'his fighting spirit and stance against injustice should at least live on in our history'.[4]

These observations make the symbolic role of Yagan in the Western Australian imaginary clear enough: Yagan (and by implication Yagan Square) stands for social justice. Yagan Square will be expected to foster inclusiveness, open access and an 'interweaving' that educates non-Aboriginal people in ways to live in amity with their Aboriginal brethren – and while there may be work to do to translate these aspirations into concrete programs, facilities and events, the social and political goals are clear. But initiatives of this kind, while commemorating Yagan, do not address Colbung's other wish – that Yagan's spirit 'join the continuum' and 'live on in a new body'. Colbung refers to Aboriginal Australian understandings of continuity. It is not simply that Yagan's repatriated head can be respectfully interred, rejoined to his mortal remains. The continuum is in a certain sense the country itself – the earth, the land and the water – that permits the migration of the soul from one generation to the next. Yagan rejoins the continuum of

Noongar existence in this place, whose history goes back thousands of years. He returns to his people after exile in a foreign country amid savage people.

However, this belief does not explain how his spirit should 'live on in a new body'; at least in the context of designing a new place of reconciliation, this prediction cannot be fulfilled through a religiously sanctioned act of reincarnation or transmigration. It implies the preparation of a new body fit to receive his spirit. As the importance of Yagan is symbolic, it implies that the new place will foster symbolic thinking, reflection and innovation. Ideally, this is not a piecemeal affair of the kind associated with most public art programs. To achieve a place-based symbolic economy capable of generating new meanings, there needs to be a new (or reminted) symbolic currency. Yagan will not live on in a new body if, for example, a statue of him is cast and erected in a prominent place. Such statues already exist in Perth, and they have the opposite effect, of confining Yagan to an old body – posed forever in anger, immobile, unresolved – they consign him to a remote and exotic past.

To become part of the collective future, the spirit of Yagan has to migrate to a new body. The function of the creative template is to propose a possible body, a new animated being, in which Yagan's spirit can circulate. Yagan Square is imagined as a giant body, with pathways for tendons, but the challenge of this spatial anthropomorphism is to demonstrate its particular and fateful connection with Yagan. This, curiously, is the function of the black swan. Rather than confront the spirit of Yagan directly – an act that risks recapitulating the colonial encounter and its fatal consequence – we must attract his animating presence by other means. Go-between articles of faith need to be found and affirmed: symbols and their narratives that facilitate imagining this world differently. The black swan allows this, its image offering in the prism of conversation pathways into the country of the collective psyche, where Yagan is reconnected to his generation, to related kinship groups and their countries, and redistributed across the region (at once psychic, social and geographical).

Brought together in this way, he suffers a second *sparagmos*, or fragmentation, but this time the sparks of his being, like grains of sand, like embers of fire, like seeds, bring out of the historical whirlwinds of great force a new community, educated to occupy the mottled landscape inherited from colonialism. In fact, dispersal back into the symbolic economy reverses the false anthropomorphism of the bronze statue, with its culturalist reduction of Yagan to a historical hero. It describes the proper approach to spirit country, which is to provide the dramaturgy of return.

Public space dramaturgy understands performance as a long-term and recursive project. The interweaving of bodies, and of bodies into place, does not have a theatrical time frame. It unfolds over months and years. The translation of the string figure into an arrangement of affordances produces a sense of place, but the modifications or evolutions in public behaviour may be hard to assess or measure. The opening gesture of scattering and gathering, stabilised in the image of the string figure, does not exist apart from its incremental realisation through a multiplicity of small acts. If, for a moment, we imagine the people who fade in and out of the frame of Yagan Square as grains of sand cast towards the water, we have a rough analogy for the intelligence of the crowd intermittently gathering there. At a macro scale, each grain belongs to a larger pattern; however, at the micro level of the individual, each follows its own trajectory. It is important that the everyday patterns of mobility which Yagan Square curates remain largely unconscious of the dramaturgical design. The assumption is that, in the absence of obstacles, people in public space self-organise: the object of the indications embedded in the arrangement of buildings, the treatment of surfaces, the thematics of public programming and the interactivity of the public artworks is to rebuild the public's confidence to make political and social decisions about the function and scope of public space.

It is an educative program in the choreotopographical sense; crossing through a symbolically re-enchanted topography, it could produce a new, enriched sense of what it means to *pass*, historically, ethically, politically and physically.

Notes

1   Philip Rowland, '"Celebration of failure": The influence of Laura Riding on John Ashbery'.
2   Neville Green, *Broken Spears: Aborigines and Europeans in the Southwest of Australia*, Focus Education Services, Perth, 1984, pp.10–11.
3   Bates, *The Native Tribes of Western Australia*, pp. 192, 199, 200.
4   *Yagan*, Kaartdijin Noongar – Noogar Knowledge, n.d., viewed 8 June 2015, <www.noongarculture.org.au/yagan/>, citing Ken Colbung, Yagan Memorial Park Newsletter, February 2010.

31

LEARNING CHOREOTOPOGRAPHY

The way of learning that choreotopography practises where undecidable difference is woven into the project of meeting can be applied in other talking places. As a technique of group ideation, it is at home in more formal teaching situations. In these cases, it serves to open up spaces in-between different creative practices, research interests and disciplinary formations. Generally, design studios (and similar forms of learning and teaching events, including masterclasses and workshops) involve the verbal paraphrase of non-verbal concepts. However, the tenor of the discussion is critical: certain implications may be drawn out, certain inconsistencies identified – hermeneutical activities that assume, in fact, the susceptibility of the drawing to principles of elaboration that are rhetorical – but the intention is to intensify and complexify (or integrate) the components of emerging ideas. Students are not usually asked to open a dialogue between their projects; even more rarely are they given an entirely novel area of concern to consider or asked to relate to it their different fields of interest. Even pedagogical techniques intended to encourage the free play of the imagination and invention usually end up consolidating competence within a particular discipline. This applies equally where the participating group is made up of people involved in a wide range of creative research, from novel writing to video art and ceramics: in this situation of eclectic, possibly incommensurable, specialisation, there is no alternative but to seek out commonalities, but these are usually assumed to be methodological.

An alternative option, however, is to take the invitation of such educational events as an opportunity to improvise something new, to imagine the *intermundia*, as it were, that must exist if the concrete 'worlds' (the various works-in-progress represented in the studio) are to exist in any logical relation to one another. And the only way to discover these realms of analogy is poetically, by the power of words to conjure up new worlds.

In a masterclass that I took at La Trobe University, Melbourne in 2012, convened by the Centre for Creative Arts and attended by twenty or so Masters and PhD candidates from a variety of disciplines, the creative brief, or script, for the day made the *intermundium* the explicit focus of the day's activities.[1] As a preliminary to inviting participants to identify shared properties of their different projects and practices, I introduced the Roman philosopher Epicurus, quoting the passage in which he speculates about the existence of worlds between worlds: 'That there is an infinite number of such worlds can be perceived, and that such a world may arise in a world or in one of the *intermundia* (by which term we mean the spaces between worlds) in a tolerably empty space and not, as some maintain, in a vast space perfectly clear and void'. Epicurus proposes that a new *between* world emerges when 'certain suitable seeds rush in from a single world or intermundium, or from several, and undergo gradual additions or articulations or changes of place, it may be, and waterings from appropriate sources, until they are matured and firmly settled in so far as the foundations laid can receive them'. This, I suggested to the participants, should be the goal of the day, to explore the 'additions' that occur when 'seeds' from different worlds or fields of research are encouraged to mingle. Among the 'waterings' of this process would be the passages I brought to the discussion, beginning with the quotation from Epicurus.[2]

Having introduced the notion of *intermundia* and seeded it with some concepts likely to attract 'additions', I asked the participants to consider what criteria would be relevant to the new combinations that emerged. How do ideas or objects, or people, for that matter, *fit* together? How do they join, coexist, mingle or merge? This is, of course, a question about the ethical hope of communication: how does communion emerge from the exchange of gestures, sounds and signs? Perhaps it begins in the recognition that the symbol of symbolic communication is made to be divided, shared and put back together again. Participants were being invited to think about the ontological basis of the group activity in which they were engaged and to consider it as a craft issue, analogous to finding 'the intrinsic logic of the composition of [an] artwork'.[3] We considered whether the *intermundium* fit manifests itself in the design of the in-between, a region or atmosphere implied by the meanings of the preposition *about*. What is fitting contributes to the creation of ambience, a quality of an environment equivalent to its affect.

Fit in this context refers to the power of the performance to make room where something can happen. An active principle of self-alteration is implied, a transformational principle favouring the formation of more complexly bound 'assemblages' analogous to the immanent structures or tendencies that Michael Tawa perceives in the materials of thinking.[4] The notion of fit extends these principles to the constitution of the situation itself. Design in this context is not an external framework and the working out of the arrangement is not like the solution of a jigsaw puzzle. Instead the design of the new ideational space in-between resembles the evolution of a line, one, however, defined relationally as a sequence of moves in which participants become bound to one another in new ways. (At this point in the class, I introduced the term *templar*, discussed above, suggesting that it captured the chiasmatic character of symbolic thinking.) Tawa draws out the character of this development when he refers to 'a region of circumstantial and combinational potential ready to be mobilised', observing that 'design constitutes firstly a playing out and unfolding of that potential in order to comprehend its relational character; and secondly an envelopment and infolding of potential into a reduced or simplified assemblage in such a way as to enable a user to reconstitute and mobilise, or to leave it unexercised according to need'.[5]

In the first phase of the masterclass, we identified some suitable seeds, some topics that seemed suspended between different interests. Catalysed by some preliminary suggestions of my own, the participants alighted upon 'engaged travelling', 'process and shadow', 'mobility and notation', 'pneuma and echo', 'cleaving', 'subjectivity and objectivity' and 'the unframed and autobiography' as combinations that seemed to capture areas of convergent interest or complementary intention. In the next phase, we tried to imagine how these phrases might come to represent unified concepts, and how these concepts might, through a second contraction or integration, relate to one another. The invitation was not solely verbal, but words that seemed telling in this second round of dialogue included 'affordances', 'animation', 'correspondences', 'repercussions', 'interference', 'relational' and 'adaptability'. These concepts have in common an attention to the vibration of surfaces and the communication of energies across intervals. They accommodate complex patternings of the interstitial and turbulent evolutions within the linear. Both in what they explore and in the way they explore it, they suggest the round-and-about, or something of the affective qualities of ambience. I reminded the participants of the peripatetic roots of the word ambience.[6] Expanding on this, I noted that the word *amble* implies a departure from the straight and narrow, a certain locomotory self-awareness; one might sway from side to side; one who ambles takes notice of things about them; their progress is measured, animated and responsive to the affordances the environment offers. The word is also used to describe certain four beat gaits some horses are able to perform: intermediate between walking and trotting, the ambling gait suggests an unusually close communication between horse and rider, an ability that riders highly prize because of the easy suppleness of progress it produces – almost as if the road had been subjected to a kind of rhythm analysis.

The first search for commonalities had created groups within the groups, and the second stage of ideation was a group exercise. It included some highly creative proposals for works of one kind another: 'Pomodoro', 'Whale's legs', 'Aporia', 'Tramping though the looking glass', 'Desire lines' and 'Water sense'. In effect, the *intermundium* was now populated with six creative communities or parts of community, which had as their shared interest the making of works adapted to the emergent creative commons they shared. But what was their social or communal value? Were they still private estates within the public domain, or did they contribute to its coming into being, maintenance and evolution? While they all had a degree of poetic surprise about them, how – reverting to the weaving metaphor – did they pattern and string figure the region? The creative proposals certainly possessed their own 'melodic' lines, but the question of texture remained to be addressed. I suggested that works proper to the *work* of art, identified here with the production of the commons, needed to be *heuristic armatures*, equipment designed in this case to detect, monitor and improve the ambience or what held the different activities together in a way that transcended their individual values. To encourage this further evolution towards the design of the commons, I asked the groups to collaborate with one another: through a second examination of commonalities, their different works were to be distilled into art concepts whose authorship was diffused across the participants and which was possessed in common. As *fit* yielded to *template*, the discursive space seemed hollowed out, able to build creative attachments in almost any direction.

Among the ideas explored in the afternoon session was one designed to 'experience *aporia*'. *Aporia* has among its connotations in logic and rhetoric ambiguity: it is associated with the undecidability of certain situations. But these branching structures of constitutional deferral provide the characteristic fretwork of ambience. If the *intermundium* is to possess ambience, it must be more than the sum of the passages that can be navigated through it: it must have resistances, appeals to the senses that cannot be translated or reduced to their melodic outline. The participants thought that the phenomenon of noise offered a way in to the materialisation of non-passage or blockage. Other templates approached the modelling of the ambient differently, but I focus here on the aural experiment, because it brings us back to the role of the dramaturg in a workshop of this kind: my job updates and adapts the skills traditionally associated with the rhapsode, the singer who patches together his new song from passages found elsewhere and in his improvisation sewn together to create a new plot. The object of this poetic gymnastic is, as it were, to fill the air with seeding concepts and to show, at least in outline, how they can fit together – generating templates that are fitting to the context.

Learning Choreotopography

Few of the masterclass ideas may have been original, but the occasion of their performance was, and the pedagogy of ambience in this environment of potentialities tending towards a more complex 'assemblage' was a skill in designing the borders between ideas in such a way that a drawing together or act of *contornare* was possible, allowing them to fit together. The catalyst of this was the 'winged word' of the orator-mentor, who, in this context, was also something of a trickster-god, beguiling the gatekeepers of the disciplines and the genres so that strange combinations and hybrids could occur. Carl Jung states that 'in several Gnostic systems, the definition of Saviour is "the maker of boundary lines"'. The power that prevents Sophia from being dissolved in the sweetness of the Abyss is called Limit (*horos*). On the other hand, there are double-handed figures, messengers, tricksters, traders who live at and across the margins, like the coast dwellers of Arnhem Land and the old Irish mystics[7] – and the instructor of *intermundia*. Oratory is usually imagined occurring in the forum but the movement of thought that inspires the orator may be anything but theatrically framed: the links the rhapsode or orator improvises between one topic and another may have the character of roped travel across a glacier: the satisfactory or reasonably secure traverse occurs when all the climbers are tightly tied together but enough rope exists to span any crevasse that is likely to open up. Part of the teacher's vocation is to envisage the metaphorical traverse while minimising the risk of falling into incoherence, to re-imagine the border as an art of parting, or rhythmic assembly, rather than as a potentially perilous containment or exclusion.

How should the educational experience of the border as parting be classified? Is the serious play of entertaining a knowledge on the rim of the abyss the kind of improvised exercise any dedicated teacher uses to free up creativity? Alternatively, is it, much more ambitiously, a group-consciousness-raising exercise aimed at social revolution? (The idea of the *intermundium* as a rhetorically ambient commons is certainly historically weighted.) Or is it something else, in-between perhaps, closer to an act of *emargination*, or mutual alteration, in the act of learning – a metaphor borrowed from the characteristic notching of the leading feathers of a bird's wing?

Oskar Kokoschka's teaching methods seem to be an example of the first possibility: 'Kokoschka didn't teach in the ordinary sense. He didn't theorise, he didn't explain, he was not prescriptive in his methods; rather he told stories, he performed. His stories changed dogs into violent wolves, charwomen into goddesses, and homeless tramps into Socratic sages. Even a crumpled piece of paper, seemingly unworthy of attention, became in Kokoschka's teaching the source of a miraculous event, "Look, LOOK!" he would say, "and you will see that this piece of paper is eternally new"'.[8]

The second alternative canvassed above endows such storytelling, or analogy-finding, with a far greater significance. In this, it corresponds to Gilles Deleuze's notion of *fabulation*. Deleuze's account of fabulation and 'genuine creativity' in Henri Bergson suggests how private dreams and hallucinations can connect to creativity to produce 'the shock of the new' in forms that implicate social theory: 'For Bergson, the "leap forward" of genuine creation is unrelated to the shock of the event that induces fabulation. For Deleuze, however, the leap forward *is* the shock of the event, and fabulation is part of the genuinely creative process that makes of the event the occasion for the invention of a people to come'.[9]

The experience I have described, though, is less imaginal than ideational. It is also more directed or plotted: the choreography of the event is consistent with the kind of outcome that is expected. Ambience as the missing discourse in contemporary architectural design is approached through a dramaturgical process that locates the unconscious outside, not inside. Deleuze's championing of fabulation is consistent with the theory of the 'irreducibly social nature of desire' he developed with Félix Guattari, where the 'group-subject' is proposed that 'forms itself from within, keeps itself open to other groups, and offers fluid and shifting roles for its members'.[10] Perhaps, in our context, the outside of the good will incubated inside the institution takes the form of Eros, the Public Worker. In *Meeting Place* a case is made for fusing the classical Demiurge, or craftsman of the universe, with the erotic potential of matter itself: complexification is immanent in materials, which are understood to be disposed to combine and self-transform.[11] Similarly, Deleuzian fabulation is 'a hallucinatory power that creates "visions and auditions", "becomings", "powers", "giants"'. The new myths created in this way are mythopoetic rather than mythological, and whether in language or image they are 'of the becoming-other of the collectivity as it fashions itself by falsifying received truths and fabricating new ones'.[12]

Fabulation of this kind is erotic, reconnective, because it disrupts the causally organised narrative of history. In this sense, it discloses 'the time of the event'. As for the event, it is also a break with history: 'The event is out of sync or in rupture with causalities: it is a bifurcation, a deviation in relation to laws, an unstable state that opens up a new field of possibilities'.[13] Certainly, these possibilities are explored in the safe place of the masterclass. In a similar way, the theoretical stance of emargination, which, through its avian reference, is connected to the rhapsodic use of the winged word, might achieve something decisively concrete when it is derived from, say, a black swan.

However, it seems to me that what can reasonably be claimed is more modest: it is that the trope of the *intermundia* reconnects pedagogy to dramaturgy. According to Marianne Van Kerkhoven, dramaturgy is 'about learning to handle complexity. It is feeding the ongoing conversation on the work, it is taking care of the reflexive potential as well as of the poetic force of the creation. Dramaturgy is building bridges, it is being responsible for the whole…a constant movement. Inside and outside'. Van Kerkhoven puts forward this definition of dramaturgy in an article that strongly rejects the 'rapprochement' between 'theory and practice' that takes place in 'the high schools of art'. She presents dramaturgy as part of a process of cultural and creative renewal characterised by breaking down boundaries – of discipline, of institution and of culture. The great failure of the art institutions, she says, is that they do not promote what she regards as the overdue conversation between *connaître* and *construire*. In principle, 'the high schools of art' *might* renovate themselves, just as theatre has, in part through a voluntary process of self-deconstruction.[14] But to do this in a way that would make a difference to the world outside, and produce work of social value in this enlarged ontological sense, the institution would need to face simultaneously inside and outside, growing like Tadeusz Kantor's 'man with two heads [who is] constantly trying to resolve for himself two "impossible" consequences of nature's excess'.[15]

A pedagogy that haunts the margin as a site of intermediality leading to the production of *intermundia* contributes to this turning inside out. It does this by surfing the edge, stepping next to the precipice: by denting the margin, sculpting gentle notches into it, it creates footholds on a future where ambience – 'the "impossible" consequences of nature's excess' – becomes accessible to discourse and imaginable to design. The Roman writer Pliny the Younger states, about rhetorical performances, 'The orator ought in fact to be roused and heated, sometimes even to boiling point, and to let his feelings carry him on till he treads the edge of a precipice; for a path along the heights and peaks often skirts the sheer drop below. It may be safer to keep to the plain, but the road lies too low to be interesting. A runner risks more falls than a man who keeps to a snail's pace, but he wins praise in spite of a stumble, whereas there is no credit in walking without a fall'.[16] The designer dramaturg who mingles choreography and topography in this perilous way risks an interruption. On the other hand, they come in contact with a nature that exceeds domination or representation.

The ideal outcome of this heady flight is love. Attacking 'the conceit of American self-conception as a democratic state', Kerry Burch explicitly links 'rising levels of student apathy and privatism, the atrophy of democracy and citizenship, the ecological devastation, the cannibalising tendencies within the American negotiation of identity' to 'the categorical denial and discursive forgetting of eros'. Citing Sheldon Wolin, she emphasises that 'the Constitutional framers explicitly, repeatedly, and passionately denounced democracy and democratic conceptions of citizenship. What they favoured was a starkly different republican model of citizenship, one in which the citizen was envisioned as a "loyal subject"'. According to Wolin, under this arrangement, in which the framers represented a kind of 'monarchy above politics', a 'father figure', democratic civic identity was bound to atrophy, and the way was prepared for 'the domesticated creature of media politics'. The founders' original design of American political identity can, writes Burch, be expressed negatively as 'Eros=Knowledge=Danger'.[17] In this case, the revolutionary potential of choreotopography emerges in a different way, as a mode of performative learning that rejoins knowledge to joy, and which the Danish artist Asger Jorn fully understands when he identifies aesthetics with 'superfluity, prodigality, munificence, surplus, the voluptuous, luxury, the generous'.[18]

Notes

1 'Reflecting on Creative Research: A Masterclass with Prof. Paul Carter', Centre for Creative Arts, La Trobe University, 26 October 2012. The Centre for Creative Arts has since been largely disbanded, such is the volatility of Australia's tertiary learning environment.
2 Diogenes Laertius, *Lives of Eminent Philosophers*, ed. and trans, R. D. Hicks, W. Heinemann, London, 1925, 2 vols, vol. 2, pp.116–17.
3 Correa & Correa, 'Whither Science?, p. 40.
4 Tawa, *Theorising the Project*, p. 234.
5 Ibid., p. 235.
6 See Chapter 17, endnote 19 above.
7 C. G. Jung, *Dream Analysis: Notes of the Seminar Given in 1928–1930*, p. 13 n. 10, p. 231.
8 James Toub, 'Kokoschka as Teacher', *Journal of Aesthetic Education*, vol. 28, no. 2, 1994, p. 35.
9 Bergson considered that creativity, or the capacity to make up stories, 'fulfils its ends by creating hallucinatory fictions – vivid, haunting images that imitate perception and induce action, and thereby counteract the operations of judgement and reason. Fabulation, then emerges in the shock of an event, a vertiginous moment of disorientation in which images bypass reason and work directly on the senses to induce action.' (Ronald Bogue, 'Fabulation, Narration, and the People to Come', in C. V. Boundas, ed., *Deleuze and Philosophy*, Edinburgh University Press, Edinburgh, pp. 202–26, 207.
10 Bogue, 'Fabulation, Narration, and the People to Come', p. 210.
11 Carter, *Meeting Place*, pp.141–6.
12 Ibid., p. 218.
13 Ibid., p. 218.
14 Marianne Van Kerkhoven, 'European Dramaturgy in the 21st century: A Constant Movement', *Performance Research*, vol. 14, no. 3, 2009, p. 11.
15 Kantor, *A Journey through Other Spaces*, p. 103.
16 Pliny the Younger, *The Letters of the Younger Pliny*, trans B. Radice, Penguin: Harmondsworth, 1967, pp. 248–49.
17 Kerry T. Burch, *Eros as the Educational Principle of Democracy*, Peter Lang, New York, 2000, pp. 3, 4, 87 (citing Sheldon Wolin, *The Presence of the Past:*

Essays on the State and the Constitution, The Johns Hopkins Press, Baltimore, 1989, p. 91).
18 Asger Jorn, *The Natural Order and Other Texts*, trans. Peter Shield, Ashgate, Farnham, 2002, p. 264.

32

PATCHING POETICS INTO POLITICS

As a poetic practice, it might be considered that choreotopography is ill equipped to venture into the realms of political theory. However, as a development of material thinking acting to shape the public realm, an aesthetic withdrawal from political considerations is illogical. There must correspond to Cameron Tonkinwise's 'poetics for this knowing-in-making-useful'[1] a corresponding politics. The beginning may lie in the kinds of affordances that are designed, in the character of the scribble, as it were; but the outreach of the program will depend on radiating alliances with increasingly diversified interest groups. Joseph Beuys's statement that his highest achievement as an artist was to be a teacher suggests that art is a kind of hospitality that draws out, that encourages creativity. In such a situation, the host or artist shares their sense of the sensible, distributing information about what matters in a way that allows the participants to find their own affordances. David Dobz O'Brien talks about this as 'the transmission of the "unknowable"'. Sarat Maharaj writes about 'xeno-epistemics', or 'non knowledges', which O'Brien glosses as 'the "immaterial affects" of the collaborative process'. Such 'non knowledge' is characterised by the fact that it does not avoid 'contradiction and difference, nor is it consumed by rational and empirical criteria'.[2] This is certainly knowledge whose social implications are 'dangerous', at least to our constituted powers, but how does it get out? Beuys alludes to this in his discussion of the 'symbolic act' of planting seven thousand oak trees. It cannot have the revolutionary effect on society that is hoped for unless it is attached to a movement for revolutionary change (the German Greens, for example): 'Appropriate associations must be linked to this action, to this symbolic act, to this creature tree'.[3] He alludes here, of course, to the necessity of systemic change in our political and administrative cultures, currently represented by the man 'without imagination'.[4]

In the other direction, to propose new forms of governance consistent with the self-realisation of a civil society able to live in the midst of it all, eager to complexify and dwell with the inevitable vortices of turbulent becoming, is to propose a new understanding of public space. If a creative community which legitimately expresses its social work through public art (or the general design of the commons) wants to wrest power back from councils, counties, states and central government, it cannot set itself up in opposition to, or in dispute with, these authorities – as if it wanted to secede. It has to define the land differently, evaluating powers it holds that the present administration neutralises and wastes. Consistent with the projects described in *Places Made After Their Stories*, it will attribute a material intelligence, or self-organising capacity, to country. Instead of treating the land as a cloth that can be progressively subdivided according to simple geometrical templates, it will appreciate the texture of the place. In the context of a statist spatial determination (the classic grid), it will assert the potential of leftover land to generate new ecologies of psychic wellbeing, post-anthropic cultures of biodiverse and sustainable vitality (big picture items that can perhaps be indicated only by analogous modes of social production).

This enlarged and somewhat animistic conception of local space as an ecology of affordances whose appeal accords with a biophiliac thesis also changes the conception of ambience. In the present ideology of place-making, ambience is a mysterious ectoplasm that invests certain designed places. It is not supposed to be a constructive principle, only a kind of lucky after-effect. In the new dispensation, where the creative community produces new kinds of living spaces through its cultivation of the self-organising principles inherent in the environment, ambience changes its character. It can be thought of almost dialectically as the principle of fusing that succeeds the historical experience of fragmentation. Ambience is the after-effect of the collective creative act and, far from being a passive background, preserves in its detection the turbulence of innovation.

A concrete way to illustrate these ideas is suggested by the practices associated with the transformation of textiles into clothes. As I have described, *Alterations* explores processes that reintroduce the fold into planar topologies: different patterns, styles and traditions of clothes-making produce a new patched-together culture of co-appearance. The present object of these practices is to conceal the patchwork, to produce new synthetic patterns that represent a successful fitting together and fitting out. What happens, though, if we attend to the craft of patching – if, instead of glossing over the challenges of the transformation, we examine the conditions that *Alterations* addresses? Patching is a practice of repair that remains visible: patching does not attempt to hide the patch but materialises repair as a creative or innovative act, introducing a new layering or patterning of reality. What happens if, more radically, we imagine a social environment composed of patches all the way down, in which patching is the primary art of socialisation and place-making? In this case, there is no prior template (the grid of longitude and latitude or the pattern the tailor uses to cut the cloth), and the materials for fitting in – for furnishing the new ecumene – have to be taken as given. Instead of cutting them to shape (square, triangle and so on) so that they form a regular patchwork quilt effect, they are accepted as they are. In this case, the new pattern is derived entirely from offcuts, the ends of rolls, the moulds of leftover portions of cloth when the panel is cut from them, and other variably shaped and sized second order figures. The new pattern or jigsaw assembled from these cannot follow any prescribed pattern: the pattern will depend on the physical shapes and colours of the scraps. Working with such a heap of leftovers, the result is unavoidably an investigation of *embellishment* itself, for the ordering and fitting together is nothing other than the examination of the creative potential of the patches themselves. In this experiment, the patches do not cover over anything; they materialise covering (the cloth of the map or the suit) as an act of continuous and endless repair. But what is repaired is not a frayed ideal pattern or geometry but the idea of the patchwork itself, as a mode of creative pattern-making whose principles are derived from the intelligence of the materials themselves.

Transpose the practice of patching to the realm of political geography. If, in a sartorial context, a patch is 'a small piece of material affixed to another, larger piece to conceal, reinforce, or repair a worn area, hole, or tear', in a geographical context it is the 'worn area' itself, the area within the broader terrain that is different, possibly the no-man's-land where something is felt to occur. What may be common to these two meanings of *patch* is roughness, the informal nature of the object's geometry. Hence *patch* is defined as 'a small piece, part, or section, especially that which differs from or contrasts with the whole: a patch of thin ice; patches of sunlight'. Although it differs from its surroundings and lacks a precise shape or stable duration, a patch is felt to be creative. There is a sense that change is focused there. A patch is a favoured horticultural unit: 'a small plot or piece of land, especially one that produces or is used for growing specific vegetation: a briar patch; a bean patch'. There is the idea that the patch is a region of strange care, that it solicits our care and our attention: the police are responsible for their own patch. The patch seems to be where something unpredictable, generative or creative may occur. Because it is associated with change, it may harbour turbulent effects of 'an indefinite period of time; a spell': it might be said that a person 'weathered a difficult patch after losing his job'.[5]

In general, patches draw attention to themselves and act synaptically: they reconfigure the ground as a pattern that communicates; they redefine it as a living network rather than as a passive ground onto which are superimposed stitches or fences. 'To patch something up' is to hasten the repair of something in order to get on. As a beauty spot, a patch draws attention to the person who sports it. It offers a focal point that leads away from itself. In radio and telephonic communications, *patching* signifies 'to connect or hook up (circuits, programs, conversations, etc.)'.[6] Critically, though, and creatively, the patch does not shy away from being noticed. As a small, contrasting part of something, it is associated with maculation, or blotting, and chiaroscuro painting technique. As the form of the *informe*, it can be defined as the unit of dwelling: as stated in *Dark Writing*, 'dwelling, then, is not simply "taking up space." It transforms the space in which one dwells. In dwelling, one must "fabricate out of what is conveniently to hand." Both improvisation and improvement work with the given in order to "create" something new. The critical point is that improvisation prevents improvement from being an act of pre-emptive enclosure. It defines a "dwelling *at the limits* of the space and transgressing those limits." The created space is context, room for performances that are always altering, transgressing, "improving".[7] Patching as repair, as the work of place-making that incorporates the trauma of colonisation, manages the passage between destruction and construction; patching is an inherently chaotic or turbulent 'turn' in social and environmental organisation.

How can this constellation of associations be demonstrated to exist? One obvious starting point is through a consideration of the kind of patching called *crazy patching*, which works precisely with leftover pieces of cloth. The challenge of creating a continuous quilt or counterpane with such scraps may cause the quilter to learn 'as much about specific embellishments as they will about crazy quilting itself'.[8] This is another way of making the point that the quilter-qua-creative dweller has to take account of the material intelligence of the patches themselves (embedded in form and colour or pattern). The instruction that the quilter receives from the process of crazy patching is analogous to the education received in navigating an archipelago: for the archipelago is also formed of patches (islands) that go together (forming an archipelago), even though the individual patches are different and unrelated. To relate the islands so that they disclose a creative region (or archipelago), the topological Gestalt or algorithm has to be found – a principle of amalgamation or regionalisation that generates a continuous field (or distinct grouping).

When the public space is conceived as a process of embellishment – a notion parallel to the valorisation of public art as cosmetic adornment – the material to hand actively informs the arrangement. The creative community cares for its patch – where *patch* has the full range of connotations indicated above. As the analogy of crazy patching suggests, a distinctive feature of the creatively conceived patch is that it is the expression of crazing, that sudden pattern of shattering seen when ice or a reinforced-glass panel cracks. In certain styles of ceramic production, a crazing glaze is characteristic – strictly, crazing is in this circumstance different from cracking, as it is not felt in the surface and does not weaken the load-bearing properties of the structure. (Here, though, crazing is assimilated to cracking, and the classic image of it is any hollow form suddenly beginning to crack and exploding into fragments.) A pattern is 'crazy' because it is defined by its proliferation of unpredictable and irregular cracks: such a pattern does not outline, cloisonné-style, a jigsaw of smaller patches; rather, it creates a labyrinthine or mazelike system of flow lines. In this context, patching is the art of putting back together something that has cracked or been shattered. However, patching does not aim to erase all evidence of breakage; on the contrary, repairing it draws attention to it. A crazy art is one that attributes value to the breakdown of form. Hence, to be *crazy* is to be shattered, but it is also to retain enough volition to make something happen. Similarly, in the intellectual sphere, a crackpot may be cracked (mad) but is acknowledged to have an exceptional if obsessive creativity.

As a phenomenon whose implications are political as well as aesthetic, crazing is the symptom of a system about to enter a phase change. It looks as if the surface is swarming, as if an unstable state is emerging in which the smallest chance perturbation may be enough to tip the whole system over into a new state. In this guise, it is a symptom of the turbulence associated with any revolutionary change, whether subatomic or social. Thus, in a report of experimental studies into particle swarm optimisation, James Kennedy and Russell Eberhart, respectively a social psychologist and an electrical engineer, group the terms *turbulence*, *craziness* and *unconsciousness*. Craziness, also referred to as turbulence, describes the change in a particle's flight when it is out of control. The authors note that when a stochastic variable called *craziness* is introduced, it brings enough variation into the system to give the simulation an interesting and lifelike appearance. They conclude, 'Particle swarm optimization is an extremely simple algorithm that seems to be effective for optimizing a wide range of functions. We view it as a mid-level form of A-life or biologically derived algorithm, occupying the space in nature between evolutionary search, which requires eons, and neural processing, which occurs in the order of milliseconds. Social optimization occurs in the time frame of ordinary experience – in fact, it is ordinary experience. In addition to its ties with A-life, particle swarm optimization has obvious ties with evolutionary computation. Conceptually, it seems to lie somewhere between genetic algorithms and evolutionary programming'.[9]

Because of its association with human behaviour, craziness is sometimes used as a bridgehead term in the application of complexity theory to the working of human systems. For instance, in their article 'The Crazy before the New: Complexity, critical instability and the end of capitalism', Kay Summer and Harry Halpin explain, 'Complexity theory is relevant to any system that links many different parts in a dynamic network, that is, a network which itself changes over time. One of the features of these systems is that they are governed by nonlinearities. This means that sometimes a small event causes a small reaction in the system, but at other times a similar event can have a massive effect. It is easy to argue that capitalism is a complex dynamic system governed by nonlinear dynamics, and so complexity theory may be a good way to understand the social world we live in'. They note that 'complex systems involve many connections between components that form loops of interaction. This contrasts with many hierarchical systems where the interactions between the various components are deliberately minimised. It is the feedback loops involving these connections that can change the system as a whole. So-called negative feedback loops tend to keep the system in its current state, while positive feedback loops may push a system to a new state, or new type of system', and they add that 'regenerating complex systems often have multiple stable states'. Applying this theory of natural systems to human society, the authors 'believe we are living through a period of *critical instability*. This term is used to describe a complex system that is behaving wildly, and seemingly chaotically. Critical instability usually signals the first detectable stage of a bifurcation point, that point at which massive systematic changes start. We are lurching towards a new yet unknown system or systems'.[10]

The same authors speculate about alternative basins of attraction into which global society will fall. Eco-fascism would be an intensification of the present 'socially authoritarian global economy that is materially steady-state for those outside the elite'. An alternative, which resembles the sociopolitical 'association' where choreotopography would be less unfamiliar, is described as follows:

> A second possible attractor would be decentralised and cooperative communities whose relations are based on affinity – that we all ultimately share the same biosphere – that maintain a high level of connectivity with each other. Unlike fascism and strangely like capitalism, this attractor bases its power and resilience on the strength of its connections. This form of social organisation is perpetually open, always seeking new connections; and in the spirit of complexity theory, and unlike previous

revolutionary movements, it embraces no determinism. The logic of autonomy allows the components of the system to optimise their own connections, and so connect to people, materials, passions, and places in manners that take optimal advantage of material and energy flows. Production is linked to a logic, not of growth, but of satisfying collective needs through 'commons'...Production and decisions about production are made via direct democracy – which maximises connectivity. Moreover, this highly flexible system of autonomy, collectivity and commons may well allow us to confront the ecological crisis.[11]

There is an intuitive connection between these descriptions of the behaviour of complex evolutionary environments and the landscape of the patch: crazy patching represents a higher order of complexity than the plain chequerboard and has non steady state potential (or the equivalent of positive feedback loops) inscribed into its fabric. Making a crazy patchwork involves operating at the bifurcation point, as every choice made is both critical and cumulative, producing a cascade of patching decisions that quickly become irreversible. At the same time, as one can build the crazy patchwork in any direction, the swarm of patches can be effected by an intervention at any number of places around the border; consequently, the new order can group and reorganise itself in a number of different ways. There is not one master plan that piecing the pieces together discovers. These features of the patchwork will inevitably reflect the governance of the dwelling place. Governance will not be prescriptive, centralised and stabilist; it will be evolutionary, algorithmic, stochastic rather than deterministic and will depend for its continuing sustainability on the participatory relationship between the actors, the network and the articulation of their always-unfinished communication in the emergence of the patchwork.

The 2008 report 'Governing Civilization through Civilizing Governance: Global Challenge for a Turbulent Future' captures the current stand-off between prevailing myths of governance and civil society and proposed steps for dismantling them. In particular, it urges respect for 'craziness' as a symptom of an emergent reality that defies linearist hierarchical thinking, embracing instead a transition to a new order of complexity and self-organisation. The task of reframing governance involves 'designing in challenging feedback loops' and 'necessarily self-reflexive fractal framing' so that the new 'non-model' is continually open to challenge. A governance system that is cognitively equipped to respond to the 'emergent reality' can 'evoke competence, insight and creative engagement wherever it is to be found', and it supports 'realistic concern to focus on higher order complementary opportunities'. Finally, and refreshingly, it emphasises the importance of reversing our present 'metaphorical impoverishment' in order to be able to think concretely and creatively, in new ways, about governance and globalisation.[12] The concrete expression of these aspirations in design practice is a choreotopography focused on the dramaturgy of encounter.

Notes

1. Cameron Tonkinwise, 'Knowing by Being-there Making: Explicating the Tacit Post-subject in use'.
2. David Dobz O'Brien, 'The Incidental Person and Collaborative Exchange', in Marilyn Lennon & Sean Taylor (eds), *Praxis: MA Space; Social Practice and the Creative Environment*, Limerick School of Art and Design, Limerick, 2012, p. 27, citing Sarat Maharaj, 'Visual arts as knowledge production in the retinal arena', lecture presented at INIVA, London, 12 November 2003.

3   Joseph Beuys, *Joseph Beuys in America: Energy Plan for the Western Man*, comp. Carin Kuoni, Four Walls Eight Windows, New York, 1993, p. 100.
4   Eliade, *Images and Symbols*, p. 20.
5   'Patch', in *American Heritage Dictionary of the English Language*, 5th edn, Houghton Mifflin Harcourt, Boston, 2011, reproduced in The Free Dictionary, n.d., viewed 8 June 2015, <www.thefreedictionary.com/patch>.
6   'Patch', in *Random House Kernerman Webster's College Dictionary*, 2010, reproduced in The Free Dictionary, n.d., viewed 8 June 2015, <www.thefreedictionary.com/patch>.
7   Carter, *Dark Writing*, p. 275, citing Bruce Ellis Benson, *The Improvisation of Musical Dialogue: A Phenomenology of Music*, Cambridge University Press, Cambridge, 2003, pp.31–2.
8   'Crazy Quilting', Project Gutenberg Self-Publishing Press at <http://self.gutenberg.org/articles/crazy_quilting.> Viewed 14 January 2015.
9   James Kennedy & Russell Eberhart, 'Particle Swarm Optimization', in *Proceedings, IEEE International Conference on Neural Networks*, vol. 4, IEEE, New York, 1995, reproduced at Tufts University, <www.cs.tufts.edu/comp/150GA/homeworks/hw3/_reading6%201995%20particle%20swarming.pdf>, p. 1947.
10 Kay Summer & Harry Halpin, *The Crazy before the New: Complexity, Critical Instability and the End of Capitalism*, Turbulence, n.d., viewed 8 June 2015, <http://turbulence.org.uk/turbulence-1/the-crazy-before-the-new.>
11 Ibid.
12 Global Governance Group of the New School of Athens, *Governing Civilization through Civilizing Governance: Global Challenge for a Turbulent Future*, Laetus in praesens, 6 April 2008, viewed 8 June 2015, <www.laetusinpraesens.org/docs00s/civilgov.php.

33

FEEDBACK AND THE MOVEMENT FORM

We say choreotopography operates at the crossing place of human time and space. But how? First, it asserts that the *non-meeting* of time and space is an ideological hangover from a Newtonian myth. Translated into social terms, that experimental approach to the construction of sociability produces a society of primarily unrelated individuals whose interactions are external to their essential identity. This conception of individuality produces the paradox of a unity achieved through indifference to the other. We are alike because we all pursue our own separate paths. Like the Newtonian laws of motion, the rules of sociability allow for collisions that change nothing. An interchangeability can occur, but it does not produce an evolving social awareness or political consciousness. One thing leads to another, endlessly. In social terms, this Newtonian dispensation is either existentialist or Marxist (or both): 'Identity is the practico-inert unity to come to the extent that it reveals itself at the moment as a *separation void of meaning*', but, to continue John-Paul Sartre's well-known analysis of the bus queue, the same separation is also a conformity to exterior conditions: 'Each is the same as the Others to the extent that he is Other than himself'. This produces what Sartre calls the 'scandalous absurdity' of 'the conflict between interchangeability and existence'.[1]

Choreotopography derives its practicability from the commonsense observation of the operational identity of time and space: human movement occurs neither in space nor in time but is their interlacing. Or, better, movement originates the possibility of separation: measurement produces a bifurcation; time and space peel back from each other to produce representation. As an eido-kinetic phenomenon, movement is never aimless but is all placing, all timing. It does not occur against a changeless temporal background or a fixed architectural set. As the order of becoming, it sees them as meeting. Everywhere is no longer the kind of planar abstraction measured by latitude and longitude; it is the quality of contingency, the potential of places to flower. Franz Kafka imagines history occurring in the mid-stride: choreotopography turns this into public space programming.[2] Instead of mapping distances, it aims to score passages, giving value to the intervals between steps, chiasmatic, always opening and closing. The self–Other dialectic falsely represents the worldly constitution of the self – its coming into being through the mother; the figure–ground convention governing the graphic representation of urban designs perpetuates a creationist myth of sovereignty, as if individuals entered public space from nowhere except the immaculate horizon of the will. However, movement is always motivated. There is no voyage without a steersman.

Beginning in movement, the mid-stride possesses momentum, orientation, inclination. As a unit of sociability, the mid-stride might be compared to the parallax effect created as people pass before and behind one another, grouping and ungrouping. Sartre's purely serial group – the bus queue, for example – defined by exterior conditions still looks like a group or bunching organised around a shared purpose. Our gaze is not omnidirectional, objectless; rather, certain primordial shapes or arrangements of sociability inform our assessment of surroundings. Alberto Giacometti does not call his arrangements of spindly figures 'queue' or 'waiting' or 'passage' or some such other descriptive title as 'interval'. He calls them 'City Square'.[3] His arrangements recall trees at the edge of a clearing: other similar groups are called simply 'The Forest.'[4] You can walk around and in-between them, rechoreographing their relationships as you come and go. So with the divagations of everyday life: an interactional grammar, a subtle custom of convergence and divergence, means that the purposeless and the purposeful revolve within broadly shared force fields.

In *Dark Writing*, I quote D'Arcy Wentworth Thompson's comparison of Brownian motion to a 'crowded market-place, always provided that the bustling crowd has no *business* whatsoever' and assimilate it to a Situationist taste for the *dérive*.[5] In the light of Sartre's critique, it could easily collapse into a kind of statistical determinism: what kind of group can evolve from this image of perpetual rebound except one unified by molecular separation? From another point of view, the behaviour of the crowd simply collectivises a mass self-absorption. In his poem 'Reflex musings: Reflections from various surfaces', the great mathematical physicist (and pioneer of cybernetics) James Clerk Maxwell tackles the problem of interaction or interchangeability from the other direction:

> In the dense entangled street,
> Where the web of Trade is weaving,
> Forms unknown in crowds I meet
> Much of each and all believing;
> Each his small designs achieving
> Hurries on with restless feet,

> While, through Fancy's power deceiving,
> Self in every form I greet.⁶

Thompson's crowd has no business whatsoever; Maxwell's crowds weave 'the web of Trade'. But the net result is potentially the same. Unlike Thompson's vision of Brownian motion, Maxwell's crowds are defined by what Sartre would call 'scarcity': in an analysis which recalls Alexis de Tocqueville's description of the paradoxes of American mercantile democracy,⁷ Sartre writes that scarcity, 'apart from any particular practice, identifies each of them as surplus, which means that Other will rival Other by the very fact of their being identical'. But the result of this competition is not necessarily murderous. It may lead instead to evasiveness, 'some practice which has as its sole aim avoiding conflict and arbitrariness by some order or other'. This 'practice', which Sartre calls 'serial unity', leads neither to an affirmation of individuality nor to a new form of social identity: 'They remain on the ground of common interest and identity of separation as a meaningless gesture; positively, this means that they seek to differentiate each Other from the Others, without adding anything to his nature as Other as the sole social determinant of this existence: so serial unity as common interest is imposed as a demand and overcomes all opposition'.⁸

The reason for reproducing this part of Sartre's critique is to highlight the political implications of the choreotopographical approach. From a dialectical point of view, the flâneur of Thompson's crowded marketplace blurs into Maxwell's 'forms unknown…Each his small designs achieving'. No account of coexistence is given, no model of mimetically induced identity formation. The queue, paradoxically, goes nowhere and has neither beginning nor ending. Sartre's initial characterisation of the bus queue as a group without critical self-awareness chooses to ignore the phenomenon of gathering. The distribution of things and people – and exchanges between them – is neither uniform nor random: arrangements are written into the constitution of places (which are, after all, collections of heterogeneous elements). Paul Kammerer's theory of seriality grows from the observation that where there is one queue, there is, as it were, very likely to be another. A series is not composed of units, one following another; some attractive energy draws the units to bunch or associate. The grouping of groups is not due to any common interest but suggests instead a transcendent desire of association. As Sartre also points out, the members of the queue may acquire a group identity, subject to 'the Rationale of series'. Sartre is pessimistic about the liberatory potential of this 'collective unity as a transcendency coming to the gathering of the future (and of the past)', because he sees it as imposed from outside (by the bus company's timetable, for example).[9]

However, the queue – to stay with Sartre's deliberately simplified simile – is not always predetermined. The late 1950s commuter or worker might experience 'seriality as the practico-inert actualization by each individual of a relationship with Others' and understand 'the objective unity of interpenetration in so far as he constitutes himself in the gathering as an objective element in a series',[10] but more recent global (and globalised) spectacles of lines of people (displaced, hungry, herded) show us queues that certainly embody a collective experience that communicates through alterity and whose crowded solitude in no way accedes to the rhetoric of common interests. This is not to belittle the critique: post 1968, Gilles Deleuze and Félix Guattari's exploration of the social nature of desire and their description of the 'group-subject' would have offered Sartre useful ways to renegotiate the existentialist-Marxist abyss. It is, though, to suggest that on the modest plateau of choreotopography the queue is no more inert than any other human arrangement.

The queue is not a neutral series: from the point of view of its appearance or becoming, it is a bunching, a differential pressure zone or interval of heightened tension. Its components can be numbered, ordered; but subjectively, it is experienced as a synchronicity, as a coming together that lacks a clear before and after. This is evident in the simple observation that queues tend to form where a lack of direction is felt. In this case, the forming queue is a kind of hunting party on the lookout for cryptic signs of purpose. It is unusually attentive to its surroundings and whatever information these afford. Besides, it could be argued that queues also have their potential: one person can be a queue. 'The homeless man, as he meanders along the street, is looking for something to break the monotony. He will stand on the curb for hours, watching people pass. He notices every conspicuous person and follows with interest, perhaps sometimes with envy, the wavering movements of every passing drunk.'[11] Queues also leave behind traces of their passing: the vortex tails of turbulent air forming at the corners of buildings, the sudden conjurings of dead leaves into miniature tornadoes: these are evidence that we navigate turbulent zones.

Seriality, like causality, is an effect of temporal and spatial linearisation. Phenomena exhibiting (according to Carl Jung) acausal synchronicity are not necessarily anti-scientific; they may simply reflect a nonlinear viewpoint, one dispersed, for example, across and between the interested parties. Discussing the history of biological speculation about the phenomenon of mimicry, Stanislav Komárek reflects, 'It is interesting that nobody from the Continental school attempted to interpret cryptic phenomena using Jung's and Wolfgang von Pauli's principle of synchronicity, or rather in this case "syntopicity", for which it would be an almost ideal subject (synchronicity is understood by Jung and von Pauli to be the accumulation of phenomena, which require joint interpretation – in this case optical phenomena) in space and time (even various other mimetic phenomena would fit into this thought system very well)'.[12]

Among these other mimetic phenomena is *fit*, as discussed earlier. The queue fits together. The exploratory queue sequences or multiplies an anxiety: it spins a thread that can link passengers through the labyrinth. An inter-psychic reciprocity occurs based on copying the other. The feedback loop intensifies and expands, creating a distinctive movement form: you could not say of this informally choreographed group that one came after the other, that one occupied the foreground, the other the background. Komárek sees the dangers of this impulse to fit in, citing 'inter-psychic connections between people who are close to one another, which causes for example the induction of psychic symptoms in otherwise healthy individuals by their sick relations (the well known phenomenon *folie à deux*)'.[13] But this may take too mechanistic a view of mimetic identity formation. Spiralling inwards like this may reflect exposure to disorienting surroundings. C. P. Oberndorf describes the *folie à deux* of a certain 'Mr. and Mrs. V' who 'had been virtually prisoners in their home for about two years – she suffered from a sensation of whirling whenever she left home, he also from whirling and a fear of slipping, or of his automobile skidding whenever the pavement was damp'.[14] But whirling, as I have pointed out elsewhere, is a classic symptom of public space alienation: 'Oberndorf's socially isolated couple' were thrown together by 'an unspoken agoraphobia': 'by not acknowledging this, they could only seek their relief in the mirror of each other'.[15]

A choreotopographical intervention shatters the mirror by providing a setting that is no longer bereft of landmarks. Ground patterns, perhaps also sound patterns, produce ambience, a sense of things forming or coming into phase. The biological parallel to this alteration of the built environment is the cryptic colouration of certain birds and animals, which, it seems, both conceals and communicates. The lexicon does not consist of primary colours and definite outlines but of crazed shadows and auditory stridulations, of second order forms (shadows, echoes) and reflected colours that produce complex, muted dappling. This is the style of dark writing. Syntopicity ceases to be an impossible concept – how can two objects occupy the same place? – when the unit of sociability is defined as the group rather than the individual. Then, all parts of the group occupy the same place but retain their difference, as Giacometti's public square does when its stalking figures are swivelled through the three hundred and sixty degrees.

An operation of this kind produces parallax effects as one figure appears to pass before another. But these instants of scission immediately yield to a new fanning out of the space in-between. These are unmarked sites of potential encounter, opening and closing cones of space where something in-between what is remarked may start to happen. Syntopicity allows for this chiasmatic phenomenon: as the topology of the mid-stride, suggesting a potential sociability beyond what has been planned, it may flood the mind with possibilities. Like the wind that buffeted René Descartes when he tried to walk in a straight line, it may produce delirium.[16]

But the *via media* between the linear and the circular remains a possible third way. We learn from Bill Hillier that when exploration opportunities occur, children 'quickly find the lacunas in the natural movement system, creating probabilistic group territories which then attract others, and this usually occurs in the most integrating lacunas within the natural movement system'. Where lacunas in the natural movement system occur in the 'local integration core', an 'explosive potential' may be created, and sudden riots. Hillier reflects, 'It does seem likely that badly designed space can create a pathology in the ways in which space is used, which a random spark may then ignite. Space does not direct events, but it does shape possibilities'.[17] In this case, the vortical movement form repeatedly recommended in *Places Made After Their Stories* ceases to be a stylistic tic, becoming instead a description of syntopicity, a phenomenon known only by inhabiting and traversing the creative region of the group. The figure that emerges in this complex passage is not the spiral ground plan of a new theory of meeting; it is a way of practising space, one that overcomes the exteriority of social relations evoked by Sartre's Other who will rival the Other 'by the very fact of their being identical'.[18]

The syntopic passage integrates what has been and what is to come through the assembly and re-assembly of what is glimpsed in passing. Perception of the Other is inseparable from a continuously revised sense of self (always suspended between what is passing away and what is yet to pass). In flight, it is any idea of fixity that makes the ground unstable.

Notes

1. John-Paul Sartre, *Modern Times: Selected Non-Fiction*, ed. Geoffrey Wall, trans. Robin Buss, Penguin Books, Harmondsworth, 2000, pp. 212–13, 213 fn.
2. 'The history of mankind is the instant between two strides taken by the traveller.' Franz Kafka, 'Third Octavo Notebook,' in *Wedding Preparations in the Country and Other Posthumous Writings*, trans. E. Kaiser and E. Wilkins, London: Secker & Warburg, 1954, 73. See also Carter, *Dark Writing*, chapter 1, for application of this aphorism to a revisionist geography.
3. For exploration of the choreotopographical significance of the name and its imagined ambience, see Carter, *Repressed Spaces*, pp. 194–200.
4. Examples of both are Alberto Giacometti, *The City Square*, 1948, The Museum of Modern Art, New York and Alberto Giacometti, *The Forest/Seven Figures, One Head*, 1950, Wilhelm-Lehmbruck Museum, Duisberg. Both are illustrated in Carter, *Repressed Spaces*, pp.198–9.
5. Thompson, *On Growth and Form*, vol. 1, p. 76. See also Carter, *Dark Writing*, pp. 178–9.
6. James Clerk Maxwell, 'Reflex Musings: Reflections from Various Surfaces', *Poems*, Poem Hunter Com. The World's Poetry Archive, 2004, p. 41.
7. Alexis de Tocqueville, *Democracy in America*, 2 vols, trans. Henry Reeve, Sever and Francis, Cambridge, Mass: 1840, vol 2, section 2, passim.
8. Sartre, *Modern Times*, p. 214.
9. Ibid., pp. 217, 219.
10. Ibid., p. 219.
11. Nels Anderson, *The Hobo: The Sociology of the Homeless Man*, University of Chicago Press, Chicago, 1923, p. 215.
12. Stanislav Komárek, *Mimicry, Aposematism, and Related Phenomena: Mimetism in Nature and the History of Its Study*, Stanislav Komárek, n.d., viewed 8 June 2015, <http://stanislav-komarek.cz/mimicry>, p. 19.
13. Ibid., p. 23.
14. C. P. Oberndorf, 'Folie à Deux', *International Journal of Psycho-Analysis*, vol. 15, 1934, p. 14.
15. Carter, *Repressed Spaces*, pp. 74–5.
16. John R. Cole, *The Olympian Dreams and Youthful Rebellion of René Descartes*, University of Illinois Press, Urbana, 1992, p. 33.
17. Bill Hillier, *Space Is the Machine: A Configurational Theory of Architecture*, Cambridge University Press, Cambridge, UK, 1996, pp. 205, 206.
18. Sartre, *Modern Times*, p. 213.

34

ON THE IMPORTANCE OF PERSONAL STYLE

I want to conclude with a return to the poetic mechanism informing choreotopography and by distinguishing between semiotic, symbolic and allegorical discourses of place-making. These can be arranged in a descending order of intimacy; in the other direction, passage from one to the other reconnects the local and contingent progressively to wider orders of coexistence. The semiotic discourse, which is the default position of design explanation in the public sphere, dematerialises the materiality of the new arrangement of space by insisting it is functional. The new steps, walkways, gardens and even public art have no independent existence of their own. They are presented as emanations of the public will, channellings of collective desire into spatial satisfactions. As the translation of forms for the conduct of movement into the behaviourist vocabulary of need, consumption and convenience is untheorised, an ersatz poetry of one-to-one *functional* resemblances is often invoked: 'The garden is *for*...', 'The lighting *meets* this need...', 'Framing the view, the portal *signifies* arrival...' and so forth. The imagined user of these useful spaces is invariably in a hurry or wheeling a pushchair or driven to have a picnic, is spontaneously given to aesthetic contemplation or a born-again regionalist. The projection of government concerns, cultures and services onto their imagined community is obvious. The acceptable new square, precinct, facility or water edge will be the look of the Medusa reflected in the mirror: the gaze of government petrifies the society of its own projection.

In *Places Made After Their Stories* the importance of the symbolic economy is argued. In an earlier book, *Dark Writing*, however, symbolic explanations of public space designs are criticised in much the way I have criticised semiotic explanations. In reality, the distinctions between signs, symbols and allegory are not hard and fast. Symbols can become conventionalised and, as Paul de Man maintains, entertain 'the possibility of an identity or identification'. In this case, they operate like signs. However, their polysemous nature means that they can also reach out to embrace a variety of associations or interpretations simultaneously. In this case, they mark out an *intermundium* where different identities (or entities) can find new common ground; the new meeting that occurs here is not necessarily definitive and retains the potential to produce further creative constellations of sense. When this propensity for further invention is foregrounded in the symbolic discourse, the symbolic is lifted into the allegorical, where the allegorical is, in de Man's terms, free of 'the nostalgia and the desire to coincide'.[1] The allegorical thinks systematically, as it were, through symbolic forms: figurative language in this expression cannot be paraphrased using instrumentalist prose. Like the 'explanation' of a metaphor – which, Paul Ricoeur states, 'is not the stereotype of positivist scientific explanation; it is less verification than validation'[2] – so with symbolic discourse generally: it cannot be exhaustively explained, but it can be understood.

To understand an identification between unlike things – as happened when different cultural formations found common ground in Shepparton and Alice Springs through the discourse of trees and rivers – requires an act of identification among the convening parties. The carapace of positivist logic has to be softened.

To pass from the harshly reductionist demands for equivalence characteristic of the semiotic turn to a less defensive, more personal identification requires the parties to delve into the soft tissue of their memories and to acknowledge the emotional pull of those historical associations that spiral up like DNA into the fabric of the present. Hence, to embrace the symbolic mode of reasoning is to enter a more intimate region of existence and coexistence. At the same time, the attractive or combinatory nature of this new attention to the genealogy of the senses we give to images and ideas means that we are not only drawn in to a consideration of past experiences but also drawn out of ourselves, becoming aware of a neighbourhood of related meanings, shared memories, habits and projections – which, in the field of public space design, could be compared to the elusive quality of ambience.

The key claim that de Man makes for the allegorical mode is that it preserves the reality of spatial and temporal disjunction. Placing the other at the heart of expression, it articulates the primary separation but for which the idea of encounter would be unthinkable, indeed unnecessary. The other speak of allegory is the discourse of meeting. It is the way in which mimetically derived identifications communicate. It is free of any nostalgia to fuse horizons or to unite differences under a common theme. It can manage the Brownian motion of a people whose sociability is turbulent, productive of higher levels of complexification. As an allegorical graph, the creative template represents nothing. Its validation depends on its usefulness as a catalyst of figurative thinking about the making of places. Its purpose is to introduce a constitutional veering away from the linear logic of planning. It retunes the edges of the time of decision-making (the period of the 'project') so that they vibrate with impulses from the past and the future, and the resulting cymatic arrangements, the distribution of social desire into centres and passages, can influence the choreo-topography of the place. The dramaturg who thinks and acts in this way still receives instructions from the others (the people, the setting), but they are received unegotistically, as the material of a forming situation which they merely stir into their proper places.

Obviously, this dramaturgical function demands a new professional attention, but, to conclude, it also depends on a new creative self-awareness. For good inventions, mythopoetically informed social and spatial innovation, depend on good remembering; and good remembering depends on an understanding of the way the imagination works on memories, reordering them into the forms of new possibility. No doubt science has gone a long way in mapping these intertwined stands of consciousness, but for our purposes the best picture of their dynamic inter-relationship and structuring remains Thomas De Quincey's description of mental involutes. The turbulence of the dream, the way it reconfigures mental experience, has a structure, which De Quincey likens to a particular kind of vortical shell. 'De Quincey used the noun "involute", borrowed from conchology, to mean a recurring complex of ideas, or as Barrell puts it, "an intricately coiled or interwoven manifold".'[3] 'Far more of our deepest thoughts and feelings pass to us through perplexed combinations of *concrete objects*, pass to us as *involutes*…in compound experiences incapable of being disentangled, than ever reach us *directly*, and in their own abstract shapes.'

These thoughts and feelings retain the traces of earlier recurrences of the same 'complex of ideas', much as a scroll might retain a palimpsest of earlier writings partially erased to accommodate newer inscriptions. A vellum palimpsest reused over centuries might well, De Quincey reflects, provoke mirth because of 'the grotesque collisions of those successive themes, having no natural connection, which by pure accident have consecutively occupied the roll'. In the 'mighty palimpsest [of] the brain', however, there cannot be such 'incoherencies': 'The fleeting accidents of a man's life, and its external shows, may indeed be irrelate and incongruous; but the organising principles which fuse into harmony, and gather about fixed predetermined centres, whatever heterogeneous elements life may have accumulated from without, will not permit the grandeur of human unity greatly to be violated'.[4] These 'organising principles' can be grasped negatively – when (as under the influence of opium) they fail. Then, 'in parts and fractions eternal creations are carried on, but the nexus is wanting, and life and the central principle, which should bind together all the parts at the centre, with all its radiations to the circumference, are wanting. Infinite incoherence, ropes of sand, gloomy incapacity of vital persuasion by some one plastic principle'. Grasped positively, though, the 'organising principles' produce 'involutes'.[5]

The value of this account here is that its description of the 'brain' might be a description of the teeming street life of a city whose 'heterogeneous elements' may exceed the capacity of any individual to order them, but which nevertheless (like the streets and squares of London) circulate around 'fixed predetermined centres'. In *The Confessions of an Opium-eater*, De Quincey describes the *liquidation* of London, the transforming of its streets and crowds into a single, oceanic figure of turbulence: in his opium visions, 'the sense of space, and in the end, the sense of time, were both powerfully affected...Space swelled, and was amplified to an extent of unutterable and self-repeating infinity'. De Quincey sees in his dreams lakes that expand: 'The waters gradually changed their character – from translucent lakes, shining like mirrors, they became seas and oceans...Perhaps some part of my London life (the searching for Ann amongst fluctuating crowds) might be answerable for this. Be that as it may, now it was that upon the rocking waters of the ocean the human face began to reveal itself; the sea appeared paved with innumerable faces…faces that surged upwards by thousands, by myriads, by generations'.[6] Such dreams transpose the 'organising principles' of the mental involute to the reorganisation of space into a figure of historical turbulence.

As a description of the way the imagination acts on memory to change the way we see the world, the involute is the ideational principle informing choreotopography. The designer-dramaturg who embraces this principle is guided in their choice of 'Images' in Mircea Eliade's sense.[7] The affective qualities of what is produced are not left to chance, although their reception and recognition are difficult to measure. Against the anti-intellectualist orthodoxy that artistic creation is a non-rational reconciliation of genius and chance, the choreotopographer studies the allegorical constitution of the scheme. The logic of the proposal is not a naïve projection of a personal history of 'fleeting accidents' any more than it is an objective synthesis of 'external shows'; it stems from the poetic logic of the selected symbolic forms. And these should be studied. The passage quoted earlier from the *Golden Grove* project notebook is a good example of rhapsodic thinking – rhetorical, running, dancing, teetering on the brink of incoherence.[8] But, despite its seeming spontaneity, it is a palimpsest of earlier complexes or compound experiences. It is a mythopoetic enquiry, a symbolic mediation of reality, a construct of the personal imagination licensed by the objective existence of the seeds brought together and transformed. The origin of *Golden Grove*, for example, is not in some metaphysical whim of my own. As the continuation of the above passage reflects, the poetic scheme of *Golden Grove* overlays those of earlier projects, continuing their symbolic mediation of the senses of place:

Stars are talismans of belonging. They let us lay claim to portions of the earth that we cannot inhabit. Canopus remains dear to me after laying its influence over a part of Docklands. I look at constellations and find associates of my dreams. They are the cities to which my inventions led. The arrangement of stars in the sky reproduces the dance of places around Lake Tyrrell. I cannot trace my history to a local genealogy, but the stars spell out a possible arrangement or association that I could share. Starlight is the principle of vision that frees the migrant to embrace new origins.[9]

In this migrant meditation, the night sky sketches the constitution of the meeting place: 'Stars herd a host of glances associated with first meeting. The passing glance, the stalwart loiterer, the figure turning away. They are migrants, dancers, explorers and children, whatever flies from the smoothness of authority and the planar death of one-to-one signs'. Among these glances is 'the gaze of the Pauline merchant and the modern migrant'.[10] As for the 'host' behind these glances, it is the ghost community, the sum of all the possible meetings that this different illumination of reality discloses: 'Everything becomes a star at night…Planets making the pathway!'[11]

When it is understood that mythopoetic practices of place-making are involuted, relating and overlaying complexes whose origins are outside the individual in the symbolic ordering of time and space, it follows that the new designer must exercise this talent if it is to flourish. A new seriousness characterises the architect's or the landscape architect's site analysis and response to the brief. Going beyond the local historical associations, the immediate identity politics of different communities and the spurious differentiations of site based on minor geological or ecological variations, they cultivate certain seeds which are suitable or fitting because they are ready to 'undergo gradual additions or articulations or changes of place'.[12] The ambient poetics practised here generate new places beyond the present one. These new spatial arrangements or mythopoetic complexes overlay earlier arrangements, other choreotopographies pervade them. In this sense they are always other places, spatial allegories, if you like, that incorporate the history of unfinished journeys. Choreotopography conceived and practised like this will always have a distinctively migrant inflection.

Notes

1   Paul de Man, *Blindness and Insight: Essays in the Rhetoric of Contemporary Criticism*, 2nd rev. edn, Routledge, London, 1989, p. 207.
2   Dan R. Stiver, *Theology after Ricoeur: Directions in Hermeneutical Theology*, John Knox Press, Westminster, 2001, p. 109, citing Paul Ricoeur, *The Rule of Metaphor*, trans. R. Czerny, Routledge & Kegan Paul, London, 1978, p. 175.
3   Frank Kermode, 'Elizabeth's Chamber', review of John Barrell, *The Infection of Thomas De Quincey: A Psychopathology of Imperialism*, London Review of Books, vol. 13, no. 9, 9 May 1991, pp. 11–12.
4   Thomas De Quincey, 'The Palimpsest of the Human Brain,' Suspiria de Profundis. https://ebooks.adelaide.edu.au/d/de_quincey/thomas/suspiria-de-profundis/chapter2.html. Originally published in 1845. Viewed 10 March 2010.
5   Ibid.
6   Thomas De Quincey, *De Quincey's Confessions of an English Opium-eater*, with introduction and notes by George Armstrong Wauchope, D. C. Heath & Co., Boston, 1898, pp. 131, 136–7.
7   Eliade, *Images and Symbols*, p. 20.
8   See Chapter 16, endnote 10 above, also Carter, *Mythform*, p. 20 and the discussion in Carter, *Ground Truthing*, pp. 210–17.
9   Material Thinking, 'Solution: A Public Spaces Strategy, Victoria Harbo★r', July 2002, pp. 1–36, p. 26. See also for full account of this project Carter,

Dark Writing, pp. 173–202.
10 Carter, *Meeting Place,* p. 65.
11 Cairns and Harney, *Dark Sparklers,* p. 64.
12 See Chapter 31, endnote 2.

BIBLIOGRAPHY

A Stone's Throw [videorecording]/a Department of Architecture student's project, documentary film, University of Sydney Television Service, 1980, University of Sydney Library, Schaeffer AV.

Adorno, T. W., 'The essay as form', trans. Bob Hullot-Kentor & Frederic Will, *New German Critique*, no. 32, 1984, pp. 151–71.

Agamben, Giorgio, *Homo Sacer: Sovereign Power and Bare Life*, trans. Daniel Heller-Roazen, Stanford University Press, Stanford, Calif., 1998.

Agamben, Giorgio, *State of Exception*, trans. Kevin Attell, University of Chicago Press, Chicago, 2005.

Allen, Richard Hinckley, *Star-names and Their Meanings*, Dover Publications, New York, 1964.

Anderson Benedict, *Imagined Communities*, Verso, London, 1983.

Anderson, Mary Elizabeth, *Meeting Places: Desert Consciousness in Performance*, Editions Rodopi, Amsterdam, 2014.

Anderson, Nels, *The Hobo: The Sociology of the Homeless Man*, University of Chicago Press, Chicago, 1923.

Andrews, Munya, *The Seven Sisters of the Pleiades*, Spinifex Press, Melbourne, 2004.

Arakawa/Madeline Gins, *Pour Ne Pas Mourir To Not To Die*, Éditions de la Différence, Paris, c.1988.

Arendt, Hannah, *The Human Condition*, Chicago University Press, Chicago, 1958.

Arendt, Hannah, *The Portable Hannah Arendt*, ed. Peter Baehr, Penguin, London, 2000.

Argyris, Chris, 'Double-loop learning, teaching and research', *Academy of Management Learning & Education*, vol. 1, no. 2, 2002, pp. 206–19.

Árnarson, Johann P. and David Roberts, Elias Canetti's Counter-Image of Society: Crowds, Power, Transformation, Camden House, New York, 2004.

The BACC II Author Team (eds), *Second Assessment of Climate Change for the Baltic Sea Basin*, Springer International Publishing, London, 2015.

Bachmann, Ingeborg, *The Thirtieth Year*, trans. Michael Bullock, Holmes & Meier, New York, 1987.

Balibrea, Mari Paz, 'Urbanism, culture and the post-industrial city: Challenging the "Barcelona Model"', in Tim Marshall (ed.), *Transforming Barcelona*, Routledge, London, 2004, pp. 205–24.

Barba, Eugenio, 'The deep order called turbulence: The three faces of dramaturgy', trans. Judy Barba, *The Drama Review*, vol. 44, no. 4, 2000, pp. 56–66.

Barcham, Manuhuia, *Working with Indigenous and Western Corporate Structures – the Central Arrernte Case*, White Paper 2012/01, Synexe, 2012, viewed 4 June 2015, <http://static1.squarespace.com/static/53b85a6ce4b046129f33a042/t/547101cee4b0922a0c042990/1416692174333/001-2012-WP-Working+with+Indigenous+and+Western+Corporate+Structures%2C+the+Central+Arrernte+case.pdf>.

Bardon, Geoffrey, 'A Place Made After the Story, The Hieroglyphic Representations of the Western Desert Painters, and their Cultural and Stylistic Significances, at Papunya, 1971-1973', typescript, 2001. Author's possession.

Bardon, Geoffrey & James Bardon, *Papunya: A Place Made After The Story; The Beginnings of the Western Desert Painting Movement*, Miegunyah Press, Melbourne, 2004.

Barnard, M., 'Introduction', *Herder on Social and Political Culture: A Selection of Texts*, Cambridge University Press, Cambridge, 1969.

Barnes, Jonathan, *The Presocratic Philosophers*, Routledge, London, 1982.

Bataille, Georges, *Visions of Excess: Selected Writings, 1927-1939*, University of Minnesota Press, Minneapolis, 1985.

Bates, Daisy, *Aboriginal Perth: Bibbulmun Biographies and Legends*, ed. P. J. Bridge, Hesperian Press, Perth, 1992.

Bates, Daisy, *The Native Tribes of Western Australia*, ed. Isobel White, National Library of Australia, Canberra, 1985.

Bates, Daisy, *The Passing of the Aborigines*, John Murray, London, 1957.

Bateson, Gregory, *Steps to an Ecology of Mind: Collected Essays in Anthropology, Psychiatry, Evolution, and Epistemology*, University of Chicago Press, Chicago, 2000.

Baudrillard, Jean, 'Two essays', essay 1, 'Simulacra and science fiction', trans. Arthur B. Evans, *Science Fiction Studies*, #55, vol. 18, part 3, November 1991, viewed 5 June 2015, <www.depauw.edu/sfs/backissues/55/baudrillard55art.htm>.

Bibliography

Benjamin, Roger, 'The fetish for Papunya boards', in Roger Benjamin, (ed.), *Icons of the Desert: Early Aboriginal Paintings from Papunya*, Herbert F. Johnson Museum, Cornell University, Ithaca, 2009, pp. 21–50.

Benjamin, Walter, *Illuminations, Essays and Reflections,* trans. H. Zohn, Schocken Books, New York, 1978.

Benjamin, Walter, *One Way Street and Other Writings*, trans. Edmund Jephcott & Kingsley Shorter, Verso, London, 1985.

Benjamin, Walter, *The Origin of German Tragic Drama*, trans. J. Osborne, Verso, New York, 1977.

Benton, Christopher P., '*Sefer Yetzirah, the Cube of Space, and the Emergence of the Tree of Life*', Paper 33, MAQOM, n.d., viewed 4 June 2015, <www.maqom.com/journal/paper33.pdf>.

Beuys, Joseph, *Joseph Beuys in America: Energy Plan for the Western Man*, comp. Carin Kuoni, Four Walls Eight Windows, New York, 1993.

Bewick, Thomas, *A Memoir of Thomas Bewick, Written by Himself*, Robert Ward, Newcastle upon Tyne, 1862.

Bharucha, Rustom, *Terror and Performance*, Routledge, Abingdon and New York, 2014.

Blake, William, *Complete Writings*, ed. G. Keynes, Oxford University Press, Oxford, 1969.

Bloch, Ernst, *Literary Essays*, trans. A. Joron and others, Stanford University Press, Stanford, Calif., 1998.

Bogue, Ronald, 'Fabulation, Narration, and the People to Come', in C.V. Boundas, ed., *Deleuze and Philosophy*, Edinburgh University Press, Edinburgh, 2006, pp. 202-26.

Böhme, Gernot, 'Atmosphere as the Fundamental Concept of the New Aesthetics', *Thesis Eleven* 36 (1), 1993, pp. 113-126.

Böhme, Gernot, *Atmosphere. Essays zur ein neuen Ästhetik*. Frankfurt: Suhrkamp Verlag, 1995.

Boundas, Constantin V., *Deleuze and Philosophy*, Edinburgh University Press, Edinburgh, 2006.

Bucklow, Spike, *The Alchemy of Paint: Art, Science and Secrets from the Middle Ages*, Marion Boyars, London, 2009.

Burch, Kerry T., *Eros as the Educational Principle of Democracy*, Peter Lang, New York, 2000.

Butler, Judith, 'Critically queer', *GLQ: A Journal of Lesbian and Queer Studies*, vol. 1, no. 1, 1993, pp. 17–32.

Cairns, Hugh & Bill Yidumduma Harney, *Dark Sparklers*, H. C. Cairns, Merimbula, 2004.

Caloni, Paolo, review of Tonino Griffero's *Atmosferologia: Estetica deli spazi emozionali*, in 'Art, objects', ed. Alessandra Galbusera & Pietro Kobau, special issue, *Methode*, vol. 1, no. 1, 2012, pp. 122–6.

Carter, Paul, *The Calling to Come*, Historic Houses Trust of New South Wales, Sydney, 1995.

Carter, Paul, 'Choreotopography; algorithms of sociability', unpublished project notebook, 2011, pp.1-31. Author's possession.

Carter, Paul, *Dark Writing: Geography, Performance, Design*, University of Hawai'i Press, Honolulu, 2008.

Carter, Paul, '"Golden Grove" project notebook', 2004-2008, pp. 1-46. Author's possession.

Carter, Paul, *Ground Truthing: Explorations in a Creative Region*, University of Western Australia Publishing, Perth, 2010.

Carter, Paul, 'Inscriptions as Initial Conditions: Federation Square (Melbourne, Australia) and the Silencing of the Mark', in B. David & M. Wilson (eds), *Inscribed Landscapes: Marking and Making Place*, University of Hawai'i Press, Honolulu, 2002, pp. 230–39.

Carter, Paul, *The Lie of the Land*, Faber & Faber, London, 1996.

Carter, Paul, *Living in a New Country*, Faber & Faber, London, 1992.

Carter, Paul, *Lost Subjects*, Historic Houses Trust of New South Wales, Sydney, 1998.

Carter, Paul, *Material Thinking: The Theory and Practice of Creative Research*, Melbourne University Publishing, Melbourne, 2004.

Carter, Paul, *Meeting Place: The Human Encounter and the Challenge of Coexistence*, Minnesota University Press, Minneapolis, 2013.

Carter, Paul, *Mythform: The Making of Nearamnew at Federation Square*, Miegunyah Press, Melbourne, 2005.

Carter, Paul, 'Participating forms: The place of myth in urban design', unpublished paper, 2001.

Carter, Paul, 'Pressure: The political economy of air', in 'City air', special issue, *The Journal of Architecture* (US), vol. 19, no. 2, 2014, pp. 168–86.

Carter, Paul, *Repressed Spaces: The Poetics of Agoraphobia*, Reaktion Books, London, 2002.

Carter, Paul, 'Showing the Word', in Michael Tawa, *Theorising the Project: A Thematic Approach to Architectural Design*, Cambridge Scholars Publishing, Newcastle upon Tyne, 2011, vii-ix.

Carter, Paul, *The Road to Botany Bay: An Essay in Spatial History*, Faber & Faber, London, 1987.

Carter, Paul, *Turbulence: Climate Change and the Design of Complexity*, Puncher & Wattman, Sydney, 2015.

Carter, Paul (ed), 'On Turbulence', *Performance Research*, 19:5, 2014.

Bibliography

Casey & Lowe, 'Non-Indigenous Archaeological Assessment', August 2004, in *University of Sydney Campus 2010*, Report to Capital Insight Ltd., Final Issue A, pp.1-32

Christine Williamson Heritage Consultants, *Point Nepean Quarantine Station Draft Management Plan*, Christine Williamson Heritage Consultants, Melbourne, 2008.

City of Gold Coast, *Gold Coast Cultural Precinct Design Competition: Design Brief, Document 2*, Gold Coast Cultural Precinct, 26 March 2013, viewed 4 June 2015, <www.goldcoastculturalprecinct.info/sites/default/files/document_2_gold_coast_cultural_precinct_design_competition_design_brief_26_march_2013.pdf>.

Clark, Ian D. & David A. Cahir, *Tanderrum, 'Freedom of the Bush': The Djadjawurrung Presence on the Goldfields of Central Victoria*, Friends of Mount Alexander Diggings, Castlemaine, 2004.

Cobbett, William, *Rural Rides*, T. Nelson & Sons, London, 1923.

Cole, John R., *The Olympian Dreams and Youthful Rebellion of René Descartes*, University of Illinois Press, Urbana, 1992.

Commission for Architecture and the Built Environment, *Creating Successful Masterplans: A Guide for Clients*, CABE, London, 2004 (reprinted 2008).

Cooper, Gregory J., *The Science of the Struggle for Existence: On the Foundations of Ecology*, Cambridge University Press, Cambridge, UK, 2003.

Copjec, Jean, 'The Sartorial Ego', *October*, vol. 50 (Autumn 1989), pp. 56-95.

Correa, Paulo N. & Alexandra N. Correa, 'Whither science? A science without origins: Nomad, minor science and the scientific method', *Journal of Science & the Politics of Thought*, vol. 1, no. 2, 2009, pp. 1–49.

Cotter, Richard, *Boon Wurrung: People of the Port Phillip District*, Lavender Hill Multimedia, Melbourne, 2001.

Darbyshire, Jo, *The Coolbaroo Club, 1947–1960*, exh. cat., City of Perth, 2010, viewed 8 June 2015, <www.perth.wa.gov.au/sites/default/files/Catalogue%20Coolbaroo%20Club.pdf>.

de Bruyn, Dirk, *Loops*, four screen video installation with Paul Carter and Soo Yeun You, Walker Street Art Gallery, Dandenong, October 2013.

de Bruyn, Dirk, *Opening*, film animation with Paul Carter & Soo Yeun You, 38 mins, Federation Square, Melbourne, 2011.

de Certeau, Michel, *The Practice of Everyday Life*, trans. S. Rendall, Berkeley: University of California Press, Berkeley, Calif., 1984.

de Man, Paul, *Blindness and Insight: Essays in the Rhetoric of Contemporary Criticism*, 2nd rev. edn, Routledge, London, 1989.

De Quincey, Thomas, *The Collected Writings of Thomas De Quincey*, ed. David Masson, 14 vols, A. & C. Black, London, 1896–97.

De Quincey, Thomas, *De Quincey's Confessions of an English Opium-eater*, with introduction and notes by George Armstrong Wauchope, D. C. Heath & Co., Boston, 1898.

De Quincey, Thomas, *Suspiria de Profundis*, *Blackwood's Magazine*, Edinburgh & London, Spring and Summer issues, 1845.

De Tocqueville, Alexis, *Democracy in America*, 2 vols, trans. Henry Reeve, Sever and Francis, Cambridge, Mass, 1840.

Debord, Guy, 'Theory of the Dérive,' *Situationist International Anthology*, ed. and trans. Ken Knabb, Bureau of Public Secrets, Berkeley, Calif., 1995, pp. 50-54.

Deakin Research Communications, *Choreotopography!*, Deakin University, 6 December 2010, viewed 4 June 2015, <www.deakin.edu.au/research/stories/2010/12/06/choreotopography>.

Dear, Michael, 'Prolegomena for a post-modern urbanism', in Patsy Healey, Stuart Cameron, Simin Davoudi, Stephen Graham & Ali Madani-Pour (eds), *Managing Cities: The New Urban Context*, Wiley, London, 1995, pp. 27–44.

Deggan, Mark, '"Not such an empty space": Cinematic ecocriticism and the performative landscape of Damon Galgut's fiction', in 'Litterature, paysage et écologie', special issue, *TRANS – Revue de littérature générale et comparée*, no. 16, 2013, viewed 8 June 2015, <http://trans.revues.org/835?lang=en>.

Deleuze, Gilles & Félix Guattari, *A Thousand Plateaus: Capitalism & Schizophrenia*, trans. Brian Massumi, University of Minnesota Press, Minneapolis, 1987.

Dérive, Wikipedia, updated 9 December 2014, viewed 8 June 2015, <http://en.wikipedia.org/wiki/Dérive>.

Derrida, Jacques, *Of Grammatology*, trans. Gayatri Chakravorty Spivak, The Johns Hopkins University Press, Baltimore, 1974.

Derrida, Jacques and Anne Dufourmantelle, *Of Hospitality: Anne Dufourmantelle invites Jacques Derrida to Respond*, translated by R. Bowlby, Stanford University Press, Stanford, Calif., 2000.

Deutsche, Rosalind, *Evictions: Art and Spatial Politics*, MIT Press, Cambridge, MA, 1996.

Devisch, Ignass, *Jean-Luc Nancy and the Question of Community*, Bloomsbury, London, 2013.

Didi-Huberman, Georges, *Le danseur des solitudes*, Éditions de Minuit, Paris, 2006.

Downarowicz, Tomasz, *Law of Series*, Scholarpedia, vol. 3, no. 11, 2008, p. 3922, viewed 3 June 2015, <www.scholarpedia.org/article/Law_of_series>.

Doxiadis, Constantinos A., 'The ekistic elements and the goals of ekistics', 1964, reprinted in *Ekistics*, vol. 33, no. 197, April 1972, pp. 237–244.

Doxiadis, Constantinos A., 'Ekistics, the science of human settlements', *Science*, vol. 170, no. 3956, 1970, pp. 393–404, reproduced at Constantinos A. Doxiadis, n.d., viewed 5 June 2015, <www.doxiadis.org/Downloads/ecistics_the_science_of_human_settlements.pdf>.

Doy, Gen, *Drapery: Classicism and Barbarism in Visual Culture*, I. B. Tauris, London, 2002.

DuComb, Christian & Jessica Benman, 'Flash mobs, violence and the turbulent crowd', *Performance Research*, vol. 19, no. 5, 2014, pp. 34–40.

Dyson, Frances, *Sounding New Media: Immersion and Embodiment in the Arts and Culture*, University of California Press, Berkeley, Calif., 2009.

Edwards, P. G., 'Charles Todd and the Adelaide Observatory', *Proceedings of the Astronomical Society of Australia*, vol. 10, no. 4, 1993, pp. 349–54.

Eliade, Mircea, *Images and Symbols: Studies in Religious Symbolism*, trans. Philip Mairet, Princeton University Press, Princeton, NJ., 1991.

Eliade, Mircea, *Myths and Symbols*, University of Chicago Press, Chicago, 1971.

El-Khatib, Mohamed Samir, 'Tahrir Square as spectacle: Some exploratory remarks on place, body and power', *Theatre Research International*, vol. 38, no. 2, 2013, pp. 104-115.

Elrick, Laura, *Poetry, Ecology, and the Reappropriation of Lived Space*, The Brooklyn Rail, 12 June 2006, viewed 4 June 2015, <www.brooklynrail.org/2006/06/poetry/poetry-ecology-and-the-reappropriation-of-lived-space>.

Estienne, Charles, *Dessins de Lapicque, La Figure*, Éditions Galanis, Paris, 1959.

Farnum, Jennifer, Troy Hall, Linda E. Kruger, 'Sense of Place In Natural Resource Recreation and Tourism: An Evaluation and Assessment of Research Findings', General Technical Report, PNW-GTR-660, Forest Service of the U.S. Department of Agriculture, Washington DC., November 2005.

Fatah gen. Schieck, Ava & Chiron Mottram, 'Collective choreography of space: Modelling digital co-presence in a public arena', in George E. Lasker & Ana Luz (eds), *Systems Research in the Arts and Humanities*, vol. 1, *On Choreographies in Music, Visual and Performing Arts, and Environmental Design*, International Institute for Advanced Studies in Systems Research and Cybernetics, Tecumseh, Canada, 2007, pp. 59–63, viewed 8 June 2015, <http://discovery.ucl.ac.uk/7487/1/7487.pdf>.

Fincher, Ruth, Paul Carter, Paolo Tombesi, Kate Shaw & Andrew Martel, *Transnational and Temporary: Students, Community and Place-making in Central Melbourne*, University of Melbourne, Melbourne, 2009.

Fincher, Ruth & Kate Shaw, 'Transnational and temporary: Place-making, students and community in central Melbourne', *Planning News*, vol. 32, no.

3, 2006, pp. 12–13.

Focillon, Henri, *The Life of Forms in Art*, trans. C.B. Hogan and G. Kubler, Zone Books, New York, 1989.

Foley, Dennis, *Repossession of Our Spirit*, Aboriginal History Inc, Canberra, 2001.

Foster, Susan Leigh (ed.), *Corporealities: Dancing Knowledge, Culture and Power*, Routledge, London, 1996.

Frazer, Sir James, *The Golden Bough, a study in magic and religion*, Macmillan Company, New York, 1922.

Freud, Sigmund, *Civilization and Its Discontents*, trans. James Strachey, W. W. Norton & Company, New York, 1930.

Gasché, Rodolphe, *Of Minimal Things: Studies in the Notion of Relation*, Stanford University Press, Stanford, Calif., 1999.

Gillam, Mike, '500 year old red gums are being lost through neglect – but the trees can't speak', *Alice Springs News Online*, 19 January 2012, viewed 4 June 2015, <www.alicespringsnews.com.au/2012/01/19/500-year-old-red-gums-are-being-lost-through-neglect-and-the-trees-cant-speak>.

Gleeson, B. & K. J. Grundy, 'New Zealand's planning revolution five years on: A preliminary assessment', *Journal of Environmental Planning and Management*, vol. 40, no. 3, 1997, pp. 293–314.

Global Governance Group of the New School of Athens, *Governing Civilization through Civilizing Governance: Global Challenge for a Turbulent Future*, Laetus in praesens, 6 April 2008, viewed 8 June 2015, <www.laetusinpraesens.org/docs00s/civilgov.php>.

Glowczewski, Barbara, 'Returning Indigenous knowledge in central Australia: "This CD-ROM brings everybody to the mind"', in Graeme K. Ward & Adrian Muckle (eds), *'The Power of Knowledge, the Resonance of Tradition': Electronic Publication of Papers from the AIATSIS Indigenous Studies Conference, September 2001*, Australian Institute of Aboriginal and Torres Strait Islander Studies, 2005, viewed 4 June 2015, <http://aiatsis.gov.au/sites/default/files/docs/asp/Indigenous_studies_conf_2001.pdf>, pp. 139–54.

Goetsch, James Robert, *Vico's Axioms: The Geometry of the Human World*, Yale University Press, New Haven, Conn., 1995.

González-Crussí, Frank, 'On my mind', *Seed*, 16 May 2006, viewed 5 June 2015, <http://seedmagazine.com/content/article/on_my_mind_frank_gonzlez-cruss>.

Grammatikopoulou, Christina, *'Shades of the Immaterial: Different Approaches to the "Non-object"'*, *Interartive*, n.d., viewed 3 June 2015, <http://interartive.org/2012/02/shades-of-the-immaterial/#_ftn10>.

Gray, John, *The Liberalism of Karl Popper*, 1976, reprinted in Philosophical Notes No. 9, Libertarian Alliance, 1988, viewed 14 February 2008, <www.

libertarian.co.uk/lapubs/philn/philn009.pdf>.

Greater Shepparton – Community Action Plan, Proposal to Department of Victorian Communities, Greater Shepparton City Council, Shepparton, Vic., July 2006.

Green, Jennifer, 'Signs and Space in Arandic Sand Narratives', in M. Seyfeddinipur and M. Gullberg, eds, *From Gesture in Conversation to Visible Action as Utterance: Essays in Honor of Adam Kendon*, John Benjamins Publishing, Amsterdam, 2014, pp. 219-243.

Green, Neville, *Broken Spears: Aborigines and Europeans in the Southwest of Australia*, Focus Education Services, Perth, 1984.

Griffero, Tonino, 'The atmospheric "skin" of the city', *Ambiances, Enjeux - Arguments - Positions*, mis en ligne le 20 novembre 2013. URL : http://ambiances.revues.org/399.

Gruenewald, David A., 'Foundations of place: A multidisciplinary framework for place-conscious education', *American Educational Research Journal*, vol. 40, no. 3, 2003, pp. 619–54.

Haeckel, Ernst, *The Evolution of Man*, 2 vols, trans. Joseph McCabe, G. P. Putnam's Sons, New York, 1905.

Hanes, Raymond, Roslynn D. Haynes, David Malin & Richard McGee, *Explorers of the Southern Sky: A History of Australian Astronomy*, Cambridge University Press, Cambridge, UK, 2010.

Harvey, David, *Justice, Nature and the Geography of Difference*, Blackwell, Oxford, 1996.

Hayter, Alethea, *Opium and the Romantic Imagination*, University of California Press, Berkeley Calif., 1989.

Healey, Patsy, 'Collaborative planning in a stakeholder society', *Town Planning Review*, vol. 69, no. 1, 1998, pp. 537–57.

Healey, Patsy, 'Planning in relational space and time: Responding to new urban realities', in Andrew Ballantyne (ed.), *Architecture Theory: A Reader in Philosophy and Culture*, Continuum, London, 2005, pp. 259–71.

Hegel, Georg Wilhelm Friedrich, *Phenomenology of Spirit*, trans. A.V. Miller, Clarendon Press, Oxford, 1977.

Herrick, Robert, 'Upon Julia's Clothes', *The Poems of Robert Herrick*, Oxford University Press, Oxford, 1924.

Heyward, Michael, *The Ern Malley Affair*, Queensland University Press, St Lucia, Queensland, 1993.

Heidegger, Martin, *Poetry, Language, Thought*, trans. A. Hofstadter, Harper & Row: New York, 1971.

Heritage Management Consultants, *University of Sydney Grounds Conservation Plan*, prepared for Facilities Management Office, University of Sydney,

Sydney, 2002.
Hilal, Sandi & Alessandro Petti, *Al-mashaa' or the Space of the Common*, Haus der Kulteren de Welt, n.d., viewed 3 June 2015, <www.hkw.de/en/programm/projekte/2013/edward_said_konferenz/multimedia_edward_said/text_workshop.php>.
Hillier, Bill, *Space Is the Machine: A Configurational Theory of Architecture*, Cambridge University Press, Cambridge, UK, 1996.
Hohl, Reinhold, *Alberto Giacometti*, H.N. Abrams, New York, 1972.
Hokari, Minoru, 'Gurindji mode of historical practice', in Luke Taylor, Graeme K. Ward, Graham Henderson, Richard Davis & Lynley A. Wallis (eds), *The Power of Knowledge: The Resonance of Tradition*, Aboriginal Studies Press for the Australian Institute of Aboriginal and Torres Strait Islander Studies, Canberra, 2005, pp. 214–22.
Holston, James, *The Modernist City: An Anthropological Critique of Brasília*, Chicago University Press, Chicago, 1989.
Innanen, Riikka Theresa, *The Ecology of Creativity and Evolution of Choreographic Strategies*, Helsinki Meeting Point, 2011, viewed 3 June 2015, <www.helsinkimeetingpoint.com/riikka/paper2.pdf>.
Institute for Infinitely Small Things, 'The analysis of infinitely small things research report', *Performance Research*, vol. 11, no. 1, 2006, pp. 76–81.
Jackson, Michael, *Minima Ethnographica: Intersubjectivity and the Anthropological Project*, Chicago University Press, Chicago, 1998.
Jarrett, Michael, *Sound Tracks: A Musical ABC*, Temple University Press, Philadephia, 1988.
Jennings, Humphrey, *Pandaemonium, 1660-1886, the coming of the Machine Age as seen by contemporary observers*, eds. M.-J.L. Jennings and C. Madge, Picador, London, 1987.
Jenny, Hans, *Cymatics: A Study of Wave Phenomena and Vibrations*, rev. edn, trans. D. Q. Stephenson, Macromedia Publishing, Newmarket, NH, 2001.
Joe, Jimmy, *Genealogy: The Pleiades (The Atlantids)*, Timeless Myths, 1999, viewed 5 June 2015, <www.timelessmyths.com/classical/family14.html>.
Jones, David, *The Anathemata*, Faber & Faber, London, 1955.
Jorn, Asger, *The Natural Order and Other Texts*, trans. Peter Shield, Ashgate, Farnham, 2002.
Jung, C. G., *The Seminars*, vol. 1, *Dream Analysis: Notes of the Seminar Given in 1928–1930*, ed. William McGuire, Princeton University Press, Princeton, NJ., 1984.
Kafka, Franz, 'Third Octavo Notebook' in *Wedding Preparations in the Country and Other Posthumous Writings,* trans. E. Kaiser and E. Wilkins, Secker and Warburg, London, 1954.

Kantor, Tadeusz, *A Journey through Other Spaces: Essays and Manifestos, 1944–1990*, trans. Michael Kobialka, University of California Press, Berkeley, Calif., 1993.

Keltner, S. K., *Kristeva: Thresholds*, Polity, Cambridge, UK, 2011

Kennedy, James & Russell Eberhart, 'Particle swarm optimization', in *Proceedings, IEEE International Conference on Neural Networks*, vol. 4, IEEE, New York, 1995, pp. 1942–8, reproduced at Tufts University, <www.cs.tufts.edu/comp/150GA/homeworks/hw3/_reading6%201995%20particle%20swarming.pdf>.

Kerényi, Carl, *Dionysos: Archetypal Image of Indestructible Life*, trans. Ralph Manheim, Princeton University Press, Princeton, NJ., 1976.

Kermode, Frank, 'Elizabeth's chamber', review of John Barrell, *The Infection of Thomas De Quincey: A Psychopathology of Imperialism*, *London Review of Books*, vol. 13, no. 9, 9 May 1991, pp. 11–12.

Kerr, Rosemary, Val Attenbrow, Cheryl Stanborough, Donald Ellsmore & Duncan Marshall, *Appendix A: University of Sydney Overview History*, in Michael Pearson, Duncan Marshall, Donald Ellsmore, Val Attenbrow, Sue Rosen, Rosemary Kerr & Chris Betteridge, *University of Sydney Grounds Conservation Plan*, University of Sydney, October 2002, viewed 5 June 2015, <http://sydney.edu.au/documents/about/heritage/gcp_appendix1.pdf>, p. A83.

Khopkar, Arun, 'Graphic flourish: Aspects of the art of *mise-en-scène*' in Ian Christie & Richard Taylor, *Eisenstein Rediscovered*, Routledge, London, 1993, pp. 151–64.

Kierkegaard, Søren, *The Seducer's Diary*, trans. H.V. Hong and E.H. Hong, Princeton University Press, Princeton, NJ., 1987.

Kimber, Dick, *Cultural Values Associated with Alice Springs Water*, Department of Land Resource Management, Northern Territory Government, 2011, viewed 4 June 2015, <http://lrm.nt.gov.au/__data/assets/pdf_file/0020/118181/Cultural-Values-of-Alice-Water-Kimber-2011.pdf>.

Kimber, Dick, 'Placenames of central Australia: European records and recent experience', in Harold Koch & Luise Hercus (eds), *Aboriginal Placenames: Naming and Re-naming the Australian Landscape*, Aboriginal History Monograph 19, ANU Press, 2009, viewed 4 June 2015, <http://press.anu.edu.au/wp-content/uploads/2011/02/ch134.pdf>.

Kimber, Dick, 'Tjukurrpa Trails: A Cultural Topography of the Western Desert', in Hetti Perkins & Hannah Fink (eds), *Papunya Tula: Genesis and Genius*, Art Gallery of New South Wales, Sydney, 2004, pp. 269-273.

Koestler, Arthur, *The Roots of Coincidence*, Random House, New York, 1972.

Komárek, Stanislav, *Mimicry, Aposematism, and Related Phenomena: Mimetism* in *Nature and the History of Its Study*, Lincom, Munich, 2003, available at *Mimicry and Aposematism*, Stanislav Komárek, n.d., viewed 8 June 2015, <http://stanislav-komarek.cz/mimicry>.

Kosho, Sabu, *On Seiko Mikami's* World, Membrane and the Dismembered Body, V2_, n.d., viewed 5 June 2015, <http://v2.nl/archive/articles/on-seiko-mikamis-world-membrane-and-the-dismembered-body>.

Kosmatopoulos, Esmeralda, *The Project*, Turbulence, n.d., viewed 4 June 2015, <http://archive.turbulence.org/Works/MARK_IT/project.html>.

Krieger, Murray, '"A waking dream": The symbolic alternative to allegory', in Morton W. Bloomfield (ed.), *Allegory, Myth, and Symbol*, Harvard University Press, Cambridge, MA, 1981, pp. 1–22.

Kristeva, Julia, *Revolution in Poetic Language*, Columbia University Press, New York, 1984.

Kruger, Linda E. Kruger, Rhonda Mazza & Kelly Lawrence (eds), *Proceedings: National Workshop on Recreation Research and Management*, General Technical Report PNW-GTR-698, Forest Service, US Department of Agriculture, Washington DC., June 2007, viewed 8 June 2015, www.fs.fed.us/pnw/pubs/pnw_gtr698.pdf.

Kulper, Amy, 'Ecology without the oikos: Banham, Dallegret and the morphological context of environmental architecture', *Field Journal*, vol. 4, no. 1, 2011, pp. 67–84.

Laertius, Diogenes, *Lives of Eminent Philosophers*, 2 vols, ed. and trans. R.D. Hicks, W. Heinemann, London, 1925.

Lawrence, D. H., *Psychoanalysis and the Unconscious*, W. Heinemann, London, 1923.

Lefebvre, Henri, *The Production of Space*, trans. Donald Nicholson-Smith, Blackwell, Oxford, 1991.

Lennon, Jane, *Point Nepean: Assessment of Its Sense of Place*, Lovell Chen, Melbourne, 2002.

Levin, David Michael, *The Listening Self: Personal Growth, Social Change and the Closure of Metaphysics*, Routledge, London, 1989.

Levinas, Emmanuel, *Ethics and Infinity: Conversations with Philippe Nemo*, trans. Richard A. Cohen, Duquesne University Press, Pittsburgh, 1985.

Levinas, Emmanuel, *The Levinas Reader*, ed. Sean Hand, Blackwell, Oxford, 1992.

Levinas, Emmanuel, *Outside the Subject*, trans. Alphonso Lingis, Martinus Nijhoff Publishers, Dordrecht, 1990.

Levinas, Emmanuel, *Totality and Infinity: An Essay on Exteriority*, trans. Alphonso Lingis, Martinus Nijhoff Publishers, The Hague, 1978.

Lewin, Kurt, *Resolving Social Conflicts: Selected Papers on Group Dynamics*, Harper & Row, New York, 1947.

Bibliography

Livingston, K. T., *The Wired Nation: The Communication Revolution and Federating Australia*, Oxford University Press, Melbourne, 1996.

Livingston, Paisley, *Models of Desire: René Girard and the Psychology of Mimesis*, The Johns Hopkins Press, Baltimore, 1992.

Lyotard, Jean-François, *The Postmodern Condition: A Report on Knowledge*, trans. Geoff Bennington & Brian Massumi, Manchester University Press, Manchester, 1984.

Maclean, Ian, *Logic, Signs and Nature in the Renaissance: The Case of Learned Medicine*, Cambridge University Press, Cambridge, 2002.

Maffesoli, Michel, *The Contemplation of the World: Figures of Community Style*, trans. Susan Emanuel, University of Minnesota Press, Minneapolis, 1996.

Maffesoli, Michel, *The Shadow of Dionysus: A Contribution to the Sociology of the Orgy*, trans. Cindy Linse & Mary Kristina Palmquist, State University of New York Press, Albany, 1993.

Maharaj Sarat, 'Visual arts as knowledge production in the retinal arena', lecture presented at INIVA, London, 12 November 2003.

Makris, Christina, *The Mapping of Meaning in Madeline Gins' and Arakawa's Architectural Body*, Arizona State University, 2005, viewed 4 June 2015, <www.asu.edu/pipercwcenter/how2journal/archive/online_archive/v2_3_2005/current/in_conference/makris.htm>.

Malbon, Ben, *Clubbing: Dancing, Ecstasy and Vitality*, Routledge, London, 1999.

Mann, Steve, Jason Nolan & Barry Wellman, 'Sousveillance: Inventing and using wearable computing devices for data collection in surveillance environments', in 'Foucault and Panopticism revisited', special issue, *Surveillance & Society*, vol. 1, no. 3, 2003, pp. 331–55, viewed 8 June 2015, <http://library.queensu.ca/ojs/index.php/surveillance-and-society/article/view/3344/3306>.

Material Thinking, 'Alterations 3, project notebook', 2011-2012, pp. 1-30.

Material Thinking, 'Alterations 4, programming Dandenong's new civic square', March 4 2013, pp. 1-17.

Material Thinking, 'Care at a Distance, strategy for delivering the Moving Alice head – Lifestyle, CBD Revitalisation project', June 2007, pp. 1-16.

Material Thinking, 'The Challenge of Integration: statement of vision for public art', submission to Lyons Architects as part of response to Perth City Link/ City Square brief, 5 March 2014, pp.1-7.

Material Thinking, 'Connecting Alice, Alice Springs Revitalisation Project', May 2011, pp. 1-14.

Material Thinking, 'Eumemerring: Aspects of Atmosphere', Dandenong Civic Square, Visioning Notes, October 2011, pp. 1-16.

Material Thinking, 'Flagging the Future: Red Ways, Alice Spring CBD

Revitalisation, Design Options Framework', January 2009, pp. 1-20.

Material Thinking, 'Golden Grove at Darlington Campus: Celebrating heritage through design', August 2006, pp. 1-15.

Material Thinking, 'Golden Grove: Design Concept for a Public Artwork Integrated into the Landscape Design, Darlington Campus, University of Sydney', May 2005, pp. 1-7.

Material Thinking, 'A New Body: Creative Template @ Yagan Square', November 2014, pp. 1-11.

Material Thinking, 'Notes for Fertile Ground feature/Functional Lighting Design' January 2005, pp. 1-5.

Material Thinking, 'Notes towards "The Society of Trees", a meeting place in Alice, September, 2008, pp. 1-6.

Material Thinking, 'Red Ways: Alice Springs CBD Revitalisation, Design Options Framework', September 2008, pp.1-70.

Material Thinking, 'The Sense of Place @ the Point Nepean Quarantine Station, Reverse Brief to the Master Plan', January 2008, pp. 1-9.

Material Thinking, 'Solution: A Public Spaces Strategy, Victoria Harbo★r', July 2002, pp. 1-36.

Maxwell, James Clerk, 'Reflex musings: Reflections from various surfaces', *Poems*, PoemHunter.Com – The World's Poetry Archive, 2004.

McGuirk, James, 'Eros, Power and Justice: William Desmond and his Others', in T.A.F. Kelly, ed., *Between System and Poetics: William Desmond and Philosophy after Dialectic*, Ashgate, Farnham, Surrey, 2007, pp. 163-174.

McIntyre Ronald and David Woodruff Smith, 'Theory of Intentionality', in J.N. Mohanty and W.R. McKenna, eds., *Husserl's Phenomenology: A Textbook*, Center for Advanced Research in Phenomenology and University Press of America, Washington DC., 1989, pp. 147-79.

McKenzie Jon, *Perform or Else: From Discipline to Performance*, Psychology Press, New York, 2001.

McMillan, Andrew, *An Intruder's Guide to East Arnhem Land*, Niblock Publishing, Nightcliff, NT, 2007.

Mead, Margaret, 'The Comparative Study of Culture and the Purposive Cultivation of Democratic values', in *Science, Philosophy and Religion, Second Symposium*, Columbia University Press, New York, 1942, pp. 56-97.

Merleau-Ponty, Maurice, *The Prose of the World: Studies in Philosophy and Existential Philosophy*, trans. John O'Neill, Northwestern University Press, Evanston, 1973.

Merleau-Ponty, Maurice, *The Visible and the Invisible*, ed. Claude Lefort, trans. Alphonso Lingis, Northwestern University Press, Evanston, 1968.

Millar, Jeremy, *Fischli and Weiss: The Way Things Go*, Afterall Books, London, 2007.
Millennium Ecosystem Assessment, *Ecosystems and Human Well-being: Synthesis*, Island Press, Washington, DC, 2005.
Moore, George Fletcher, *A Descriptive Vocabulary of the Language in Common Use amongst the Aborigines of Western Australia: With Copious Meanings, Embodying Much Interesting Information Regarding the Habits, Manners, and Customs of the Natives and the Natural History of the Country*, Wm. S. Orr & Co., London, 1892.
Moore, George Fletcher *Diary of Ten Years Eventful Life of an Early Settler in Western Australia; and also a Descriptive Vocabulary of the Language of the Aborigines*, M. Walbrook, London, 1884.
Morin, Marie-Eve, 'Nancy, Violence and the World, *Parrhesia*, Number 16, 2013, pp. 61-72.
Mountford, Charles, *Nomads of the Australian Desert*, Rigby, Adelaide, 1976.
Munn, Nancy, 'Excluded Spaces: The figure in the Australian Aboriginal landscape', *Critical Inquiry*, vol. 22, no. 3, 1996, pp. 446–65.
Musil, Robert, *Young Törless*, trans. Eithne Wilkins & Ernst Kaiser, Pan Books, London, 1987.
Myers, Fred, 'Graceful transfigurations of person, place, and story: The stylistic evolution of Shorty Lungkarta Tjungurrayi', in Roger Benjamin (ed.), *Icons of the Desert: Early Aboriginal Paintings from Papunya*, Herbert F. Johnson Museum, Cornell University, Ithaca, 2009, pp. 51–64.
Nancy, Jean-Luc, *The Inoperative Community*, trans. P. Connor, University of Minnesota Press, Minneapolis, 1991.
Nechita, Elena, 'Some Considerations on Seriality and Synchronicity', *Brain*, Issue 1, January 2010, pp. 49-54.
Negri, Antonio, *Reflections on Empire*, Polity, Cambridge, UK, 2008.
Nelson, John S., 'Strategy studies: Explications of rhetorical performance', *Poroi*, Essays on Poroi's Set of Occasional Features, Iowa Digital Library, August 2003, viewed 5 June 2015, <http://digital.lib.uiowa.edu/poroi/poroifeaturetypes.htm#strategystudies>.
Northern Territory Government Department of Planning and Infrastructure, Cardno Willing, *Alice Springs Traffic Management and Parking Study*, Cardno Willing, Darwin, December 2004.
Northern Territory Government, *Moving Alice Ahead: Lifestyle*, brochure, Northern Territory Government, Darwin, 2007.
Oberndorf, C. P., 'Folie à deux', *International Journal of Psycho-Analysis*, vol. 15, 1934, pp. 14–24.
O'Brien, David Dobz, 'The incidental person and collaborative exchange', in

Marilyn Lennon & Sean Taylor (eds), *Praxis: MA Space; Social Practice and the Creative Environment*, Limerick School of Art and Design, Limerick, 2012, pp. 26–9.

Olson, Charles, *Collected Prose*, University of California Press, Berkeley Calif., 1970.

Papastergiadis, Nikos, *Cosmopolitanism and Culture*, Polity, Cambridge, UK, 2012.

Pearson, Michael, Duncan Marshall, Donald Ellsmore, Val Attenbrow, Sue Rosen, Rosemary Kerr & Chris Betteridge, *University of Sydney Grounds Conservation Plan*, vol. 1, University of Sydney, October 2002, viewed 5 June 2015, <http://sydney.edu.au/documents/about/heritage/gcp_vol1.pdf>.

Plato, *Timaeus*, in *Plato in Twelve Volumes*, trans. W.R.M. Lamb, W. Heinemann, London, 1925, vol. 9.

Pliny the Younger, *The Letters of the Younger Pliny*, trans B. Radice, Penguin: Harmondsworth, 1967.

Popoaca-Giuran, Anca, 'Mircea Eliade: Meanings (the apparent dichotomy: scientist/writer)', PhD thesis, King's College London, London, 1998.

Positive Solutions, 'Southbank Cultural Precinct Draft Audit', Melbourne, August 2012.

Potter, Emily, 'Postcolonial atmospheres: Recalling our shadow places', in Paul Ashton, Chris Gibson & Ross Gibson (eds), *By-roads and Hidden Treasures: Mapping Cultural Assets in Regional Australia*, University of Western Australia Publishing, Perth, 2015, pp. 75-86.

Pound, Ezra, *Antheil and the Treatise on Harmony*, P. Covici, Inc., Chicago, 1927.

Powell, J.M., *Environmental Management in Australia: 1788-1914*, Melbourne University Press, Melbourne, 1976.

Quinn, Edward, *Max Ernst*, Éditions Cercle d'Art, Paris, 1976.

Rainio, Kullervo, *Kurt Lewin's Dynamical Psychology Revisited and Revised*, Goertzel.org, 2009, viewed 4 June 2015, <http://goertzel.org/dynapsyc/Rainio-Lewin's-psych-pdf-6-8-09.pdf>.

Rajchman, John, '*Les Immatériaux* or How to Construct the History of Exhibitions', *Tate Papers* No12, October 2009, viewed 3 June 2015, <www.tate.org.uk/research/publications/tate-papers/les-immateriaux-or-how-construct-history-exhibitions>.

Rancière, Jacques, 'The emancipated spectator', paper presented at the Fifth International Summer Academy of Arts, Frankfurt, 20 August 2004, transcript at Maryland Institute College of Art, n.d., viewed 4 June 2015, <http://digital.mica.edu/departmental/gradphoto/public/Upload/200811/Ranciere%20%20spectator.pdf>.

Read, Sir Herbert, 'The Personality of the Poet', in *Selected Writings of Herbert Read*, Faber & Faber, London, 1963.

Rickert, Thomas, *Ambient Rhetoric: The Attunements of Rhetorical Being*, University of Pittsburgh Press, Pittsburgh, 2013.

Ricoeur, Paul, *The Rule of Metaphor*, trans. R. Czerny, Routledge & Kegan Paul, London, 1978.

Riding, Laura, 'A Last Lesson in Geography', *Art and Literature*, Autumn 1965, pp. 28-43.

'Riemann for Anti-Dummies Part 54, The Dramatic Power of Abelian Functions', http://www.wlym.com/antidummies/part54.html. Viewed 14 March 2015.

Rieff, Philip, *The Feeling Intellect: Selected Writings*, ed. Jonathan B. Imber, University of Chicago Press, Chicago, 1990.

Roberts, David, see Árnarson, Johann P.

Rockel, Rosie, 'A Mysterious Accord: 65 Maximiliana, or the Illegal Practice of Astronomy', http://rosierockel.com/2015/01/27/a-mysterious-accord-65-maximiliana-or-the-illegal-practice-of-astronomy/. Accessed 23 February 2015.

Rollinson, Philip, *Classical Theories of Allegory and Christian Culture*, Duquesne University Press, Pittsburgh, 1985.

Rosen, Stanley, *Metaphysics in Ordinary Language*, Yale University Press, New Haven Conn., 1999.

Rouse W.H.D., 'Introduction', Lucretius, *De Rerum Natura*, trans. W.H.D. Rouse, W. Heinemann, London, 1966, pp. vii–xxi.

Rowland, Philip, '"Celebration of failure": The influence of Laura Riding on John Ashbery', *Flashpoint*, no. 6, 2004, viewed 8 June 2015, <www.flashpointmag.com/riding.htm>.

Sacks, Oliver, *Seeing Voices*, Harper Perennial, New York, 1990.

Sallis, John, *Chorology: On Beginnings in Plato's Timaeus*, Indiana University Press, Bloomington, 1999.

San Roque, Craig, 'Coming to terms with the country: Some incidents on first meeting Aboriginal locations and Aboriginal thoughts', in Maria Teresa Savio Hooke & Salman Akhtar (eds), *The Geography of Meanings: Psychoanalytic Perspectives on Place, Space, Land, and Dislocation*, International Psychoanalytical Association, London, 2007, pp. 104–40.

San Roque, Craig, 'The yard', in Ute Eickelcamp (ed.), *Growing Up in Central Australia: New Anthropological Studies of Aboriginal Childhood and Adolescence*, Berghahn Books, Oxford, 2013, pp.156-79.

Sartre, John-Paul, *Modern Times: Selected Non-Fiction*, ed. Geoffrey Wall, trans. Robin Buss, Penguin Books, Harmondsworth, 2000.

Satter, Todd Jerome, 'The Black Box in the White Cube: Lyotard's *Les Immatériaux* as Machinic Theater', 2011, http://www.anyspacewhatever.com/the-black-box-in-the-white-cube-lyotards-les-immateriaux-as-machinic-theater, viewed 10 February 2012.

Sayers, Sean, *Dialectic and Social Criticism*, EServer, May 1992, viewed 3 June 2015, <http://govt.eserver.org/dialectic-and-social-crit.txt>.

Schuster, John A., '"Waterworld": Descartes' vortical celestial mechanics', in Peter R. Anstey & John A. Schuster (eds), *The Science of Nature in the Seventeenth Century: Patterns of Change in Early Modern Natural Philosophy*, Springer, Dordrecht, 2005, pp. 35–81.

Sengoopta, Chandak, 'Dr Steinach coming to make old young!' Sex glands, vasectomy and the quest for rejuvenation in the roaring twenties', *Endeavour*, vol. 27, no. 3, 2003, pp. 122–6.

Sennett, Richard, 'Destructive Gemeinschaft', in Alan Soble (ed.), *The Philosophy of Sex*, Rowman and Littlefield, Totowa, 1980, pp. 291–321.

Shafer, Glenn, *The Art of Causal Conjecture*, MIT Press, Cambridge, MA, 1996.

Shearer, Ann, *Athene, Image and Energy*, Viking Arkana, London, 1996.

Simmel, Georg, *Simmel on Culture: Selected Writings*, ed. David Frisby & Mike Featherstone, Sage, London, 1997.

Skeat, Walter W., *An Etymological Dictionary of the English Language*, Clarendon Press, Oxford, 1888.

Slochower, Harry, *Mythopoesis: Mythic Patterns in the Literary Classics*, Wayne University Press, Detroit, 1970.

Smith, David Woodruff, see MacIntyre, Ronald.

Smithson, Robert, 'The Spiral Jetty (1972)', *The Collected Writings*, University of California Press, Berkeley, Calif., 1996, pp. 143–153.

Smyth, Robert Brough, *The Aborigines of Victoria*, 2 vols, Government Printer, Melbourne, 1876.

Spencer, Tracy, 'Stories from the Street: Todd Mall/Todd Street, At the heart of Alice Springs', July 2008', 1-17.

Spencer, Tracy, for the Uniting Church in Alice Springs, 'The Heart of Alice: a place for welcoming, connecting and encountering', draft statement, December 2006, 1-4.

Spirituality, Kaartdijin Noongar – Noogar Knowledge, n.d., viewed 8 June 2015, <www.noongarculture.org.au/spirituality/Spirituality>.

Spivak Gayatri Chakravorty, 'Translator's Preface', Jacques Derrida, *Of Grammatology*, Baltimore: Johns Hopkins Press, Baltimore, 1976, pp. ix-lxxxvii.

Stanford Encyclopedia of Philosophy, Stanford University Press, Stanford, Calif, http://facstaff.uww.edu/mohanp/popper.html.

Stanner, William E. H., *The Dreaming and Other Essays*, Black Inc. Agenda, Melbourne, 2009.
Stanner, William E. H, *White Man Got No Dreaming: Essays 1938-1973*, Australian National University Press, Canberra 1979.
Steinberg, Michael, *The Fiction of a Thinkable World: Body, Meaning, and the Culture of Capitalism*, Monthly Review Press, New York, 2005.
Stephenson, Peta, *The Outsiders Within: Telling Australia's Indigenous-Asian Story*, University of New South Wales Press, Sydney, 2007.
Stewart, Kathleen, *A Space on the Side of the Road*, Princeton University Press, Princeton, NJ., 1996.
Stiver, Dan R., *Theology after Ricoeur: Directions in Hermeneutical Theology*, John Knox Press, Westminster, 2001.
Strehlow, T.G.H., *Comments on the Journals of John McDouall Stuart*, Adelaide: Libraries Board of South Australia, 1967.
Strehlow, T. G. H., *Songs of Central Australia*, Angus & Robertson, Sydney, 1970.
Summer, Kay & Harry Halpin, *The Crazy before the New: Complexity, Critical Instability and the End of Capitalism*, Turbulence, n.d., viewed 8 June 2015, <http://turbulence.org.uk/turbulence-1/the-crazy-before-the-new>.
Tarkovsky, Andrey, *Sculpting in Time: Reflections on the Cinema*, trans. Kitty Hunter-Blair, Faber & Faber, London, 1994.
Tawa, Michael, *Agencies of the Frame*, Cambridge Scholars Publishing, Newcastle upon Tyne, 2010.
Tawa, Michael, *Theorising the Project: A Thematic Approach to Architectural Design*, Cambridge Scholars Press, Newcastle upon Tyne, 2011.
Taylor, Nigel, *Urban Planning Theory since 1945*, Sage, London and Thousand Oaks, 1998.
Tennyson, Alfred, 'Locksley Hall,' *Poems and Plays*, Oxford University Press, Oxford, 1968.
Terzidas, Kostas, *Algorithmic Architecture*, Routledge, London, 2006.
Thass-Thienemann, Theodore, *Symbolic Behavior*, Washington Square Press, New York, 1968.
Thomashow, Mitchell, *Bringing the Biosphere Home: Learning to Perceive Global Environmental Change*, MIT Press: Cambridge, MA, 2003.
Thompson, D'Arcy Wentworth, *On Growth and Form*, 2 vols, Cambridge University Press, Cambridge, UK, 1942 (first published 1917).
Thrift, Nigel, 'Movement-space: the Changing Domain of Thinking Resulting from the Development of New Kinds of Spatial Awareness,' *Economy and Society* 33: 4, November, 2004, pp. 582-604.
Todd, Charles, 'Observations of the phenomena of Jupiter's satellites at the observatory, Adelaide, and notes on the physical appearance of the planet',

Monthly Notices of the Royal Astronomical Society, vol. 37, 10 November 1876, pp. 284–300.

Tonkinwise, Cameron, 'Knowing by being-there making: Explicating the tacit post-subject in use', *Studies in Material Thinking*, vol. 1, no. 2, 2008, viewed 3 June 2009, <www.materialthinking.org/sites/default/files/papers/Cameron.pdf>.

Toub, James, 'Kokoschka as teacher', *Journal of Aesthetic Education*, vol. 28, no. 2, 1994, pp. 35–49.

Townley, John & Robert Schmidt, 'Paul Kammerer and the Law of Seriality', in Stephen Moore (ed.), *Fortean Studies*, vol. 1, John Brown Publishing, London, 1994.

Troy, Jakelin, *Australian Aboriginal Contact with the English Language in New South Wales: 1788 to 1845*, Pacific Linguistics, Series B, No. 103, Australian National University, Canberra, 1990.

Trudinger, David, 'Demythologising Flynn, with love: Contesting missionaries in central Australia in the twentieth century', in Frances Peters-Little, Ann Curthoys & John Docker (eds), *Passionate Histories: Myth, Memory and Indigenous Australia*, ANU Press, 2010, viewed 4 June 2015, <http://press.anu.edu.au/apps/bookworm/view/Passionate+Histories%3A+Myth,+Memory+and+Indigenous+Australia/8271/Text/ch07.html>.

Turnbull, Robert G., *The Parmenides and Plato's Late Philosophy*, University of Toronto Press, Toronto, 1998.

Turner, Margaret Kemarre, *Iwenhe Tyerrtye: What It Means to Be an Aboriginal Person*, IAD Press, Alice Springs, 2010.

Valéry, Paul, 'Analecta', *Selected Writings of Paul Valéry*, trans. Stuart Gilbert, New Directions, New York, 1950.

Valéry, Paul, 'Philosophy of the dance', trans. R. Manheim, in Roger Copeland & Marshall Cohen (eds), *What Is Dance? Readings in Theory and Criticism*, Oxford University Press, New York, 1983, pp. 55–65.

Van Kerkhoven, Marianne, 'European dramaturgy in the 21st century: A constant movement', *Performance Research*, vol. 14, no. 3, 2009, pp. 7–11.

van Toorn, Penny, *Writing Never Arrives Naked: Early Aboriginal Cultures of Writing in Australia*, Aboriginal Studies Press, Canberra, 2006.

Virgil, *Aeneid*, in *Virgil*, trans. H. Rushton Fairborough, W. Heinemann, London, 1947, 2 vols.

Walker, Louise, *Gender, Age and Class in the Hospitality Industry, Victoria, 1900–1914*, Australian National University, n.d., viewed 5 June 2015, <www.anu.edu.au/polsci/marx/interventions/wagesboards.htm>.

Wallace, Kathleen Kemarre, *Listen Deeply, Let these stories in*, IAD Press, Alice Springs, 2009.

Wallace, Marina, Martin Kemp & Joanne Bernstein, *Seduced: Art and Sex from Antiquity to Now*, Merrell, London, 2007.
Warner, Marina, 'The writing of stones', *Cabinet*, no. 29, 2008, viewed 5 June 2015, <http://cabinetmagazine.org/issues/29/warner.php>.
Von Sturmer, John, 'Aboriginal Singing and Notions of Power', in *Songs of Aboriginal Australia*, eds. M. Clunies Ross, T. Donaldson, S.A. Wild, University of Sydney Press, Sydney, 1987.
Watson, Christine, *Piercing the Ground: Balgo Women's Image Making and Relationship to Country*, Fremantle Arts Centre Press, Fremantle, 2003.
Weekley Ernest, *An Etymological Dictionary of Modern English*, Dover, New York, 1967.
White Eric Charles, *Kaironomia, On the Will-to-Invent*, Cornell University Press, Ithaca, N.Y., 1987.
Whitehead, Alfred North, *Science and the Modern World*, Cambridge University Press, Cambridge, UK, 1926.
Wind, Edgar, *Pagan Mysteries of the Renaissance*, Penguin, Harmondsworth, 1967.
Winslow, C. E. A., *The Conquest of Epidemic Disease*, Princeton University Press, Princeton, NJ., 1943.
Wisser, Max, 'Gregory Bateson on deutero-learning and double bind: A brief conceptual history', *Journal of the History of the Behavioral Sciences*, vol. 39, no. 3, 2003, pp. 269–78.
Wolin, Sheldon, *The Presence of the Past: Essays on the State and the Constitution*, The Johns Hopkins Press, Baltimore, 1989.
Wordsworth, William, 'Intimations of Immortality from Recollections of Early Childhood', *Poetical Works*, ed. T. Hutchinson, Oxford University Press, Oxford, 1969.
Wright, John P., *The Sceptical Realism of David Hume*, Manchester University Press, Manchester, 1983.
Wurzer Wilhelm S., 'Nancy and the Political Imaginary after Nature', in *On Jean-Luc Nancy: The Sense of Philosophy*, eds. D. Shephard, S. Sparks, and C. Thomas, Routledge, London, 1997.
Yagan, Kaartdijin Noongar – Noogar Knowledge, n.d., viewed 8 June 2015, <www.noongarculture.org.au/yagan/>.
Žižek, Slavoj, *Welcome to the Desert of the Real*, Verso, London, 2002.

INDEX

Adorno, Theodor 378–9
Agamben, Giorgio 297–8, 299, 306–7
Albrecht, Friedrich Wilhelm 125
Alice Springs, *see* Material Thinking, *Red Ways*
Anaxagoras 95, 98
Arakawa, Shūsaku 50, 136–7
Arendt, Hannah 241–2
Argyris, Chris 65
Arnheim, Rudolf 282
Bachmann, Ingeborg 292
Balbuk (Noongar) 351–3, 356, 357
Balibrea, Mari Paz 289–90
Barak, William (Wurundjeri) 264, 265 [Fig. 28]
Barba, Eugenio 63
Bardon, Geoffrey xiii–xvi, 125, 128–9, 132–3, 319–20
Bataille, Georges 12
Bates, Daisy 351–2, 380
Bateson, Gregory 46, 65, 330, 331, 332
Baudrillard, Jean 329–30
Benjamin, Roger 124
Benjamin, Walter 165, 193, 295, 330
Benton, Christopher 156–7
Bergson, Henri 282, 392
Beuys, Joseph 398–9
Bewick, Thomas 336

Bharucha, Rustom 226
Blake, William 249
Böhme, Gernot 369
Boon Wurrung people 338–9
Botticelli, Sandro 192
Bunjil (Kulin nation creator deity) 17, 91–6, 339, 350
Burch, Kerry 395
Butler, Judith 226
Cadigal people 193
Cain, Seymour 318
Canetti, Elias 10, 50
Carter, Paul
    Dark Writing 402, 412, 421
    Ground Truthing 79
    Material Thinking 3–4, 12
    Meeting Place 9, 10, 321, 375, 393
    Road to Botany Bay, The 35
Centre for Creative Arts, La Trobe University 32, 386
choreotopography 15–17, 30, 33–4, 43–52, 55, 385–96, 406–7, 410–11
Choreotopography multimedia performance 71–5, 73 [Fig. 5]
Colbung, Ken (Noongar) 381
Copjec, Jean 261
Correa, Paulo and Alexandra 60–2, 331–2
Da Vinci, Leonardo 65 [Fig. 2]
Dandenong, Victoria, *see* Material

Index

Thinking, *Alterations*
Deans, Bruce 109
de Bruyn, Dirk 76–7, 80, 81–3, 91, 269–70, 278, 78 [Fig. 6]
de Certeau Michel 276
de Clérambault, Gaëtan Gatian, 261–2, 263
de Man, Paul 421, 422
De Quincey, Thomas 64, 423–4
Debord, Guy 352, 373
Deleuze, Gilles 60–2, 392–3, 414–15
Derrida, Jacques 157, 206–7, 243
Descartes, René 34, 96–9, 170–1, 417, 97 [Fig. 10]
Desmond, William 205
Deutsche, Rosalind 58, 154
Didi-Huberman, Georges 344–5
Doxiadis, Constantinos 47, 280, 315
Dyson, Frances 370–1
Eberhart, Russell 404–5
Eisenstein, Sergei 335
Eliade, Mircea, 316–20, 325, 329, 342, 357, 359, 425
El-Khatib, Mohamed Samir 226–7
Elrick, Laura 47, 70
Eno, Brian 204, 370
Epicurus 32, 386–7
Eratosthenes 247–8
Ernst, Max 178–80, 179 [Fig. 17])
Flynn, John 130–1
Focillon, Henri 317
Foster, Susan Leigh 52, 70
Frazer, Sir James 167
Freud, Sigmund 50, 323
Ganai people 339
Gasché, Rodolphe 99, 346
Giacometti, Alberto 51, 259, 412, 417
Gillam, Mike 105, 107, 132
Gins, Madeline 50, 136–7

Girard, René 218
Glowczewski, Barbara 123–4
'Governing Civilization through Civilizing Governance: Global Challenge for a Turbulent Future' 408
Gray, John 51
Green, Jennifer 321
Green, Neville 379
Griffero, Tonino 369–70, 375
Gruenewald, D. A. 304
Guattari, Félix 60–1, 62, 393, 414
Gurindji people 353
Haeckel, Ernst 322
Halpin, Harry 405–8
Harney, Bill Yidumduma 108
Healey, Patsy 150, 229
Hegel, Georg Wilhelm Friedrich 11
Heidegger, Martin 135
Herrick, Robert 257
Hilal, Sandi 224–5
Hillier, Bill 418
Hokari, Minoru 353
Holston, James 155
Houël, Jean 308, 308 [Fig. 36]
Hume, David 44
Husserl, Edmund 202
Hutchinson, William 165–6
Innanen, Riika Theresa 46, 372
Institute for Infinitely Small Things 64
Jackson, Michael 276
Johnson, Richard 166
Jonson, Ben 98
Jorn, Asger 396
Jung, Carl 346, 391, 415–16
Kafka, Franz 411
Kammerer, Paul 216–18, 414
Kantor, Tadeusz 50, 394
Kennedy, James 404–5

Kerényi, Carl 109
Kierkegaard, Søren 214
Kimber, Richard E. (Dick) 117, 119
Koestler, Arthur 217
Kokoschka, Oskar 392
Komárek, Stanislav, 415–16
Kristeva, Julia 95–6, 98
Kulper, Amy 282–3, 328
Lapicque, Charles 361–2
Le Bon, Gustav 50
Lefebvre, Henri 47, 70, 71
Lennon, Jane 299
Levin, David 99, 135–6
Levinas, Emmanuel 49, 99, 361
Lewin, Kurt 65–6, 97
Loops, see de Bruyn, Dirk
Lucretius 63
Lyons 229
Lyotard, Jean-François 12
Macquarie, Lachlan 165
Maffesoli, Michel 45, 180
Maharaj, Sarat 398
Mann, Steve 373–4
Material Thinking
   Alterations 25–6, 33, 56, 222–7, 244–54, 256–65, 269, 277, 280, 400, 223 [Fig. 22], 245 [Fig. 23], 247 [Fig. 24], 250 [Fig.25], 253 [Fig. 26], 257 [Fig. 27], 265 [Fig. 29], 270 [Fig. 30], 271 [Fig. 31, 32]
   Golden Grove 23–5, 30, 56, 156–60, 164–72, 174–86, 188–208, 351, 425–6, 159 [Fig. 13], 170 [Fig. 14], 171 [Fig. 15], 172 [Fig. 16], 179 [Fig. 17], 182 [Fig. 18], 184 [Fig. 19], 190 [Fig. 20], 197 [Fig. 21]
   Nearamnew (Federation Square, Melbourne) 16–17, 68–70, 80–1, 93, 102–4, 200, 339, 69 [Fig.3], 90 [Fig. 8]
   New Body, A 31–2, 56, 342–53, 359, 377, 379–84, 349 [Fig. 37], 359 [Fig. 38]
   Opening, see de Bruyn, Dirk
   Passenger (Yagan Square) 56
   Pearl 71, 206, 72 [Fig.4]
   Relay 200
   River Connect 16, 58–60, 136, 59 [Fig. 1]
   Red Ways 18–21, 23–4, 30–2, 56, 113–19, 137–43, 149–52, 207, 213, 320, 142 [Fig. 11]
   Turning Point (Point Nepean Quarantine Station) 28, 298–310, 328, 338–9, 298 [Fig. 33], 301 [Fig. 34], 302 [Fig. 35], 308 [Fig. 36]
Matta-Clark, Gordon 352
Maxwell, James Clerk, 412–13
McAuley, James 357
McLeod, Shaun 276
Mead, Margaret 331
Merleau-Ponty, Maurice 259, 362–3
Metropolitan Redevelopment Authority 358
Moore, George Fletcher 346–50, 353, 356
Morin, Marie-Eve 8
Mottram, Chiron 373
Munn, Nancy 215
Musil, Robert 82–3
Myers, Fred 124
mythopoiesis 17–19, 76–7, 323, 324
Namatjira, Albert 131
Nancy, Jean-Luc 8, 43, 132
Negri, Antonio 310
Neilson, John Shaw 79, 81
Nelson, John S. 207–9

Index

Nolan, Jason 373–4
Noongar people 342, 347–50, 358, 379–82
Oberndorf, C. P. 416–17
O'Brien, David Dobz 398
Olson, Charles 351
Pallas Athene 143, 263–4
Panofsky, Erwin 192
Paracelsus 203
Perth (Western Australia), *see* Material Thinking, *A New Body*
Petti, Alessandro 224–5
Philpot, Arthur, 130–1
Piper, Graham 109
Pliny, the Younger 394–5
Popper, Karl 51
Pound, Ezra 56
Powell, Dani 129–30
Rajchman, John 12–13
Rickert, Thomas 134–5, 190, 222–3, 227, 330
Ricoeur, Paul 421
Riding, Laura 362–3
Rockel, Rosie 178
Rollinson, Philip 192
Rosen, Stanley 329
Rush\Wright Associates 229, 223 [Fig. 22]
Russell, Bertrand 332
Sacks, Oliver 74–5
San Roque, Craig 106, 114
Sartre, Jean-Paul 410, 411–14, 418
Saxl, Fritz 192
Schieck, Ava Fatah gen. 372–3
Seduced: Art and Sex from Antiquity to Now 214
Sefer Yetzirah 56–7, 157 [Fig. 12]
Shearer, Ann 264
Shepherd, Thomas 167
Shepparton (Victoria), *see* Material Thinking, *River Connect*
Simmel, Georg 217–18
Smithson, Robert 170, 176–7
Smyth, Robert Brough 92
Stanner, W. E. H. 114
Stewart, Harold 357
Stewart, Kathleen 288–9
Stone's Throw, A 174–5
Strehlow, T. G. H. 108, 116–18, 124–5, 141, 319
Stuart, Doris Kngwarraye 107–9
Stuart, John, McDouall 116
Summer, Kay 405–8
Tarkovsky, Andrey 308–9
Tawa, Michael 11–12, 202, 303, 371, 387–8
Taylor Cullity Lethlean 158, 171 [Fig.15], 172 [Fig.16], 182 [Fig. 18], 184 [Fig.19], 190 [Fig.20], 197 [Fig. 21]
Taylor, Nigel 296
Terzidis, Kostas 206–7, 208, 334
Thass-Thienemann, Theodore 323
Thomas, William 338
Thomashow, Mitchell 303–4, 305
Thompson, D'Arcy Wentworth 63, 204, 282, 412–13
Thrift, Nigel 55
Tjupurrula, Johnny Warrangkula 125, 133, 141
Todd, Charles 18, 116, 119–21
Tonkinwise, Cameron 3–4, 35, 152, 153, 398
'Transnational and Temporary: Placemaking, Students and Community in Central Melbourne' 27–9, 283–92
Trudinger, David 132
Turnbull, Robert G. 95–6
Turner, Margaret Kemarre 108, 122

Valéry, Paul 262–3
van Hoorn, Penny 192
Van Kerkhoven, Marianne 394
Vertov, Dziga 83
Vico, Giambattista 335–6
von Pauli, Wolfgang 416
Wallace, Kathleen Kemarre 160–1
Walley, Richard 358
Warminski, Andrzej 99
Warner, Marina 262
Watson, Christine 128–9
Wellman, Barry 373–4
Whadjuk Working Group 358–9
White, Eric Charles 222
Whitehead, Alfred North 44, 61, 270
Wind, Edgar 98, 192
Wolin, Sheldon 395
Yagan (Noongar) 342, 346–8, 351, 380–3
You, Soo Yeun 78, 91, 269–70, 276, 79 [Fig. 7]
Young, Thomas 360
Žižek, Slavoj 301

www.ingramcontent.com/pod-product-compliance
Lightning Source LLC
Chambersburg PA
CBHW051347220526
45469CB00001B/140